AF572003

Morality and Economic Growth in Rural West Africa

For Gavin Williams and Vicki Ann Cremona

Morality and Economic Growth in Rural West Africa

Indigenous Accumulation in Hausaland

Paul Clough

NEW YORK • OXFORD
www.berghahnbooks.com

Published in 2014 by
Berghahn Books
www.berghahnbooks.com

Library of Congress Cataloging-in-Publication Data

Clough, Paul, 1948– author.
Morality and economic growth in rural West Africa : indigenous accumulation in Hausaland / Paul Clough.
pages cm
Includes bibliographical references and index.
ISBN 978-1-78238-270-6 (hardback : alk. paper) —
ISBN 978-1-78238-271-3 (ebook)
1. Hausa (African people)—Nigeria, Northern—Economic conditions—20th century. 2. Hausa (African people)—Social networks—Nigeria, Northern. 3. Economic development—Nigeria, Northern. 4. Social networks—Nigeria, Northern. 5. Nigeria, Northern—Economic conditions—20th century. 6. Nigeria, Northern—Social conditions—20th century. I. Title.
DT515.45.H38C56 2014
330.966976—dc23

2013023284

British Library Cataloguing in Publication Data

A catalogue record for this book is available from the British Library

Printed on acid-free paper

ISBN: 978-1-78238-270-6 hardback
ISBN: 978-1-78238-271-3 ebook

Contents

ILLUSTRATIONS

Tables

Charts

Figures

Preface

This book has two concerns – an African framework for economic growth, and the distinctive ways in which Africans in their lived localities go about achieving it. An intellectually exciting search has been on for some time among Africanist scholars for new approaches to growth, which backs away from the assumption that the only viable pathway to growth is the increasingly homogenous market with ever larger private organizations and concentrations of capital (for example, Jane Guyer's model of the 'niche economy' [Guyer 1997, further explored by many scholars following Guyer 2004b], or Sarah Berry's concept of 'political accumulation' [Berry 1985, 1993]). This book draws on the close engagement of the author for over thirty years with one particular region of the West African Savannah to offer a different framework for growth in Africa – the *trajectory of accumulation*. Through a careful examination of the economic institutions in a hamlet in Nigerian Hausaland from 1976 to 1998, it uncovers a historically specific pathway to growth. Instead of an ineluctable process of transition to agricultural capitalism, the author found that three kinds of accumulation have woven together to constitute a distinctive trajectory – (1) the expansion in the number of wives and children; (2) the search for ever more clients and trading friends; and (3) the accumulation of capital. This book shows how the historical sequencing and combination of these different kinds of accumulation together constitute a particular trajectory of noncapitalist accumulation.

Four realities make this model of noncapitalist accumulation interesting. First, land, labour and produce markets are highly developed in the hamlet economy. It is therefore interesting that a transition to capitalism is not taking place. Secondly, the accumulation of wives and children, clients and trading friends, actually *encourages* the accumulation of capital. Thirdly, (in counterpoint), the financial obligations arising from polygynous households and widening trade networks act as a constraint on the individualization of goals – and of wealth itself. Instead, accumulators seek growth through the mutual exchange of services and money loans.

Fourthly, the outcome of this trajectory of accumulation is a very particular lived idea among the people of what economic growth is about: the multiplication of social bonds more than individual material wealth. The accumulators of Marmara hamlet were materially acquisitive. But their acquisitiveness was channeled by the moral priorities of a polygynous, cliental and increasingly Islamic society.

In short, this book shows how the trajectory of noncapitalist accumulation leads to wealth in people *as well as* in things. It argues that different societies can have different trajectories of accumulation. They are different because they are driven by different moral paradigms. 'Growth' itself should be theorized in heterogeneous and culturally multiple terms. In contesting the axiom behind the New Institutional Economics, this book argues that formal rationality and individualization of decision making are not the only path to growth.

Why a Study from Hausaland?

The specific nature of Hausaland makes its economic ethnography important in the comparative endeavour to develop relevant models of African growth. The depth of the Hausa historical record shows that Hausaland has the long-term potential for locally based growth, and change, in agriculture. The size of Hausaland has meant that it constitutes a large market undergoing constant expansion through a multiplicity of trading networks. This dimension of market size has led scholars to realize that Hausaland has distinctive growth poles – large cities; hundreds of rural towns; and (as this study shows, in line with the pioneering work of Polly Hill), markets between different *rural* ecological zones. It is all the more interesting, then, to explore how Hausa localities have achieved economic growth. Furthermore, Hausaland has a long tradition of Islamic belief and lively religious debate. The region therefore becomes relevant to our understanding of how religious and economic change affect each other.

Hausaland has been the focus of classic studies of African logics of economic change and integration with international capitalism. These often reach opposing conclusions about growth possibilities and the survival of indigenous economic institutions – from the positive (Polly Hill) to the negative (Michael Watts, Robert Shenton). This book adds to the debate. It follows in the footsteps of Polly Hill, by showing the durability of indigenous agriculture. At the same time, it complements Hill by demonstrating the significance of trading networks to local farmers.

In an important recent contribution to theories of economy, Stephen Gudeman has argued for a dialectical relationship between the base and the market of any economy (Gudeman 2008). On the one hand, the base is an economy's realm of mutual and communitarian relations, including the relations that establish trust, where people are connected through practices of sharing, and a stock of ideas and things is produced through communication between persons and groups. On the other, the market is the abode of calculative reason, where persons compete to maximize their individual advantage. Although the market actually depends on trusting and promissory behaviour which emanates from the base, competition for individual gain on the market erodes the base. Thus, there is tension between base and market in any economy. In contrast, this study shows how in Hausaland, the expansion of markets has not eroded communally based relations of production and marketing or the cooperative ideas that animate local economic institutions. Despite competition among traders for the purchase and sale of produce, the forging of personal bonds of obligation between larger and smaller traders and between traders and farmers has been essential to the operation of produce and capital markets. Thus, markets are not inevitably driven by an ethos of individual utility maximization, but can rather encourage an ethic of reciprocal assistance and mutual benefit. One of the main reasons for a complementary relationship between communitarian base and competitive markets is that in rural Hausaland, polygyny engenders a socially extraverted approach to social obligation and thus to economic growth (see especially chapter 2).

It is critical to distinguish between the neoliberal praxis and the Hausa praxis of the market. In the former, individual advantage is defined by a short term. All market agents make their calculations in order to maximize advantage in that short term, and divest themselves of any assets or relationships which do not optimize individual short-term gain. In the latter, however, individuals establish alliances of interpersonal dependence in order to seek mutual income growth in the long term (see also Clough 2012). In the Hausa praxis, market and base enhance each other.

Why This Particular Village?

Marmara is on main roads directly connecting the agriculturally thriving, highly commercialized region of southern Katsina to most economic regions of Nigeria. Thus, a study of Marmara shows the impact of long-distance communication and transport networks on local rural economy. Partly because it is a transport hub, its size has grown significantly in the thirty years that the author has studied it. The comparison in this book is between different periods of time – in different national economic cycles, from the expansion of the 1970s petroleum boom to the contraction following the Structural Adjustment of 1985. This adds to our understanding of growth over time in the Nigerian rural economy. And yet, Marmara has remained small enough to take further the comprehensive empirical method of Polly Hill – adding to her work particularly in the study of credit and trading networks. The significance of a comprehensive study in a small place is that the dynamics of economic differentiation over time, which emanate from successive national economic cycles, can be tracked and interpreted.

The people of Marmara converted to Islam from the indigenous Hausa Maguzawa religion as recently as the decade 1960–1970. In consequence, Islam is still a very self-conscious part of local consciousness. Islam has a particular impact on the economic thinking and practices of local people. Muslim ideas, as filtered through the teaching of the local mallams, have had a special effect on local trading and on the relations between richer and poorer households. Islam has thus contributed significantly to the trajectory of accumulation for which this book argues.

Why Pay Particular Attention to Local Terms of Growth?

Throughout this book, the focus is on institutions at the local level. The book shows that these are flexibly adaptive and changeable in line with material needs and local ideas of the moral purposes of economic life. Local institutions have been durable over time – despite great changes in political regime from the colonial to the postcolonial era, and movements in and out of cycles of prosperity and decline at the level of the state. The author's approach differs from that of the New Institutional Economics (NIE). NIE tends to stress the importance of state-level institutions to the expansion of a homogenous impersonal market. In contrast, this book argues that local-level, rural institutions generate lively but personal markets in land, labour, capital and skills.

Since 2008, the global financial crisis has put pressure on the availability of international credit for investment in Africa at a time when, ironically, Africa appears to be entering a phase of comparatively high macroeconomic growth in statistical terms. If the flows of private international investment and interstate assistance are under pressure, it becomes all the more necessary to understand where and under what institutional circumstances African farmers and traders are themselves investing in production and marketing. By using a descriptive analysis of a highly commercialized district of Hausaland, this book demonstrates that an indigenous trajectory of noncapitalist accumulation, heavily influenced by Islam, is generating productive expansion while at the same time ensuring the social security of small farming households.

ACKNOWLEDGEMENTS

The work on this book has turned out to be the work of a lifetime. I did the initial fieldwork in Nigeria in 1977–79, for a D.Phil. dissertation at Oxford University. After return visits to my village, Marmara, in 1985, 1996 and 1998, I began to write a book, the first draft of which was completed in 2003. The second draft was finalized in early 2008, and the third and final draft in December 2011. This book has collected so many debts on the long road to completion that it is almost impossible for me to thank appropriately all those who have helped.

I am grateful beyond telling to Gavin Williams, the supervisor of my doctoral dissertation. The generosity with which he discussed the ideas and information which went into the dissertation, and subsequently his powerful encouragement of my research and writing all the way to the completion of this book, are acts of friendship which can never be repaid.

In 1977–79, the initial fieldwork in Nigeria was financed by a research fellowship from the Leverhulme Trust, which was generously extended to a third year back at Oxford when I began the analysis of my data. I am truly grateful to Tom Forrest, also a Research Associate at Queen Elisabeth House Oxford at the time, for stimulating discussion over the period 1977–83 which enabled me to keep abreast of new and interesting work, not only on the political economy of Nigeria, but more generally on that of West Africa. In 1985, Edward Rice at the World Bank sought me out as a consultant rural sociologist. His open-minded leadership of the mission 'World Bank Agriculture Sector Memorandum for Nigeria' enabled me to return for a month to Nigeria as a consultant and work again in the villages and marketplaces of Hausaland – above all, in Marmara. In September 1996, Bayero University Kano kindly gave me the research affiliation which made possible my fieldwork in Marmara at that time. In September

1996, and over the Christmas vacation of December 1997–January 1998, employment at the University of Malta gave me the resources to return again to Marmara. I am very grateful to Dr. Yahaya Hashim for facilitating my return to Nigeria and fieldwork there in December 1997–January 1998, and for advice given to me in preparation for that visit by Dr. Abdul Raufu Mustapha and Dr. Kate Mustapha. From October 2007 through September 2008, I had my first sabbatical from the University of Malta, after fourteen years of full-time service; I was given a further four-month study leave from October 2011 through January 2012. In that final study leave, Mr. Malcolm Borg-Galea of the university's IT Services gave me essential help in preparing the final manuscript. I am very grateful to my ex-student J.J. Vella, and to academic colleagues Matthew Montebello and Sandro Spina for their help in preparing the maps.

I am deeply grateful to Veena Das, head of the Department of Anthropology at Johns Hopkins University, for her hospitality in giving me a place in her department over the four-month period in which I finalized the second draft of this book at the end of 2007 and the beginning of 2008. I gratefully acknowledge Jane Guyer, professor at Johns Hopkins, for her detailed comments on the organization of the first draft of this book, and her encouraging reading of the theoretical chapter in the second draft.

This work would never have reached completion without the sympathy and very often the practical advice or assistance of friends. In this regard, special thanks go to Richard Bruce, Ian and Jane Linden, David Napier and Judith Okely. Richard Bruce took time out from his own research to visit me during my initial fieldwork and demonstrate fieldwork techniques which turned out to be essential. Back in England, continuous discussion with Richard clarified the importance of off-farm occupations to rural society. Ian's and Jane's love and support over many years, and their trenchant comments on my key ideas, were essential. Ian also facilitated my return to Nigeria in 1997. Without the strong encouragement of David Napier and Judith Okely, I would have despaired of this manuscript ever finding a publisher. They pushed me to spend my last four-month study leave returning to and revising the third and final draft of this book. And warm thanks to Michael Herzfeld, who gave me the courage to pick up the phone in December 2012 in order to find out that the manuscript was, indeed, going to be published.

Jon Mitchell of the University of Sussex, visiting lecturer at the University of Malta and a long-serving member of the International Editorial Advisory Board of its *Journal of Mediterranean Studies*, has been a constant source of wisdom and very necessary practical assistance over the many years that I have been teaching, and editing the *Journal of Mediterranean Studies,* at the University of Malta. Jeremy Boissevain has been unfailing in the generosity of his practical advice. I am very grateful to Alex Strating, who prompted me to publish an overview of the main argument of this book in the Dutch journal *Etnofoor* in the summer of 2003; it was heartening when Alex and the other members of the editorial working group at *Etnofoor* published my article. I thank Martin Roessler, head of the Department of Anthropology at Cologne University, for inviting me to give a seminar at its Anthropology Colloquium in December 2003; I was much encouraged by its enthusiastic reception of my ideas on debt in Hausaland.

At the University of Malta, my special thanks go to colleagues and dear friends – Sibyl O'Reilly Mizzi, David Zammit and Vicky Sultana. From 1994 to 1997, Sibyl, my anthropology programme head, constantly encouraged me to continue my writing, and helped provide the time in which I could do so. From an early date, David was crucial in giving intellectual direction, by insisting that this was a 'study in moral praxis' that needed to see the light of day. Vicky was an unfailing source of wine, food and courage over the many years spent trying to find time for writing from the rigours of running the anthropology programme at the University of Malta from 1997 to 2009, and editing there the *Journal of Mediterranean Studies.* In Malta, I am deeply grateful to my sisters and brothers-in-law, Vicky and Albert Anastasi and Maggie and Ray Gerada, for continuous support and wise counsel.

Other friends in Malta provided invaluable assistance. David Grech gave his time freely in the small hours of many mornings to computerize the trade data on which chapter 7 is based. Terry Gosden, friend and neighbour, kept insisting that I devote my scarce free time to the completion of the manuscript. Students and ex-students at the University of Malta were tremendously helpful: Marguerite Pace Bonello prepared the index; Olivia Vella showed me that my thought was more Weberian than I cared to admit; Martin Cassar was deeply encouraging in the period of 2009–11 when the manuscript could not find a publisher.

Two intellectual debts are vital in their very different ways – to Polly Hill and to Robert Shenton. Polly Hill was the inspiration behind this book, in her insistence on the existence of 'facts', and the importance of collecting them. Robert Shenton's thinking, decisively delivered, was vital to the genesis and evolution of my thought. Most of the arguments in this book developed out of my growing disagreement with Bob over the nature of change in rural Africa.

Vicky Ann Cremona, my colleague at the University of Malta and later, Maltese Ambassador to France, was indispensable. Particularly during two stressful periods, in 2000 and 2007, she provided the strength and, indeed, the guidance, without which I would have been unable to finish the writing of key chapters.

I remember especially my friendship with the late Ndamodu Alhassan of Ahmadu Bello University, Nigeria, and his wife Patti, through whom, in the 1970s, I came to love Nigeria. In Marmara, I acknowledge the generous support of the Village Head Ciroma Alhaji Hamza and the vital assistance of Isa Dan Kaka, Alhaji Sale Marmara, Abdulhamidu Jikan Zaki, Mallam Audu Mai Tafsiri and the late Mallam Nasiru during my long, two-year stretch of fieldwork. They were far, far more than 'informants' in the light that they shone on Hausa economic life, and in the unfailing friendship with which they supported my fieldwork. During my return to Marmara in 1996 and 1997–98, I was given crucial research help by Alhaji Habu dan Alhaji Yahaya. My overwhelming and unrepayable debt is to the late Yvonne Clough. Without her continuous financial assistance, and moral strength, the writing of chapters 1, 3 through 7 and much of the final chapter, would never have been begun, or completed.

I am grateful to publishers and journals for permission to use in this book parts of my previously published work: to Taylor and Francis for re-use of pages 16–32 of 'The Social Relations of Grain Marketing in Northern Nigeria', *Review of African Political Economy* No. 34 December 1985, in chapter 7; to Palgrave Macmillan for re-use of most of 'The Relevance of Religion and Culture to Commercial Accumulation: Fieldwork on Muslim Hausa Exchange and Agricultural Trade in Northern Nigeria', in Barbara Harriss-White (ed.). 1999. *Agricultural Markets From Theory to Practice,* in the Introduction; to the journal *Etnofoor* for re-use of most of 'Polygyny and the Rural Accumulation of Capital: Testing a Model Based on Continuing Research in Northern Nigeria', Volume XVI (1) 2003, in chapters 2 and 8; to Berghahn Journals for re-use of pages 139–40 of 'The Relevance of Kinship to Moral Reasoning in Culture and in the Philosophy of Ethics', *Social Analysis* Volume 51 Issue 1 Spring 2007, in chapter 2, and parts of 'Tension, Reflection, and Agency in the Life of a Hausa Grain Trader' in a forthcoming issue of *Social Analysis*, in chapter 7; and to the journal *Africa* for re-use of pages 598 and 600–606 of 'The Impact of Gender Relations in Islamizing Hausaland, Nigeria', Volume 79 Number 4, 2009, in chapter 1.

Maps

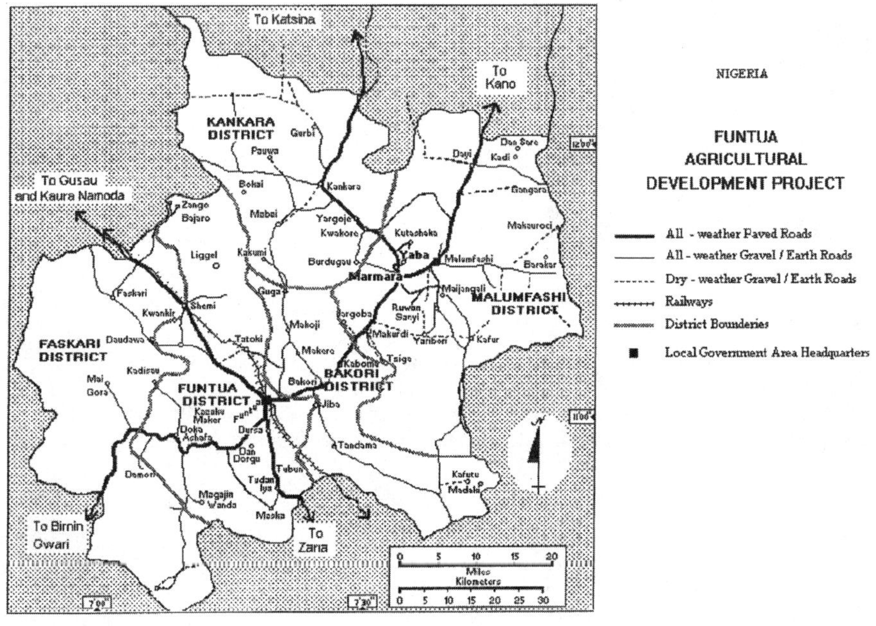

Map 1. Nigeria: Funtua Agricultural Development Project

Source: The World Bank: report IBRD 15862, July 1981, as simplified and prepared by Joseph J. Vella.

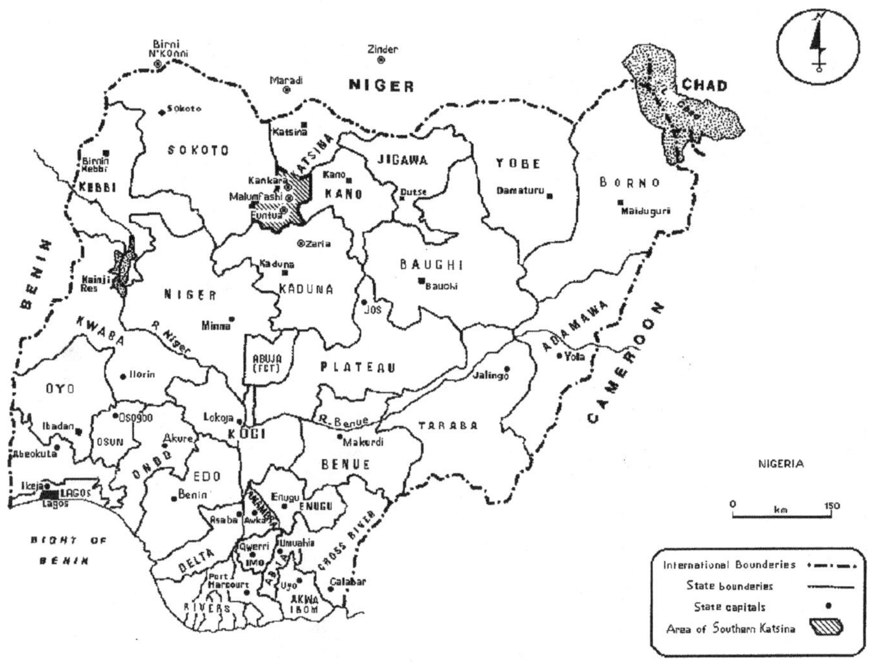

Map 2. Nigeria

Source: © International African Institute, as modified and prepared by Joseph J. Vella. The map on which it is based was first published in Tom Forrest (1994) *The Advance of African Capital: the growth of Nigerian private enterprise*. Edinburgh University Press for the International African Institute. Reproduced by permission of the International African Institute, London.

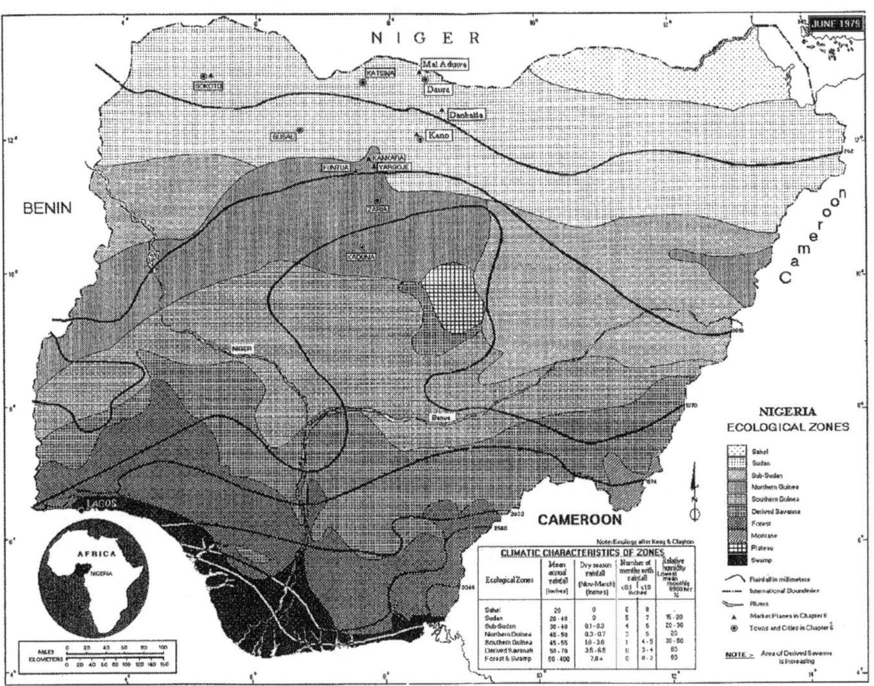

CLIMATIC CHARACTERISTICS OF ZONES

Ecological Zones	Mean annual rainfall (inches)	Dry season rainfall (Nov-March) (inches)	Number of months with rainfall <0.1 inches	Number of months with rainfall <1.0 inches	Relative humidity Lowest mean monthly 0900 hrs %
Sahel	20	0	6	8	-
Sudan	20 - 40	0	5	7	15 - 20
Sub-Sudan	30 - 40	0.1 - 0.3	4	6	20 - 30
Northern Guinea	40 - 50	0.3 - 0.7	3	5	20
Southern Guinea	45 - 55	1.0 - 3.0	1	4 - 5	30 - 60
Derived Savanah	50 - 70	3.6 - 6.8	0	3 - 4	60
Forest & Swamp	60 - 400	7.0 +	0	0 - 2	65

Map 3. Nigeria: Ecological Zones

Source: The World Bank*:* report IBRD 14343R, September 1986, as simplified and prepared by Joseph J. Vella.

Introduction

Methods of Fieldwork and Analysis

Introduction

For ten weeks in 1976, and for almost two years from October 1977 through July 1979, I did fieldwork in the rural Hausa hamlet of Marmara in Katsina Emirate of northern Nigeria. I followed up this research with return visits in December 1985, September 1996 and December 1997–January 1998. Thus, my involvement with Marmara has spanned over twenty years – years of turbulence in the Nigerian economy. The main research, of 1977–79, took place when the economy was undergoing heady expansion. Subsequent visits from 1985 to 1998 occurred during a period when national economic contraction had begun (1985) or was deep (1996 and 1997–98), accompanied by reductions in real government expenditure on the rural areas. The analysis which I developed to explain rural economic relationships in Marmara during the period of expansion and considerable government investment in the rural economy, has had to be tested and refined by attention to economic change, especially after 1986, when Structural Adjustment policies and the sharp devaluation of the currency were consequential. Thus, the anatomy of rural economy outlined in the two concluding chapters of this book weighs both change and continuity in agrarian relationships between 1976 and 1998.

My fieldwork began as a study of long-distance produce trading between Marmara hamlet and other parts of Nigeria. However, it grew into a general investigation of patterns of production and exchange inside the hamlet, because the degree to which not just produce, but also land and labour, were sold on the market, highlighted long-term changes in rural economy. In consequence, the research developed three geographical poles:

- Marmara hamlet,
- nearby marketplaces,
- Danbatta marketplace, over 120 miles to the north, not far from Kano city, where Marmara traders sold their produce in an economic region with very different characteristics.

These three poles are all within the geographical and cultural zone of central Hausaland (Map 3). Chapters 1 and 3–7 focus on the research from 1976 through 1979. Within that period, they analyse households (chapter 1), land distribution, labour practices and credit relations (chapters 3–5); while the marketplaces are more thoroughly explored in the studies of long-distance produce marketing (chapter 6) and rural produce traders (chapter 7). Chapter 8 extends the analysis to the period 1996–98.

Chapter 2 offers a paradigm to explain the intriguing economic particularities of this rural economy, comparing it with competing perspectives. Chapter 9 tests the paradigm by reviewing change and continuity in production and exchange relations between 1979 and 1996–98 in this part of the West African savannah.

Questions Guiding the Research

From 1976 through 1979, I was preoccupied with uncovering relationships of exploitation between traders or wealthier farmers, and the majority of villagers. In the years spent analysing my evidence, however, and in return visits to Marmara, three overlapping questions came to dominate research:

- Are the relations of rural production and exchange characteristic of central Hausaland, changing into capitalist relations?
- If not, can we specify, from the evidence, a different way of understanding how the rural economy has evolved?
- What is the nature and extent of economic inequality in the rural society of central Hausaland?

I have treated answers to the third question as being dependent on answers to the first two.

This book uses two very different approaches to address these questions – a hamlet study of economic relationships between richer and poorer farmers; and an inquiry into a general *field* of activity – agricultural marketing between the economic region of which the hamlet forms a part, and other economic regions. The analysis is limited to the evolution of production-and-exchange relations from *within* the rural society of Marmara hamlet, where my fieldwork on production was focused. It does not analyse the agricultural investments of traditional rulers, urban merchants, the Nigerian political elite, or foreign companies, because these were not present in the area of my fieldwork.[1] It is important for the reader to understand this. Their absence makes it possible for me to argue for a descriptive economics of the common people.

Theory and Practice in Fieldwork

This chapter explores how the fieldwork experience during the main period of research, 1977–79, and equally, the subsequent period of analysis, led me to reject the theoretical perspective on economic change in Africa with which I began, and to search for an alternative mode of explanation. The questions just outlined grew out of debates in Marxist political economy. Two schools of thought influenced the interpretation of findings from my pilot research in 1976. Gunder Frank's development of the 'metropole-satellite' metaphor stressed the reorganization of rural economies under the impact of capitalist industry, in such a way that their surplus was channelled to regional, national and international centres of capital (Frank 1967, 1969). In contrast, theorists of 'articulation' between modes of production sought to define precapitalist economic relations in ex-colonial countries, and then show how these were preserved in a dependent fashion, because they provisioned capitalist industry with low-paid labour or inexpensive produce (Dupre and Rey 1980; Clammer 1978; and Meillassoux 1980, 1981). Combining both perspectives, I explained rural traders as the 'brokers' between a precapitalist mode of production in Hausaland based on family labour, and the capitalist mode based in Western Europe and North America (cf. Long 1975). The precapitalist mode exchanged produce for manufactured goods from the capitalist mode. In this exchange, imported textiles were especially important, because they were used as marriage goods in the rites which reproduced farming households as the basic units of production. Because of their privileged position in this exchange, rural traders accumulated trading profit (merchant's capital) and then used it to expand their landholdings and employment of hired farm labour – an insertion of Marxian 'capital' into the production process. At the same time, these 'farmer-traders' acted in their rural communities both as clients of urban merchants and as patrons of rural producers. Thus, they mediated an 'exchange of cultural meanings' between two different kinds of society. In short, they preserved rural cultural forms, while pushing capitalist transformation beneath the surface (cf. Clough 1981). I carried this theoretical framework into my extended fieldwork of 1977–79.

The Research Area

Marmara is situated in the broad flatlands of the northern Guinea Savannah. It is 100 miles south of the border with the Niger Republic, and sixty miles west of the ancient city of Kano. The hamlet includes a central settlement of farming households – the focus of this study – and many dispersed homesteads. The hamlet is part of the village of Yaba, in the administrative area of Malumfashi Division, in Katsina State (Maps 1 and 2). Most villagers are Muslim Hausa farmers, although there is a sizeable minority of Fulani who mix farming with cattle rearing, and a small number of pastoral Fulani.

I was introduced to Marmara by a neighbour and friend in Zaria township, where I was a teacher. He was born and raised in the hamlet. The choice of Marmara for fieldwork was accidental. It turned out to be a good one, because the original aim of my research was to study agricultural marketing. Marmara is at the centre of an economic region known as southern Katsina, producing large amounts of guineacorn (sorghum) for sale in other parts of Nigeria and in Niger, and cotton for sale to textile companies in Nigeria and to overseas markets.

In 1976, the compound which I rented was part of the storerooms of the hamlet's largest grain trader. I soon discovered that he engaged in weekly trade by lorry over long distances – to Danbatta marketplace, 126 miles to the northeast, and occasionally to Sokoto marketplace, 240 miles to the northwest. I travelled by motorcycle fortnightly to Danbatta to explore his trading contacts there. I also began to explore his relationships with wealthier produce traders living in other villages. I kept records of changing prices and volumes in two big marketplaces near Marmara which bulked produce for long-distance traders. Inside the hamlet, I began to investigate relationships of indebtedness between farmers and traders.

During my second, much longer stay, from October 1977 through July 1979, I enlarged my study, for I decided that the organization of produce marketing could only be understood in the wider context of the social relations of production and exchange. With regard to production, I broadly categorized farmers, on the basis of landholding, into 'large', 'middle', 'small' and 'very small', and toured the farms of volunteers, recording inputs and outputs. Furthermore, I surveyed the farms, and learnt as much as I could about the lives, of a few wealthy traders living in other villages, who had important economic relations with Marmara traders. In 1979, using aerial photographs, I mapped and measured most of the fields used by farmers in the central roadside settlement. With regard to exchange, I worked through informants to chart household expenditure patterns. I spent much time collecting information on the financing of marriage expenditure, the greatest single expense in the life-cycle of most households.

In December 1985, I returned to Marmara, as a consultant working on the World Bank's ten-year Agricultural Sector Memorandum for Nigeria. This gave me the opportunity to catch up with people who had been central to my earlier research, and especially with their involvement in land transfers. For three weeks in September 1996 and for two weeks in December 1997–January 1998, on research leave from the University of Malta, I returned to Marmara to gain a sense of the changes in the rural economy since 1985. It gave me the chance to look more particularly at changes in the lives of individuals across a wide range of income and economic power.

General Comments on My Field Practice

During my first stay, in 1976, I was accompanied everywhere by an interpreter. Moreover, I was largely dependent for ideas on a young part-time trader. He became my key informant. He told me about flows of commercial credit from urban merchants, government contractors and hereditary rulers to the patron of the main grain trader in Marmara, and through him, to other hamlet traders. He obtained for me numerical data concerning the extent to which traders bought produce at harvest and stored it against a price rise in the next farming season. He also explained the pervasiveness of a form of 'high-interest' credit, whereby traders advanced money to farmers in return for grain at harvest.

During my second, much longer stay, three general changes emerged in the character of my fieldwork. First, the hamlet head and other villagers insisted that I work without an interpreter, that my spoken Hausa was good enough to be getting on with, and that they would 'teach me what I did not know'. This experience was itself instructive. They distrusted the interpreter as an outsider, though he was from a town only twenty miles away. And they regarded me partly as an insider, through their kinsman who had introduced me to the hamlet. Second, the 'key informant' of my earlier fieldwork was no longer there. I therefore had to make direct acquaintance with farmers and traders for information. Much more than in 1976, I was more immediately exposed to the necessity of forming personal relationships.

Learning Hausa more fully, with the aid of a dictionary, was itself a part of fieldwork. People were self-conscious about expression, sought forcefully to convey personal meanings through words, and enjoyed demonstrating different ways of expressing an idea. Members of a Muslim society, rural Hausa not only describe actions but also like to reflect upon them, and justify them in religious or moral terms. Confronted with some new idiom that they would give me, I had to ask many questions as to its meaning, while they laughed and urged me to get out my dictionary. Learning the ways in which they verbally encapsulated the meaning of their actions turned out to be a way of gaining insight into their sense of 'value'.

Thirdly, it was soon apparent that villagers regarded me differently once they realized that I was in the hamlet for an extended time. If in my initial fieldwork I was treated as a guest, now I was treated as a mystery. For a foreigner to spend ten weeks among them, asking questions, was flattering. For the same foreigner to spend two years was unsettling. They knew that my stay was sanctioned by the relevant hereditary rulers – the village head of Yaba and the district head of Malumfashi – and by the police and government authorities. I explained that I had come from the university in Zaria (seventy miles away) with which some were familiar, and that I wished to write a book about their 'history and their work'. This did not reduce their suspicion that I was a government spy (*mutumin siyasa*) prying into their incomes and political views. Traders, with their contacts in the urban world, felt more comfortable in my company than did farmers anchored in the rural community. But all were evasive in giving economic information. After several months, their political fears were replaced by a more deep-seated belief – that I was simply mercenary. I was writing down their affairs in my 'little books', which I would 'carry back to England and there make profit'. In this way, I would 'eat (*ci*) the village'.

Under these conditions, I emphasize the very gradual nature of collecting information. The quality and quantity of information grew with trust and acceptance by particular individuals. It was greatest among those villagers who became personal friends – but these were not necessarily the ones in whom I was most interested. Quite separately, the experience of distrust made me question the accuracy of my earlier short-term fieldwork. A long stay was needed to pry open, partially, the 'secrets' (*asiri*) of wealth and poverty.

The Course of the Fieldwork

The need to proceed through personal relationships conditioned the course of fieldwork. Here, I summarize it very briefly by reference to the period 1977–79. I used two kinds of notebook – pocket notebooks, which I always had with me, and large notebooks in which, at the end of the day, I tried to sort out complex social relationships or transcribe numerical data jotted down earlier. Facing distrust, I soon decided only to bring out the pocket notebook in particular circumstances – when asking questions about linguistic usage, when interviewing friends who accepted my research, and when noting produce prices in marketplaces. Otherwise, I looked and listened and wrote from memory in the evening (this inevitably produced the remark: 'Now you watch, he's going to go away and write all that down in his big book.')

Through the first fifteen months, I made a point of attending the nearby periodic marketplaces whenever they met, and openly recording produce prices. It was a way of confirming publicly my identity as a researcher (even to myself) and gradually accustoming people to the fact. Thereafter, it was easy to rely on villagers who had been to market for this information, so saving time. I travelled to the Danbatta weekly marketplace north of Kano, on nine weekends through the two years, spread over different seasons of the annual marketing cycle.

In Danbatta, I watched the activities of Marmara's long-distance grain traders. I established a close relationship with the extremely helpful retailer through whom they wholesaled most of their grain. I got to know his marriage arrangements, toured his farms, and noted the details of his farm expenditure and output. This helped me to establish similarities in culture between the economic regions of Northern Kano and Southern Katsina, and contrasts in their agronomic systems (chapter 6).

My fieldwork changed as I increased the number of my friends. During October–December 1977, I made my three best friends in the hamlet. Two were farmers with relatively small landholdings, and they gave me much information about their total income and expenditure. The third was the most enterprising entrepreneur in the hamlet, and had used his earnings from trade to rapidly expand his engagement in farming and transport. He was very patient in showing me his farms while harvesting was underway and discussing inputs, outputs and profit margins. A maize trader and bus transporter, he explained the different types of commercial lending.

During January–February 1978, I carried one of my 'small farmer' friends on my motorcycle on all his cotton buying and selling expeditions, noting bargaining practices, and observing and discussing conditions of cotton production as well as marketing. Through the postharvest dry season from January through April, I spent much time at marriage ceremonies, and developed comparative records of marriage expenditure among different categories of farmer. Hausa society is polygynous, so I found throughout my stay that the pursuit of marriage partners was a constant preoccupation of men. I paid attention to their conversations surrounding marriage negotiations, and their understanding of the causes of marital stability and instability.

During the farming season of May–August 1978, my relationship with my landlord, the hamlet guineacorn trader, had become sufficiently close that I could follow him through all farming operations. I also recorded the production expenditure of friends in different categories of farmer. Nevertheless, I was still casting about for information about the grain trade. When the leading trader in the adjoining village sent a consignment by lorry to distant Sokoto, I volunteered to take him there on my motorcycle. The trip enabled me to make comparisons between the long-distance trade to Sokoto and that to Danbatta (chapter 6). Thereafter, he took to dropping into my room, and I gradually developed a picture of his trading relationships and of his 'high-interest loans' to farmers (chapter 5).

During September–December 1978, I was able to obtain detailed information from my landlord about the guineacorn trade. Moreover, I established a working relationship with an older villager who knew much about this trade and the general history of the hamlet. At the same time, I became part of a group of neighbouring household heads who ate their evening meals together. Hausa Muslim men eat dinner in friendship groups in front of their compounds. In the hush of darkness, they would quietly discuss Islam, living conditions past and present, the past injustices of hereditary rulers.

From January through April 1979, my main work was to map the farmland of the hamlet, using aerial photographs given to me by the World Bank agricultural development project providing fertilizer in the area. This exercise, utterly exhausting, had unforeseen advantages. My paid assistants included an older man who knew much about the history of land sales in the hamlet. Both assistants gave 'high-interest' loans. Only after months of working with me did they divulge their lending (chapter 5).

Before leaving Marmara in July 1979, I completed my survey of household size and composition in the central settlement by interviewing all household heads whom I did not know well. I spent much time listening to the Qur'anic mallams, and visiting my landlord's patron, a much richer trader in another hamlet.

In summary, necessity led me to conduct research through a technique of 'branching out'. One person led to another. No one person had the knowledge to be a 'key informant'. After a full year, a few case studies began to emerge in detail. Quantified information could be collected from friends, but universal surveys – for example, of family size – were more reliable if they developed gradually through a network of friends. Only after this branching out had become ramified, could I expect reasonable cooperation and the likelihood of accurate responses from villagers who did not know me personally. They trusted me – to a degree – because they knew one or more of my friends.

Case Studies of Three Farmer Traders

My landlord, a hamlet produce trader, was a difficult man to get to know. Put more honestly, I did not realize until I left Marmara just how helpful he had been from the beginning. He was always busy. Until the farming season of 1979, I had to be content with friendly banter and occasional explanations – and the advantage of living in his warehouse. I had to watch without asking questions. However, he eventually invited me to join him when he indulged in *kewaya,* the Hausa habit of doing a circuit of the fields under cultivation. Then, he would discuss not only economic details but also his broader purposes.

The real breakthrough came as a result of advice given by Mr Richard Bruce, doing fieldwork on the Jos Plateau. To better understand the reasons for borrowing and the ethics of lending, I started loaning small sums to friends in the hamlet. Once I began lending money to my landlord for trade, his approach to me became more serious. I gathered details of his relations with other farmers. He would tell me about other traders – and was interested in doing so. Through him, I learnt much about his patron, an inter-village wholesaler of grains, and about a long-distance grain trader who was the servant of a hereditary ruler. I became what the Hausa call a 'friend-in-trade' (*abokin ciniki*). I had accomplished a partial transition to the inside of the web of trading networks (chapter 7).

Gradually, I became an extended member of his household, invited for dinner in front of his personal compound. I became close to his younger brothers. They were part of his family farming unit (*gandu*). At the minor and major harvests, they told me his output on each farm.

I had been on friendly terms with the intervillage wholesaler during my first stay in Marmara. But on my return to Southern Katsina in 1977, when I started questioning him about 'high-interest' credit, he reacted like an angry bear. Later, his personal retainer befriended me. The master treated me courteously if distantly whenever I visited his hamlet at the end of the market day at Kankara. I could observe the circle of Qur'anic mallams surrounding him, the mosque at the entrance to his compound, the continual religious discussions.

My personal friendship with him was revived indirectly. Once he heard from his client, my landlord, that I was mapping the farmland in Marmara, he called me to his hamlet and set me to measuring his fields. He wanted a careful assessment of his fertilizer requirements from the development project. He became for me an acute commentator on economic trends, the result of a long career shifting trade between commodities. The servant of the hereditary ruler was the most relaxed and engaging of the three traders, perhaps because his social position rendered him more secure. I used his warehouse in Kankara marketplace as a base for observation. I asked him few questions.

My interpretation of the actions of the intervillage wholesaler was partly based, and of the servant of the hereditary ruler largely based, on the accounts of the hamlet trader. He focused on the various relationships into which they entered in the course of trade. To say this is to say that I was entering the mind of a trader. But furthermore, I was entering the mind of a trading system. That is a large claim.

My landlord discussed trade in terms of the gains and losses arising out of social relationships, and in terms of his main preoccupation – strategies for success. But I came to see that he was always *pointing* – to what counted as 'success', 'wealth' or 'gain'. Through him, I was gradually redefining 'value' in rural Hausa terms.

An obvious criticism of my method is that it looks upward at the marketing system through the mind of the man at the bottom.

Against this, I would offer three points. The hamlet view was for me the most useful, since my main concern was the impact of commodity exchange on rural relations of production. Second, the merit of hamlet-based research is that it enables the fieldworker to establish what, if any, value 'community' has for the various levels of rural trader. Lastly, I note that there was nothing exceptional or unique in my landlord's observable actions. I therefore inferred, buttressed by general experience of other traders, that his account of motives and values was 'typical'. Following the usage of J-F Bayart (1993), my logic is that social analysis traces collective *mentalities* as much as social interactions.

Fieldwork, and Rural Society, as Political Process

Villagers often recounted the past extortions of the hereditary ruling class, and the use of forced labour on the rulers' farms (euphemistically called *gayya,* or 'communal labour'). These practices were called *zalinci* (oppression). The rulers had 'eaten the country' (*ci kasa*). It was sometimes blurted out that I, too, was 'eating the village'. Clearly, I would profit from the information (*labari*) in my little notebooks, in the same manner, they said, as colonial merchants had profited from export crops. What was humbling was their ability to separate my person – which they liked – from their view of my political function.

I got very depressed. I spent a week in May 1978 enclosed in my room, reading the least taxing material I could find. Then, the villagers themselves buoyed me up. Led by the hamlet head, they urged me to farm. Belatedly, I rented two small fields and planted and harvested with hired labourers. Again, the hamlet head urged me to start an evening class in English. Many villagers felt that in their dealings with the police, the burden of bribery would be lessened if they could speak some English. So, for three months in the village schoolroom, I chalked out Hausa phrases and English translations. They were very serious. I was nonplussed by the range of pupils – from the richest farmer, a cloth trader with at least forty acres, to the poorest, a butcher with half an acre. I was surprised when the pupils called communal labour (*gayya*) to weed my farms. The richest farmer weeded alongside the poorest.

These experiences engendered in me the sense that, despite differences in income, villagers constituted a 'community'. I felt pressed inside myself to establish some measure of equivalence in my exchanges with this community: villagers had become for me more than just a collection of individuals. My motorcycle became an ambulance to the divisional hospital. Having antiseptics and bandages, I tended cuts. These are, of course, the common experience of fieldworkers. I also gave gifts at marriage ceremonies – a source of confusion as they correctly pointed out to me that once I had left the village, they would be unable to reciprocate at my ceremonies.

There were seven Qur'anic mallams in the hamlet. All villagers attached themselves to at least one mallam, from whom they received charms and detailed advice in their personal lives. Most traders and rich village farmers, like their poorer kin, followed the local mallams in identifying with the populist political party of northern Nigeria at that time, the PRP. They referred to Aminu Kano, its leader, as *shehu* (Islamic scholar and leader). Beneath differences in landholding and economic practice, there was community of 'value' – beliefs about right action and the nature of God, much discussed between mallams and other villagers. For example, people accepted that the hamlet head, their kinsman and a commoner, represented the political interests of the hereditary rulers. After all, he relied on them for advances as a cotton buyer. But on other occasions, he organized the protest against corruption in the agricultural development project.[2] He also led the pressure for me to start an evening class for all villagers.

Error in Fieldwork

I was twenty-eight when I entered the hamlet, and gravitated at first to its young men. I often cursed this mistake. Income and social power corresponded rather closely with age. Given my wealth and power in rural eyes, I ought to have avoided the company of young men. They took to dropping into my room for chats which consumed time. I felt an irritated bystander to their conversations. But in retrospect, I see that I was in fact 'overhearing' their expressions of what was valuable in sexual, domestic and economic life.

I spent too much time with poorer men, not enough with the most successful farmers. This resulted at least partly from my Marxisante political bias and the accompanying theoretical frameworks. Within the village much of my information came too low on the scale of income and economic power. This gave me difficulties in the initial period of analysis and writing up after leaving Nigeria. In consequence, it took me years to unravel what was at first, in my head, a thesis which took 'poor and middle peasants' as the defining categories from which to reason a perspective on change in the rural economy.

My awareness that appropriate fieldwork involved branching out, came very slowly. For the first eight months, I treated villagers as receptacles of data which needed ferreting out. Only after that week alone in my room did the intervention of the hamlet head make me realize how hard people were trying to understand me – and be helpful. Only thereafter did I begin to see individuals as interesting in their own right. While they differed in their ability to articulate observations and opinions, in varying degrees each person carried within himself a consciousness of community structure, values and history. More accurately, each person had developed a picture somewhat different from the others. The point for the researcher was to accord individuals the time to allow their picturing to unfold.

In this respect, the four months toward the end of fieldwork spent mapping and measuring all farms within the hamlet area marked a reversion to my old, instrumental approach to research. The mapping exercise revived much of the distrust toward me. Only toward the end of the exercise did a number of farmers volunteer to show me their fields, because they realized that a knowledge of their acreage increased their chances of obtaining fertilizer from the agricultural project. It would have been more revealing had I undertaken farm mapping much earlier, and gone about it more gradually, by branching out from one person to another.

Now, I accept that mistakes are inherent in the social learning which is intrinsic to fieldwork. I was helped from the beginning by accident and luck. My greatest mistake was a failure to perceive at the time. Importantly, then, the period spent away from the research site, trying to achieve a written argument out of the material collected, enables the fieldworker to confront mistaken judgements in fieldwork and try to overcome them.

Analytical Method

The Example of Polly Hill

My manner of thinking through findings resulted from continuously rereading the work of Polly Hill. In *Rural Hausa* (1972), she analysed the economy of a village of relatively low population density. In *Population, Prosperity and Poverty: Rural Kano 1900 and 1970* (1977), she shifted her attention to hamlets in an area of extremely high population density. In *Dry Grain Farming Families* (1982), she extended her method of inquiry to south India, to communities which shared with her Nigerian villages a type of production based on rain-fed food grains and permanent, manured cultivation. Throughout these studies, she had a basic aim, the measurement and explanation of inequality among village farmers, and to achieve it she focussed on three features of village economy: land distribution; relations within households between the heads, their wives and subordinate kinsmen; and relations between employers and hired labourers. These studies have a thematic unity – the impact of varying population densities on a 'dry grain' type of production.

From Polly Hill, I take my analytical method: valid statements about economy can only be derived from painstaking measurement of key economic indicators, and careful descriptions in plain language of the variety of activity. Hill's method was to establish a village boundary and then measure, for all households inside it, basic features of their economic life. While doing this, she developed a descriptive picture of economic relations and how they vary from rich to poor. Through her works, she evinced a botanical enthusiasm for details. This, more than anything else, marks her method – sheer interest in the actual diversity of human conduct.

Two further features of her method can be singled out for their relevance to economic analysis. First, the general categories she developed to explain her findings did not derive from existing literature. Rather, she developed them by combining discussion with village people and her own observations. For example, in *Rural Hausa,* she based her analysis of inequality on a practical question: how do various households withstand the hunger resulting from a late, or very poor, harvest? Asking this question of local people, she constructed four 'groups' of farmers – those helping others with loans or gifts, those 'neither suffering nor helping', those 'suffering somewhat', and those 'suffering severe hunger'. Her eventual classification of all household heads showed systematic variation in measured assets and activities. It therefore enabled her to generate conclusions about the extent and causes of inequality.

Secondly, Hill's method was open-ended: she was prepared to be surprised by what she found. Then, she allowed unexpected findings to change her general assumptions ('theoretical postulates') regarding rural economy. She contrasted this approach with the 'deductive method' of economists. They begin with a priori postulates, work out the logical inferences, compare these with observed phenomena and then 'qualify' both postulates and inferences accordingly (Hill 1982: 7–8, 14).

Hill's method implies that analysis of 'the local' is as important as analysis of the regional, the national and the international, in explaining economic change. Using the metaphor of 'structure', writers in the political economy tradition of West African history and anthropology explain local structures in terms of larger structures (e.g., Hart 1982; Shenton 1986). Following an ethnographic tradition, Hill's analysis of 'the local' illuminates larger structures. Using the metaphor of 'picture', a true picture of economic change in larger structures can only be generated out of local pictures.

The Logic of the Method

My method of analysis is empirical, in so far as I seek to arrive at general statements about the nature of rural economy from specific descriptions of attitudes, persons, activities and social relationships. I present a series of indices covering all households in the central settlement of Marmara hamlet to enable comparison with other areas, and set the framework for further analysis (chapters 1, 3 and 4). Thereafter, I increasingly use case study material to isolate what I regard as significant to understanding the relations of production and exchange (chapters 4, 5, 7 and 8). At the same time, conversations with villagers are reported in order to convey their social consciousness – regarding their attitudes to economic activity, the proper goals of economic life and the moral beliefs attached to those goals. Thus, the interpretative generalizations in the theoretical introduction (chapter 2) and the reflections on change (chapter 9) are the product of *different* kinds of observation – universal surveys, partial samples and case studies. A further point has to be made. The *weight* given to the various kinds of observation relies on my overall judgement of what was 'crucial' or significant'. This judgement, intrinsically subjective, derives from my accumulated experience of living in the hamlet.

Universal samples, partial samples and case studies, across the range of economic processes and institutions, showed a consistency of pattern. This book does not seek to persuade the reader through an additive piling up of detail. Rather, it tries to demonstrate that under each sphere investigated – land, labour, household expenditure, credit, marketing and the acquisition of wealth – careful attention to empirical detail points in the same analytical direction: existing theories of underdevelopment or transformation are inadequate; a new synthesis is needed to explain structure and change. Put differently, measurements, descriptions of action and reports of conversation all dovetail. There were gaps in my information. But the information available to me showed remarkable internal consistency.

Like Hill, I developed categories for descriptive analysis which arose from the conditions of the research area. Thus, the characteristics of my 'large', 'middle' and 'small' farmers were defined by farmers' differing capacities to solve local problems. The book also develops a key distinction between villagers engaged in long-term wealth acquisition and those not so engaged. These categories arose out of the crucial contribution of off-farm occupations to income. Because of the greater scale of their off-farm activity, some villagers were better placed to invest farm and off-farm earnings in various sorts of wealth acquisition.

My method departs from Hill's in four ways. First, my arguments are not based to the same extent on the demarcation of a village boundary. My concern with agricultural marketing took my research outside the boundaries of any one village and into the other economic regions where villagers marketed their produce. Secondly, Hill measured the assets and activities of discrete units (usually households) in order to reach conclusions about socioeconomic relations. I am more preoccupied with descriptions of interaction. Hence, 'social relations of production and exchange' is my focal concept for generalising out of concrete descriptions. It allowed me to capture the quality of interaction. Thirdly, I make much greater use of case studies in arriving at generalizations. My case studies include both 'social situations' – a combination of interconnected events in a restricted time span – and 'extended case studies' – sequences of events over a long period (a distinction drawn by Gluckman 1961: 5–17, quoted in Clyde Mitchell 1983: 193–94).

Finally, Hill called her method 'inductive' (Hill 1982: 4) – general principles of behaviour are inferred from the empirical investigation of particular instances. For a writer like myself, who relies more heavily on case studies, the logical basis for arguing the truth of generalizations is more complicated. For the hamlet of Marmara, an inductive method was at work. Consistency between different kinds of sample allowed for extrapolation to most individuals and groups inside the hamlet. Beyond it, chapter 1 demarcates a small zone which appeared to share with Marmara a similar population density and an agronomic system. There, I would argue that extrapolation is safe. However, to extrapolate from my samples to the entire region of southern Katsina pushes induction too far. People of the region shared a common history (as the march between the emirates of Kano and Katsina) and a propensity to produce crop surpluses for markets. These similarities might make my conclusions interesting. They do not make them valid.

In this book, I do not extrapolate from one area to a wider one. Rather, I use my descriptive analysis[3] of economic processes to suggest a model of the way in which rural relations of production and exchange have evolved under certain general conditions. These conditions had emerged in a specific history. They were true during the period of research:

- high and rising population density;
- low real tax burdens;
- private control of land *by villagers* – *without* outside encroachment;
- a road system linking the ecological zone of which the hamlet studied is a part, to other ecological zones;
- in consequence, a large market for agricultural products;
- the importance of off-farm occupations to rural income;
- diverse systems of credit based on the negotiation of personal ties;
- men's widespread use of increased income to expand the number of wives, for themselves and their sons

I argue that there are causal interconnections between these conditions which generate a certain dynamic of economic change. Thus, my generalization is from a descriptive analysis to a model.

Is such generalization epistemologically sound? J. Clyde Mitchell attempted to show how the unique material of a case study can form the basis for inference about some more general social process. He argued that worries about the logical basis of extrapolation from case studies stem from a failure to distinguish between statistical inference and 'logical or scientific' inference. This failure comes from the belief that extrapolation is only achieved through statistical inference – procedures whereby an analyst draws conclusions about the existence of two or more characteristics in some wider population from their existence in a small sample of that population. In contrast, 'scientific or causal – or perhaps more appropriately, logical inference', is the act whereby an analyst draws conclusions about the essential linkage between two or more characteristics in terms of some systematic explanatory schema (Clyde Mitchell 1983: 199–200). The process of inference from case studies to like situations in general can never be statistical. 'We infer that the features of the case study will be present in a wider population because our analysis of the case study is unassailable' (Clyde Mitchell 1983: 200).

Here, Clyde Mitchell clearly implies a conditional statement: *if* the key conditions, and causal interconnections between them, specified in a case study are found elsewhere, *then* the analysis of the case study is applicable elsewhere. The explanatory power of a case study depends on its logical connections with the explanatory principles of a theory (Clyde Mitchell 1983: 204). His account implies that the 'predictions from an analysis based on case study techniques tend to be theoretical rather than empirical' (Clyde Mitchell 1983: 205). Thus he proceeds to his main conclusion: 'The validity of extrapolation depends not on the typicality or representativeness of the case but upon the cogency of the theoretical reasoning' (Clyde Mitchell 1983: 207).

Clyde Mitchell dwells on the particularity of case studies. The very *detail* of case studies provides optimum conditions for the exploration of the principles and processes developed in a general theory (Clyde Mitchell 1983: 206). Thus, the 'a-typical' case, if sufficiently detailed, can be highly significant, precisely because the 'concatenation of events is so idiosyncratic as to throw into sharp relief' the principles of a theory, so making possible its revision (Clyde Mitchell 1983: 204). In providing a theoretical framework for the rich material of the case study, the case researcher is addressing the workings of wider systems.[4]

Description and Theory

A constant worry for ethnographers is the view that their descriptions do not constitute an independent witness to the strengths or weaknesses of existing interpretations, precisely because the descriptions are themselves theoretically evolved and therefore, constructed. Here, I argue my disagreement with this view, by resorting to a brief chronology of my analysis.

I was not an anthropology student at the time of my fieldwork. Neither anthropological theory in its breadth, nor any training in fieldwork techniques, illuminated my fieldwork. Rather, I was collecting evidence to help develop the corpus of Marxian theories of political economy and underdevelopment. Only through analysis *after* fieldwork did I discover in my memories and field notes:

- the importance of 'face-to-face' interaction in societies where most economic, political and religious transactions proceed through personal relations;
- the extent to which people's notions of 'gain' and 'loss', 'wealth' and 'poverty' are socially defined;
- the extent to which the complex of human actions and relations, and the contacts between 'local' and 'extra-local', form a seamless web[5] and so invite an holistic analysis.

It is mainly an analysis of economic activities and relations. With difficulty, these could be described and connected to each other. Their explanation, however, required recourse to the meaning that actions had for the doers. I invoked 'meaning' by trying to rediscover during analysis the beliefs of farmers and traders concerning what was desirable and what was obligatory. I did not *assume* logical consistency between desires and moral views. That villagers were trying across time to achieve consistency between action, desire and moral belief stemmed from my later interpretation of the field notes. My sense of their desires and beliefs is based partly on actions and partly on oral statements – often mutterings and musings[6] overheard. Fragments of conversation were essential to my personal reconstruction of belief and desire.

Thus, this book reports conversations which I deem to encapsulate their beliefs. My explanations thus rely on discourse. But I do not use 'discourse' in the sophisticated sense of a semiotics (Geertz 1973: 3–20) or of fine-grained discursive analysis (Foucault 1972: 21–70, 199–211; Lutz and Abu-Lughod 1990: 1–10). In a sentence: my analysis focuses on observed actions, but in a frame of heard conversations where I attended to those desires and beliefs of the doers which go beyond short-term economic or political calculation.

For me, then, the period of analysis and writing after going back to England was a part of fieldwork. I mean to say that, bewildered by old and familiar surroundings, I was not just taxing my original theoretical frameworks with the numerical evidence that I had collected but, more deeply, I was making an effort to recall to mind all whom I had known – and what they had expressed with force.

From 1979 through 1983, I increasingly found that my overall impression of village life and large amounts of my numerical evidence did not agree with existing interpretations of agrarian change in northern Nigeria or rural West Africa. And my initial theoretical perspective – farmer-traders as the brokers of capitalist agricultural transformation – did not integrate all of my experiences into a meaningful whole. I sought to fill the interpretative vacuum by a descriptive reconstruction which involved an enormous number of numerical calculations. From 1987 to 1995, I reworked this reconstruction into a framework for a doctoral thesis in sociology. Return visits to Marmara in 1996 and 1997–98 gave me the chance to test and further refine my analysis. Chapter 2 offers a very different model of economic change from the thesis of capitalist transformation with which I began fieldwork in 1976.

From this chronology, I take exception to the argument which holds that description presupposes a theoretic framework. That neglects the extent to which socioeconomic researchers tax their information as archaeologists torture their relics (John Goldthorpe's phrases in a seminar in 1983). Certainly, my written descriptions do incorporate assumptions. But those were analytic decisions taken *after* thousands of calculations. To neglect these is to discard the open-ended years of factual rediscovery. In this sense, the distinction between 'empirical' and 'theoretical' *is* vital. It is, perhaps, under-recorded in Clyde Mitchell's account of inference from a case study. The intrinsically theoretical nature of 'description' is true of the final writing, but is false of the preliminary analysis in which the argument evolves.

I offer a summary justification for my method of analysis. Based on all of his information and personal experience, the student uses imagination to frame generalizations. These offer 'explanation' by endowing particular events or attitudes with causal significance, or by showing the connections between different social spheres. 'Truth' refers to the consistency of the explanations offered. The behaviour patterns derived from any one kind of observation – for example, case studies – must be consistent with the patterns implied by other types – universal and partial samples, local conversation and habits of speech, and evidence collected over the wider area of social interaction in which the fieldwork site is located.

The metaphor of 'pictures' is helpful. Very briefly, my main method of fieldwork was to spend time with those farmers and traders who were willing to talk to me. While I could record produce prices and volumes in marketplaces or measure farmland with assistants, I could not construct pictures of economic interaction until I had related these measurements to the lives of people. In consequence, much of my time was spent waiting for individuals to find it convenient or interesting to discuss their lives with me. As a result, there are many gaps in my knowledge. But if the pictures of economic life drawn from different sources are consistent with each other, this enables me to fit them into a broader canvas.[7] This book is a plea for the study of 'patterns' intermediate between theory and description.

The Mode of Analysis: Thinking in a Tabular Fashion

My analytical reconstruction of the rural economy is based on an effort to think through and integrate the many measurements – of land, labour use, credit, trade turnover, agricultural yields and profit margins in trade and agriculture – collected during the main period of research. In chapters 3 through 7, I present my reconstruction of the rural economy through a large number of tables which constitute my final decisions regarding the significance of those measurements. My argument proceeds *through* the tables. They are designed to convey to the reader the key cause-effect relationships which I discovered during analysis *after* fieldwork had ended.

The tables are of different kinds. Using chapters 3, 4 and 7 as examples, the reader can distinguish between:

- aggregations of data
- analytic comparisons
- argumentative analyses
- summaries
- synopses
- financial processes over time
- descriptive charts

For example, Table 3.2, 'Land distribution among household heads, Marmara, 1978', is an *aggregation of basic data,* because it presents the acreage range for each of the ten deciles of land-using household heads, from that using most land to that using the least. Table 3.4, 'Land distribution among household heads, Village Studies, 1949–79', is an *analytic comparison,* because land distributions across all village studies up to and including my own, are presented so as to compare the degree of inequality in landholding in the different villages, with differences in their population density. Tables 3.8 and 3.9, 'Intergenerational depth of residence', may be termed *argumentative analyses,* because there, I explore the effect on the amount of land used, of the length of residence in the hamlet of the progenitors of each land user. On other occasions, I conclude a series of tables with a *summary table,* which allows me to convey the pattern of behaviour for the hamlet as a whole. For example, having previously tabulated the different kinds of land seller and land buyer, in Table 3.25, 'Summary of land purchases', I group together all purchases in terms of a social typology of transactions, in order to assess the relative significance of each type. Then, again, there are important *synoptic tables,* which bring together different kinds of evidence in order to explore causal relationships. For example, Table 3.19, 'Landholding, number of wives and household size', is designed to reveal how, as landholding increased among all household heads, the number of wives and the size of households tended to increase. Finally, there are tables which convey *financial processes over time.* Thus, in Tables 7.10A through 7.10E, 'M.'s Income and nontrade expenditure', the trader's total income and his expenditure inside each of the five trading periods of the year are compared so that the reader can gauge the extent of his dependence on credit.

Charts are more descriptive than tables. On some occasions, they make it possible to outline the criteria I use in analysis – for example,

Chart 4.1, 'Categories used in analysing arrangements for labour hiring'. On other occasions, a chart makes it possible to concisely describe an activity over time – for example, Chart 4.2, 'Farm operations for the two main crops of the Marmara farming season'. Charts are designed to allow the argument of each chapter to proceed in a clearer fashion, because necessary information has been conveyed.

In short, I developed my framework for analysing the rural economy by thinking through the evidence in a tabular fashion. Tabular thinking about a small population is a way of directly confronting and comparing evidence. It thus keeps the analyst close to the evidence. Furthermore, it allows unexpected economic behaviour to be compared with less surprising behaviour, so as to assess their relative significance within the same table. Finally, it enables the analyst to quickly capture key economic relationships in a small population. The tabular method is innovative because it makes tables and charts not an appendix to the argument, but the core of the argument. They are the pivot around which the argument turns.

Notes

1. For accounts of these, see, for example, Andrae and Beckman 1987; Beckman 1987; Forrest 1994.
2. For an account of this, see Clough and Williams 1987: 184–92.
3. The term is from Jane Guyer. See Guyer 1997: 221–34.
4. To my mind, Hammersley's critique of Clyde Mitchell involves a misreading. He argues that Clyde Mitchell provided no solution to the problem of induction (Hammersley 1992: 180). His misreading is understandable. Clyde Mitchell does use words like 'extrapolation' and 'prediction'; and approvingly refers to Znaniecki's account of 'analytical induction' (Clyde Mitchell 1983: 200–201). However, a close reading shows that 'causal or logical inference' from case studies does not involve induction at all.

   Hammersley will not allow that a presentation of logical relationships between characteristics in a case study is sufficient to show the plausibility or otherwise of a theory. He would require that the evidence be sufficient to show that the interpretation is the '*most* plausible of those available' (1992: 177). But surely, this amounts to an unrealistic account of theory building in the social sciences. Rather, theories have been found useful, or illuminating, until cases have arisen wherein causal connections are incompatible with existing theory. When this has occurred, conditions in the incompatible case study have been used to develop new theory.
5. I take the term from Murray Last (personal communication).
6. These were typical terms of Gilbert Ryle (in lecture).
7. The term is from Gavin Williams (personal communication).

Chapter 1

An Introduction to the Political Economy and Culture of Marmara Hamlet

Introduction

Any model of the production and exchange relations in the area around Marmara will only be clear once key patterns of historical change in the wider political economy have been introduced. Thus, this chapter surveys changes in the much larger contexts of the Nigerian state, of northern Nigeria as an historical formation and within it, the economic region of southern Katsina of which Marmara forms a part.

From its independence in 1960 until 1966, Nigeria was governed by civilian politicians. Thereafter, a succession of military governments continued, apart from a brief return to elected government between 1979 and 1983, until 2000, since when the country has once again returned to civilian government. In 1967, a military government split four regions into twelve states; in 1976, a subsequent military regime divided the country into nineteen states. By 1991, a further eleven states were created, making thirty in all (Map 2). By 1996, the number of states had expanded to thirty-six.

Nigeria can be distinguished from most countries in sub-Saharan Africa by three features – its enormous population, its petroleum wealth and its steady pursuit since independence of policies favouring a market economy. The main emphasis of government spending has been on infrastructure rather than direct investment in industrial or agricultural enterprises. Before the onset of the oil boom in 1970, Nigeria was the world's premier producer of groundnuts and palm oil, and its second largest cocoa producer. From 1970 to 1983, petroleum royalties financed a rapid growth in government services and imports. The result was a fourth distinctive feature of Nigeria in Africa – the rapid growth, not just of large cities, but also of hundreds of smaller towns, each with its own rural hinterland.

My main research, from 1977 to 1979, occurred during the petroleum boom. From 1970 to 1981, the price of Nigerian petroleum rose by 1,940 per cent; from 1970 to 1979 (the peak), petroleum output increased by 112 per cent (Forrest 1995: 134). This windfall, combined with the consequent appreciation of the naira, led to a vast increase in state spending and in the import of capital and consumer goods. These changes had profound effects on the rural economy. The development of an excellent road system, and the importation and local private ownership of buses and lorries, connected the northern agricultural hinterland to hundreds of towns and cities and to the major ports. The rapid appreciation of the naira also rendered the traditional export crops, like cotton and groundnuts, uncompetitive on world markets. This led to a shift in production in the northern states from cotton to high-yielding varieties of yellow maize. This shift was accelerated by the distribution of highly subsidized imported fertilizer through the state Agricultural Development Projects (ADPs).

Chapters 3 through 7 focus on economic relations between a stratum of 'farmer-traders' and other rural people during this period, when increasing financial liquidity in the rural areas allowed farmer-traders to prosper through the sale of grains. The petroleum boom also created conditions for an expansion in the rural 'capital market', whose workings are explored in chapter 7. Chapter 8 tests the analysis by reference to a more recent period, 1996–1998, when financial support from government for agriculture fell steeply.

While chapter 8 compares a period of austerity with the previous period of prosperity, we should not lose sight of the continuous growth of Nigeria's internal market. This provides a degree of continuity between the two periods. Nigeria had some 88 million people according to the 1991 census (Forrest 1993: 21, 30). Perhaps 70 per cent were still rural. Since before the Second World War, there has been increasing specialization between export crop, food crop and livestock-producing regions. Thus, over the long term, a large internal market has been developing for agricultural goods and services, not just between urban and rural areas, but also between different, essentially rural ecological zones. Surprisingly, then, chapter 8 reveals much evidence of rural economic growth in a period characterized by urban decay.

Northern Nigeria

From the fourteenth through the eighteenth centuries, a group of Hausa-speaking kingdoms increased their capacity for warfare on horseback through two ecological zones south of the Sahara – the flat Sudan and the park-like Guinea savannah. They shared a common religion, based on a pantheon of spirits (Greenberg 1941, 1946; Usman 1974). However, Islam became increasingly popular in the walled towns and cities. At the beginning of the nineteenth century, an urban class of Muslim scholars with kinship ties to Fulani pastoralists declared jihad and overthrew the Hausa dynasties. They established the Sokoto Caliphate over most of northern Nigeria. By 1832, their domain included the Nupe-speaking Emirate of Bida and the Yoruba-speaking Emirate of Ilorin; although not the Tiv-, Jukun-, Idoma- or Igala-speaking peoples south of the Benue river or the ancient Muslim state of Bornu. The Muslim emirates owed allegiance to the Caliph, and were subject to supervision by his Vizier (Last 1967; Usman 1974). They shared a common official language, Hausa. A common social system divided the ruling class (*masu sarauta*) from the commoners (*talakawa*), who paid labour service, taxes and dues of various kinds.

The uniting of most of Hausaland in the Caliphate increased security for the growth of a large market in the central savannah and Sudan, despite the continuance of wars and slave raiding (Iliffe 1995). Long-distance trade was essential to the economy of nineteenth-century Hausaland. It included both rural caravans carrying agricultural products, leather goods and woven cloth, and 'international trade' based on Kano city which involved non-Hausa traders (Hill 1977). Cowries had constituted a widespread currency as early as the eighteenth century. The cowrie was not just a medium of payment but also a unit for reckoning comparabilities in the value of goods and services in local marketplaces and long-distance trade (Johnson 1970).

In the Caliphate, slave holding encompassed hereditary rulers and wealthy traders (Lovejoy 1978; Lovejoy and Hogendorn 1993) and also small-scale owners with no more than four slaves (Hill 1977). The category of 'surplus labour' was a reality in this market. It was supplied by slaves and by subordinate members of free households. Trade and 'accumulation' were going on in nineteenth-century Hausa society (see also chapter 2). They were based, not on a movement of capital, but on surplus product supplied by a variety of economic systems, including slave, lineage and individual household units (see chapter 2).

After the conquest of 1900, the British abolished slavery, though in practice the effects of abolition took time to work through the economic and social system (Lovejoy and Hogendorn 1993). Abolition had profound effects on the rural economy (see chapter 2). The British sharply reduced the power of the Caliph. However, the emirates maintained their identity under the colonial system of indirect rule. The emirates contained the majority of people in the Northern Provinces, reconstituted as the Northern Region under the 1951 Constitution. Although much undermined by populist politics and the subdivision of the Northern Region in 1967, their political and social system was still in place through the duration of my research.

Changes in the Political Economy of Southern Katsina

Marmara hamlet was one of hundreds in Malumfashi District. Yaba, its superior village, was on the border with Kankara District immediately to the north. These two districts were part of the economic region known historically as southern Katsina. For centuries, it has been known for its relatively fertile clay soil, *laka*, and hence its old name – Katsina Laka. Before the twentieth century, southern Katsina was a centre for the production of guineacorn (sorghum), indigo and indigenous cotton (*bagwandara*). It was also a centre of weaving and dyeing. Its products were sold in northern Katsina, Daura, Damagaram and to the west, in Kebbi; they were also sold for salt from Bilma and Abzin in the Sahara, and for slaves from Zaria to the south (Usman 1974: Ch. 3.1, 3.2). During 1976–79, southern Katsina consisted of five administrative districts – Faskari, Funtua, Bakori, Malumfashi and Kankara (Map 1). It was distinguished from the surrounding regions because it produced guineacorn surplus to local requirements, and was one of the premier cotton-producing areas of Nigeria.

People began to produce groundnuts for export when the railway was extended to Funtua and to Kaura Namoda in eastern Sokoto Emirate, which it reached in 1929, and when roads were built in the 1920s. Cotton gins were established in Funtua in 1926 and Malumfashi in 1927 (Schatzl 1973: 80). Cotton production expanded during the commodity boom of the 1950s. The trade in groundnuts and cotton was dominated by Hausa traders who sold the crops to foreign firms. In the postwar period, government marketing boards took over the export of groundnuts and cotton. They fixed prices for each season, generally below world market levels. In the late 1950s, Nigerian traders replaced the foreign firms as Licensed Buying Agents (LBAs) for the boards. Licenses were allocated to supporters of the Northern People's Congress (NPC), which governed the Northern Region from 1951 to the advent of military rule in 1966.

After World War II, the regional market for grain expanded together with the rise in prices and output of export crops. The clay soil of southern Katsina is excellent for guineacorn; the dry, sandy soil of northern Kano (*jan kasa*) is ideal for groundnuts. Guineacorn was now exported from Malumfashi and Kankara Districts to the groundnut-producing district of Danbatta in northern Kano. In the 1960s, the market for grain was extended to Maradi in the Republic of Niger (van Apeldoorn 1981: 102). The widening of the grain trade between southern Katsina and grain-deficit regions to the north created opportunities for villagers who combined farming with trade. Urban merchants and local rulers advanced money to them as a way of profiting from the inter-rural grain trade, which they could not enter for lack of the necessary knowledge and contacts.

From the 1950s onward, there was a sharp rise in conversion from the indigenous Hausa Maguzawa religion to Islam. Maguzawa culture is based on the maintenance of large households in which men and women farm together. Women brew and sell guineacorn beer, which is purchased and exchanged by men. Islamic conversion has resulted in two changes in the rural economy. First, abstinence from guineacorn beer has released grain for sale on the market. Therefore, it has increased both the commercialization of production and the money wealth of those households with grain surpluses. Secondly, Islamic conversion has led to the withdrawal of women from most farm work except planting and some aspects of harvesting. This has stimulated the demand for hired labour among richer households (chapter 4). Thus, conversion has generated a capacity to accumulate capital, and a concern to do so.

In 1975, southern Katsina was one of three regions chosen for their agricultural potential by the federal government and the World Bank for the joint financing of pilot projects. The Funtua Agricultural Development Project (FADP) (Map 1) had three general aims – raising yields; 'integrated development' of the farming and pastoral populations; and the selection of a segment of rural society for inputs and extension advice, on the theory that the 'demonstration effects' of innovative farming practices would later 'trickle down' to other farmers (World Bank 1981: 53). Accordingly, a limited number of richer farmers in each village area, called 'progressive farmers', were chosen as project recipients, and a much smaller group of 'large-scale farmers' was also defined, who received special attention (Clough and Williams 1987: 172–77).

The specific objectives of the FADP were the increase in cotton yields by expanded use of insecticides and fertilizers; the revival of groundnut production; the introduction of high-yielding varieties of 'yellow maize' through the use of technologies developed at the Institute of Agricultural Research at Samaru; and the retention of the pastoral population during the dry season. Accordingly, FADP built many Farm Service Centres in village areas for the distribution of input packages at highly subsidized prices, built over 500 km of feeder roads, and constructed a number of shallow dams.

During the period 1977–79, changes in federal policy combined with intense village pressures from ordinary farmers, mobilized by farmer-traders, to undermine the selective approach to input distribution and widen considerably the range of farmers who received fertilizer. The project did bring major changes to the rural areas. It extended the mileage of feeder roads and thereby assisted agricultural marketing. It dramatically increased the number of village farmers growing 'high-yielding' maize. And by magnifying the physical presence of officials and inputs in village areas, it set up a new political interaction between the rural population and the government (Clough and Williams 1987: 184–201).

From the 1950s to the present day, immigrant mallams from older Muslim areas have been influential in moulding the political consciousness of rural households. They preach a populist ethic. Many villagers have been active supporters of the two radical populist parties of northern Nigeria – the Northern Elements Progressive Union (NEPU), and its successor, the People's Redemption Party (PRP). In the 1950s, NEPU campaigned against the extortionate practices of the hereditary rulers, who were a bastion of the ruling party, the NPC. In the federal election of 1959, it gained more than 30 per cent of the vote in twenty-four constituencies, fourteen of which made a contiguous block in the frontier areas of eastern Sokoto, southern Katsina, northern Zaria and western Kano Emirates (Post 1963: 451 ff.; map at 222–23). In the Malumfashi constituency, dominated by Malumfashi town, a stronghold of the ruling party, NEPU did not win the parliamentary seat. However, the neighbouring constituency of Kankara-Kogo (on whose border Marmara hamlet sits) returned a NEPU member.

In 1967, the military government incorporated the Native Authority Courts and police into the new state administrations. These reforms reduced the capacity of hereditary rulers to levy exactions on villagers. Successive military governments greatly reduced the level of rural taxation. Fear of a return to extortionate practices led the majority of people in Malumfashi and Kankara Districts to support the PRP in the 1979 elections. Thereafter, the PRP state governor abolished the annual head tax on adult males (*haraji*).

In summary, four changes in the regional political economy affected rural economy and social stratification in southern Katsina over the period from 1945 to 1979. (1) The growth in the interregional grain trade increased the wealth of a stratum of rural farmer-traders who engage in long-distance trade. (2) Islamic conversion increased the commercialization of production and, through the withdrawal of female labour from most farming, the demand for hired labour. (3) The FADP increased the supply of inputs to village farmers, widened the production of grains for sale on the market and intensified the interaction between rural people and government. (4) Populist agitation, military government and oil revenues led to a sharp reduction in the pressure of hereditary rulers on rural people.

Malumfashi Division

Malumfashi and Kankara Districts composed the Malumfashi Local Government Area, or Malumfashi Division (Map 1). It was the largest division in Kaduna State. One of the new states carved out of the Northern Region in 1967, Kaduna State (at first named North Central State) retained its boundaries until 1987. Then, a military regime divided it into two states and the division became part of the new Katsina State. During periods of civilian rule, village areas elected representatives to local authority councils, whose chairmen were often a key link between the state government and local interests. But through much of their existence – and certainly during my periods of fieldwork (1976–79, 1996 and 1997–98) – divisions were governed by divisional officers or sole administrators appointed by the state Ministry of Local Government.

Beneath these changes, the enduring political organization has been an hierarchical and hereditary system of authority – the Emirate of Katsina. The rural population is subject, through hamlet heads appointed from among the commoners, to village heads, who form the lowest tier of the hereditary ruling class. Village heads are subject to district heads (*hakimai*, sing. *hakimi*) who in turn owe allegiance to the emir of Katsina (*Sarkin Katsina*). The British constituted the emirates as 'native authorities'. They made district heads reside in their districts. The military government subdivided the native authorities into 'local government authorities' corresponding to one or more districts. Hamlet heads assisted village heads in the collection of the annual head tax on adult males (haraji). Village heads adjudicated many disputes. Otherwise, rural people took their disputes directly to the Muslim area court, presided over by the Alkali.

Malumfashi town was only established in the reign of the Emir Musa between 1883 and 1888 and administered by his official slaves, subject to a hereditary fief holder. It was near the boundary between Katsina, Kano and Zaria emirates. In the colonial period former slaves, and talakawa who had lost control of their slaves, migrated into the area from northern Katsina and Kano Emirate. During the 1930s there was still free land and abundant game. But by 1952, Malumfashi District was described as 'fully settled' (Grove 1957). Thereafter, migrants continued to be attracted into the region by farming and trading opportunities.

Malumfashi Division lies mainly within latitudes 11 to 12 degrees north and longitudes 7 to 8 degrees east. Most of Kankara District, and the western portions of Malumfashi District, constitute the northernmost tip in Nigeria of the Northern Guinea savannah ecological zone (Map 3). From Malumfashi Division, this zone extends south and southeast about 150 miles, and southwest over 300 miles. Mean annual rainfall in this zone varies from 50 inches in the south to 40 inches in the north (about 1,000 mm).[1] Directly to the north of the division, the ecology changes to that of the Sudan, a vast zone extending over 100 miles northwards across the width of Nigeria, and then into the Republic of Niger. In that zone, mean annual rainfall declines from 40 inches to 20 inches.

In Malumfashi Division, rainfall is confined to four and a half months, from May into September. There are sharp periodic changes in the amount of rainfall. In 1973, the division was severely affected by the Sahelian Drought. In 1976–79, rainfall was excellent. In 1984, there was again severe drought, from which the division recovered in 1985 and 1986. The people distinguish four seasons:

- *Rani* – mid-December through February – the cold, dry season when harmattan winds blow from the Sahara.
- *Bazara* – March and April – the hot, dry season of the harmattan.
- *Damina* – May through mid-September – the rainy season.

- *Kaka* – mid-September through mid-December – the main harvest period, at first hot, then cool.

In 1975–6, the FADP attempted a listing of all communities of the division, and the number of families in each. It defined the family in terms of the Hausa notion of *iyali* – those living under an authority figure and eating from the same food supply. It found the *unguwa* to be the basic unit in the organizational structure of rural communities – an individual settlement, or a group of settlements in close physical proximity. *Unguwa* refers to all those people, usually living in a number of separate settlements, who are subject to a common *mai unguwa,* or hamlet head. 'Village' refers to all those who are subject, through their hamlet heads, to a common *mai gari,* or village head. *Gari* has been translated as 'town', in contrast to *birni,* a 'large and walled town' (Abraham 1962; Robinson 1925). In Malumfashi District, *mai gari* was the usual term for a village head as well as the ruler of a town.

In the FADP exercise, Malumfashi town had 3,494 families. The twenty-three village areas had 209 *unguwayi* and 26,039 families. Kankara town had only 869 families. Kankara District contained twelve village areas with eighty-two unguwayi and 17,824 families. If we apply the mean family size of seven that I found in Marmara, then the population of Malumfashi District was roughly 207,000 people. Kankara District had about 125,000 people.[2]

Malumfashi town was the headquarters of Malumfashi Division, the seat of a district head, *Galadiman Katsina,* and the location of the Muslim area court. The market in the town met twice weekly. It was not a major bulking centre for grain or other produce. To the north, Kankara town was the seat of a district head, *Sarkin Pauwa.* Its market, which met once weekly, was much larger, and drew farmers and produce buyers from a much wider area, than that of Malumfashi town. It had the only cattle market in Malumfashi Division, attracting buyers from as far as Zaria. Kankara marketplace was one of the largest centres for bulking grains in northern Nigeria, attracting many wholesale buyers from Niger.

During 1976–79, the main crop throughout Malumfashi Division for consumption and sale was a type of yellow guineacorn called *kaura.*[3] Before the 1973 Sahelian drought, farmers throughout the division sold large amounts of groundnuts to the Northern States Marketing Board. After the drought, the widespread incidence of rosette disease and aphid infestation led to a sharp decline in sales. Moreover, marketing board prices could not compete with prices on the private market. The private market in groundnuts continued to flourish on a smaller scale than before the drought.

Farmers throughout Malumfashi Division had been used to planting large amounts of cotton. They sold it to the marketing board. In the summer of 1978, farmers throughout the division gave up growing cotton. (The only exceptions were a few Maguzawa farmers, and some large-scale, town-based farmers who had undertaken to grow cotton in return for bank loans.) Village farmers forsook cotton for three reasons.[4] First, the returns to growing cotton had become unfavourable compared with the returns to guineacorn. The producer price paid by the Cotton Board remained virtually unchanged over 1976–79 whereas guineacorn prices on the private market increased greatly (Table 1.1). Secondly, fertilizer supplied by the FADP had enabled many farmers to increase their planting of yellow maize. Thirdly, village farmers were incensed at their inability to obtain compensation from the Alkali Court when seasonally migrant pastoralists grazed in their cotton fields.[5] The decline in cotton production in Malumfashi Division was a more dramatic version of the trend in Nigeria (Table 1.2).

The marketing system was connected to the local political structure. In 1976–79, the Nigerian Cotton Board granted large advances to LBAs to buy cotton at official prices. LBAs were paid a buying allowance on every tonne delivered to the ginnery, which covered overheads plus a margin for 'reasonable profit'. While the national number of LBAs had been greatly increased by the government, there were local semi-monopsonies because of the role of the hereditary rulers in the marketing system.

In Malumfashi town, three of the four LBAs were members of the family of the district head during 1976–79. Three of them were also village heads. Before his death in 1976, the largest LBA was the *Magajin Gari,* or town head, of Malumfashi. LBAs operated through their 'agents' (*yara*), themselves well-placed town merchants. *Yara* distributed hundreds of thousands of naira in advances sanctioned by the Cotton Board, to hamlet cotton buyers (*yan baranda*). Cotton buying was highly competitive in the hamlets. Farmers had a good idea of the official price. As a result, the profit margins of hamlet cotton buyers were small (Clough 1986: 108–12). LBAs and their agents benefited from the distribution of Cotton Board advances and local semi-monopsony in cotton purchase over the large zones determined by the Cotton Board. The Cotton Board, like other marketing boards, was abolished in 1986.

Table 1.1. Local guineacorn prices and Cotton Board producer prices, 1975–79 (N)

	Guineacorn: Marmara		Seed cotton: Nigerian Cotton Board	
	Price per sack		Producer price, Grade 1 cotton	
Year	Lowest December	Peak July	Per lb.	Per metric ton
1975–76	8	16	0.14	308
1976–77	12	24	0.15	330
1977–78	18	30	0.15	330
1978–79	18	20	0.15	330

Table 1.2. Nigerian cotton production, 1976–82

Year	Output (bales)
1976–77	465,101
1977–78	216,152
1978–79	206,039
1979–80	161,620
1980–81	149,820
1981–82	115,820

Source: Nigerian Cotton Board: *1983/84 Market Prospects*

Hereditary rulers were also active in the grain trade. They loaned money to client traders in the villages. They also benefited from access to urban merchant capital and to government contracts for the supply of grain.

Marmara Hamlet

Now, let us enter the hamlet of Marmara. In 1978, I counted 120 families in the central roadside settlement.[6] The remaining families lived in a smaller settlement a mile to the west, or were dispersed over the countryside in 'big houses' (*manya gidaje*, sing. *babban gida*) named after the founding ancestor. These were themselves closely packed settlements, headed by brothers or the sons of brothers. Encircled by fences of guineacorn stalks, they rose out of the surrounding farmland like miniature villages.

The FADP listed 266 families under the hamlet head (mai unguwa) of Marmara. Yaba village area contained 1,770 families.[7] It ranked third in population among the rural village areas of Malumfashi District. The village head (mai gari, with the title of *Ciroma*) lived in the main settlement of Yaba, a mile to the east of the central roadside settlement of Marmara.

According to old men who took great interest in preserving historical memories, in the late nineteenth century, slave raiding was common. The raiders were *yan samame,* small bands of horsemen, usually from Maradi. If people put their ears to the ground and heard the sound of horses' hooves, they would flee to Malumfashi town. The raiders would capture 'children, never grown men, and they ran quickly'. Pastoralists controlled most of the land. They had Maguzawa slaves. (Some families in Marmara originate from nearby Unguwa Rinji, formerly a slave hamlet owned by pastoralists.)

In the early twentieth century, the land remained sparsely populated. In the 1920s and 1930s, the wealthiest figures in the area were the Fulani owners of large herds and the heads of large Maguzawa farming units. When Gambo, the founder and head of a big house near Marmara, went to sell his groundnuts at Malumfashi, he would be accompanied by 'ten horses, thirty donkeys and many drummers'. The truly formidable figures were the pastoral Fulani who owned herds of biblical size, men like Bello na Mammman, Ango Gafuri, Shapatu, and Bassa dan Pampa. These four could not meet together at one place 'for the magic would be too much'.

Old informants dated the growth of the grain trade to Danbatta to the 1940s. The largest farmer in 1979 originally bought land with money from this trade. Other farmers travelled as far as Kano city to buy European cloth for retailing in Marmara and nearby marketplaces. The second largest farmer in 1979 grew rich in this way. Others specialized in local cotton buying, operating with the advances of LBAs. As of 1976, three of the five hamlet cotton buyers received their advances from the agent of the magagin gari of Malumfashi town. Three became relatively well-off but hardly rich – and only by combining cotton buying with goat trading, trading in yellow maize or retailing from small shops.

In the 1950s and 1960s, the in-migration of farmers and increasing population density caused the out-migration of most Fulani pastoralists. They moved with their cattle to more sparsely populated areas further south. They sold most of their landholdings to the richer village farmers (see chapter 3). Many of the cattle tended by remaining Fulani are the property of local farmers. Thus, the area has witnessed a historic change in social stratification. From being a rural society dominated by Fulani pastoralists, it has become one where the wealthiest are Hausa farmer-traders.

The roadside settlement established in 1960 consisted of Maguzawa indigenes and Muslim immigrants. Shortly thereafter, most Maguzawa converted to Islam. In 1978, only four of the 120 household heads, and their wives, continued to brew and drink guineacorn beer.

In 1978, I could define four sections. The northernmost section comprised twenty-one families descended from a settler called Marmara, who arrived from Kano Emirate in the late nineteenth century. Originally dispersed among big houses, they built their compounds on the present site when the roadside settlement was formed. The central part consisted of nine families descended from a slave, who was purchased by a local Maguzawa farmer in the late nineteenth century. His freed son founded a big house whose baobab tree is the tallest landmark in the settlement. Opposite, on the eastern side of the road, Gidan Kwale and Gidan Dan Bako contained thirty families. Their progenitors had arrived early in this century and carved farms out of the bush. Again on the western side of the road, the southern section comprised twenty-eight families whose progenitors came in the middle of this century or had arrived from nearby hamlets after 1960; and thirty-two immigrant families from Kano Emirate and other parts of Katsina.

During 1976–79, the people of Marmara defined themselves as talakawa (commoners) in contrast to the *sarakuna* (rulers). They also referred to themselves as '*mu, Habe*' ('we, the Habe' – i.e., Hausa commoners) in opposition to '*su, Fulani*' ('they, the Fulani rulers'). These angry phrases expressed a difference which was political rather than ethnic, for they did not apply them to local Fulani pastoralists. The people of Marmara continually brooded over former practices of the village and district heads which had only been abandoned under the military regime. The rulers had employed retainers (*fadawa,* sing. *bafada*) and used them to enforce *gayya* (which could mean any voluntary work gathering, but in this context meant that every family provided free labour on the fields of the rulers). It was also called literally *aikin tilas* (forced labour). Older farmers recalled how, years before, the rulers had forced people to head-load goods long distances during the dry season. Also, rulers practiced the custom of *mazada* in touring their domains. They and their retainers would occupy the houses of the wealthiest farmers and receive gifts from the village wherein they rested the night. Furthermore, they extorted 'license fees' from farmers who engaged in the grain trade to Danbatta. Local people called these practices *zalinci* (oppression).

In the 1950s, NEPU activists in the area were inspired by the tradition of the *jarumi*, or brave man, who was prepared to challenge the rulers. In 1979, I was in Marmara during the national elections for a return to civilian rule. Overtly, the local campaign had the appearance of factional conflict. The main leader of the People's Redemption Party (PRP) gathered public support from his section of the settlement, while the main leader of the National Party of Nigeria (NPN), the party of the rulers, gathered his from kin and neighbours. Privately, most people spoke strongly in favour of the PRP. The PRP drew its natural leaders from the farmer-traders and mallams. In Marmara, they were the second largest farmer (a cloth trader); a cotton buyer who had diversified into retail trading; and the most learned mallam, a *mai tafsiri,* able to translate and comment on the Qur'an. The NPN drew its leaders from the hamlet clients of the ruling class, among them the hamlet head. They were all cotton buyers. The divisional leader of the NPN – who was also chairman of the local authority, a village head, and an LBA – had promised that their cotton advances would be returned to them as general trading loans if they campaigned actively for the party. The chagrin of the hamlet head at the election results can be imagined when his wives told their friends that even they had voted for the PRP.

Population

Henceforth, I use the term *household* in place of 'family' (*iyali*). Their meanings are equivalent, involving three features – a domestic group, i.e., those living together in the same place; a head, or authority figure; and dependence on a common food supply. *Household head* refers to any independent person, married or unmarried – i.e., anyone not farming under the leadership of another person, and not dependent on a food supply other than that of his own production or purchase. Of the 120 households in Marmara, three consisted of unmarried men with no dependents, their previous wives having left them. There was one household headed by an unmarried man, whose previous wives had left him, responsible for the food of eleven dependents. The remaining 116 households consisted of domestic groups of two or more persons, headed by a married man. There were no domestic groups headed by women.

Gida (house) denotes the space occupied by the domestic group, and the people therein. Gida is the place where the domestic group lives, eats and stores its food supply, as bundles of unthreshed grain in earthen granaries (*rumbuna,* sing. *rumbu*) or as sacks of threshed grain in storerooms (*shaguna,* sing. *shagu*). Among the Maguzawa, where several generations of men and their wives farmed together, there was no physical partition between the space occupied by each conjugal family. The entire domestic group was surrounded by a fence of guineacorn stalks, and thus formed a 'big house'.

In 1978, the total population of the central settlement was 813 people. A quarter lived in relatively small households, with five or fewer members. At the other extreme, over a third lived in households with eleven or more people. The mean household size was 7, the median, 5.5 (Table 1.3).

Population Density

All users of farmland in Marmara farmed a total of 964 acres. Most fields were within a radius of one mile from the settlement, though

Table 1.3. Size of households in Marmara, 1978

	No. of households				Total:	
No. of persons	With land	Without land	Total	Per cent	Population	Per cent
1	3		3		3	
2	5	3	8		16	
3	8	4	12	}47%	36	}25%
4	14	1	15		60	
5	17	1	18		90	
6–10	42	3	45	38%	337	41%
11–15	13		13	11%	163	20%
16–20	5		5	4%	86	11%
Over 20	1		1	—	22	3%
Total	**108**	**12**	**120**	**100%**	**813**	**100%**

	With land	Without land	All
Mean number per household:	7	4.2	6.8
Median number per household:	6	3.0	5.5

some were more distant. As distance from the settlement increased, the extent of land use by its inhabitants declined, their fields becoming more interspersed with those of farmers in nearby settlements. The closest bush land was two and a half miles to the west. Within a three-mile radius of the central settlement, where I mapped and measured all land used by Marmara household heads in 1979, there was no fallow land (chapter 3).

Four Fulani grazing trails crossed the surveyed area. These trails are relevant to population density, since farmers are continually encroaching on the remaining grazing land. Within a one-mile radius of Marmara, they amounted to perhaps 100 acres. Altogether, about 1,100 acres were available to the 813 inhabitants of the central settlement as farmed land or potential farmland. This gives a population density of approximately 470 per square mile in 1979 (183 per square km).

Marmara hamlet was on the southwestern side of a rectangle which, broadly speaking, extended northeast for a length of fifteen miles, and had a width varying from ten to fifteen miles. It was roughly bisected by the main road running through Malumfashi town (Map 1). My travels suggested that all of the land in this area was in continuous cultivation. To the northwest, in Kankara District, population densities were visibly lower.

Thus, Marmara had a high population density in the absolute sense that fallow land had disappeared; and in the relative sense that its density was comparable with those found in other zones where fallow land had disappeared – the Kano and Sokoto Closely Settled Zones (Mortimore 1968: 298; Goddard et al. 1976: 6, 20; and Table 3.5). An increasing population of farmers was reducing the remaining pasture land, and so widening the area under permanent cultivation.

The relatively high population density in the area around Marmara may be crucial to explaining an important fact. When I mapped and measured the fields used by Marmara farmers within a three-mile radius of the settlement (chapter 3), I never encountered fields controlled by members of the ruling class like the Ciroma Yaba or farmland owned by urban merchants or by agribusiness companies. Local farmers had bought the major share of land from departing pastoral Fulani, and thus preempted the purchase, when population density was still relatively low, of large areas by traditional rulers or outside investors.

An Overview of Economic Activity

In the literature on northern Nigeria, the agronomic system followed in Marmara is referred to as *mixed farming* and *permanent cultiva-*

tion. Under mixed farming, farmers own manufactured ploughs and teams of oxen; they use these for ploughing and ridging their own fields and hiring out their ploughing services to other farmers. Soil fertility benefits from the application of cattle manure. In Marmara, ridging by oxen had almost entirely replaced ridging with the hand-hoe (*garma*).

Under permanent cultivation, all of the fields are cultivated annually and to maintain the fertility of the soil, farmers apply considerable quantities of household manure. This consists of household sweepings and goat and sheep droppings, brushed into a mound inside the compound, ready for application on the fields around the time of the first rains. It is called *takin gargajiya* ('old', or traditional fertilizer) to distinguish it from chemical fertilizer – *takin turawa* (fertilizer of the Europeans). Cattle manure is highly prized. Farmers enter into annual agreements with local pastoral Fulani to establish cattle camps on their fields during the dry season, in return for a sum of money. Chemical fertilizer used to be scarce and costly. After the establishment of the FADP in 1975, farmers of almost all income levels bought it at highly subsidized prices. They applied it mainly to guineacorn, the major food and cash crop, and to high-yielding yellow maize (Clough and Williams 1987: 184–201).

Among the 108 household heads with land, twenty-nine headed joint farming units containing married sons or other married male kinsmen (*gandaye,* sing. *gandu*). Most married sons with living fathers were in gandu – 77 per cent (chapter 4). Many more household heads had young, unmarried male adults forming an important part of their workforces. The few remaining Maguzawa household heads had working for them seventeen women, seven being their wives, ten the wives of male dependents (Table 1.4).

The increasing commercialization of production and conversion to Islam had together stimulated changes in the relations of production. The distribution of land use in Marmara had become very unequal. In 1979, when I mapped and measured the fields of Marmara household heads, the top 10 per cent of land users controlled 40 per cent of the land. In a hamlet where the mean acreage was 7.8 and the median 4.1, their holdings ranged from 16 to 50 acres. The bottom 40 per cent of land users controlled only 10 per cent of the land. Their holdings ranged from 0.5 to 3.1 acres (see chapter 3). According to villagers, hired labouring had become a widespread practice since the mid-1960s. In the 1978 farming season, when I surveyed patterns of labour use, 22 per cent of household heads were frequent hirers of labour during weeding, the farming operation that most critically influenced

Table 1.4. Size of household adult work groups, Marmara, 1978

Number of farming adults	Number of households	Per cent	Total number of farming adults	Per cent
1	66	61%	66	33%
2	21	19%	42	21%
3	9	8%	27	13%
4	5	5%	20	10%
5	2	2%	10	5%
6	2	2%	12	6%
7	—	—	—	—
8	3[a]	3%	24	12%
Total	**108**	**100%**	**201**	**100%**

a. These three Maguzawa households deployed three household heads, three married sons, one male kinsman and 17 wives.

the harvest yield, and they controlled 50 per cent of total hamlet acreage. Conversely, 21 per cent of household heads frequently hired out their labour, and they controlled only 8 per cent of hamlet land. In the middle were 57 per cent of household heads who controlled 42 per cent of hamlet land (see chapter 4, especially Table 4.2).

Most household heads had at least one off-farm occupation (*sana'a*) which yielded a money income. Young men from an early age were seeking to develop an off-farm niche where they could learn a skill or apply their strength. Not just small farmers (chapter 4) but also farmers with substantial landholdings (chapter 7) might have earnings from their off-farm occupations which were considerably greater than the market value of their total agricultural output. I give below a list which shows the diversity of off-farm occupations (Chart 1.1). It spans the range of production, exchange and services. It does not include auxiliary activities by general labourers who assisted such specialists as house builders. Often, men and women were learning from other more practiced specialists through participation (e.g., praise singers).

Mixed Farming and the Ownership of Oxen and Ploughs

Between 1933, when the colonial government first introduced loans for ploughs, and 1966, the number of mixed farmers using oxen and ploughs rose to an estimated 40,000 throughout the Northern Region, by which date a quarter of all ploughs were said to be in the

Chart 1.1. Off-farm occupations in Marmara, 1976–79

Barbering
Blacksmithing
Bus driving
Bus ownership
Butchering
Carpentry
Cotton buying
Cooking foods and snacks
Donkey transport
Grain milling
Groundnut decorticating
Head retailing of women's jewellery cosmetics (*kolli*)
Herbal healing
House building
Leather crafting

Midwifery
Oxen-cart and hand-art transport
Loading/unloading vehicles
Pillow and mattress making
Praise singing
Qur'anic teaching
Roof making
Rope making
Retailing cooked foods and snacks
Table retailing (*teburi*) of vegetables, fruit, condiments
Tailoring
Shop keeping

Specialized trading:
- Chaff
- Cloth
- Grains, groundnuts, cowpeas
- Goats and sheep
- Hides and skins
- Fowl
- Locust beans

Specialized wholesaling:
- Cassava
- Kerosene
- Kolanuts
- Sugar cane

Specialized retailing:
- Dried fish
- Kerosene

Water carrying
Well digging

northern part of Katsina Emirate (King 1939; Anthony and Johnstone 1968, quoted in Hill 1972: 307–8). In southern Katsina, the number of mixed farmers was small but growing by 1952 (Grove 1957: Figure 9), and by 1979 was visibly widespread. In Marmara, the first farmer purchased a plough in 1960, and by 1979, 21 of the 108 landholding household heads – 19 per cent – owned forty-seven oxen and twenty-three ploughs. Sixteen owned at least one team of oxen with plough. A further five owned one ox each and had part shares in a plough together with a full sibling. The top quarter of land users owned 80 per cent of oxen and ploughs. Their holdings spanned from 10.2 to 50 acres. The remaining 20 per cent were owned by household heads in the second quarter of land users. Their holdings were from 4.5 to 7.7 acres. Yellow maize production using fertilizer supplied by the FADP widened significantly the ownership of these tools: four of the twenty-one owners and part-owners were two sets of full siblings who used their 1979 maize earnings to jointly purchase a plough, while each brother bought an ox.

In a hamlet where most farmers are related by ties of blood, marriage, friendship or clientage, the notion of a purely commercial relationship is difficult to apply. Nevertheless, we can distinguish between farmers who were closely related by ties of blood or marriage, and the rest. 'Close relationship' included father; son; brother; half-brother; sons of brothers, half-brothers, sisters or half-sisters; and son of the plough owner's brother or sister. It also included affinal relationships: father-in-law; son-in-law; brother of plough owner's wife or of plough owner's father-in-law or mother-in-law. Finally, it included close personal friends regardless of consanguineal or affinal tie, and long-standing patrons or clients.

Table 1.5 summarizes my evidence for all known cases where plough owner and hirer were *not* related or were *distantly* related – a small sample of twelve hirers and twenty-six fields. Among these, plough owners tended to charge hirers who were 'large farmers' (with more than 10 acres) distinctly more than hirers who were 'smaller farmers' (with less than 10 acres).[8] For the first ridging just after the onset of the rains, large farmers tended to pay almost N2 per acre more than smaller farmers. For the second ridging one-to-two months later, large farmers tended to pay at least N1 more than smaller farmers. The significance of the difference is heightened by the fact that, between these two groups in the sample, there was little difference in average or median field sizes. Plainly, among plough owners and hirers who were not closely related, the uppermost consideration in the mind of the plough owner was the relative wealth of the hirer – a significant fact, for among the twenty-five Marmara farmers with more than 10 acres, ten did not have oxen and required ploughing services.

With regard to plough hirers and owners who *were* closely related, a small separate sample of eleven hirers and thirty-one fields shows that the most closely related kin in the sample paid no fees – fathers, fathers-in-law and sons-in-law. Moreover, close friends of plough owners paid little or nothing. Where the hirer was related to the plough owner as half-brother, first cousin, nephew or client, the average/median fees were N3.60/3.85 per acre for the first ridging. This was considerably less than the average/median fees for those who were not closely related – N5/5.30 per acre. Across all thirty-one fields in the sample, the average fee paid for the first weeding was N1.40 per acre. This figure is significant compared with the N5 average paid by hirers who were not closely related, because any plough owner had to calculate before the start of the rainy season that many of his contractual agreements would be with a range of close kin and friends. Across this range, he would make much less money than he did with more distantly related hirers and non-kin.

In summary, the relative wealth or poverty of the hirer, and his kinship or friendship with the plough owner, were considerations that

Table 1.5. Ploughing fees (N per acre) among unrelated or distantly related parties: 11 hirers, 26 fields, Marmara, 1978

Hirers	Average/Median fee	Average/Median field size (acres)
First ridging:		
Large farmers[a]	6.60/5.80	3.0/2.2
Smaller farmers[b]	4.70/4.20	2.0/2.1
All[c]	5.00/5.30	2.7/2.2
Second ridging:		
Large farmers	6.00/5.00	2.5/2.0
Smaller farmers	4.10/4.00	2.7/2.5
All[d]	5.40/5.00	2.6/2.1

a. Farmers with 11.6 – 35 acres.
b. Farmers with 2.0 – 9.6 acres.
c. 85 per cent of all farmers performed the first ridging.
d. 65 per cent of large farmers, and 55 per cent of smaller farmers, did the second ridging.

limited the gain from plough hiring. The hiring out of ploughing services was embedded in the claims of kinship, friendship and clientage – highly ramified in a polygynous culture. Furthermore, as the size of landholding of the plough owner increased, the number of wives and children, and therefore, of present and eventual affinal kin, tended to increase significantly (see Table 3.19). As a strategy for capital accumulation, hiring out ploughing services therefore had limited usefulness. Taking into account the cost of maintaining oxen, the most likely effect of *hiring out* plough and oxen since the first arrival of the plough in 1960 was to introduce a new 'income-earning off-farm occupation', or sana'a, to Marmara.[9]

Culture and Community in Marmara

Because their conversion to Islam was very recent, the indigenes of Marmara were part of a culture in transition in 1976–79. On my first night in Marmara, I witnessed one of the last displays of *sauran marke* – athletic dancing by young girls wearing only brief skirts, accompanied by superb drumming – and this at a wedding feast in the house of the hamlet head. When I returned to Marmara in 1977, the drumming was still intricate and haunting. But there was less of it: the mallams said that it turned people's minds away from God.

As a result of conversion, the nature of community had changed. People had formerly been dispersed among big houses related by ties of blood or marriage, between which men rotated on fixed afternoons in order to exchange beer. Now, they formed a concentrated settlement. Cultural transition and community change were overlapping mutations: in the concentrated settlement, indigenous households were exposed to the ideas and habits of immigrant families from Kano with a longer tradition of Muslim belief.

So we need to ask, did the people of Marmara see themselves as a community? And if so, in what terms? In answering these questions, I use 'culture' to indicate the deep 'values' of the people – their beliefs concerning what is desirable, dutiful and forbidden – and following from this, the local patterns of certain basic human relationships. Here, I can only sketch the contours of culture to alert the reader to those features of social life which were so compelling as to influence my whole analysis.

People were keenly conscious of new kinds of both division and integration (Clough 2009: 599–601). As Maguzawa, their economic differences had derived from the number of wives and children a household head could deploy in farming. As Muslims, they saw themselves as bifurcated – between a small number of relatively rich villagers who combined farming with trade, and the rest, who were dependent on the rich for credit. By 1979, there was considerable inequality in land use. While the top 10 per cent of land users controlled from 16 to 50 acres, half of all households used 4.1 acres or less (see Tables 3.2 and 3.4).

At the same time, villagers, saw themselves as constituting a new kind of community, much larger and more abstract than before conversion. Islam in Marmara was collective and self-conscious. It gave detailed form to the day, week and year. All men gathered five times a day for prayer in one of the earthen mosques which had been built by villagers. On Friday, they travelled to the mosque at Yaba village or the central mosque in Malumfashi town for the early afternoon prayer (*azahar*). All adults fasted during Ramadan (*azumi*). All boys gathered in front of the houses of various mallams for several years of instruction in the Qur'an. Men would frequently gather in small groups to listen to preaching (*wa'azi*), or the recitation of and commentary on the Qur'an (*tafsiri*). Then, again, there were special gatherings, very strange, at which men and women shouted out their sense of the presence of God. Older boys from immigrant families often spent several years as begging Qur'anic students (*almajirai*) in far-away Borno or Hadejia. When infants were given their Muslim names, most of the settlement would gather for the prayers at the ceremony (*suna*). Men would travel miles to attend the suna of a friend's child.

The local practice of Islam laid emphasis on three activities. *Sadaka* was the giving of alms. Infrequently, this took the impressive form of giving a daughter in marriage without marriage payments (*auren sakaka*). Frequently, people gave very small gifts of money or food to those less fortunate, or simply to groups of friends. *Zaka* was the giving of one-tenth of each harvest crop to the mallams and poor households of one's choice though in practice, the proportion varied from 5 to 10 per cent (chapter 5). *Hajji* was the pilgrimage to Mecca, thus transforming pilgrims into *Alhazai*. Before 1976, the five largest Muslim farmers, a farmer-trader of middle income, and the hamlet head, were already Alhazai. During 1976–79, the sixth largest Muslim farmer made the Hajji. Before 1985, the seventh and eighth farmers in terms of land use, the most successful young farmer-trader and a general retailer of middle income went to Mecca. In 1979, Hajji involved a total expense of N1,000 – usually more than the N600–1,000 which would be spent on the marriage of a rich villager's son (chapter 5).

Seven household heads were mallams – religious teachers with the power to elicit divine intercession through prayer. All were immigrants from Kano Emirate. With landholdings of less than four acres, they all depended on harvest contributions and gifts from the rest of the hamlet. People gave more respect to the one mai tafsiri, who was able to translate the Qur'an from Arabic into Hausa and interpret it in the light of other holy books, than they did to the *liman*, the official leader of prayer appointed by the village head. Most men had a particular mallam whom they favoured for advice and charms. All enterprising men developed a close association with at least one mallam, whose supernal assistance they believed essential to material success.

Yet cultural change, and the restructuring of community, did not obscure continuity in the conduct of certain human relationships. The main preoccupation of men and women was the development of a stable relationship between husband and wife and the pursuit of new marriage partners. These goals are not as contradictory as they may seem. Incorrigibly, a man with one wife sought a second and, if he had the income, a third. Divorce was easy, if legally tedious. It entailed wearying trips to the Alkali, in which he urged reconciliation (*'Ku daure! Ku daure!'* – 'Be patient!'), followed by a final trip at which the divorce was settled. Most men and women had been through several marriages.

The thinking of both men and women was dominated by the social prestige of polygynous marriage (Clough 2009: 603–7). In 1978, among the 108 household heads with land, the majority, 55, had two or more wives. Among the 12 without land, 9 had one wife, 3 had two wives. The prevalence of polygyny was in marked contrast to Batagawara in northern Katsina, where Hill found that only a third of heads of farming units had more than one wife (Hill 1972: 23). Polygyny must also be seen from the women's perspective: almost 70 per cent of the wives of household heads had co-wives (Table 1.6).

Polygyny was a crucial dimension of 'wealth' (*dukiya*) in the eyes of men and women. Later chapters will show how men devoted rising income from farming, trade or other services to increasing the number of their wives. Here, I cite the basic pattern, using landholding as a very approximate index of material wealth: among the bottom three deciles of land-using household heads, 74 per cent had only one wife; the proportion of polygynous household heads gradually increased with increasing land use until, in the top three deciles of land-using household heads, 85 per cent were polygynous. Among the 108 household heads with land, 16 had three or four wives, of whom 8 were in the top three deciles of land users (see Table 3.19).

For Muslim men, as for Maguzawa, wives were the source of children, and therefore of a household work force. Because of the high rate of infant mortality, there was all the more reason to seek out additional wives in order to expand the household farming unit. After conversion to Islam, the withdrawal of women from most forms of farm labour actually enhanced the prestige of polygyny among men, for it signified a man's capacity to maintain more than one wife. In women's eyes, entry into a polygynous marriage for the first time often increased their economic security and social prestige, since a man's capacity to have more than one wife depended on his income.

Table 1.6. Number of wives of household heads, Marmara, 1978

	Number of household heads			Number of wives in each category	Per cent of wives in each category	Per cent of household heads in each category
Marriage category	**With land**	**Without land**	**Total**			
No wife	4	—	4	—	—	3%
1 wife	49	9	58	58	30%	48%
2 wives	39	3	42	84	43%	35%
3 wives	13	—	13	39	20%	11%
4 wives	3	—	3	12	6%	2%
Total	**108**	**12**	**120**	**193**	**99%**[a]	**99%**[a]

a. The discrepancy with 100 per cent is due to rounding.

Moreover, it meant that they were sharing domestic chores with co-wives. Partial seclusion did not prevent wives from visiting their women friends in other households or hamlets, their heads covered with a shawl which fully exposed the face.

Muslim wives had a high degree of economic independence. From the sale of cooked foods and snacks – retailed in the hamlet by their unmarried daughters – they accumulated savings which they invested in small livestock and fowl. Indeed, they owned most of the small livestock and fowl in Marmara. Most wives belonged to women's revolving savings and credit associations (*adashi*). These helped them to save and withdraw lump sums.

Mothers and sons remained close, regardless of the mother's divorce and remarriage or removal to a distant place. It was customary for a mother to finance from her savings a specific share of the marriage expenses of her sons – *lefe,* the new clothing provided for the bride (chapter 5). The close bond engendered an important distinction – between full brothers (*yan daki daya* – sons of the same marriage room) and half-brothers (*yan riga daya* – sons of the same robe). Full brothers retained a strong sense of social and economic obligation to each other, whereas relations between half-brothers were more distant. Full brothers often formed a unit of joint investment in trade, livestock or oxen for ploughing.

Husbands fed their wives. For the marriage to endure, they also had to provide them with a stream of small gifts of cosmetics and jewellery, and large gifts of cloth at the festival marking the end of Ramadan (*Salla*). Husbands clothed their sons and fed, provided medicines for and paid much of the marriage expense of their sons and daughters.

Mothers provided their daughters with clothing, cosmetics and spending money. A daughter's sense of obligation to her mother was so strong that the mother usually remained throughout her lifetime the arbiter of her daughter's marriages. Her consent to a daughter's marriage marked a new development in her social and economic position. The son-in-law had to give her a continuous stream of gifts, and defer to her advice, if his marriage were to last. The wife's mother was a central figure in rural society. She was to be seen striding across the countryside, statuesque in winding veil, haranguing above the head of some kneeling son-in-law. She not only made the marriages. She broke them.

Because marriage was central to economy and culture, the reciprocal exchange of gifts of money and grain (*gudummawa*) at marriage ceremonies was an important institution linking people related by consanguineal or affinal ties. An important kind of friendship also flowed from the centrality of marriage – *biki* partnership. Biki partners contributed money at each other's marriage and naming ceremonies. Over the long term, the relationship was symmetrical regardless of income differences: equal amounts had to flow in both directions. In the short term, one partner might be giving more because of the disparity in the number of their respective ceremonies (chapter 5).

Every man and woman had a number of biki partners. As a person's income increased, the number of his biki partners rose – often poorer than himself. Biki provided insurance. The total donations which a person made in the interval between two of his own ceremonies were returned to him by his various partners at his second ceremony. Since smaller farmers generally had smaller households, several years usually elapsed between their own ceremonies. The total donations which they had made to biki partners in the interval – returned to them at their second ceremony – therefore defrayed a considerable share of its cost.

Beneath great changes in community and culture, the men and women of Marmara manifested continuity in their ideas of what was ultimately desirable and morally obligatory. The achievement of a stable polygynous household arrangement remained the major goal of life. As wives or potential wives, mothers, sources of household saving and mothers-in-law, women were still the central focus of social exchanges arising out of farm or off-farm income.

Conclusions

This chapter enables us to define the parameters in which the economy and culture of Marmara had evolved by 1976, when I began fieldwork: (1) high population density, (2) a particular *dynamic* of population change – the in-migration of farmers and the out-migration of pastoralists, (3) highly developed integration with national and international markets, (4) the disposal of produce by rural farmer-traders rather than by outsiders, (5) the liberation of villagers from most exactions of the hereditary ruling class, (6) the absence of outside landowners, whether traditional rulers, urban merchants or agribusiness companies, (7) a farming population that was open to technical change and (8) the influence of Islamic thought and practice on political and economic action. Given these parameters, we can now establish the questions which will guide the subsequent analysis in this book:

- What was the extent of the economic power of those rural talakawa who had acquired wealth and combined farming with trading?
- To what extent were smaller farmers able to achieve a degree of autonomy in their relations with farmer-traders? In other words, to what extent were smaller farmers viable – i.e., able to meet necessary household expenditures without alienating land or going severely into debt to farmer-traders?

Notes

1. Grove reported mean annual rainfall between 35 and 40 inches in the area of Malumfashi Division in 1946–51 (Grove 1957: Figure 2).
2. Projecting from the 1963 census, the population of Malumfashi District was officially estimated at 256,400 in 1978; of Kankara District, at 146,300 (Kaduna State 1976). However, the 1963 census was massively inflated (Hill 1972: 310).
3. Groundnuts were still abundant in the north of Kankara District. On the western fringe of Malumfashi District, farmers sold surpluses of pepper and white guineacorn (*mori*); on its eastern fringe, locust beans and okra.
4. A more extended discussion is in Clough 1986: 5–13, 28–67, 120–28.
5. This is an under-researched problem in Nigerian social sciences.
6. In this thesis, 'Marmara' always refers to the central roadside settlement, unless otherwise indicated.
7. In 1976, the village head told me that Marmara hamlet had 250 taxpayers while the total village area of Yaba contained about 2,000 farmers.
8. For the rationale behind designating those with more than 10 acres 'large farmers', and those with less 'smaller farmers', see the explanation at the beginning of Part II of Chapter 3. Essentially, those with over 10 acres had an income from *both* farming and off-farm occupations that left them in surplus after meeting a range of basic household requirements; those with less than 10 acres either managed to balance their income from *both* farm and off-farm occupations with their expenditure on basic household requirements (frequently with a small surplus or deficit) or they were in annual deficit, which had to be met by borrowing cash, repayable out of harvest earnings. The reason for combining farm with off-farm income in demarcating 10 acres as the cut-off point between those who were or were not in surplus is that as farmers' income from off-farm occupations increased, they tended to invest part of the increase in farmland.
9. Bearing in mind the differences in agrarian pattern between the Hausa of southern Katsina and those in the Maradi valley of the Niger Republic, my conclusion agrees with that reached by Guy Nicolas in a far larger and more rigorous survey of the effects of the introduction of oxen ploughs for hiring: the objective of the Hausa plough owner in Niger 'was to acquire an external source of income, analogous to that obtained from craftwork or trade' (Nicolas 1968: 126, cited by Hill

1972: 308). It disagrees with the analysis of Kritsman and the School of Agrarian Marxists, who, in the evidently extraordinary circumstances of the Soviet peasantry in the 1920s, argued on the basis of many surveys and intricate analysis that the plough owner was a 'hidden capitalist' because he appropriated part of the (labour) product of plough hirers, even when they had much larger holdings than the plough owner (Kritsman as summarized by Cox in Cox 1984: 13–14, 22, 31, 56–58). Such an analysis might have been true of the Soviet peasantry of the time, but to extend this analysis to Hausa farmers risks the conclusion that hiring out oxen and plough is fundamentally a *successful* strategy of capital accumulation in Hausaland. Such a conclusion neglects the reality that hiring is embedded in an array of kinship and cliental relations which are onerous in a polygynous culture, and therefore neglects the *difference* between monogamous and polygynous societies – the fundamental point in the entire argument of this book.

Chapter 2

The Cultural Logic of Noncapitalist Accumulation

The Patterns of Production and Exchange

On the surface, chapter 1 has shown signs of a capitalist agrarian transition in Marmara as a result of changes in the regional and wider political economy since colonial times. The process of commoditization had extended chronologically from the sale of produce (well before the onset of colonialism) to the widespread selling of farmland and the frequent hiring of labour in the mid-twentieth century. Some villagers had grown rich by engaging in an interactive cycle of investment, such that trading profit was invested in farmland and the hiring of labour, while money income from the sale of produce became working capital for investment in trade or transport. As we have seen, by 1979, there was great inequality in land use.

Changes in politics appear to support the idea of an ongoing transition to agrarian capitalism. As a result of populist agitation and more recently, rural prosperity during the oil boom, there had been a certain shift in the balance of power from the hereditary overlords (*sarakuna*) to the common people (*talakawa*) – and particularly to their local leaders, the rural farmer-traders.

Marmara, and the district of Malumfashi around it, comprise an area of Hausaland which, historically, was a frontier between the three Muslim emirates of Katsina, Kano and Zaria, and thus, did not become a centre of agricultural production and trade until the twentieth century. Therefore, it has been heavily influenced by colonial contact and the shift in trading patterns from production for the West African Savannah to production for European markets. Nevertheless, I discovered extraordinary patterns incompatible with a model wherein commoditization generates a capitalist agrarian transition. 'Signs' of capitalist transition, probed more deeply, were curiously opaque.

Increasing inequality in land distribution was not the result of land transfers from 'small' farmers (those in net annual financial deficit) to 'large' farmers (those in net annual financial surplus). Rather, large farmers had bought most of their land from a departing pastoral population – and from *other* large farmers (chapters 3 and 8).

The term 'wage labour' makes little sense of a society where hired labouring was predominantly part-time. Family heads who frequently hired out their labour had land. Labouring tended to be a phase in their life cycle. This was because they were seeking to acquire one or more of the off-farm occupations in the hamlet. The great majority of hired labourers were boys or youths released occasionally by their fathers from family farming (chapter 4).

Ecologically, the existence of different rainfall zones in Nigeria enabled smaller farmers to earn extra income when not engaged in their own farming, through southward seasonal migration to areas with longer rainy seasons. At the level of social consciousness, ecological differences encouraged them to treat hired labouring as a *complement* to family farming. A second dynamic was the continuous search by household heads for a remunerative off-farm occupation (*sana'a*). The income from a sana'a increased the viability of smaller farmers. It enabled many of them to engage in limited land acquisition, by purchase or by loaning money in return for pledged land (chapters 3 and 5). Moreover, the development of a sana'a with increasing age tended to restrict the supply of hired labourers to a workforce of younger men (chapter 4). This raised the bargaining power of men who frequently hired out their labour power. Thus, key dynamics actually increased the viability of smaller farmers and prevented them from being reduced to landless or semi-landless labourers.

The monetization of bridewealth, and the consequent increases in bride-price (Bernstein 1977: 63), had not caused a crisis in the social reproduction of small farmer households. Indeed, by the time that a typical villager married off a son or daughter, he tended to be middle aged, and to have acquired enough land through his lifetime to be, at least, a 'middle' farmer (in annual financial balance) (chapter 5).

He was deeply involved in the *biki* system of marriage gift exchange which meant that his marriages were partly financed by cash and kind from gift partners. Moreover, women, with their own sources of income, paid a vital part of the marriage expenses of their children. When farmers did transfer land in order to finance a marriage, they tended to pledge it rather than sell it, with a good expectation of reclaiming it several years later (chapters 3 and 5).

Farmer-traders were involved in intricate arrangements, based on a series of traditional relationships, for the supply of marketing credit, which provided them with a high degree of forward security (chapter 7). Commercial credit relationships took the form of either patron-client ties between men of very unequal income; or 'trading friendships' between those of broadly similar income (chapter 7). Notionally, there were two kinds of trading loan – interest-free, short-term credit (*rance*) repayable in a week or less, usually granted by 'friends in trade'; and interest-free, long-term credit of some size (*jali*) usually granted by patrons at harvest and repayable before the next farming season. But in practice, periods of repayment could be extended where a long-standing personal relationship had engendered mutual services based on trust.

The most interesting fact about commercial credit is that enormous sums were circulating in the rural areas without interest being charged. Islamic injunctions against 'interest' were part of the reason for this. However, the basic reason for the absence of a rate of interest on commercial loans is that borrowers were subject to such fluctuating claims on their own income – from kin, from other trading friends or from their own clients – that they could not guarantee lenders the reinvestment of borrowed funds over a specific period in such a way as to generate a predictable return. Because lenders and borrowers were subject to the same diverse set of social pressures, it made little sense to charge interest on loans. Their attention was rather focussed on a concept of *mutuality*. Through the personal loyalties of patronage or trading friendship, they aimed by lending to generate a return flow of services in the long term. In a real sense, I saw them 'accumulating together'.

'Profit' (*riba*), as the margin of earned income over incurred costs, was indeed their universal preoccupation. But at least as much profit flowed into the polygynous marriages of themselves and their children, and into their growing commitments to clients and friends, as flowed into the purchase of land and hired labour-power. In assessing economic process, it is as important to study the uses to which profit is put, as it is to study the ways in which it is acquired (chapter 7).

The most revealing evidence concerned the patterns of expansion among households. As money income increased among villagers, it was invested in farmland. It was also used to finance a larger number of wives and larger households (chapters 3 and 7). Thus, as income increased, so, too, did the number of consanguineal and affinal kin. The greater a villager's wealth, the more gift (biki) partnerships he established with poorer men, which helped them to defray their own marriage and naming ceremony expenses (chapter 5).[1] The totality of these patterns shows that, on the one hand, small farmers were able to maintain their hold on land by combining farming with off-farm occupations; on the other, the kinds of expansion in which farmer-traders engaged involved them not just in the multiplication of material assets but also in the extension of their marriage ties with the rest of the community – and their immersion in a form of gift exchange with the rest of the community (biki) which helped small farming households meet the financial burden of bridewealth without selling land.

These patterns do not imply the progressive reduction of small farmers to agricultural labourers. Nor do they suggest that rich villagers were becoming a distinct class with enterprises that separated the pursuit of profit from personal relationships. Patterns presented paradoxes which could not easily be accommodated within a logic of transition to capitalism.

Islamic Conversion, Trading and Accumulation

We saw in chapter 1 that the people in the immediate area around Marmara had converted to Islam in the mid-twentieth century from the indigenous Hausa religion. Before conversion, farming had been based on the very extended family work unit (*gandu*) comprising up to three generations of men and their wives. Wives in these units had significant rights to land and working time, linked in a special economic relationship with their married sons. The male head of the extended ensemble only fed its members from the common granaries during the farming season. Thereafter, until the next farming season, his wives would feed him and his unmarried dependents from their own granaries, while married dependent men, their wives and children would live off the food from their own farmland (chapter 4).

After conversion, women withdrew from most farming operations. The gandu contracted to a smaller male unit linking mainly fathers and sons. Islamic conversion exposed smaller households to economic deficits resulting from the absence of female labour. In most cases, it necessitated the development of an off-farm occupation (sana'a) to provision the household. At the same time, it opened up opportunities for larger households to enter Muslim trading networks and use the profits therefrom to hire labour and purchase land (see also Last 1979: 240–42). For these men, Islamic conversion made possible a process of capital accumulation. But it drew them into other processes as well.

To succeed in trade, in whatever line, required access to commercial credit, sources of supply, wholesale or retail outlets, storage facilities. It required the ability to develop networks of trust in borrowing and lending. The aspiring trader needed patronage for long-term funds, and if this endowed him with sufficient credit to gradually develop trading profit, he was thereafter drawn into trading friendships, wherein he loaned and borrowed short- and medium-term funds. Through Islamic conversion, therefore, he entered the world of clientage and trading friendship.

He also added to his home community at least two other regular communities of interaction – that of other traders in his vicinity, and the group of men with whom he did business at the marketplaces to which he journeyed. He became exposed to the religious and political discussions of an Islamic world much wider than that of his home. And he adapted to the habits of commerce entrenched in those marketplaces. Thus, conversion gradually changed him from a farmer (however successful) confined to the convivial rural world of the Maguzawa (non-Muslim) big houses (*manya gidaje*) into a more cosmopolitan being learning the practices and modes of communication inside trading networks – and their moral expectations.

Moral Concepts and Accumulation

My concern with moral assumptions stems partly from ethnographic experience. In Marmara, I was struck by certain kinds of private and public behaviour. In the quiet of my room, men would insist on a course of action using the word *gara* ('you had better' with the meaning 'you really should') or *dole* ('it is necessary' with the sense of 'compulsory'). Men engaged in a loud and public justification of their actions whenever they felt these would be subject to question. The voice would be raised and points would be couched in an interrogative, almost rhetorical, plea. They would compare each other's behaviour in terms of *hali*. While dictionaries translate this generally as 'character, temperament, disposition, mode' or even just 'peculiarity', the lexical examples all point to adjectival contrasts between good and bad, spiritual and physical, courageous and cowardly, liberal and mean (Abraham 1962: 366; Robinson 1925: 149). In Marmara, there was certainly an emphatic quality to the continual explanation of other people's behaviour in terms of *kyan* (good) or *mugun* (bad) hali. My experience of the Hausa language was that people reserved their highest approval for those who undertook *hidima* (pronounced 'hid'ima', with the accent on the first syllable). Dictionaries translate this simply as 'serving a person' (Abraham) or 'service, administration' (Robinson). But in Marmara, it seemed to have the special connotation of 'responsibility' and was used of a range of personal responsibilities – especially the responsibility to provide oneself and one's children with marriage partners.

Before the military government opened up public debate in 1978, villagers were privately obsessed by the rightness or wrongness of the traditional ruling class: *Abun da sarakuna suke yi, haram ne* ('What the rulers do is unlawful [by the Muslim code]'). During the 1979 national elections, most villagers supported the parties opposed to the party of the rulers, and would compare their respective merits in these terms: *Adalci muke nema* ('We are seeking justice'). This seemed to denote not just a more even distribution of power and wealth, but a more reciprocal interaction between governors and governed.

Most of these terms have an Arabic derivation. The long exposure of Hausaland to Islamic concepts emanating from beyond the Sahara has affected the forms of discourse. Not long before my fieldwork, the people of the area had converted to Islam. This may have given their discourse some of its self-consciously ethical form. The mallams of Marmara were at the centre of discussion concerning the whole range of human behaviour.

Focussing on farmer-traders, the arrangements for lending, borrowing and repayment among them must be seen in their context – a form of Islam which placed great value on communal intercourse and prayer among abstemious men. Muslim marketplaces and trading networks, as much as Muslim villages, were sites of religious discussion and public prayer. Every man seeking wealth attached himself to at least one mallam for supernatural assistance and personal advice. These activities reveal a society with strongly held notions of right and obligation – and a concomitant sense of guilt when those notions were transgressed.

In assessing the prospects for future cooperation, farmer-traders paid great attention to each other's character (hali). Personal reliability was one measure of character. A more important measure was willingness to enter personal relationships marked by generosity in providing commercial credit which would improve the life-chances of borrowers – in short, an acceptance of responsibility (hidima) for borrowers as clients or friends in trade. Time and again, rural Muslims discussed the success of a particular farmer-trader in terms of an almost mystical sense of causation: *because* he had developed a web of dependent juniors (*yara*), *therefore* he grew rich. In brief, men gave commercial credit because they calculated that in the future borrowers would help them; and because they believed that their generosity would attract God's favour.

Although any short-term credit relationship was dyadic, borrowers were typically situated in the middle of three-way relationships, such that the credit flowed from a richer person through the borrower to poorer persons with whom he himself had dyadic ties (chapters 5 and 7). This reflected a collective understanding of the social process of enrichment, and a corresponding sense of reciprocal justice. Since the success of most farmer-traders depended on the willingness of others to lend them money, it was right that they lend to others still struggling to succeed. The failure to acquire clients or junior trading friends was seen to undermine the workings of the whole process, and therefore incurred moral disapproval. 'Bad character' (*mugun* hali) was imputed to borrowers who failed to lend. The operation of this norm was so dramatic that traders could have out on short-term loan so much money that they needed to borrow to cover their subsistence needs (chapters 5 and 7).

Thus, the rural community of Marmara and the trading networks to which its farmer-traders belonged can be said to comprise a 'society of lenders'. Lending expressed the effort to establish bonds of reciprocal obligation: A. gives to B. so that later he can receive from B. Lending of short-term credit involved an ebb and flow of subsistence as well as investment funds, away from and back towards persons, because lenders knew that they in turn could borrow from trading friends.[2] The social relations of production and exchange through which this society was reproduced thrust up a need to borrow, and a concomitant duty to lend. Among farmer-traders, it is not misleading to speak of a process of 'collective enrichment'.

The duty to lend was related to the notion of 'working capital' among the rural Hausa. Jali denoted the liquid assets which could be invested in all economic or social spheres which contributed to the growth of 'wealth'. The rural Hausa idea of wealth (*dukiya*) included both monetizable resources and the range of persons to whom there were varying ties of responsibility (hidima). Thus, jali referred to investment funds, set aside from spending on personal consumption, but its range of application incorporated the sets of personal relationships which the possessor of jali was seeking to expand. It was subject to a diffuse range of social claims, including the requests for loans from clients and trading friends. Equally, its possessor could make claims on the jali of others. A farmer-trader's investment capacity was the result of the net combination of his jali, the claims of others on his jali, and his claims on the jali of others. Thus, expenditure of jali on, say, marriages, or lending, could actually expand investment capacity in so far as it attracted the jali of others who respected the investor's willingness to shoulder responsibility (hidima) for others.

For the ambitious man to convert to Islam was to enter a community of traders and thus, a society of borrowers and lenders. Particularly for those who were expanding their trade, the moral obligations attached to lending were therefore seen as part of the life of the good Muslim. Thus, the clientage and trading friendship of Muslim trading networks gave new meaning and added point to ideas of hali and hidima.

This account parts company radically with the analyses of Polly Hill, M.G. Smith, and Guy Nicolas in one respect – their emphasis on the Hausa concept of *arziki* as reflecting the tendencies of the rural economy (Smith 1955: 14–15; Nicolas 1964: 105 cited in Hill 1972: 185–86). Arziki incorporates the idea of life as a game of chance which some win and others lose. It denotes the highly individual quality of good fortune, which is here today and gone tomorrow. It cannot be transmitted from its holder to his children. In dwelling on arziki those authors gave the impression that rural Hausaland consisted of individuals struggling in a lonely combat with natural and market forces. They reiterated the elements of chance, accident and coincidence because of the vagaries of climate and market uncertainties. In contrast, my account reveals a pattern of social relations imbued with moral obligation. The rural Hausa with whom I worked were embedded in moral practices whose regularity and coherence make possible individual enrichment.

A Model of Noncapitalist Growth

Chapters 1 and 2 have revealed a specific historical sequence of economic change and continuity in the area of southern Katsina of which Marmara forms a part. In the nineteenth century, the area was sparsely populated, but immersed in the circuits of long-distance trade whereby its grains, cotton and crafts were sold in other parts of Hausaland through the medium of a widely accepted currency, the cowrie. It was dominated by slave production, with Fulani pastoralists as the major slave owners. They lived alongside Maguzawa (non-Muslim) polygynous farming households of considerable size. In the early twentieth century, imposition of colonial rule led to the abolition of slavery. With this security, Maguzawa (non-Muslim) Hausa farmers spread over the land, and small farmers from other parts of Hausaland migrated in – many of them ex-slaves. The imposition of tax in colonial currency and the introduction of capitalist manufactures (particularly textiles) disrupted local craft production and intensified the production of agricultural commodities – a relative shift away from the sale of grains and traditional cotton to other parts of Hausaland, toward the export of groundnuts and colonial cotton to the European market. This created the conditions for the expansion of a particular kind of small farmer organization – the polygynous household in which men, their wives and children farmed together.

By the mid-twentieth century, grain surpluses were being sold once again to more northerly regions with grain deficits, as in the precolonial period. This, combined with the post–World War II rise in world commodity prices, made possible the profitable employment of part-time hired labourers to supplement the family workforce. From this time onward, conversion to Islam led to the withdrawal of female labour from most farming operations. This compelled larger households with grain surpluses to increase their employment of hired labourers to work alongside the male family workforce. By entering Muslim trading networks, the heads of these households could develop trading margins and acquire loans which enabled them to intensify their employment of hired labour and their purchase of farmland. Richer households could engage in a new kind of expansion – the accumulation of capital.

At the same time, success in Muslim trading networks depended upon acquiring a growing circle of patrons, clients and trading friends, to whom many obligations were attached. We can thus outline an historical sequence of overlapping changes in economic organization – polygynous expansion, cliental expansion (the consequence of entering Muslim trading networks), and capital accumulation (the result jointly of colonial commodity production and conversion to Islam). Today, the successful farmer-trader interweaves all three forms of expansion in the development of his enterprise.

There are complex transfers going on between the three forms of expansion. Trading profit made on the basis of loans from patrons and trading friends is invested in farmland and hired labour. Profit from agriculture is extended as interest-free loans to clients and trading friends. Profits from both trade and agriculture provide the bridewealth for the expansion of the household through marriage and procreation. Over time, the growth of a household workforce provides not just labour for farming, but more importantly, a team which the household head will deploy as agents or managers in trading and farming (chapters 7 and 8).

This book argues that polygynous marriage and the relationships of patronage and trading friendship have deflected a potential agrarian capitalist transition into a distinctive pattern of noncapitalist accumulation. This pattern emerges from the sequence of changes in economy, polity and religion which characterize the history of southern Katsina and the manner of its insertion in the world market. Islam in particular introduced a style of commercial interaction and a notion of personhood which emphasized multiple partnership in the acquisition of wealth. Islam as taught and practiced in southern Katsina has strongly supported polygynous marriage. Moreover, conversion to Islam profoundly changed notions of gender, so that women moved off the farm and stayed in the house. This, in turn, accelerated the need for small farmers to acquire off-farm occupations in order to supplement farm income. But off-farm income enabled them to retain their hold on land, to even engage in small-scale land acquisitions themselves (chapter 3), and so prevented wealthy farmer-traders from having at their disposal a landless or semi-landless labour force.

In contesting the inevitability of capitalist agrarian transformation, I have in mind a composite model of 'capitalism' derived from Marx and Weber – a set of production relations in which the pursuit of profit transforms human labour into a commodity. Various changes may lead to these production relations. But they are rooted in a particular kind of rationality – the numerical calculation of ends as well as means to ends (Weber 1992 [1930]: 21, 26). Money profit results from the action of 'capital' as social process – the production of surplus value through the employment of workers who generate more exchange value than they receive. They accept these unequal terms of exchange because they have been dispossessed of means of production and therefore depend on wage labour for survival (Marx 1976 [1867]: 716, 719).

'Capital' as social process is reproduced and expanded in so far as employers reinvest profit in the extension of the work force – the *accumulation* of capital (Marx 1976 [1867]: 732). This involves, concomitantly, the purchase of other forces of production, including land. Slowly, or rapidly, the social forces of production are reorganized under the control of capitalist accumulators.

In a model of noncapitalist accumulation, however, the accumulation of capital is impeded, and so, too, are capitalist production relations. Since other forms of accumulation are connected to capitalist accumulation, noncapitalist production relations continue to reproduce themselves. Other cultural purposes persist alongside money profit as organising goals of economic life. In the model I am proposing, a historically specific trajectory of noncapitalist accumulation prevents the full development of capitalist production as theorized by Marx and Weber.

Long ago, Terence Ranger's review of peasant research in central and southern Africa (Ranger 1978)[3] cautioned against the assumption that 'accumulation' was necessarily the result of European colonialism and capitalism. He outlined a process of accumulation in precolonial southern Africa, whereby a man's power and wealth were defined by his success in building up herds of cattle. His article effectively demolished the idea that 'accumulation' is intrinsically a capitalist characteristic. It opened the way to showing that distinctive kinds of indigenous accumulation characterize different kinds of society.

My general definition of accumulation draws on, but goes beyond, Marx. Once 'capital' has emerged as a social relationship, Marx defines the accumulation of capital as the *expanded* reproduction of this social relationship. Capitalist employers do not consume the surplus value appropriated from the workforce, but reinvest it in payment for additional workers, and additional or more efficient means of production. The reinvestment of appropriated value triggers off continual expansion in the production of surplus value, and hence of production itself. If 'capital' is the relationship of value appropriation and realization, 'capitalist accumulation' is the reproduction of capital on an extended scale (Marx 1976 [1867]: 732). Marx also calls this 'valorization', whereby the value realized in exchange is reconverted into capital (Marx 1976 [1867]: 725).

Citing work on nineteenth-century India, where agricultural surplus was appropriated as rent and tribute, Marx briefly extends his discussion of accumulation to other economic systems. "In economic formations of the most diverse kinds . . . [there is] . . . reproduction on an expanded scale. More is produced and consumed. Therefore, more products are converted into means of production (Marx 1976 [1867]: 744–45)." Thus, Marx used 'accumulation' to refer to the expanded reproduction of any economic relationship.

Combining insights from Marx and Weber, I define accumulation as that process which generates a self-sustaining increase in the objects or relations that are socially defined as desirable, and in their forces of production. Thus, 'accumulation' implies a self-sustaining increase in the number of persons who produce or procure those objects or relations. It follows that one process of accumulation may be distinguished from another by

- the objects or relations that are socially construed as desirable;
- the manner in which labour power is obtained to produce or procure them;
- the balance of power and obligation between those who control labour power (in all of its different forms) and those who provide it.

Accumulation, like other economic processes, is seen as being the product of distinctive social and moral totalities (Weber 1992 [1930]: 21–27).

From Marx's idea of accumulation I take the notion of a process that is self-sustaining and expanding within an otherwise-defined cycle of economic activity. My disagreement with Marx is that I do not treat *appropriation* as essential to the definition of accumulative process (Marx 1976 [1867]: 725–46). Some forms of accumulation are intrinsically exploitative or appropriative. For example, under slave, feudal and capitalist economic systems, part of the product of labour is appropriated by the controllers of labour power in order to invest in the further expansion of land, technology or other productive forces. But under other forms of accumulation, we can think in terms of a common fund in which part of the product of labour power is set aside from general consumption and invested. Moreover, we can think of accumulation by individuals based on savings and investment – and thus, an internal augmentation of the productive forces at their disposal from the proceeds of a particular activity, rather than from the appropriation of the labour product of others. Thus, I propose a cross-cultural definition under which deferred consumption and the reinvestment of the surplus thus acquired is the common criterion of accumulation. Provided that a cycle of economic activity can be specified, and provided that part of the product of this activity is reinvested in the expansion of productive forces, then there is 'accumulation' – i.e., re-production of the activity on an expanded scale. While appropriation, or exploitation, is essential to the expanded re-production of capitalism, it need not be essential to the expanded re-production of all economic activities or systems. This perspective on accumulation allows for processes that are distinctly different from the accumulation of capital.

Capital accumulation may be contrasted with other kinds. Under *household* accumulation, household heads enlarge the family work force through marriage and procreation. Under *pastoral* accumulation, pastoralists seek a self-sustaining increase in the size of herds but to achieve this goal, they use livestock to obtain wives and children, or clients, or contracted labourers who are given a share of the herd. Under *cliental* accumulation, patrons attract clients by providing protection, gifts and loans, and use the product of cliental labour to further expand their circles of clients. This typology is not exhaustive.[4] However, the manner in which labour power is procured, and the balance of rights and obligations between those who provide labour power and those who control or seek to control it, are essential considerations for any typology.

Because it directs attention to the balance of power between providers and controllers of labour power, 'accumulation' entails a reference to politics. I use 'politics' in the wide sense – the distribution of the capacity to influence people, and equally important, the struggles over that distribution (Foucault 1983: 220–21). We are drawn to examine intrahousehold negotiations or conflicts between fathers and sons, husbands and wives, as well as the extrahousehold conflicts between employers and labourers, patrons and clients, and trading friends. Secondly, 'accumulation' implies a reference to the conceptual systems of a society. It draws us to consider how people construct their sense of the ultimately desirable – the goals which animate work. That leads us to reflect on people's sense of those ultimate demands which cannot be avoided – their sense of obligation.

The usefulness of 'accumulation' as a central concept in cross-cultural comparison is that it unifies the analyses of economic action, desire and morality. Accumulation as social process takes the gain from labour, however labour is organized in a particular society, and reapplies it to the expanded production of what is wanted and ethically esteemed. Collective moralities strongly inflect the social construction of desire. At stake are the distinctive ways in which people *desire to acquire* and *institute acquisitive desire as a process over time.* By redefining accumulation in a more general way than is found in Marx and Weber, I am seeking to locate economic action in a socially constructed, morally inflected hierarchy of desires.

I apply this cross-cultural definition of accumulation to the Hausa society around Marmara which shared with it a relatively high population density and an agronomic system based on permanent, manured cultivation (chapter 1). During the period 1976–98, 'profit' (*riba* in Hausa, the concept used by all farmers to measure the relative money worth of different undertakings) fuelled three processes of accumulation:

1. *Household* accumulation: surplus in the form of cash or kind resulting from transfers between the household head and his male and female dependents, was used for the polygynous marriages of himself and his sons and daughters, in order to enlarge the household through marriages and procreation. More particularly, surplus generated out of the labour of male and female dependents was used to expand the household through marriages and procreation.
2. *Cliental* accumulation: surplus in the form of cash or kind resulting from transfers between patron and client, was used by the patron to expand his circle of clients through the recruitment of new clients. Where patrons and clients were part of extended patron-client chains, the patron used long-term, interest-free credit from superior patrons, and medium-term, interest-free credit from lateral trading friends, to generate money profit in the sphere of trade; this trading profit was then invested in the recruitment of new trading friends and clients for trade or agriculture.
3. The accumulation of *capital*: the farmer-trader reinvested value appropriated from hired labourers and exchanged on the market, in the expansion of the hired work force and other productive forces.

It is important not to confuse the accumulation of capital with the acquisition of 'wealth'. 'Wealth' (dukiya) was a broad concept among the rural Hausa among whom I lived. As a local concept, it incorporated wives and children and their provisioning; social relations which included friends, patrons and clients; living, growing realities like crops, animals and farmland; productive equipment, and new technologies and means of transport; and media of exchange like money which could be the instrument for achieving an increase in all of these. In contrast, 'capital' in the strictly Marxian sense refers to the process whereby employers appropriate exchange value from employees through the institution of labour contracts specified in money terms, in a sphere of production which enables appropriated value to be realized through the sale of commodities. Comparing the local concept of 'wealth' with a cross-cultural concept of 'capital', we see that Hausa people strove for 'wealth' in many directions, only one of which was the accumulation of capital. Throughout this book, I will therefore refer to the 'social process of long-term wealth acquisition' to capture the integrated way in which farmer-traders pursued the three processes of accumulation that I have outlined.

Farmer-traders were not 'incipient capitalists' because the household and cliental processes of accumulation were just as essential as capital accumulation to the development of 'wealth' in the terms of the rural Hausa of southern Katsina. The process of capital accumulation was embedded in, and limited by, the claims on resources resulting from household and cliental accumulation. Household and cliental accumulation involved farmer-traders in marriage ties with the rest of the community, and created bonds of moral obligation between patrons, clients, trading friends and kin. The obligations incurred were consistent with making profit through commodity production, but reduced the level of profit.

The model specifies the emergence of this complex pattern of accumulation in very particular parameters of geography, history and human agency. The relatively rich clay soil of southern Katsina had made it attractive to prospective emigrants. The abolition of slavery and, thereafter, the continuous in-migration of liberated slaves and other small farmers from less-fertile areas (e.g., Kano Emirate) led to rising population density. Crucially, population density was *already* high around Marmara when the petroleum boom of the 1970s led the World Bank and the Nigerian government to make large investments in support of agriculture and encouraged private agricultural investment by members of the traditional ruling class, the Nigerian political elite and agribusiness companies. Thus, in the period 1940–70, when the demographic structure of local society was shifting from one dominated by pastoralists to one dominated by local farmers, it was the farmer-traders who expanded cultivation. By the 1970s, when investment in capitalist agriculture first became attractive, local farmer-traders had already preempted opportunities by the traditional ruling class, alone or in alliance with outside capital, to establish large landholdings in the area.

Political dynamics are a necessary part of this model. The in-migration of Qur'anic mallams who gave Islam a populist interpretation, inspired local farmers in their struggles with the traditional ruling class from at least the 1950s to the end of fieldwork by this author (chapter 1). Thus, it would be a mistake to reduce the parameters of the noncapitalist pattern of accumulation to structural changes in human ecology and demography. Distinctive qualities of social consciousness were part of the human agency that interacted with structural changes to produce a politically active population, not a passive one. In consequence, it was difficult for traditional rulers, or outside capitalists, to profitably invest in large landholdings.

In the model, three further dimensions of household, cliental and capital accumulation need to be considered. First, under each of these processes, there is a different balance of power and obligation between the controller and providers of labour power. Under household accumulation, the husband and father must attend to a wide range of demands from his wives and children. These are personal relationships in which the wives in particular require a stream of gifts for the marriage to endure. And standard gifts and occasional assistance to affinal relations cannot be avoided. Under cliental accumulation, the patron must be attentive to the requests for loans and other forms of assistance of his client, because the client can transfer his loyalty to another patron. Again, personal negotiation is essential. Under capital accumulation, the relationship between employer and hired labourer is more impersonal. It terminates with the end of the work for which they have agreed a rate of pay.

Secondly, household, cliental and capital accumulation differ in the extent to which there is appropriation. Under household and cliental accumulation, there are highly significant clusters of economic relationship that are not appropriative. Under household accumulation, the household head appropriates part of the product of the family workforce in order to get the bridewealth needed to acquire more wives for himself. However, against this must be set the bridewealth that he provides to the sons who work for him, and his gifts to his daughters at their weddings. Moreover, where the farm labour of women in Hausa Muslim households is limited to planting and some harvesting operations, the extent to which the household head appropriates the product of their labour must be balanced against the provisions and gifts which he makes available to them. It follows that – while there may be elements of appropriation in the relations between the household head and his dependent members – the product of their joint labour is more realistically approached as a common fund upon which all members have a claim in their efforts to achieve polygynous marriage and more children.

Under cliental accumulation, two conceptual distinctions ought to be made for the sake of clarity – between patron-client relations and lateral trading friendships (see chapter 7 for a full discussion) and between political and economic clientage. In this model, the patron-client relation emerges between rural commoners who were historically excluded from political power by the Hausa-Fulani ruling class. Thus, the relationship is distinctively economic and flexible. It is closer in nature to the relations described by Abner Cohen in his classic study of commoners engaged in livestock and kolanut trading (Cohen 1969) than to the inherently political, aristocratic patronage analysed by Nadel and M.G. Smith in their studies of political economy in northern Nigeria (Nadel 1942; Smith 1955). Moreover, an analytical distinction should be made between trading friendships among social equals, where transfers are expected to balance in the long term, and patron-client relations, where there is an element of command over the labour or services of the client; the client understands that the balance of economic and social advantage will be with the patron and accepts this arrangement because through clientage he plans to be upwardly mobile economically, and thus become a patron himself. Under lateral trading friendship, it is understood that assistance rendered will reap profit in trade; and thus, trading friendship becomes part of cliental accumulation when the profit is reinvested in trading friends or in clients.

The patron plans in the long term that the profit made from the sale of products received from the client be greater than the value of the interest-free loans which he gives to the client. However, in the short term the patron may be extending as interest-free credit or other assistance more value than he receives from the client as money profit on the sale of the produce generated by the client (chapter 7). Similarly, trading friends may expect balanced reciprocity of their transfers in the long term, but in the short term, the transfers can be very unbalanced, one person showing more generosity. Thus, under both forms of cliental accumulation, the speed of accumulation is likely to be slow, and *material* success likely to be associated with increasing age. In contrast, compared with either household or cliental accumulation, under capital accumulation there are not the same personal encumbrances. Therefore, the speed of capital accumulation is likely to be faster. It will depend largely on the ratio between product prices and the price of hired labour power on the market, which in turn will depend on the variable confluence of supplies and demands.

Thirdly, there are complex transfers between these three processes. Net profit accruing under cliental accumulation is likely to be partly converted by the patron into agricultural investments under capital accumulation, because in the long term, his credit standing as a borrower depends on the scale of his landholding (chapter 7). At the same time, profit arising from capital accumulation will be used to extend his circle of clients and trading friends. Profit made under either cliental or capital accumulation will be converted partly into more household marriages.

The interconnections between these three processes of accumulation make it possible to speak of a *trajectory* of noncapitalist accumulation. It emerged from the totality of social relations and values in rural society. It both resulted from, and incorporated, changes in rural economy. I borrow the term 'trajectory' from J-F Bayart. Bayart has developed the idea of 'trajectory' in order to group real political systems and thereby understand them in terms of their historical evolution and cultural attitudes (Bayart in Manor 1991: 51–71). A political trajectory can be coterminous with a single state while others can encompass many states. In a trajectory, the field of action is structured by long-term evolution and to that extent, exhibits continuity. At the same time, it is radically inflected by short-term changes – including those emanating from the global arena. Nevertheless, the significance of any recent 'rupture' can only be fully understood in terms of a distinct history (Bayart 1991: 54). Continuities in human geography provide one key to understanding this (see also Bayart 1993: 252–59). And the concept does not *assume* the overriding importance of the global as against the local in structuring the field of action (Bayart 1991: 51–52). For example, in outlining a political trajectory for sub-Saharan Africa, Bayart links recent upheavals with popular beliefs of great antiquity – a 'concatenation' of old and new, local and extralocal, which has 'concurrent' effects (Bayart 1991: 60–61, citing Anderson 1978 and Balandier 1959).

There is continuity of practices beneath the multiplicity of meanings given by different social actors to a trajectory's 'discursive genres' – its 'relatively stable types of expression' (Bayart 1991: 64, citing Bakhtin in Todorov and Bakhtin 1981: 65–66). The historicity of a trajectory consists in the ways whereby elements of action and relationship from a distant past are strangely compatible with recent elements. This compatibility engenders continuity in the linguistic expressions characteristic of the ensemble. More deeply, it allows for a perpetuation of desires (Bayart 1991: 66) through changing circumstances. Thus, discursive genres play their part in enabling the past to continue in the present. Bayart is illustrating the circularity of causal sequences which permit an expressive idiom to surface and sit.

In transferring the term 'trajectory' from the political to the economic domain, I seek to convey the sense that relations and actions constitutive of accumulative process are part of a social whole which is both persistent and expressive. Historically, the gradual abolition of slave labour by the British, the resultant spread of the rural population over the land and the consequent wide diffusion of land ownership made it more difficult for farmer-traders to command nonfamily labour. Demographically, rising population density increased the price of land and made it more expensive for farmer-traders to expand their landholdings. The commoditization of labour power has been conditioned by the articulation of geographical space. For the pattern of different rainfall zones, from the Sahel to the rainforest, enabled small farmers to complement work on their own farms with hired labouring in other ecological zones (chapter 4). A further condition of human ecology is important. The long postharvest dry season in southern Katsina generated the widespread pursuit of off-farm occupations. These tended to limit the supply of hired labour in relation to the demand, even during the rainy season (chapter 4). Therefore, they increased the bargaining power of hired labourers.

Morally, the value placed on extended ties of personal obligation, rooted in polygyny and confirmed by recent conversion to Islam, was expressed in the idiom of hidima (service, responsibility). Political change was crucial. The struggles between commoners and rulers were part of an historical process inspired by the preaching of the rural mallams (chapter 1). The decline in the extortionate practices of the hereditary ruling class – dated by villagers to populist agitation in the 1960s and the advent of military rule in 1967 – opened up fresh possibilities for farmer-traders to engage in accumulation. Thus, my model relates a noncapitalist trajectory of accumulation to a specific historical-cultural context. Different contexts might generate different accumulative trajectories.

If the traditional rulers had intruded significantly on territory used by the common people in this part of southern Katsina, or continued with the forced labour (*gayya*) abolished by the military regime that came to power in 1967, a different accumulative trajectory, more akin to that of capitalist agriculture, *might* have emerged. Avoiding speculation, the noncapitalist or polygynous trajectory of accumulation outlines an economics of the Hausa *talakawa,* the common people, in the absence of elite or capitalist encroachment.

The Conceptual Connections between Polygyny and Clientage

The acquisition of more wives and through them, more children, was an economic strategy among the farmers of Marmara before conversion to Islam – and among the non-Muslim Hausa nearby with whom I was familiar. Among non-Muslims, women worked, and so marriage expenditure was a direct economic investment. After conversion, the withdrawal of women from most forms of farm labour actually enhanced the value of polygyny among men, for it signified their ability to attract and maintain more than one wife.

Nevertheless, polygynous marriage was much more than an economic strategy. It had social prestige and moral significance in itself.

In order to acquire further wives, for themselves and their sons, men sold land, went into debt and diverted funds from trading or farming into marriage expenditure, without regard for the material gains. In my experience of Marmara, the desire for polygynous marriage had a compulsive quality among men. Men married more – and wealthy men, sometimes many more – than the Muslim limit of four wives through the course of a lifetime, because of the frequency of divorce and remarriage. In contrast to Weber's stress on the capitalist monetary calculation of ends as well as means, the desire for polygynous marriage took precedence over other desires. It structured the pursuit of other desires.

Polygyny provided the image and inspiration behind a local 'model' of economic activity (for local 'modelling', see Gudeman 1986: 29–44, 90–154). The value placed on polygyny generated a peculiarly *outward* sense of obligation. It defined economic growth in terms of a continuous extension of circles of relationship. The relations between the household head and the members of his household engendered a paradigm of social relations, intrinsically both domestic and economic. It was extended outward, beyond the household, and served as a mental guide in the conduct of other economic relations – between those who sought and those who provided the various kind of subordinate labour.

In his study of the Hausa landlords who controlled the cattle and kolanut trade, Abner Cohen stressed that their expenditure on client agents was the major form of their 'investment in primary relationships' (Cohen 1969: 86–92). It went through various stages. The most important were the financing of the client's marriage, and subsequently, the fostering of the client's first child. This added the dimension of 'kinship' to a relationship which became 'intense and highly personalized. In the process the client will be called by the community after the name of the landlord, in the same way that a son of the landlord would be called' (Cohen 1969: 90). Cohen actually argued that employment of unrelated clients was a preferred alternative to the employment of the tensely competitive sons of the landlord's polygynous marriage. Clientage was assimilated to sonship in every respect except inheritance. The cliental relation was 'an inescapable moral bond … governed by an "ought", by a categorical imperative, and is an end in itself, … the moral relation becomes a kinship relationship proper, serving multiple interests, and making use of primary kinship terms and patterns of behaviour' (Cohen 1969: 91).

Among the farmer-traders around Marmara, as in the cattle or kolanut trade, a process of analogous thinking assimilated personal economic relations to kinship relations. More deeply, the pursuit of material ends through the extension of personal bonds was the enactment of a moral paradigm grounded in polygyny.

Accumulation and 'Value'

Since the term 'noncapitalist' refers to such a wide variety of possible economic systems, the trajectory in this part of Hausaland could be called more specifically a *polygynous* trajectory of accumulation. Not that the process of cliental accumulation can be reduced to the accumulation of wives and children, for we have seen the crucial influence of Islam in generating a particular kind of trading relationship. And yet, I argue, polygyny generates a peculiarly outward and multiple sense of obligation toward others, in which patron-client bonds are assimilated (with understood differences) to father-son relations. Nor that capital accumulation is negligible: far from it, and in chapters 4, 7 and 8 we will see the extent of capital accumulation. It is rather that capital accumulation is contained and constrained by the actions and attitudes intrinsic to household accumulation. More deeply, the three processes of accumulation are integrated by a moral outlook which emphasizes hidima – personal responsibility for known others in the household, among wider kin and in work. That is to say that the first call on profits generated through capital accumulation is to meet the socially sanctioned demands of known others, beginning with the wives, children and *potential* wives of the accumulator's household. Provided that the reader bears in mind that 'polygynous accumulation' more graphically reveals the moral priorities of this historical trajectory, and that polygyny structures cliental and capital accumulation, I will continue to intersperse the more general term 'noncapitalist accumulation' in order to stress that the underlying economic dynamic is not capitalist.

One of the most fully developed analyses of polygyny as part of an indigenous form of accumulation is implicit in the classic work on the Tiv of central Nigeria by Paul Bohannan (1955, 1959; he does not use the term 'accumulation'). There were three 'spheres' of exchange among the Tiv – separate but not insulated sets of 'things' or realities, each having a different moral evaluation. These were the 'subsistence' sphere (including foods, craft products, tools and raw materials), a 'prestige' sphere (including slaves, cattle, special textiles and brass rods), and the highest sphere (rights in marriageable women). 'Conveyances' consisted of exchanges within any sphere, 'conversions' of exchanges between spheres. 'Conversions' were subject to strong moral evaluations, favourable when a man converted 'up', disapproving when he converted 'down'. The ultimate upward conversion occurred when a man paid brass rods from the prestige sphere in order to contract a *kem* marriage. Quite separate from 'wife exchange' between lineages, kem marriage gave the man *individual* rights to the wife's sexual and domestic services and, upon further payment of brass rods, the rights of a father over any child she bore him. Clearly, the whole process whereby a man converted food into brass rods, and brass rods into individual rights over women and children, increased the labour power under his control in the short term (the kem wife) and in the long term (the working children resulting from the kem marriage). We have here, I argue, a local process of accumulation – a self-sustaining increase in the objects or human relationships valued by society. At its heart is a socially sanctioned process for expanding the labour power at the disposal of accumulators.

Through colonial rule and the increasing circulation of Western currency, both 'wife exchange' marriages and kem marriages were replaced by bridewealth marriages accomplished with money. That did not stop women from remaining the highest 'value'. This is shown by the continuing inflation in bridewealth payments, which were consistently far greater than payment for any other object or service. Despite great changes in the extent of the market and in the forms of marriage, there was a continuity in 'value' and accumulative pattern before and after the intervention of colonialism. Women remained the most highly desired and positively evaluated goal in Tiv social life. Thus, accumulation refers to *both* moral evaluations and material process. Tiv said that a man who was successful at upward conversions had a 'strong heart' (Bohannan 1955: 67). In other words, accumulation is a process of acquisition shaped by the culturally constructed goals of local society.

Gudeman provides a slightly different interpretation of accumulation in the precolonial Tiv economy. It is more attentive to different regimes of 'value'. For Gudeman, upward conversion between the three spheres was accumulation in the sense of arbitrage between different value domains (Gudeman 2001: 8–9). Fundamentally, Tiv accumulators were converting material wealth into sacra – realities of special, sometimes symbolic significance deemed to be essential to the existence of the community. Among the Tiv, the sacra were women (Gudeman 2001: 134–36).

Gudeman's analysis focuses on the discrepancy in the value attached to different activities. Accumulation occurs when value is secured from one domain and transferred to another (Gudeman 2001:

9). Considering the trajectory of polygynous accumulation that I have outlined for the Hausa of Marmara, I derive from Gudeman the insight that there was, indeed, an incommensurability of value between three accumulative processes – money profit in the sphere of agriculture based on hired labour, mutuality in the sphere of clientage and trading friendship and the pleasures and economic support of wives and children in the household sphere. Hausa accumulators were seeking all of these values. They sought to mediate the differences between them through multiple conversions; when possible, they converted the profit based on hired labour and that based on cliental relationships into wives and children in the household sphere.

While we can read Bohannan's upward conversions as a process of accumulation, equally, I argue, we can understand accumulation as including the upward conversion of less-valued realities into more valued ones. Furthermore, this interpretation of upward conversion gives us a more complete understanding of what it means to say that different processes of accumulation are 'integrated' by a single moral outlook (e.g., an outlook that emphasizes personal responsibility to known others among the rural Hausa). Here, moral integration means that the different objects or relations in society are perceived as constituting a hierarchy of value. Some are given more value than others. In consequence, men seek to convert less-valued objects or relations into more valued ones, through an indigenous trajectory of accumulation.

Wealth in People

My argument for a noncapitalist trajectory of accumulation in a part of the African savannah needs to be related to the 'wealth in people' model elaborated for Equatorial Africa, because there are crucial similarities and differences. Focussing particularly on the precolonial and early colonial period, the idea of 'wealth in people' emerged in scholarly discussions of the various kinds of conversions between people and things (through, for example, conditions of slavery; cf. Miers and Kopytoff 1977). This culminated in Vansina's statement that in Equatorial Africa, wealth in things was converted into wealth in followers (Vansina 1990).

Guyer and Belinga have added a new dimension to the concept, arguing that wealth in people was wealth in knowledge (Guyer and Belinga 1995). They stress the wide range and growth of knowledge in that part of precolonial Africa and its loss under colonialism. Without denying that some accumulation did occur, they emphasize that the key element in 'wealth as people' was 'composition', as opposed to dominance and appropriation. The ecology behind the process of 'composition' is important: people survived in the rainforest by a wide array of knowledge – and tapping into the knowledge of others (Guyer and Belinga 1995: 109). The kinds of special skills ranged from esoteric knowledge to medicine to music to craft production. The need to combine the special knowledge of a diversity of persons was rooted in the absence of centralized power through most of the region. The authors epitomize this condition by referring to 'an information society without hierarchical controls' (Guyer and Belinga 1995: 112).

In an earlier exploration of the dimensions of self-realization behind the idea of wealth in people, Guyer's stress was on the singular authorship needed to create 'value' in exchange (Guyer 1993). Equatorial Africa was 'profoundly commercialized' at the start of the colonial era (Guyer 1993: 256), yet the terms of each exchange were unique because they rested on the individuality of the authors of the items exchanged. To such an extent was this true, that the alternative to unique exchanges was capture – of women, slaves and animals. This itself required exceptional daring. The aim of exchange, as of warfare, was self-realization – the achievement of a 'singular personhood' (Guyer 1993: 246).

Guyer and Belinga allow that 'wealth in people' incorporated an accumulative dynamic as well as a compositional one – the addition of increasing numbers, necessitating methods of control. This dynamic can be seen in the addition of children, wives, servants and clients. But they wish to emphasize the singular contributions which were sought for in particular additions, and thus the special skill which any wife, for example, brought into a polygynous marriage (Guyer and Belinga 1995: 116, 118).

Not much attention is paid to crop production or trading. This perspective on the connections between wealth in people, knowledge and self-realization appears to be the consequence of a particular forest ecology, where artisanship is privileged over crop surpluses, where movement is difficult and for these reasons, the inimitable qualities of exchanged objects are admired. Equally, the political skill to mobilize people and their knowledge in a difficult environment is locally praised. Whether we are dealing with the broad concept of wealth in people, where goods are converted into followers, or the more specific, knowledge-based concept, it follows that 'wealth' is essentially a political reality – the capacity to negotiate skills and supporters.

There are correspondences between the Hausa notion of wealth (dukiya) and certain kinds of wealth in people in Equatorial Africa. Moreover, the compositional aspect of 'wealth' adds to our knowledge of economic process. In Marmara, composition was at work as well as accumulation – for example, in choosing potential wives for their particular skills, or clients for their knowledge of trade conditions in an area. More generally, the entire world of off-farm occupations in southern Katsina – including trade in various lines – gives witness to the importance of different knowledge niches. Nevertheless, comparing wealth in people in its sophisticated form with the noncapitalist trajectory of accumulation that I have outlined, there is a very different *balance* between composition and accumulation. This balance is rooted in a series of realities.

First, there is the difference between rainforest and savannah environments. The savannah allows for the production of vast amounts of standardized products, including various crops and kinds of livestock, which are comparable by measure or weight or other agreed criteria. The 'uniformity' of 'large lots' (to use the language of Guyer and Belinga [1995: 119]) was not a feature imported into the savannah as a result of colonialism but was characteristic of it. This made possible thinking in terms of incremental addition and linear material growth.

Connected to the relative ease of movement across the savannah and Sahel and the space for trade enabled by large kingdoms or emirates, a large market for agricultural products facilitated the standardization and comparison of values through the cowrie as a medium of exchange and store of value. This expedited large transactions. It also added a cross-temporal dimension to personal economic planning, since value could be stored in the form of a widely accepted and relatively stable currency. This had two linked implications. First, individual commoners could think long term because of the possibilities for transaction on the market. Secondly, they could think in terms of material acquisition. To be sure, long-term material acquisition was only achieved through the establishment of personal relations. However, a large market with an accepted currency enabled thinking in terms of the growth of material assets – not just in terms of the combination of skills and personal qualities.

Secondly, the political context of the two regions is profoundly different. Hierarchy was a defining feature of many savannah polities, certainly of Hausaland, for centuries. Denied political participation until very recently, Hausa commoners have had to focus their energies on whatever economic success was permitted. (As we saw in chapter 1, their economic space has been greatly enlarged since independence.) Put differently, the *externality* of political control (chapter 1) led Hausa commoners to focus on the multiplication of local social relations as well as material assets – an accumulative dynamic more than a compositional one.

Thirdly, Islam has exerted a vital influence on the Hausa trajectory of noncapitalist accumulation, particularly on the process of cliental accumulation, but also in its confirmation of the desirability of polygyny. In their capacity as traders, accumulators are part of a community with an all-encompassing rhythm of prayer five times daily and of fasting during Ramadan. This induces a certain solidarity that shapes the particular morality of commercial credit outlined earlier. Guyer and Stiansen comment that

> to trade is itself to emulate the Prophet, and can be seen as imbued with spiritual value. It follows that a religious credo is used to evaluate commercial practices and to relate them as a system. Islam provides both a comprehensive set of interlocking concepts and ideas that are mutually meaningful to the community and a manual for business conduct. (Guyer and Stiansen 1999: 7)

The regularity of pattern and the density of social networks resulting from this ethical system are very different from the emphasis on singular authorship, novelty, daring and virtuoso performance characteristic of the system of beliefs and practices called wealth in people (Guyer 1993: 259).

Various models of wealth in people aim, of course, to explain how wealth was conceived and related to valuations of personhood in a period now past, whereas the noncapitalist, or polygynous, trajectory of accumulation is an account of the present which incorporates the deep changes in economy and society underway since before the twentieth century. Its salience is that it seeks to explore how some rural people do accumulate capital, but in a way that is embedded in the relations and ethics of polygyny, clientage and trading friendship. It is a model of how rural economic growth proceeds and rural inequalities unfold inside a market and a state system, in a particular ecology, under the influence of Islam.

Alternative Perspectives on Commoditization and Economic Change

This and the previous chapter have been concerned with three realities – the long-term process of market expansion in one part of Hausaland; the manner in which markets work their way through local relations of production and exchange; and the ways in which market expansion confronts and is inflected by local moral concepts regarding rightful conduct. In order to clarify what the trajectory of noncapitalist accumulation entails, it is useful to compare it with two contrasting perspectives on commoditization in Africa. The first, the Marxian perspective, argues that commoditization has displaced or is displacing noncapitalist modes of production in a way that leads to impoverishment of the small farmer or his complete dependence on outside forces. The second perspective, that of the New Institutional Economics, shares with Marxism a belief in the power of the market, but stresses that it displaces group modes of producing and thinking with the individual, 'rational' decision maker, and so contributes to both freedom and material welfare.

Commoditization and the Penetration of Capitalism

The argument for a noncapitalist trajectory of accumulation inevitably opposes the theory that commoditization necessarily leads to pervasive capitalist relations of production. With regard to Africa, one form of the theory is associated with Henry Bernstein and the late Michael Cowen: the reorganization of African economic systems by Western capital has relocated a variety of forms of peasantry within international capitalist relations of production, because all of these different forms contribute to the international accumulation of capital. Based on a labour theory of value, Bernstein argued that Western capital disrupted a 'natural economy' based on the production of subsistence goods, and created the category of 'simple commodity production' in Africa (Bernstein 1977: 61–63). Western capital was receiving increasing amounts of the labour time of African small farmers, embodied in their commodities, relative to the labour time incorporated in the capitalist manufactures which they were buying in exchange (Bernstein 1977: 64–69).

Bernstein has recently revised this argument – drastically. Because peasant production in Africa is fully 'commodified', '(p)etty commodity producers are capitalists and workers at the same time' (Bernstein 2005: 129). They exemplify 'non-class agrarian capitalism'. Either they engage in simple reproduction by combining household labour with 'wage labour'; or they engage in a form of accumulation (expanded reproduction) by investing in trade or transport – but not in an expanded scale of agriculture (Bernstein 2005: 131). Hence, Bernstein's new formula for petty commodity production – the 'self-reproduction of African small farmers as ... *both* capital and labour' (Bernstein 2005: 133)! African small farmers are 'capitalist' because they appropriate value from themselves (self-exploit) or contribute to the appropriation of value from other farmers through trade and transport.

Cowen argued that rural capitalism, as a part of capitalism in general, depends on the development of the 'capital-labour relation'. This need not take the form of wage labour – it can equally well be developed among petty commodity producers, using family labour and land, and selling their product to capitalist industry (Cowen 1981: 59–61). For Cowen, capitalist accumulation can be achieved by the employment of a landless proletariat, but it can equally well be accomplished by the 'expanded circulation of commodities': household producers become increasingly specialized, and therefore dependent on the sale of their products to capitalist industry in order to obtain items of necessary consumption and farm inputs (Cowen 1981: 70).

Bernstein's and Cowen's perspectives on commoditization treat 'capital' at a global level of generality. Both commoditization and accumulation are treated as entirely capitalist and driven from *outside* the rural areas. Particular changes in production relations inside rural Africa are given secondary significance. Nor do they evince interest in local African ways of conceptualizing economic activity. This prevents them from considering whether other forms of accumulation might be present. It denies to Africans the reality that their engagement with the market is on terms that draw from local cultural logics. In contrast, the noncapitalist trajectory of accumulation reveals profit making on the market as prioritizing the expansion of the polygynous household and the circles of clients and trading friends.

A second form of commoditization theory is associated with the work of Michael Watts and Robert Shenton. It gives critical attention to specific changes in production relations in northern Nigeria. They argue that colonial and postcolonial economic reorganization has created a crisis in the social reproduction of the Hausa peasantry, leading to its impoverishment. This paves the way for a possible development of agrarian capitalism. Watts's *Silent Violence: Food, Famine, and Peasantry in Northern Nigeria* (1983) sets forth his research findings from one year in the village of Kaita in northern Katsina Emirate, in 1977–78. His dominant tone is that the peasantry is in permanent crisis. This tone is amplified because he paints a picture of nineteenth-century rural Hausaland as dominated by subsistence and gift exchange (1983: 112, 123). This underplays the historical literature on complex, long-distance trading networks between rural areas, on the cowrie as the medium of exchange and unit for comparative evaluation, and on the prevalence of slave labour for the production of surplus (chapter 1). Watts asserts that the 'uncertainties' of the grain trade led to a strong system of famine insurance through state redistribution of grain (1983: 135). This picture of social security in nineteenth-century Hausaland sets the scene for treating the twentieth century as dominated by peasant insecurity. Nevertheless, his own research from Kaita does not show that the 'poor' have been under severe pressure in times of food shortfall. Indeed, land sales and land pledging were rare during the 1973 drought (1983: 432). There was plenty of evidence of adaptive flexibility in times of drought in a village with a variety of irrigation systems (1983: 418–41). Moreover, a 'broad spectrum' of 'middle peasants' was able to withstand both a fickle climate and a rapacious elite (1983: 441). It is hard to be persuaded of his overarching themes: the persistence of small-scale commodity producers is in question (1983: 489); commoditization is destroying the peasantry (1983: 513).

Robert Shenton's *The Development of Capitalism in Northern Nigeria* (1986), argues that Western capital prompted a reproduction crisis through commoditization. In consequence, the colonial export-crop economy transformed the relations of production in Hausaland into capitalist relations. The core of his argument is that the mid-colonial period (1930–45) was a time of severe financial crisis for Hausa 'peasants'. During the Great Depression beginning in 1929, village farmers greatly increased their production of groundnuts and cotton, the two major export crops, to compensate for falling producer prices paid by colonial trading companies. In consequence, most village farmers grew less grain and therefore became severely indebted to traders and richer farmers for the first time in their history. As a result, they were forced to perform 'wage labour' for richer farmers. Thus, relations of production were fundamentally transformed.

This perspective underestimates the capacity of small farmers to devise their own adaptations to the market. To better appreciate the resilience of small farmers, it is useful to compare Shenton's evidence with that from other sources. It is true that from 1927–29 to 1943–45, groundnut producer prices more than halved while the import price index (referring mainly to cloth) more than doubled. Total groundnut exports more than doubled (Williams 1981: 75, 79). However, the *number* of groundnut farmers seems to have risen considerably (Shenton 1986: 95). If we discount the rise in the number of groundnut farmers from the rise in total exports, then the increase in *individual average* production was probably modest. Over the same period, cotton producer prices fell 28 per cent. However, total cotton exports, and, thus, very likely, the production of most farmers, also fell (Heillener 1966: Tables II-B-6 and IV-A-8).

More interesting than the response of supply to price changes over the whole period was the reaction of supply in any *one* year to price changes between the two *previous* years.[5] There were three years in which groundnut exports increased despite price falls between the two previous years – 1931, 1932 and 1934. Otherwise, groundnut exports rose or fell as producer prices rose or fell, and from 1936 to 1945, exports in any one year moved sharply in direct response to price changes between the two previous years (Williams 1981: 75, 79). The reaction of cotton supply to price changes, as reflected in export figures, was even more pronounced (Shenton and Lennihan 1981: 19). Producers were usually able to adjust output in response to price changes. They were not locked into *increased* commodity production.

Shenton underestimates the Hausa farmers' capacity for innovation in response to new market conditions. He claims that the general effect of groundnut cultivation was a sharp decline in food production. However, he does not consider the effect on average food consumption of increasing specialization between export crop and food crop zones. Nor does he consider the effect on food production of *intercropping* grains with export crops – a standard practice.

Colonial reports relayed by Forde do not suggest a shortfall in food supply resulting from the combination of taxation and falling crop prices. These reports give limited evidence of the real burden of tax on 'average' households in 1939 – in Misau, 7 per cent of cash income; in northern Sokoto, 8 per cent of cash income (Forde 1946: 129, 153, 155). The Sokoto report also stated that the payment of tax and tithe forced farmers to sell 44–61 per cent of their annual grain *surplus* (Forde 1946: 153), not their total output.

An increasing proportion of export crop earnings must have been used to pay tax during the Depression. The main effect of falling producer prices was not a shortfall in food grain output. Rather, it was a general decline in the purchase of imports (Shenton 1986: 96). On the evidence, village farmers were not locked into growing dependence on capitalist manufactures.

We need to consider the rich complexity of occupations and income sources in the economy of the rural Hausa. Household budgets compiled by Forde from colonial reports show that rural people combined a variety of farm and off-farm income sources in the mid-colonial period (Forde 1946: 138–62). In Kazaure Emirate, farmers obtained income from tobacco, sugar, other irrigated crops and 'weaving of great skill' as well as from groundnuts. In Dawakin Kudu district of Kano Emirate, an 'average household' obtained a third of its total income from sylvan produce, livestock and secondary occupations. Farmers commonly combined a variety of farm and off-farm income sources.

The findings from these sources are in accord with my more recent evidence from Marmara: the combination of farming with off-farm occupations renders viable small farming households in a highly commoditized economy where many necessities must be purchased. Farmers were adept at reacting to changes in relative prices on the market. As we saw in chapter 1, farmers throughout southern Katsina forsook cotton for grains in the late 1970s because of the comparative price advantage. As we will see in chapter 3, scholars have shown that rural Hausaland is often marked by inequality in landholding and income. Nevertheless, inequality need not imply a crisis in the social reproduction of small farming households (chapters 1 and 3).

Marxian analyses have tended to assume that commoditization – the sale, first, of the agricultural product, then of land and finally, of labour power – inevitably results in agrarian capitalism. And yet, present-day agricultural and marketing relations are influenced by habits of thought and methods of calculation much older than the impact of Western capitalism. They are also deeply influenced by conversion to Islam. In contrast to commoditization theory, this book argues that the widening of the market in products, land and labour is proceeding through, rather than in opposition to, indigenous ideas about the purposes of economic life, the rightful conduct of personal relationships and changes in religious belief.

The Spread of the Market and the New Institutional Economics

A profoundly different approach to the impact of the market assumes that the market optimizes economic growth and eventually individual welfare. It is associated with the New Institutional Economics and Rational Choice theory. The new institutional economics (NIE) argues that transaction costs are a key to understanding the constraints on market growth. Social and political institutions, formal and informal, can raise or lower the costs of transaction, and thereby hamper or expedite market growth (Williamson 1975, 1985; Wallis and North 1986; North 1981, 1990).

In *Making a Market: the Institutional Transformation of an African Society* (1992) Jean Ensminger uses the NIE as her framework for analysing the historical and ethnographic evidence which she collected over time among the pastoral Orma of northern Kenya, who had sedentarized to the extent that the majority of livestock owners were living in villages, while a minority remained nomadic. A series of institutional changes had reduced transaction costs by making markets more secure, transactions more reliable. For example, almost total conversion to Islam between 1920 and 1940 had increased trust among men unrelated by kinship ties and so, their willingness to consign cattle or credit to fellow Muslim traders (Ensminger 1992: 60–62). Thus, Islam is analysed for its effect – the reduction in the individual's transaction costs on the market. In contrast, Islam as I encountered it in Marmara underlined a new form of solidarity and an ethic of connectedness, wherein traders had a duty to lend. Thus, while conversion to Islam may have lowered transaction costs, it also added new costs in the form of clientage and trading friendship (chapter 9).

A key component of the NIE which Ensminger introduces into her analysis is agency theory. This compares the costs to employers (principals) of various kinds of worker (agent) in order to understand the type of labour contract which is actually chosen. Ensminger shows that among sedentary livestock owners, the great distance between villages and cattle camps and the consequent difficulties of supervision led them to distinguish between ordinary hired labourers and client labourers (1992: 112–20). The latter were given far greater rewards and were associated to the owner in a quasi-kinship relationship. Thus, Ensminger treats clientage as a special form of individual labour contract which reduces agency costs to the principal. It could decline if changes in property rights allowed for greater supervision of cattle by employers (1992: 122). In contrast, patronage and clientage in Marmara involved a deep morality – an extension of personal ties locally modelled on the expansion of relations characteristic of the polygynous household. Moreover, the exchange of loans and other assistance by patrons for labour service by clients reflected a long-term cycle whereby younger men achieved income growth. This complex attitude to clientage, drawing on layers of pre-Muslim and Muslim tradition, encouraged the upward mobility of the client, rather than consigning him to a position in a labour contract.

Ensminger argues that changes in relative prices transformed Orma 'ideology' – the society's view of legitimate social order, and the behaviour flowing from it (1992: 144, 156, 172–73). And yet, 'ideology' is a simplistic way of handling cultural specificities. It prevents her from following up some of her own evidence on kinship and marriage. For example, because of their close link, mothers of the sons of sedentary livestock owners prevented them from joining the cattle camps (1992: 116). This must surely have increased the need for livestock owners to associate clients to themselves in a quasi-kinship relationship. Furthermore, her account of the dismantling of the Orma commons actually shows that a communitarian ethic persisted *within* the boundaries of any village of sedentary livestock keepers (1992: 138–42). Clearly, there are continuities as well as changes in social relationships and beliefs which get lost when an attempt is made to homogenize them into an 'ideology'.

The tendency to simplify institutions, and to see them in terms of their functional response to the market, may be related to her acceptance of Rational Choice Theory, the behavioural axiom undergirding the NIE (1992: 12–13). One formulation of Rational Choice Theory is that individuals, in making choices, seek to maximize the *difference* between the benefit of the ends chosen and the cost of the means chosen, where both ends and means are changeable. I draw this definition out of Marshall Sahlins. He stressed that the axiom of 'scarcity' relates to a psychology special to capitalist society – an anxious state in which wants are *always* greater than the means to satisfy them (Sahlins 1974: 1–9).[6] Some rational choice theory draws from neoclassical economics the axiom that individuals seek to maximize net 'utility' (satisfaction) from any given level of expenditure of time, effort and resources – or to minimize these expenditures for any given level of net utility (Plattner 1989: 10).[7] Crucially, anthropologists arguing in favour of 'maximization' set the context as transactional: individuals are acting from within interpersonal relationships where they give as well as receive. In other words, they exchange, and seek through doing so to receive at least as much as they give (Barth 1966: 5).

The problem with Rational Choice Theory is that, even if we were to concede that people are always 'maximising', their very definition of ends and means is so heavily informed by family upbringing, ideas of appropriate gender behaviour, social notions of personhood, local cosmology and familiarity with a range of existing institutions (from the domestic to the political), that a theory of maximization is inherently vague beyond situations involving calculations of strictly measurable and material benefit and cost. If economic behaviour were restricted to these situations, then theories of maximization would be explanatory. But people's effort to maximize or optimize in response to relative prices does not just seek net individual material satisfaction, but also invokes a wide range of existing beliefs and practices. People do engage in cost-benefit analysis, but their very perception of costs and benefits is collectively, culturally, shaped over a long term. Among the Orma, one response to the rising shortage of herding labour occasioned by sedentarization was an increase in polygyny; another was child adoption and cooperative herding with other members of their settlement (Ensminger 1992: 114). These were deeply rooted cultural practices. Ensminger underplays the persistence of collective modes of thought and action in her account of people's choices in a market.

In exploring the rationality of economic action, more useful than Rational Choice Theory is Max Weber's distinction between 'substantive' and 'formal' rationality. In his posthumous *Economy and Society,* substantive rationality is true of any economy where calculations are made in the light of some set of ultimate values; in contrast, formal rationality is the subjection of all economic actions to calculation in numerical terms (Weber 1978: 85). Under formal rationality, the ultimate criterion of choice, not just the means of choice, is the numerical comparison of the calculable net gains from alternative potential actions (Weber 1978: 86). In his discussion of Weber's distinction, Jeff Pratt writes that for Weber, a necessary condition for the complete development of formal rationality is the technical practice of accounting, most fully attained under capitalism (Pratt 1994: 15). What is fascinating about the Hausa rural economy of southern Katsina is that *particular subspheres* of economy were characterized by formal rationality in the period 1976–98 – decisions over crop choice, the extent of labour hiring, the use of mechanical and chemical inputs and the choice of markets in which to sell the product of labour. Nevertheless, the *integration of all economic subspheres* depended on a substantive rationality wherein the accumulation of wives, children, clients and trading friends was given preference over the accumulation of capital in the total distribution of time, energy and material resources. This entailed a *moral unity* or *consistency in decision making,* whereby there was an upward conversion of less-valued material and monetary realities into more valued personal and relational realities.

Two motifs run beneath Ensminger's account of change among the Orma – the primacy of the individual, and transience. The individual is seen as the mover of institutional change, calculating his 'best advantage', and so influencing other individuals (Ensminger 1992: 8, 12–13). The individual is also seen as the terminal point of social change, in the end result of a highly ramified market in which individuals offer their specialist goods and services to all other individuals (e.g., Ensminger 1992: 124). The effect of rational choice based on the relative prices of goods and services is the eventual erosion of what Ensminger calls 'ideologies' – i.e., collective cosmologies and moralities – in so far as they stand in the way of the individual calculating his optimum personal advantage (e.g., 1992: 11).

We may doubt the necessary truth of these motifs. In the case of Marmara, the widespread circulation of products from at least the nineteenth century, and the intensified commoditization of land and labour power in the twentieth, have led to a market which is far more comprehensive than that among the Orma. Yet the growth of this market, and capital accumulation within it, has been accompanied by the persistence of polygyny – with the particular responsibilities experienced by polygynous accumulators. In the area around Marmara, the spread of the market encouraged the spread of Islam and, with it, social networks of clientage and trading friendship – with their own model of 'good character' (kyan hali) and right action. Thus, new morally inflected collectivities have grown up alongside older ones inside an expanding market.

The argument of this book is that different trajectories of accumulation encourage markets to grow in different ways. The 'acquisitive drive' is a universalizable term that describes human motivation in most economic systems – apart, perhaps, from hunter-gatherers. Nevertheless, the priorities for acquisition can differ profoundly between economic systems. If acquisition is directed significantly to expanding families and circles of clients and friends, this can lead to *slower growth in per capita material income,* but *faster growth in multiple social bonds of mutual trust and obligation,* than would occur under a trajectory of capitalist accumulation. The evidence from Marmara suggests that the very meaning of 'economic growth' varies between societies, according to their sense of the ultimately desirable and morally obligatory.

At stake are two issues – the ways in which people construct morality, and desire. Wendy James has insisted on the importance of the collective transmission of a moral 'tradition' via teachers. Cultural 'construction' goes on at many levels; thus, a distinction between the collective social body and individual inter-actors has got to be retained (James 1996: 111). What individuals regard as deeply desirable has, too, a collective dimension. Rational Choice theorists are mistaken in assuming that desires in a monogamous society correspond to the desires between genders or age groups in a polygynous one. Any theory of change needs to pay attention to the durability of collective modes of morality and desire as well as the power of individuals to effect change.

Themes

A comparison of my account of economic change in Marmara with the account of change among the Orma and with reconstructions of precolonial life in Equatorial Africa suggests the historical specificity of economic formations. Their specificity consists in particular sequences of change. The particularity of these sequences stems from different constellations of human ecology and collective thought – and impact from the international sphere of political economy. Secondly, economies are moral systems. This goes deeper than saying they harbour ideologies of appropriate social order. They contain distinctive notions of right and wrong behaviour, rooted partly in notions of personhood and partly in notions of the relation between humans and the divine. Different systems of moral belief inflect the acquisitive drive in different ways, so that different trajectories of accumulation emerge. The outcome will be different systems of meaning in terms of which economic growth is defined. In opposition to the NIE, I do not see growth as a unilinear process leading to the homogenization of markets and the individualization of decision making.

This book will examine a series of economic institutions in Marmara – for the transfer of land (chapter 3), labour (chapter 4), credit (chapter 5) and produce and investment funds (chapters 6 and 7). Throughout, it aims to explain how the spread of the market, local collectivities of thought and practice, and the discovered institutional patterns mutually constitute each other. The historical specificity of the noncapitalist, or polygynous, trajectory of accumulation is that it has generated institutions that express and enable indigenous moral priorities.

The New Institutional Economics and its anthropological advocates tend to focus on a different conceptual scheme, wherein there is change from weakly developed institutions that impede market formation, to more strongly developed ones that promote it. They see the state, its subinstitutions (e.g., courts, or police), and its infrastructure (e.g., roads) as the crucial level of institutional analysis for understanding the growth of the market (cf. Ensminger 1992: 26–27, 143–65). In contrast, I will be focussing on small-scale microinstitutions as patterns of behaviour that grow, adapt and change to solve local problems. By shaping transfers, they actually generate markets – especially in land, labour and credit.

In summary, this chapter has identified a noncapitalist trajectory of economic growth that has emerged in a part of the West African savannah where, due to rising population density, elite and capitalist agriculture were not a serious force. It has specified within this trajectory a fluid group, or stratum, of individuals who were the agents of accumulation – the Hausa farmer-traders of southern Katsina. It has delineated that group's motivation – the desire to accumulate, in *increasing* order of local value, capital, clients and trading friends, children, and marriageable women. They used the accumulation of capital for the development of domestic and extradomestic circles of dependents. Farmer-traders have expressed and satisfied these desires within the ethical constraint – and compulsion – of personal responsibility (hidima) for known others. Hidima encourages multiple bonds of obligation between farmer-traders and the other members of rural Hausa society. The noncapitalist, or polygynous, trajectory of accumulation is a model of three things at once – material growth and technical change, upward mobility among those in trading networks and social security for those who do not trade. Thus, it disputes the axioms and implications of both Marxian commoditization theorists and the New Institutional Economists.

Notes

1. Among the lowest tenth of land users, the great majority had one wife, and mean household size was 3.3; among the top decile of land users, the great majority had at least two wives, and mean household size was 14.5. See Table 3.19.
2. For me, this recalls the systemic and emotional sense of the ebb and flow of gifts in M. Mauss, *The Gift*.
3. I am indebted to Ian Linden for having provided me with this reference.
4. Even among pastoralists, anthropologists have shown sharp differences in the nature of the labour force and its social relations with herd owners. (Compare Stenning's emphasis on husband-wife relations among the Fulani of northern Nigeria with Barth's emphasis on the terms of contract between livestock owners and shepherds among the Basseri of south Persia: Stenning 1958; Barth 1964).
5. The data is in terms of export volumes, only a partial reflection of supply conditions.
6. This corresponds closely to Weber's definition of 'instrumental' and 'formal' rationality (Weber 1978: 24–26, 85–86). Jeff Pratt surveys the debate about the meaning of these terms, and comments that in Weber's earlier writings, 'ultimate values … are driven out as formal rationality takes hold' in the modern world; whereas in his later writings, substantive and formal rationality are 'dichotomous principles inherent in the historical process at all times' (Mommsen 1987: 43, cited in Pratt 1994: 14–15).
7. Theories of rational choice have been exhaustively debated and overlap with earlier debates between formalists and substantivists in economic anthropology. For bibliographies, see Plattner 1989: 14, and Ensminger 1992: 8–9.

Chapter 3

Land Distribution and Land Transfers

Part I: Land Distribution

The Nature of the Evidence

From January through early May 1979, I mapped the farms of Marmara by using aerial photographs lent to me by the FADP. I surveyed all fields on foot. With the help of my paid assistants, I determined the boundaries of each field and marked the corresponding boundaries on the aerial photographs, listing the name of the owner of each field.

The purpose of this exercise was not just to obtain a strong idea of the extent of inequality in land distribution. Land measurement, as a universal survey, was to be combined with other universal surveys – of all household sizes, of the number of wives per household head and of the estimated ages of household heads, to see if there was an extent to which these varied with the size of landholding. Moreover, land measurement was to be combined with a study of how the land had been acquired, and of the other, off-farm income-yielding activities of all household heads, in order to see if there was an extent to which the ability to increase landholding was attributable to the nature of nonfarm occupations. Thus, land measurement was one of a series of surveys mounted in order to detect key dynamics of wealth acquisition among villagers.

The first assistant was a farmer who knew the ownership of fields to the south and east of Marmara, because his own fields were there, and he had, years before, accompanied his father in surveying farm ownership at the behest of the village head. The second assistant and I mapped the ownership of fields to the north and west. As a donkey transporter he was in a good position to know their ownership because he transported *taki* and crops to and from them, and his own fields were located there. In this way, all fields owned by farmers within a radius of three miles of Marmara were marked. To map fields at a greater distance, it was necessary to ask the owner and go with him to the site.

While my knowledge of ownership is based on these two assistants, I was able to confirm their statements for half of the fields. First, in April and May, it was possible to ask the owners because at that time they were clearing, ploughing or planting while I was mapping. Secondly, a number of farmers themselves showed me their fields because they wanted to know the acreage in order to estimate their fertilizer requirements from the FADP. Thirdly, many farmers for this reason came to my compound in early May. Talking with each farmer alone, I reviewed my written descriptions of the location of their fields. In almost all cases, this review confirmed the statements of my two assistants. Where a farmer was able to correct their statements, it was because the field in question belonged to his wife. Thus I learnt the extent of women's land ownership.

I was also able to cross-check the holding size of a number of farmers with the local agricultural assistant of the FADP. He had conducted a much smaller survey. He had rounded field sizes to the nearest whole number, whereas my raw data, calculated from an aerial measurement overlay superimposed on the photographs, were expressed to the third decimal point. Apart from this difference, the results of our surveys agreed. Because of these various cross-checks, I am confident in the statements of my assistants.

There is a certain amount of undermeasurement, because I did not know some fields beyond the three-mile limit of the photographs. Still, through many visits to distant farms, and my general experience of Marmara farmers over two years, I believe that most of the distant fields have been listed.

One hundred and eight household heads controlled 829 of the 964 acres recorded as being used by the various categories of farmer (Table 3.1). The size of holding ranged from 50 acres for the largest farmer to 0.5 acre for the smallest. The mean size of holding – 7.8 acres – is misleading because it obscures the extent of inequality among household

Table 3.1. Landholding survey, Marmara, January–April 1979

	Number with land	Total acreage (*acres*)	Holdings size range (*acres*)	Mean holding size (*acres*)	Total no. of fields	Mean field size (*acres*)
I. Household heads	108	829	49.9 – 0.5	7.8	445	1.9
DEPENDENT MARRIED MALES:						
II. Fields from household heads	24	36.6	3.8 – 0.1	1.5	42	0.9
*[1]**III.** Fields from other sources	3	31.3	16.5 – 2.2	—	11	2.8
IV. Women	49	66.9	4.1 – 0.3	1.4	72	0.9
Totals:	**182**	**963.8**	**49.9 – 0.1**	**5.3**	**570**	**1.7**
Hectares		390.2	20.2 – 0.4	2.1		0.7

**1* These men are included with respect to 'number' under II., with one exception, who had no field from his household head. See the text.

heads. A more useful reference point is the median acreage among household heads – 4.1 (1.7 hectares). Almost half of household heads controlled less than 4 acres each.

Throughout this book, the index-numbered land rank of household heads – as HH 1 to HH 108 – will normally be used to name them. As long as the reader bears in mind that the biggest land user, HH 1, had 50 acres, the smallest land user, HH 108, had 0.5 acres, and that half of all land users had 4.1 acres or less, the land rank of each household head, as measured in 1979, provides a convenient reference to his approximate economic position.

Thirty-eight dependent married men farmed as part of larger farming units, usually under the supervision of a father, but occasionally under a senior brother or a brother of their deceased father (chapter 4). Of these dependents, twenty-four were recorded as having been given fields, usually small, by their household heads for their own personal use (*gayauni*, sing. *gayauna*).

Very interesting are two of the three dependent men recorded under Category III. One married son, farming together with his father, had gradually purchased 16.5 acres for his own use which, had he been an independent household head, would have placed him among the top 10 per cent of land users. Another married dependent, farming together with the brother of his deceased father, had inherited a sizable 12.6 acres which he farmed in his private time. (The third man had acquired 2.2 acres by pledge [*jingina*].)

Forty-nine women were found to control some 67 acres of farmland. Of these 44 were wives of household heads or of their dependent sons. Thus, of the 243 married women in Marmara, 18 per cent were recorded as having farms. Five of the women landholders were mothers or sisters of household heads. Most women had received their fields from husbands. Two were recorded as having inherited their holdings from a parent or a deceased former husband, and two had been given farms by their fathers upon marriage.

This survey probably underestimates the extent to which household heads gave *gayauna* fields to married dependent men. However, further inquiries would have changed the results only marginally, because it was easy to observe existing field boundaries from ploughing patterns and boundary plants. Again, probably more wives and mothers of household heads had farmland than was recorded. The survey is likely to have recorded too many dependents' fields as *gayauni*, and too few as their private purchases. However, the small size of most dependents' holdings implies that the overall division of farmland between household heads and their dependents is close to what was recorded.

Modes of Acquisition of Farmland

The farm survey revealed eight modes of land acquisition in Marmara:

1. Inheritance (*gado*). The most common form of land transfer was by paternal inheritance from fathers to sons. Little land was transferred from fathers to daughters or by maternal inheritance, from mothers to sons or daughters.
2. Sale (*sayarwa*). This was the second most common form of transfer. Farmland sold became the permanent possession of the buyer. Whenever land was sold, buyer and seller called witnesses to the transaction, who were paid a commission. It was not necessary for transactions to be witnessed by the hamlet or village head.
3. Pledge (jingina). Under the third most common type of land transfer, farmland was pawned to a creditor in return for a loan of money. The land was reclaimed by the owner if and when the loan was repaid in full. Frequently, the owner demanded additional sums of money in subsequent years, and if the receiver did not agree, the owner was free to transfer the field to a new receiver provided he repaid in full his loan from the first

receiver. If the owner could not repay the loan, after some years he negotiated the sale of the field to the creditor in return for an additional sum of money, which was included with the original value of the loan in the full sale price.

4. Loan (*aro*). Small fields were occasionally lent by larger farmers to smaller farmers. Fields were given aro for a small sum, much below the annual value of field produce. The transfer was for one farming season, but was often renewed continuously by mutual agreement.
5. Gift (*kyauta*). Occasionally, a farmer gave a small field to a friend in need, or more often to a mallam. The transfer was permanent.
6. Bush clearing. Some farmland was still held by the original owners who had cleared it from bush when the population density was much lower than it is today.
7. Field exchange. Occasionally, two farmers exchanged fields of roughly equal size or produce value (sometimes to consolidate a larger holding). The resulting transfers were permanent.
8. Gayauna (pl. gayauni). It was common for household heads to give dependent married sons, or other married male kin who farmed with them, small fields for their own use. Some husbands gave their wives small fields to farm.

Besides the general survey of all farmland, I developed a smaller record of land transfers which distinguished between the various types of tenure under which household heads had acquired particular fields (Part II below). But with regard to the survey of all farmland, I was not able to determine how household heads had acquired all of their fields. Thus, the general survey describes the distribution of land *use* rather than land ownership. Throughout most of the book, the landholding of any particular farmer refers to his *effective acreage,* i.e., to the farmland he actually used, without distinguishing between the various types of tenure under which he held it. The distinction between ownership and use will be important.

Land Distribution among Household Heads

For analytical convenience, the total group of household heads is arbitrarily broken down into deciles. (Given the total number, the tenth and last 'decile' throughout the book contains only nine persons, each of the others, eleven persons.)[1] Tables 3.2 and 3.3 show that farmers in the first decile of landholding used over 40 per cent of the land. Williams brought together all village studies from northern Nigeria

Table 3.2. Land distribution among household heads, Marmara, 1978

Decile	I.	II.	III.	IV.	V.	Totals
Rank	1–11	12–22	23–33	34–44	45–55	
Total acreage	336.2	138.3	106.4	75.2	54.7	
Acreage range	49.9–16.3	14.4–11.6	11.5–8.3	7.7–6.2	6.0–4.0	
Mean acreage	30.6	12.6	9.7	6.8	5.0	
Total no. of fields	116	70	61	47	39	
Mean no. of fields	10	6	6	4	4	
Mean field acreage	2.9	2.0	1.7	1.6	1.4	
	VI.	VII.	VIII.	IX.	X.	I–X.
Rank	56–66	67–77	78–88	89–99	100–108	1–108
Total acreage	38.2	31.3	25.1	16.4	7.2	829
Acreage range	3.9–3.2	3.1–2.6	2.5–2.0	2.0–1.1	1.1–0.5	49.9–0.5
Mean acreage	3.5	2.8	2.3	1.5	0.8	7.8
Total no. of fields	34	25	22	21	10	445
Mean no. of fields	3	2	2	2	1	4
Mean field acreage	1.1	1.2	1.1	0.8	0.7	1.9

Table 3.3. Land distribution among household heads, Marmara, 1979

Decile	Acreage total	*1Acreage range	Share of land use
I	336.2	50–16	40.5%
II	138.3	14–12	16.7%
III	106.4	11–8	12.8%
IV	75.2	8–6	9.1%
V	54.7	6–4	6.6%
VI	38.2	4–3	4.6%
VII	31.3	3.1–2.6	3.8%
VIII	25.1	2.5–2.0	3.0%
IX	16.4	2.0–1.1	2.0%
X	7.2	1.1–0.5	0.9%
I–X	acreage: **829**	range: **50–0.5**	share: **100%**

**1* Figures for the first six deciles are rounded from those in Table 3.2

for which there were land surveys (Williams 1988: 368, summarized in Table 3.4). Clearly, land distribution in Marmara was more unequal than in other villages studied. The pronounced degree of inequality had two facets: the relatively high share controlled by the top 10 per cent of land-using household heads, and the relatively low share controlled by the bottom 40 per cent.

Is it possible to explain the inequality in Marmara in relation to the other villages? One possible explanation is that differences in population density may largely account for differences in the degree of inequality. It might be argued that as population density rises, the process of subdivision of land among inheritors affects differently inheritors near the top and bottom of the land-using scale. Those inheritors among, for example, the top tenth will still have enough land to meet most household requirements. In some cases, they will even be left with enough land to have the economic power to acquire more. But those inheritors, for example, among the bottom 40 per cent of

Table 3.4. Land distribution among household heads, Village Studies, 1949–79

				PERCENTAGE USED BY:	
Date	**Source**	**Place**	**Size**	**Top 10%**	**Bottom 40%**
1949	**Smith**	*Zaria:* 4 sites	58	29%	17%
		7 sites	109	26%	15%
1966	**Norman**	*Zaria:*			
		Dan Mahawayi	103	33%	13%
		Hanwa	64	27%	11%
		Doka	153	29%	14%
1967	**Hill**	Batagawara,			
		N.Katsina	171	34%	14%
1968	**Goddard**	Sokoto:			
		Gidan Karma	103	27%	17%
		Kaura Kimba	170	27%	12%
		Takatuku	98	26%	19%
1971	**Hill**	Dorayi	544	38%	12%
1974	**Huizinga**	Giwa, *N.Zaria*	103	32%	13%
	Kohnert	Bida	210	34%	13%
1975	**Ross**	Hurumi, *E.Kano*	50	31%	18%
1979	**Clough**	Marmara, *S.Katsina*	108	40%	10%

Source: Williams 1988: 368. See notes in Williams

land users will be left with such small holdings that the pressure of household needs will force them to eventually sell land to richer farmers. Thus, increasing population density in and of itself causes a net transfer of land from poorer to richer. However elegant the argument, the evidence from the few village land surveys for which there are population density statistics does not support it (Table 3.5).

All these villages had 'high' population densities, in the restricted sense that there was little or no fallow land. Clearly, the mean holding size fell as population density rose. But there was no tendency for the shares of land used by the top 10 and bottom 40 per cent of landholders to vary with population density. These figures suggest that the degrees of inequality must be explained by the particular historical dynamics of different areas.

In chapter 1, we saw three processes at work in southern Katsina:

1. The gradual nature of in-migration over time meant that earlier immigrants found more land available for acquisition than those who followed them.
2. The expansion of interregional grain trading after the second world war gave farmer-traders the funds with which to acquire more land by purchase, particularly from the pastoral population which departed as increasing population density reduced the land available for grazing.

Table 3.5. Land distribution and population density, Village Studies, 1949–79

					PERCENTAGE USED BY:	
Date	**Source**	**Place**	**Density**		**Top 10%**	**Bottom 40%**
1967	**Goddard**	Gidan, Karma, Sokoto	274	11.4	27%	17%
1979	**Clough**	Mamara, S.Katsina	470	7.8	40%	10%
1967	**Goddard**	Takatuku, Sokoto	479	7.6	26%	19%
1975	**Ross**	Hurumi, E.Kano	518	5.2	31%	18%
1967	**Goddard**	Kaura Kimba, Sokoto*1	557	3.0	27%	12%
1972	**Hill**	Dorayi *nr. Kano City*	1500	2.2	38%	12%

Persons per square mile

Mean acres

**1* Figures are for upland areas only. The village also had a large floodplain which, if included, reduced population density to 306 per square mile (Goddard 1976: 6)

Source: Table 3.4; Goddard et al. 1976: 6; Hill 1977: 77; Ross in Watts (ed) 1987: 225.

3. Recent conversion to Islam, by causing the withdrawal of women from most kinds of farm work and abstinence from guineacorn beer, gave advantages to farmers with large grain reserves which could be sold on the market, and to those with large numbers of dependent males, which placed those groups in a position to buy land.

Here, I focus on the first of these processes: the staggered process of in-migration. I combine the specific evidence from the landholding survey with information about the immigrant status of household heads and with genealogical evidence. In Marmara, rising population density proceeded through two particular changes: a pastoral population left the area, selling its farmland to those in the sedentary population with money to buy; each successive wave of immigrants found less land available for acquisition, and found it more costly, than the preceding wave.

Tables 3.6–3.8 focus on the distribution of land as between indigenous and immigrant household heads. In these tables, 'immigrants' are those household heads who were not born within ten miles of Marmara; 'indigenes' are those who were. The term 'indigene' includes farmers who settled in Marmara as adults, but retained land in their hamlet of origin, provided it was within ten miles of Marmara. Their fields have been mapped and measured in the land survey. Most 'immigrants' have come to Marmara from distant places, mainly from rural areas in Kano State. But I use a 'ten-mile limit' to distinguish immigrants from indigenes because anyone who settles in Marmara from a place more than ten miles distant will find it very difficult to supervise or arrange for the cultivation of fields in his place of origin.[2]

Three-quarters of landholding household heads were indigenes, and one-quarter were immigrants (Table 3.6). But indigenes used much more, while immigrants used much less, than their proportionate shares of farmland. While half of indigenous household heads used 5.9 acres or less, land use among immigrants was much more circumscribed: half used 2.7 acres or less.

Almost all of the top half of land-using household heads were indigenous. Almost half of the bottom 40 per cent of land-using household heads and three-quarters of the bottom 10 per cent were immigrant, although immigrants were only a quarter of all household heads (Table 3.7).[3]

Unequal land distribution reflected the fact that immigrants had found land difficult to obtain. But the fact that the proportions of indigenes and immigrants in the *median* 40 per cent corresponded

Table 3.6. Land distribution among indigenes and immigrants, Marmara, 1979

Status	Indigenes	Immigrants	Total
Household head	81	27	108
Percentage	75%	25%	100%
Total acreage	729.5	99.5	829
Share of land	88%	12%	100%
Median acreage	5.9	2.7	4.1 (1.7ha.)
Mean acreage	9.0	3.7	7.8 (3.2ha.)
Total range	**49.9–0.6**	**22.3–0.5**	**49.9–0.5**

Table 3.7. Composition of landholding, percentile categories, Marmara, 1979

Percentile category:	No. of indigenes	No. of immigrants	Total
Top 10%	10	1	**11**
Top 30%	30	2	**32**
Top 50%	48	6	**54**
Bottom 50%	33	21	**54**
Bottom 40%	25	18	**43**
Bottom 30%	19	13	**32**
Botom 10%	3	8	**11**

closely to their proportions of all landholders (Appendix 1), also suggests that we are observing a gradual process: immigrants had found it very difficult to enter the top 30 per cent of landholders, less difficult to form part of the median 40 per cent and least difficult to find their place in the bottom 30 per cent.

Immigrants have added to the population a new group who clearly have less land than the descendants of previous immigrants. At the same time, their entry into the community has limited the land available to the descendants of previous immigrants. In studying the impact on land distribution of successive waves of immigrants, we are thus dealing with a continuous and interrelated stream of events. Can we push our analysis backwards in time, to gauge the impact on land distribution of previous immigrants? As people were coming into Marmara continuously, it is impossible to do this accurately. Furthermore, genealogical information can give only a very approximate idea of how long the progenitors of any current household head were in the area of Marmara, for household heads varied in age and, moreover, it is not known at what age their ancestors in Marmara died in each generation. Still, using genealogies, it is possible to say for how many generations the progenitors of present household heads lived in the area. Then, we can link this information with the known size of present landholdings so as to compare, in broad terms, the historical depth of residence of household heads with the size of their holdings.

By examining family histories it was possible, for 106 household heads, to trace the number of generations the progenitors of present heads had lived in the area. The results are striking. Those household heads whose families had lived longest in the area had experienced the impact of subdivision upon inheritance much more than those whose families arrived more recently. Even so, as one links the landholdings of present heads to the intergenerational depth of their progenitors' residence in Marmara, the size of holdings tends to rise as the number of generations increases.

Of the 29 household heads in the first three deciles whose pedigree was known, 83 per cent had been in Marmara for three or more generations. Of the 29 household heads known in the bottom three deciles, 65 per cent were either immigrants or second-generation residents.[4] Table 3.8 reveals that as the number of generations rises, there is a marked movement away from small holdings and landlessness, through the middle ranges of landholding, and into the largest holdings. (The two farmers in the fifth generation were exceptional, being the youthful successors of recently deceased fathers.) Table 3.9 dem-

Table 3.8. Intergenerational depth of residence, Marmara, 1978: 106 household heads

		Deciles:				
		I–III.	IV–VII.	VIII–X.	Landless	Total:
Number of generations in residence	1	6%	37.0%	41.0%	16%	**100%**
	2	19%	37.5%	37.5%	6%	**100%**
	3	37%	37.0%	19.0%	7%	**100%**
	4	45%	38.0%	17.0%	0%	**100%**
	5	50%	0.0%	0.0%	50%	**100%**

Table 3.9. Intergenerational depth of residence, Marmara, 1979: 106 household heads

	Number of generations					
Household heads:	**1.**	**2.**	**3.**	**4.**	**5.**	**Totals:**
With land	27	15	25	29	1	97
Without land	5	1	2	0	1	9
Total:	32	16	27	29	2	106
Total acreage:	99.5	125.9	168.6	278.4	41.5	**713.4**
Mean acreage	3.1	7.9	6.2	9.6		
Median acreage	**2.7**	**3.6**	**5.9**	**6.8**		

onstrates the marked tendency for the median size of landholding to rise as depth of residence increases.

The figures themselves clearly reveal other processes to have been at work, since immigrants and second-generation household heads are among the biggest land users, while third- to fifth-generation heads are among the smallest and the landless. However, first-generation and second-generation residents are so heavily excluded from the first three deciles as to suggest that land availability *at the time of immigration* is a key factor in explaining unequal land distribution.

The Effect on Land Distribution of Subdivision Among Inheritors

Polly Hill has raised the important possibility that there is 'intergenerational instability' with regard to economic position. As a man grows wealthier in rural Hausa society, he is likely to have an increasing number of wives, and partly for this reason, an increasing number of children. At death, the landholding of a wealthier man is likely to be divided among a larger number of male inheritors than is the land of a poorer man. So it is at least possible that the sons of relatively large landholders inherit as little land, or even less, than the sons of relatively small landholders. In general, this mechanism would contribute to a process whereby the sons of smaller landholders are able to attain as high an economic position, or higher, than the sons of larger landholders (Hill 1972: 181–83).

Hill presented estimates for three-quarters of the farming units in Batagawara village, of the number of brothers (other than the head of farming unit himself) between whom the father's farmland is believed to have been divided on his death. She related this information to the economic position of 'heads of farming units'. In her analysis, there were four Economic Groups among these heads, corresponding with a range of economic factors rather than landholding alone; the acreage range of each overlapped. But by virtue of her careful investigations, her Economic Groups represent a stratification from 'rich' to 'poor'. With regard to the number of inheriting brothers of each head of farming unit, her findings are simplified in Table 3.10 to allow comparison with my evidence.

Hill argued that if (as seems reasonable) a high proportion of fathers who had three or more inheriting sons at their death would themselves have been in Groups 1 and 2, then it is likely that many of these sons are in lower economic groups than their fathers. In Marmara, however, a similar exercise yielded very different results. The deciles used in analysis do not correspond to Hill's broad Economic Groups. They are strictly landholding categories. Nevertheless, that is sufficient for our purpose – which is to relate present landholding among household heads to the number of male inheritors upon the death of their fathers. Here, we necessarily exclude immigrants. Among the 81 indigenous households, there were 71 whose fathers were no longer alive. Among these, the number of brothers (other than the household head himself) between whom the father's farmland is believed to have been divided, is known for 65 household heads.[5] In contrast to Hill's study, Table 3.11 shows that a disproportionately small per cent of sole inheritors, and a disproportionately large per cent of household heads with three or more brothers, were in the top three deciles.

Notwithstanding the difference in the categories used by Hill and Clough, their evidence points to opposite conclusions. In contrast to

Table 3.10. Number of brothers sharing inheritance at father's death, Batagawara, 1967

	Per cent of heads of farming-units		
Economic group of head of farming-unit:	1–2	3–4	Total:
Sole inheritor:	47%	53%	100%
One brother:	32%	68%	100%
Two brothers:	41%	59%	100%
Three or more brothers:	24%	76%	100%
Total:	**37%**	**63%**	**100%**

Source: Hill 1972: 182, table XIII.5

Table 3.11. Number of inheriting brothers at father's death, 65 indigenous household heads, Marmara, 1979

Decile	I–III.	IV–X.	Total:
Sole inheritor:	15	85	100%
No. of brothers as a percentage of household heads:			
One brother:	42	58	100%
Two brothers:	23	77	100%
Three or more brothers:	64	36	100%
Total:	**34**	**66**	**100%**

Source: Appendix 1

Hill, I found that relatively large landholders tended to have shared their inheritance with many others. Why should researches have yielded such different results?

Hill's hypothesis of 'inter-generational instability in economic position' is too mechanistic. Granted, large landholders tend to have more children than small ones, and so the inheritance of larger landholders tends to be split more ways. But to infer from this that the sons of large landholders receive an inheritance which is less than the sons of small landholders, is to push a hypothesis to its extreme. An example illustrates the point. A decile I farmer in Marmara had over 16 acres. If on death his land was split equally among four sons, they each received over 4 acres. A decile VI–X farmer had less than 4 acres. If on death his land was partitioned between two sons, they each received less than 2 acres. We may plausibly argue the opposite hypothesis to Hill's: relative economic positions are, broadly speaking, bequeathed to, not reversed among, inheritors. Secondly, Hill uses the category of 'three or more inheriting brothers'. But this grouping is too inclusive. It is necessary to subdivide it into its component parts – 3, 4, etc., brothers (Table 3.12).

Sixty-four per cent of household heads with three inheriting brothers were in the first three deciles, which strongly suggests that a relatively high economic position tends to be bequeathed to inheritors. But Table 3.12 also reveals the limits to this tendency. Only 14 per cent of household heads with six or seven inheriting brothers were in the top three deciles. If a relatively large landholder found it easy to pass on his economic position to three, or possibly four or five, sons, he would find it very difficult to pass it on to six or seven. Had Hill subdivided her category 'three or more brothers' into its components,

Table 3.12. Number of inheriting brothers at father's death, 65 indigenous household heads, Marmara, 1979

Decile:	I–III.	IV–X.	Total:
Sole inheritor:	15	85	**100%**
One brother:	42	58	**100%**
Two brothers:	23	77	**100%**
Three or more brothers:	64	36	**100%**
Five brothers:	33	67	**100%**
Six to seven brothers:	14	86	**100%**
Total:	**34**	**66**	**100%**

Source: Appendix 1

she might have revised her view of 'inter-generational instability of economic position' in rural Hausaland.

The sons of a relatively large landholder had other advantages over the sons of a small holder – larger gayauna acreage, inheritance of some livestock or cash, access to his father's financial and trading contacts. These factors also improved their relative economic position.

This evidence is consistent with my earlier findings. For if those farmers whose progenitors had lived longest in the area tended quite strongly to have larger holdings than those whose progenitors arrived more recently; and if these, in their turn, had more land than immigrants, then it is consistent with this pattern that the present generation tend to have inherited their relative landholding positions from the previous generation.

Age and Land Distribution

I now consider the connection between land distribution and age among household heads. Again, a comparison with the work of Polly Hill gives useful insights into the dynamics behind inequality in land use. She cast her conclusions in terms of 'economic group' in her research in Batagawara in 1967 but in terms of 'rich', 'middle' and 'poor' in her work in Dorayi in 1971. Comparison is still useful, because each of her income groupings tended to have more land per household than the subsequent and lower group. In Batagawara, Hill found that the association between the age of heads of farming units and their economic group was generally not close. In Dorayi, she found that older men had a much greater chance of being rich than younger men. In my own research in Marmara, I found that the connection between age and land distribution was even closer than that which Hill had discovered in Dorayi (Table 3.13).

Table 3.14 relates land distribution to age distribution for all household heads in Marmara. To test the significance of age, we should really confine our attention to those household heads who had spent their entire economic life in Marmara. Thus, we need to separate in-

Table 3.13. Summary comparison, 3 village studies: The connection between age and economic position

Study	Household head	Economic group		Wealth		Landholding (*decile*)	
	Age:	1–2	3–4	Rich	Poor	I–III.	IV–X.
Hill 1967	50 and over	28%	72%				
Sample size:	40–49	43%	57%				
169	under 40	31%	69%				
Hill 1971	50 and over			23%	77%		
Sample size:	40–49			11%	89%		
544	under 40			4%	96%		
Clough 1979	50 and over					37%	63%
Sample size:	40–49					26%	74%
120	under 40					12%	88%

Source: Hill 1972: 80; Hill 1977: 113–14

Table 3.14. Ages of household head by landholding group, Marmara, 1979

	Landholding Deciles									
	I–III.		IV–VII.		VIII–X.		Landless		Total:	
*[1]Age:										
Under 30	1	(3%)	1	(2%)	1	(3%)	0	(0%)	**3**	(2%)
30–39	3	(9%)	13	(30%)	7	(23%)	7	(58%)	**30**	(25%)
40–49	8	(25%)	11	(25%)	10	(32%)	2	(17%)	**31**	(26%)
50–59	11	(33%)	11	(25%)	9	(29%)	3	(25%)	**34**	(28%)
Over 60	10	(30%)	8	(18%)	4	(13%)	0	(0%)	**22**	(19%)
Totals:	**33**	(100%)	**44**	(100%)	**31**	(100%)	**12**	(100%)	**120**	(100%)

**1* Estimated age in years

Mean age: 47 years; Median age: 45 years

digenes from immigrants, and look more closely at the connection between age and landholding among household heads born into the community. As my main interest lies in the chances of a man's land increasing with age, I simplify the land distribution to a comparison of deciles I–III, IV–X and the landless, and reduce the number of age groups (Table 3.15).

Indigenous household heads present a much sharper picture of the relationship between land and age than the picture given by all household heads. As would be expected, immigrants drop out mainly from the older age groups. A very high proportion of indigenes in deciles I–III were aged fifty or more, and a very low proportion of I–III were under forty, compared with the proportion of all indigenes in those age groups. Conversely, the percentage of Deciles IV–X who were under age forty was significantly higher, while the proportion of IV–X who were fifty and over was significantly lower than those age groups' share of all indigenes. When only indigenes are considered, the landless become significantly younger: 71 per cent of landless indigenes were under age forty compared with 33 per cent of all indigenes.

It is equally interesting to look at the age-land connection among indigenes in reverse fashion. Over half of all indigenes aged fifty and above were in the first three deciles. 70 per cent of indigenes aged less than forty were in deciles IV–X. Moreover, the percentage of 'young' indigenes who were landless (17 per cent) was significantly higher than the percentage of all indigenes who lacked land (8 per cent).

Taken together, Tables 3.14 and 3.15 present striking evidence. The chances of being landless among indigenes were lower than they were for all household heads. The correspondence between increasing age and increasing land size was closer for indigenes than it was for the

Table 3.15. Landholding and age: Indigenous household heads only, Marmara, 1979

	Range	Under 40		40–49		Over 50		Total:	
Deciles: I–III	50–8 acres	4	*13%*	7	*23%*	20	*64%*	31	*100%*
		13%		**33%**		**53%**		**35%**	
IV–X.	8–0.5 acres	20	*40%*	14	*28%*	16	*32%*	50	*100%*
		70%		**67%**		**42%**		**57%**	
Landless		5	*71%*	0	*0%*	2	*29%*	7	*100%*
		17%		**0%**		**5%**		**8%**	
Total:		29	*33%*	21	*24%*	38	*43%*	88	*100%*
		100%		**100%**		**100%**		**100%**	

whole population. So strong was the correspondence, that it is worth pursuing the inquiry one further step. For deciles I–III, referring as they do to an acreage range as wide as 50–8, can connote little more than 'economic security'. Decile I – those household heads with more than 16 acres – was a grouping which was seen as 'successful' in the eyes of the community; and, moreover, a grouping some half of whom were regarded as 'wealthy'. As Table 3.16 shows, 21 per cent of indi-

Table 3.16. 'Wealth' and age: Indigenous household heads only, Marmara, 1979

	Range	Under 50		Over 50		Total:	
Deciles: I.	50–16 acres	2	*20%*	8	*80%*	10	*100%*
		4%		**21%**		**11%**	
II–X.	14–0.5 acres	43	*61%*	28	*39%*	71	*100%*
		86%		**74%**		**81%**	
Landless		5	*71%*	2	*29%*	7	*100%*
		10%		**5%**		**8%**	
Total:		50	*57%*	38	*43%*	88	*100%*
		100%		**100%**		**100%**	

Table 3.17. Landholding and age: All household heads and indigenous household heads compared, Marmara, 1979

	All household heads		Indigenous household heads	
Decile	**Number**	**Average age**	**Number**	**Average age**
I	11	54	10	54
II	11	47	10	48
III	11	52	11	52
IV	11	46	9	43
V	11	43	9	40
VI	11	46	7	44
VII	11	46	7	40
VIII	11	45	8	44
IX	11	45	7	46
X	9	48	3	38
Landless	12	40	7	42
Total	**120**	**47 years**	**88**	**45 years**

genes aged fifty and over were in decile I, though only 11 per cent of all indigenes were in the top decile. Eighty per cent of indigenes in decile I were fifty or over, though only 43 per cent of all indigenes were in that age group.

In summary, there was a close association between land distribution and age distribution, such that as age increased, landholding tended to increase. Over half of the landless – and 71 per cent of indigenes without land – were less than forty years old, suggesting that they likely obtained land as they grew older. At the same time, increasing age was no guarantee of a larger landholding. Obviously, the factors which caused age to be associated with increased landholding were neither rigid nor all-determining. What those factors were – and what different processes existed – will be explored in the later chapters. Here, I simply stress the consistency in the patterns. If indigenes tended to have more land than immigrants, and if indigenes whose families had been long resident possessed more than those whose progenitors arrived recently, then we now can add: those with greater age tended to have more land than those with less (Table 3.18).

Landholding, Polygyny and Family Size

I end Part 1 with evidence which concerns the effects of inequality in landholding rather than its causes. But I present it here because it is essential to the subsequent analysis in this book. Table 3.19 shows that as landholding increased, so, too, did the number of wives of the household head, and the total number of his dependents. Among the bottom half of land users, only 26 per cent had two or more wives. Among the top half of land users, 71 per cent had two or more wives. Mean household size doubled from the bottom through the sixth

Table 3.18. Age and landholding: Land-using household heads, Marmara, 1979

Estimated age	Number	Mean acreage	Median acreage
60 or over	22	10.3	6.9
50–59	31	9.0	4.5
40–49	29	5.9	3.6
30–39	23	4.4	3.3
Under 30	3	16.9	7.7
Total:	**108**	**7.8**	**4.1**

Table 3.19. Landholding, number of wives and household size, household heads, Marmara, 1979

Deciles:	I.	II.	III.	IV.	V.	VI.
Acreage range	49.9–16.3	14.4–11.6	11.5–8.3	7.7–6.2	6.0–4.0	3.9–3.2
Number	11	11	11	11	11	11
Mean no. of wives	2.4	2.3	1.8	1.9	1.5	1.7
*[1]Mean household size	14.5	10.1	6.6	7.6	6.5	6.6
Number of wives: 0	0	0	0	0	1	0
1	2	0	3	4	4	6
2	4	8	7	5	5	3
3	4	3	1	1	1	1
4	1	0	0	1	0	1

Deciles:	VII.	VIII.	IX.	X.	Landless	Totals
Acreage range	3.1–2.6	2.5–2.0	2.0–1.1	1.1–0.5	0	
Number	11	11	11	9	12	**120**
Mean no. of wives	1.2	1.1	1.4	1.1	1.2	**1.6**
*[1]Mean household size	5.4	4.6	4.4	3.3	4.2	**6.8**
Number of wives: 0	1	1	0	1	0	**4**
1	7	9	7	7	9	**58**
2	3	1	3	0	3	**42**
3	0	0	1	1	0	**13**
4	0	0	0	0	0	**3**

*1 Includes household head

decile, and then stabilized through the third decile. From the third through the first decile, mean household size more than doubled.

Two patterns should be emphasized. As landholding increased *above* 11.5 acres, there was a significant increase in the number of household heads who had more than two wives and a sharp increase in his household size. Conversely, as landholding declined below 3.2 acres, there was a significant drop in the number of household heads who had more than two wives and a sharp drop in their household size. These figures are related to land use rather than total wealth. But they permit us to say that as wealth increased greatly, so did the number of wives and the size of household; conversely, men of restricted means tended to limit the number of their wives and other dependents.

The ensuing chapters will show that these patterns strongly influenced the levels of household expenditure, and the consequent degree of indebtedness.

Part II: Land Transfers

Part II outlines the surprising conclusions of my investigation into the nature of land transfers. It examines the types of land transfer through which Marmara farmers arrived at their relative landholding positions. It looks particularly at the two most common forms of commercial transfer – selling and pledging. It is guided throughout by a major question: to what extent did changes in the wider economy lead via selling and pledging to a net transfer of land from smaller to larger landholders?

The Evidence for Land Transfers in Marmara

Terms of Classification

Farmers are classified in three categories: Small, Middle and Large. Commercial land transactions are analysed in two ways: the degree to which sales were 'upward' or 'downward' between categories or 'lateral' within a category; secondly, the extent to which land sold or pledged constituted a net loss to Small Farmers and a net gain to Middle and Large Farmers.

Here, 'Small Farmer' refers to those household heads whose annual farm and off-farm income combined was usually less than they needed to meet their annual expenditures on a range of household needs – both personal (e.g., family food) and social (e.g., ceremonial contributions). By 'annual', I mean the year from one harvest to the next. As a result, they borrowed cash credit annually, repayable out of harvest earnings (For a full discussion of credit, see chapter 5). 'Middle Farmer' is confined to those household heads whose annual total income was broadly equivalent to their expenditure on household needs, or left them with a small surplus or deficit. 'Large Farmer' refers to those heads whose annual total income usually exceeded considerably their expenditure on household needs. 'Farm income' refers to output from landholdings as surveyed in the postharvest dry season of January–April 1979. Translating these criteria into their rough equivalents in terms of land sizes, I classify farmers[6] as follows:

- Small Farmer: used less than 5 acres (2 ha.)
- Middle Farmer: used 5–10 acres (2–4 ha.)
- Large Farmer: used more than 10 acres (4 ha.)

By 'household needs', I mean the entire range of possible expenditures which a man, his wives and children were likely to face. By a combination of farm and off-farm earnings, farmers with less than 5 acres generally managed to pay for certain household needs – food, tax, clothing, alms (zaka). But they usually needed credit to meet a variety of urgent additional expenses – including marriages, naming ceremonies and legal and medical expenses (chapter 5). They also needed credit to defray the annual deficit resulting from major purchases, such as land, earlier in the year.

There are two reasons why farmers with less than 5 acres were usually able to pay for food, tax, clothing and alms:

1. Farmers combined farm income and off-farm earnings.
2. Farmers showed a tendency to restrict the number of their wives, and as a result, the number of their children, in accordance with their total income in general, and their size of landholding in

Table 3.20. Categories of farmer, Marmara, 1979

Category	Large	Middle	Small	Totals
Acreage range	Over 10	5–10	under 5	
Number of farmers	25	24	59	**108**
Total acreage	507	177	145	**829**
Per cent of hamlet acreage	61%	21%	18%	**100%**

Table 3.21. Record of land transfers, Marmara, 1979

Farmers:		Fields:		Acreage:	
Total no. of farmers:	108	Total no. of fields:	445	Total acreage:	829
Farmers included:	79	Fields included:	244	Transfer known:	447
Per cent of farmers:	**73%**	Per cent of fields:	**55%**	Transfer known	**54%**

Note: For only 31 per cent of farmers in the Land Transfer Record, was the mode of acquisition known for all of their acreage.

> particular (Table 3.19). There were exceptions. Indeed, the exceptions – farmers with unusually large families in relation to landholding – tended to be most heavily in debt.

The acreage ranges adopted correspond with my general experience of the economic condition of Marmara men. Farmers with less than 5 acres did tend to be in deficit from both farm and off-farm income with respect to the whole range of household expenditures. Men with 5–10 acres usually balanced financially or generated small savings; those with more tended to have a substantial aggregate financial surplus over household expenditure. This was so, because as farmers' income increased from off-farm work – butcher, tailor, trader, etc. – they tended to invest part of the extra income in farmland. Because of this tendency to invest increasing income in farmland, I refer throughout the book to three categories of 'farmer' rather than villager.

In summary, the three categories are broad and loose. But they better reflect the changing realities of economic power in the hamlet than would acreage ranges referring to surplus-generating capacity from farming alone.

Methods

Much of my evidence for the means whereby farmers acquired their use of fields came in the course of the Landholding Survey. Each of my two assistants had a specific knowledge of how some of the present users had obtained some of their land. I also went with a number of farmers to their fields to survey their farming operations. These surveys took place on the fields, and sometimes led to questions about the means of acquisition. Occasionally, information about a field came from a brother or father of the current user.

Finally, the aerial photographs used in the Landholding Survey were a source of information. I sometimes found while measuring fields that brothers used adjacent fields of almost identical size. In those cases, I assumed that the brothers had inherited these from their father – 5 per cent of all fields listed among land transfers. Two per cent of all fields in the Land Transfer Record, classified in this indirect fashion by aerial photograph, were independently confirmed by the users.

For 50 per cent of the fields discussed below, my record depends on one of the two land survey assistants. For 82 per cent of the fields, information is derived from one source. For 18 per cent, information came from two or more sources.

To what extent is the recorded pattern of land transfers likely to be true of the remaining half of fields and acreage? The results incorporate a bias toward Large and Middle Farmers. Only three in five Small Farmers but most Large and Middle Farmers are represented in the land transfer record (Chart 3.1).

Large Farmers acquired most of their acreage by purchase or pledge, while Small Farmers relied mainly on noncommercial forms (Table 3.23). Therefore, the aggregate results overestimate the percentage of land acquired by commercial forms of transfer and underestimate the percentage acquired by noncommercial forms. Moreover, the results under-record the percentage of real acreage purchased by Small Farmers, because of the record's bias toward the Large and Middle Farmers. Therefore, 'lateral' transfers within any category and 'downward' transfers from the higher categories are (mostly) underestimated. Nevertheless, Chart 3.2 shows crucially that the distribution in the land transfer record is very similar to that for the total acreage in the landholding survey.

Chart 3.1. The land transfer record, Marmara, 1979

A. FARMERS	Large	Middle	Small	Totals
Total number of farmers	25	24	59	**108**
Included in transfer record	22	22	35	**79**
Per cent in record	88%	92%	59%	**73%**
B. ACREAGE				
Total of farmers in record	440	160	106	**706**
Transfers known	288	101	58	**447**
Transfers known	65%	63%	55%	**63%**
C. TOTAL ACREAGE				
In Marmara	507	177	145	**829**
Transfers known	288	101	58	**447**
Transfers known	57%	57%	40%	**54%**

Chart 3.2. The landholding survey and transfer record compared, Marmara, 1979

Farmer categories	Large	Middle	Small	
Landholding survey: acres	507	177	145	829
Landholding survey: per cent	61%	21%	18%	100%
Land transfer record: acres	288	101	58	447
Land transfer record: per cent	64%	23%	13%	100%
Totals:				

Means of Acquisition of Farmland

Table 3.22 presents the distribution of acreage and fields according to means of acquisition for the total area in the land transfer record. To understand the area transacted commercially, we add Purchases and Pledges and exclude the area Borrowed – small fields given annually for a notional sum. Purchases and Pledges accounted for 45 per cent of the area acquired, noncommercial forms for 55 per cent.

Table 3.23 reveals that the distribution of types of acquisition was very different for the three categories of farmer. Large Farmers had inherited a low proportion of their land for which transfers are known, whereas Middle and Small Farmers had inherited relatively high proportions. Large Farmers had often purchased and received as pledge more than they inherited, unlike Middle and Small Farmers.

Table 3.22. Means of acquisition of farmland, Marmara, 1978

	Inheritance (*gado*)	Purchase (*saye*)	Pledge (*jingina*)	Loan (*aro*)	Gift (*kyauta*)	Other	Totals:
Number of acres:	221	147	54	5	3	17	**447**
As a percentage:	49%	33%	12%	1%	1%	4%	**100%**
Number of fields:	139	60	30	7	3	5	**244**
As a percentage:	57%	25%	12%	3%	1%	2%	**100%**

Table 3.23. Means of acquisition of farmland, Marmara, 1979

Farmers:	Large	Middle	Small	Total
Inheritance:				
acres:	111	75	35	221
percentage:	**38%**	**73%**	**61%**	**49%**
Purchase				
acres:	120	20	7	147
percentage:	**42%**	**20%**	**12%**	**33%**
Pledge				
acres:	38	6	10	54
percentage:	**13%**	**6%**	**17%**	**12%**
Loan				
acres:	4	0	1	5
percentage:	**1%**	**0%**	**2%**	**1%**
Gift				
acres:	0	0	3	3
percentage:	**0%**	**0%**	**5%**	**1%**
Other				
acres:	15	1	1	17
percentage:	**5%**	**1%**	**2%**	**4%**

Note: Discrepancy of the total percentage with 100 percent is due to rounding

Given the bias of the record toward Large and Middle Farmers, and that in the record they had purchased a higher percentage of their land than had Small Farmers, the proportion of all farmland purchased would likely have been less than a third, and the proportion inherited would have been over a half. Correcting for the partial and biased nature of the record, it still appears that the area obtained through Purchase and Pledge was nearly as great as that obtained through noncommercial forms of transfer.[7]

Land Purchases

Part I showed more unequal land distribution in Marmara than in any Hausa village previously studied. Part II has shown the high degree of development of the land market. But beneath the surface, there are surprising patterns. The users of 1979 had acquired over half of their

Table 3.24. Summary of purchases among known transactors, Marmara, 1979

Buyer:	Seller:	Fields	Acres		Average acreage
Large Farmers	1. Departing Fulani.	11	34.9	40%	
	2. Inheriting women	3	32.0	36%	
	3. Large Farmers.	3	10.4	12%	
	4. Middle Farmers.	4	7.8	9%	
	5. Small Farmers.	0	0.0	0%	
	6. Departing farmer.	1	0.6	1%	
	7. *Not known.*	1	2.0	2%	
	Sub-totals:	**23**	**87.7**	**100%**	
	Average acreage:				**3.8**
Buyer:	**Seller:**	**Fields**	**Acres**		
Middle Farmers	1. Departing Fulani.	2	4.0	16%	
	2. Inheriting women.	0	0.0	0%	
	3. Large Farmers.	3	5.5	22%	
	4. Middle Farmers.	1	2.5	10%	
	5. Small Farmers.	3	3.9	16%	
	6. Departing farmer.	3	1.6	7%	
	7. *Not known.*	4	7.0	29%	
	Sub-totals:	**16**	**24.5**	**100%**	
	Average acreage:				**1.5**
Buyer:	**Seller:**	**Fields**	**Acres**		
Small Farmers	1. Departing Fulani.	2	4.6	13%	
	2. Inheriting women.	1	0.6	2%	
	3. Large Farmers.	3	5.0	15%	
	4. Middle Farmers.	3	4.5	13%	
	5. Small Farmers.	5	6.9	20%	
	6. Departing farmer.	0	0.0	0%	
	7. *Not known.*	7	12.8	37%	
	Sub-totals:	**21**	**34.4**	**100%**	
	Average acreage:				**1.6**
	GRAND TOTALS:	**60**	**146.6**	**100%**	

purchased land from departing pastoralists and inheriting women. More particularly, those purchasers who were Large Farmers at the time of transaction had acquired over three-quarters of their purchased land from departing pastoralists and inheriting women – less than a quarter from other farmers (Table 3.24). Of equal interest, less than half of the acreage recorded as purchased was transacted between *farmers*. Furthermore, in terms of farmers' positions at the time of transaction, the acreage transferred 'laterally' within categories or 'downward' from higher to lower categories was much greater than the amount transferred 'upward' (Table 3.25; see Appendix 6, Table 1 for the data on all buyers and sellers).

Focusing on transactions between farmers, there had been no significant land transfer from Small or Middle Farmers to Large Farmers. On the contrary, Small Farmers were gaining land, while Middle and Large Farmers were both losing slightly, viewed in terms of the positions of transactors at the time of transactions (Table 3.26, derived from the data in Appendix 6, Table 1).

Analysis of upward mobility among buyers reveals more interesting patterns. Immigrants participated more actively than indigenes in land purchase. They added a dynamic element to the land market. Arriving without any local holding, they proceeded to buy more energetically than indigenes (Table 3.27).

A second distinction helps explain upward mobility in land purchase – that between buyers engaged in a process of 'land accumu-

Table 3.25. Summary of land purchases: The pattern of transactions between sellers and the owners of 1979

Type of purchase:	Acres	Per cent	No. of fields	Per cent
From departing Fulani	43.5	30%	15	25%
From inheriting women	32.6	22%	4	7%
By upward transfer	11.7	8%	7	11%
By lateral transfer	19.8	14%	9	15%
By downward transfer	15.0	10%	9	15%
*1From departing farmer	2.2	1%	4	7%
*2*From unknown*	21.8	15%	12	20%
Totals:	**146.6**	**100%**	**60**	**100%**

**1* One farmer was recorded as selling fields when he emigrated south to a village in Zaria Emirate.
*2 Mainly farmers in neighbouring hamlets. Since 6 of the 12 fields measured at least 2 acres, it is likely that the majority were Large or Middle Farmers.
See: average field sizes, Table 3.2

Table 3.26. Summary of the land purchases: The pattern of transactions between sellers and the owners of 1979

	Sales		Purchases		Net Transfers
	Acres	Per cent	Acres	Per cent	Acres
Small Farmers	10.8	23%	16.4	35%	+5.6
Middle Farmers	14.8	32%	11.9	26%	−2.9
Large Farmers	20.9	45%	18.2	39%	−2.7
Totals:	**46.5**	**100%**	**46.5**	**100%**	

Source: Table 3.24 and Appendix 6, Table 1

lation', and those engaged in more limited purchases. In Table 3.28, the first seven buyers – HH 2 through HH 25 – can be described as 'land accumulators'. The remaining ten – HH 38 through 66 – were involved in more limited acquisitions.

The combined earnings from farm and off-farm sources of HH 2 through HH 25 placed each of them in a position where, over time, they could greatly expand their landholdings. With the possible exception of HH 3 – a young bus driver who had recently inherited from

Table 3.27. Land purchase by immigrants, transactions between farmers: The land transfer record

A.	**Total acreage purchased**	**46.5 acres**
	By immigrants	**15.9**
	Percent purchased by immigrants	**34%**
	Share of all land used by immigrants	**12%**
B.	**Total number of buyers**	**17**
	Buyers who were immigrants	**8**
	Percent of buyers who were immigrants	**47%**
	Share of all farmers who were immigrants in 1979	**25%**
C.	**Acreage purchased by Small Farmers**	**16.4 acres**
	By immigrant Small Farmers	**10.4 acres**
	Percent purchased by immigrant Small Farmers	**63%**
D.	**Acreage purchased by Middle Farmers**	**11.9 acres**
	By immigrant Middle Farmers	**5.5**
	Percent purchased by immigrant Middle Farmers	**46%**

Table 3.28. Buyers in interfarmer transactions, Marmara, 1979

	Buyer*1	Total holding (*acres*)	Position, first purchase (*left*) Position in 1979 (*right*)	Total purchased acres*2	Total purchased acres*3	Indigene (I) or Migrant (M)	Age and description (*1979*)
1.	HH 2	43.3	L-L	4.0	**14.9**	I	**50,** bus owner, cloth trader, 3 oxen teams
2.	HH 3	41.5	L-L	0.5	**20.7**	I	**25,** 2 oxen teams
3.	HH 6	35.0	L-L	9.6	**11.6**	I	**55,** kolanut wholesaler
4.	HH 7	22.4	S-L	2.3	**6.2**	M	**55,** grain wholesaler
5.	HH 9	19.0	L-L	4.1	**4.1**	I	**40,** corn miller, cotton buyer
6.	HH 20	12.0	M-L	2.3	**9.8**	M	**40,** maize trader, cotton buyer, bus owner
7.	HH 25	10.1	S-L	6.4	**9.1**	I	**35,** goat and maize trader, oxen hire, corn miller
8.	HH 38	6.9	M-M	0.8	**0.8**	I	**30,** kolanut retailer
9.	HH 40	6.7	S-M	3.7	**3.7**	M	**55,** goat trader, butcher
10.	HH 42	6.4	S-M	1.9	**1.9**	M	**65,** small retailer
11.	HH 45	6.0	S-M	2.7	**3.5**	I	**40,** housebuilder
12.	HH 49	5.1	S-M	1.7	**3.1**	M	**55,** kolanut retailer
13.	HH 51	4.6	S-S	0.2	**0.2**	I	**35,** donkey transporter
14.	HH 56	3.9	S-S	1.3	**1.3**	M	**50,** retailer, tailor, smuggler
15.	HH 62	3.3	S-S	1.3	**1.3**	M	**60,** Qur'anic mallam, teacher
16.	HH 64	3.3	S-S	2.3	**3.6**	I	**55,** roof-maker, farm labourer
17.	HH 66	3.2	S-S	1.4	**1.4**	M	**40,** tailor
			Total:	**46.5**	**97.2**		

*1 Described in terms of their index-numbered land rank in 1979.
*2 Acreage purchased in recorded intra-farmer transactions only.
*3 Acreage purchased in all recorded transactions, including purchases from pastoralists, women and unknown farmers in neighbouring hamlets.
S, M, L = Small, Middle and Large Farmers

his father – these men had developed extraordinary positions in the hamlet with respect to the supply of or demand for goods and services. HH 2 was one of the three owners of motor transport in 1979. His combined earnings from motor transport, cloth trading and oxen hire enabled him to gradually build up the second largest holding in

Marmara. HH 6 was the only hamlet wholesaler of kolanut, buying in distant markets and selling to retailers in Marmara. HH 7 was the biggest wholesaler in the long-distance grain trade. HH 9 had invested in land part of his combined returns from agriculture, cotton buying and his ownership of one of the two corn-grinding mills in Marmara. HH 20 was the most active maize trader and cotton buyer. He invested part of his earnings after 1975 in high-yielding yellow maize supplied by the FADP, and thereafter invested his income from maize production in a bus. HH 25 began as a goat trader, shifted out of goats into maize trading with the development of maize production under the FADP, and finally invested part of his farm and off-farm income in a team of oxen and a corn-grinding mill. With the possible exception of HH 3, the unifying feature of this group of buyers was an interactive cycle of wealth acquisition. Earnings from off-farm activity flowed into agriculture, and from agriculture into off-farm activity.

In contrast, the second group of buyers, HH 38 through HH 66, had off-farm occupations which yielded them much smaller earnings. As a result, their aggregate incomes enabled them to make smaller acquisitions than the first group (Table 3.28).

Thus, the scale of off-farm occupation distinguishes 'land accumulators' from 'limited land purchasers'. 'Scale' refers to the size of income from a diversity of sources. In making this distinction, four points are important:

1. This typology refers in reality to a spectrum of purchasers. For example, HH 38 – on the boundary between the two groups in terms of landholding – was young, had limited family responsibilities, a relatively large holding by hamlet standards and a steady source of earnings from kolanut retailing. He was thus poised to begin a process of land accumulation.
2. Off-farm earnings fuel land accumulation as one part of a more general process of long-term wealth acquisition.
3. There is a very real difference between 'land accumulation' and 'long-term wealth acquisition'. For example, HH 40 – the goat trader – was later to become rich by hamlet standards. But he chose not to invest heavily in land.
4. I use inverted commas deliberately in referring to 'land accumulators'. In chapter 2, I defined accumulation as a total social process which is self-sustaining. Its goal consists of objects or relationships ranked as desirable by specific societies. It depends upon culturally approved procedures for the appropriation of labour power. I am not suggesting that in 'land accumulation', the

purchase of land necessarily leads to the purchase of more land. Rather, I am pinpointing the combination of farm and off-farm income as a factor which makes possible the expanded purchase of farmland.

The distinction between 'land accumulators' and 'limited land purchasers' helps explain the high degree of upward mobility among buyers in interfarmer transactions. Of the land bought in these transactions, 63 per cent was acquired by land accumulators. The significance of this figure cuts two ways. On the one hand, land accumulation explains many purchases. On the other, land accumulators were subject to genuine competition from farmers making limited purchases.

Analysis of downward mobility among land sellers explains why more land had been sold by Large Farmers than by any other category. Chart 3.3 below explores the connection between family size

Chart 3.3. Family size in 1979 of former land sellers

Farmer		Acreage Sold			Age 1979		Family size 1979	
	No.	Total	Mean	Median	Mean age	Median age	Mean size	Median size
A. Category at sale:								
Large Farmers	5	15.5	3.1	1.7	53	50	10	11
Middle Farmers	7	14.8	2.1	2.0	42	45	7	7
Small Farmers	5	8.1	1.6	1.3	43	45	4	4
Total:		**38.4**						
B. Sellers' family size:								
11 to 13:	3	15.7	5.2	5.3				
8 to 9:	2	2.8	1.4	—				
6 to 7:	5	12.0	2.4	1.7				
2 to 4:	5	7.9	1.6	1.3				
C. All Marmara Farmers:								
Large Farmers, 1979:	25				51	50	12	13
Middle Farmers, 1979:	24				47	47	7	6
Small Farmers, 1979:	59				46	45	5	5

Note: This table excludes the four sellers who were from neighbouring hamlets or else deceased in 1979.

and land selling. It shows that those who had sold as Large Farmers tended to have considerably larger families in 1979 than those who had sold as Middle Farmers, who in turn tended to have larger families than those who had sold as Small Farmers. Admittedly, Chart 3.3 lists family sizes as these were in 1979, not at the time of sale. Still, there is a pattern. We saw in Part I that larger landholders tended to have markedly larger families (Table 3.19). The greater prominence of higher categories in land selling may be connected with the greater financial burdens of increased family size.

The pattern of variation between amount of land sold on the one hand, and position at time of sale and 1979 family size on the other, suggests a partial explanation for the prominence of Large Farmers in land selling. As income increases, both the size of landholding and family size tend to increase. This exposes some Large Farmers to increased financial risk as their family commitments exceed their total resources. Severe imbalance may result from a short-term increase in commitments over resources – for example, the need to finance several marriages in a much enlarged household. Or it may result from a short-term fall in resources in relation to commitments – for example, drought, or failure in trade. In a society where polygyny is a highly valued goal in life, the larger landholder's accumulation over time of wives and children may leave him exposed to continuing deficits in the long term.

In this society, men not only acquire land, cattle, equipment and money. They also acquire people to whom they are tied by the deepest bonds of moral obligation – 'wives and children' are an inherent part of their definition of wealth. Once a man has reached the level of (for example) HH 2, who had 43 acres in early 1979, the financial burdens of a large family are no longer a serious problem. But until a man has scaled the local heights of acquisition, his expansion will be marked by a tense balance between resources and family commitments.

Let us look more closely at the five living Marmara sellers who had sold land as Large Farmers (Table 3.29, see Appendix 6, Table 1 for the data on all sellers and buyers). HH 16, HH 50 and HH 82 exemplify the financial difficulties of farmers with large families. HH 59 exemplifies the problems of a young farmer with too much land in relation to resources for farming. He began with a holding of 14.3 acres. In 1964, when he was thirty years old, he sold 1.9 and pledged 1.1 acres to immigrants. In 1969, he sold 2.1 acres to an indigenous Large Farmer. Thus, by 35 he was reduced to a Middle Farmer. He later sold 2.0 and pledged a further 2.2 acres, reducing his position in the hamlet to that of a Small Farmer.

Table 3.29. Sellers in interfarmer transactions, Marmara, 1979

Seller[*1]	Total holding (*acres*)	Position, first sale	Position 1979	Acreage sold	Family size	Age, (*description*[*2])
HH 16	12.6	**L**	**L**	0.9	**13**	**65** Part-time grain trader, 5 working sons. Obtained a pledge of 11 acres in 1979
HH27	9.9	**L**	**M**	1.5	**7**	**50** Bus owner, cotton buyer, hamlet head. Sold 1.5 acres and pledged 13.5 acres in 1978 because his bus ws seized in a dispute with the police chief.
HH 34	7.7	**M**	**M**	2.0	**6**	**25** Oxen team, 2 working brothers.
HH 36	7.4	**M**	**M**	0.8	**7**	**45** Part-time labourer, working son.
HH 46	5.9	**M**	**M**	1.7	**6**	**45** Oxen team, working son.
HH 50	4.9	**L**	**S**	5.3	**11**	**50** Chief of motor park, 1 working brother. He had pledged or sold 8.6 acres (reclaimed 3.3 pledged acres in 1979).
HH 59	3.6	**L**	**S**	6.0	**7**	**45** Donkey transporter. He had pledged or sold 10.7 acres since 1964. Reclaimed 2.2 pledged acres in 1979.
HH 63	3.3	**M**	**S**	0.1	**9**	**30** Survey worker, part-time labourer. He pledged 3.5 acres in 1978 due to debts as a cotton buyer.
HH 79	2.5	**S**	**S**	2.0	**4**	**55** Herbalist and part-time labourer.
HH 80	2.5	**M**	**S**	2.5	**4**	**45** Farm labourer, one working son.
HH 82	2.3	**L**	**S**	9.5	**13**	**55** professional Lagos beggar, part-time labourer, one working son.
HH 92	1.5	**S**	**S**	1.3	**2**	**25** Petty trader, smuggler, marijuana seller.
HH 94	1.5	**S**	**S**	1.0	**3**	**60** Part-time labourer.
HH 103	0.9	**S**	**S**	1.1	**4**	**30** Bus driver.
HH 105	0.8	**S**	**S**	2.7	**8**	**45** Leather worker.
Total:				**38.4**[*3]		

*1 By their index-numbered land rank in 1979.
*2 Sellers were indigenes.
*3 Excluded from this table are the four sellers who were Large Farmers in neighbouring hamlets or deceased in 1979.

Finally, HH 27. He had been a goat trader who used his accumulated trade earnings to buy a second-hand bus. A keen politician and notorious gambler, he had neglected his farms and focused his energies on the bus. But his constant disputes with the local police chief led to it being impounded. An abrasive man, his quarrels with his son deprived him of any help from that quarter. To raise cash, he sold 1.5 acres as a Large Farmer in 1978. At the same time, he pledged 13.6 acres to various farmers. His holding was thus reduced from 25 to 9.9 acres. Through his contacts with the local aristocracy, he made money as a cotton buyer in 1979. He then deliberately relinquished his post as hamlet head in order to organize the local campaign of the NPN in the 1979 elections. He was a risk taker! But if we try to disentangle a pattern from his exuberant personality, it is surely that the process of long-term wealth acquisition can expose a hitherto successful man to serious financial risk.

With the exception of HH 59, who sold or pledged much of his inheritance as a young man, the sellers who were Large Farmers exemplify two types of 'exposure to risk': firstly the financial risks resulting from increasing family size, and secondly, the risks arising from enterprise. Thus, my surprising conclusion is that Large Farmers are likely to account for a higher per cent of land sold than Middle or Small Farmers.

Land Pledges (Jingina)

Land pledging also reveals the efforts of immigrants to acquire land. In transactions between Marmara farmers, eight of the fifteen receivers were immigrants. They took 22.3 of the 44.1 acres pledged. Hill found that in northern Katsina, pledging was often a prelude to sale by farmers in severe need (Hill 1972: 273). In contrast, I found that Large Farmers were both the major receivers and the major givers of pledged land (Table 3.30). The proportion of pledged land which was reclaimed by givers over the period of fieldwork, or by December 1985 when I made a return visit to Marmara, suggests that much pledged land would eventually be recovered (Table 3.31). The relative youthfulness of givers compared with receivers further supports this view (Chart 3.4). I conclude that pledging should be analysed primarily as a credit institution whereby farmers borrow money to finance big expenditures (e.g., marriage) with the reasonable expectation of reclaiming the land when their circumstances improve.

Table 3.30. Summary: Pledged land given and received by category of farmer, May–December 1978

	Given:		Received:	
	Size	**Per cent**	**Size**	**Per cent**
Small Farmers	5.8 acres	13%	13.8 acres	31%
Middle Farmers	13.2 acres	30%	1.2 acres	3%
Large Farmers	25.1 acres	57%	29.1 acres	66%
Totals:	**44.1 acres**	**100%**	**44.1 acres**	**100%**

Note: Of the 54 acres pledged in the land transfer record (Table 3.22), 9.9 had been given by farmers in neighbouring hamlets, whose economic status was not known.

Table 3.31. Summary: Reclamations of pledged land by category of farmer, December 1985

	Acreage given	**Reclaimed**	**Per cent reclaimed**
Small Farmers	5.8 acres	0.8 acres	14%
Middle Farmers	13.2 acres	7.2 acres	54%
Large Farmers	25.1 acres	10.8 acres	43%
Totals:	**44.1 acres**	**18.8 acres**	**43%**

Chart 3.4. Ages of all living transactors of pledged farmland in the land transfer record, Marmara, 1979

Pledgers:	**Transactions:**
Younger to older	**16** (*12: age difference ten years or more*).
Giver and receiver same age	0
Older pledges to younger	9
Ages of both known:	25

Givers: Average age: 46. Median age: 45

Receivers: Average age: 47. Median age: 50

Changing Inheritance Customs

Changing patterns of land transfer had provoked major alterations in the disposition of inherited property. Increasingly, siblings were postponing the division of inherited farmland. They were dividing it for use only, which allowed them to pledge it but not sell it (Ross found this trend far advanced in the Kano Closely Settled Zone – Ross 1987: 226, 229, 235). Furthermore, male inheritors had recently prevented their female counterparts from inheriting land. Instead, they offered women a share of the money, livestock or other goods.

Two causes were at work. Male inheritors had noticed that Large Farmers were buying land from inheriting women (Tables 3.24, 3.25). Secondly, conversion to Islam made it increasingly necessary for women to farm indirectly, by paying their husbands or labourers. When they could not afford to do so, and they had no sons to whom they could give the land, they were tempted to sell it.

Final Comments

Reviewing the evidence, it is true that a process of land accumulation by farmer-traders and rural transporters had been at work in an area where land and produce are highly commercialized. Nevertheless, the pastoralists from whom they had bought land had departed, and local inheritance custom had been changed to reduce the possibility of women inheriting land. Therefore, most purchases by Large Farmers had been part of a unique historical shift unlikely to be repeated. Secondly, the tendency of Small Farmers to acquire commercially more land than they sold or pledged suggests a high degree of viability among them. Finally, the problem of selling arose mainly as some farmers became more successful, and were in consequence exposed to greater financial risks from household, trading or transport deficits. I conclude that commercial land transfers had not led to a net transfer of land from smaller to larger landholders.

The study of transactions and transactors isolates four dynamics at the heart of this economy:

1. Population movement and growth. In-migration brought into the community individuals who participated more actively than indigenes in land acquisition. The out-migration of a pastoral population in response to rising demographic pressure helps explain why so much land had been concentrated in the hands of the top tenth or third of landholding household heads.

2. The constant search among Hausa farmers for new or more remunerative off-farm occupations. This explains why those engaged in wholesale trade or transport could accumulate land; and why those engaged in retail trading or specialized skills (e.g., house building, tailoring, roof making, Islamic teaching) could participate in limited land purchases.
3. The increased exposure to risk of those engaged in wealth acquisition. If in-migration, off-farm occupations and a variety of credit mechanisms explain upward mobility among land buyers, the risks resulting from enterprise and increasing family size explain at least some downward mobility among sellers.
4. Institutional flexibility. Hausa villagers are capable of altering the social institutions governing land transfers in response to changing circumstances. They acted reflectively and decisively on their individual and social reality. Reacting against diverse pressures toward land alienation, they were resilient in preventing the selling off of family land.

The interaction of these features of Hausa rural economy leads me to risk three further conclusions. Land accumulators are operating under increasingly severe constraints. The future distribution of land is likely to be less unequal than it has been in the past. The long-term effect of increased integration with a wider market economy is likely to be greater equality in landholding.

Notes

1. The index-numbered Land Rank of land-using household heads in 1979, from 1 to 108, is a convenient way of referring to them, which enables the reader to quickly assess their position on the land-holding scale. It will be used throughout the book.
2. Occasionally 'immigrants' farmed in a distant place of origin. Thus, HH 52 still travelled about fifteen miles to his former hamlet to pay a farmer there to cultivate a field. And HH 56 claimed to pay his kin to cultivate a field in their hamlet eighty miles away. But these cases were exceptional.
3. For basic data, see Appendix 1.
4. For basic data, see Appendix 1.
5. For basic data, see Appendix 1.
6. In the remainder of the chapter, I drop the term 'household head'. 'Farmer' will always mean 'household head' unless otherwise explained.

7. My limited and scattered evidence shows little difference between selling prices and pledging sums. Receivers of pledged land could not apply manure but were free to use artificial fertilizer. Selling and pledging prices both varied with farmers' assessments of land potential and actual fertility:

Table 3.32. Land values per acre (N), Marmara

	1977	1978	1979
A. Selling prices:	31	40	54
			219*2
B. Pledging sums:	24	5*1	36
	40	11*1	48
	40	21	50
		28	195*2
		39	
		47	
		50	—

**1* These fields, over four miles from the hamlet, were pledged at a discount because of the cost of transporting labour and fertilizer.

**2* These fields, adjacent and of similar size, were acquired by the same man at the same time from the same farmer.

Chapter 4

FARM LABOUR

Forms of Agricultural Production

As with land, so, too, with labour power: the market has become highly developed. Since the mid-1960s, the use of hired labourers in farming (*yan kwadago,* sing. *dan kwadago*) has become widespread. Many Small and Middle Farmers make occasional daily use of hired labour. Richer farmers frequently hire labour. A form of production making frequent use of hired labour has grown up alongside the form based on family labour. This chapter will be especially concerned to analyse the connections between the two forms.

Farming is commonly pursued through three time periods:

- *Rana:* The 'long morning' of 5–6 hours.
- *Yin mace:* The afternoon of 2–3 hours
- *Kwana:* The full day of 7–9 hours.

Over 1976–79, a majority of hired labourers worked for the long morning or the afternoon, a minority for the day. Concerning modes of payment, employers paid the majority of workers on a daily basis; a minority were paid a piece rate. Large Farmers preferred to hire as many labourers as would get the job in hand done quickly, and pay them a piece rate, but they were often restricted by lack of cash to employ three or four labourers over a week or more, and pay them daily.

During the course of my stay in Marmara, I developed a definite view of the nature of the hired labour force and the relations between employers and labourers. It was based on general discussion with villagers and my observations of the sequence of tasks during the farming season. I also studied a prominent grain trader and farmer in the adjacent district of Kankara (chapter 7). I measured part of his landholding and in doing so, had the opportunity to observe his labour force. I begin by giving my general impression of the evolution of agrarian labour relations. It strongly influenced my subsequent analysis of the numerical data.

Before the mid-1960s, Marmara people did not perform much hired labour. They felt 'shame' (*kunya*) to be seen working on the farms of others. If they needed money in the farming season, they would obtain credit (*bashi*), to be repaid with twice as much money at harvest, on the old principle that 'a cowrie draws a cowrie' (*wuri ya jawo wuri*). In those days, hired labourers were usually seasonal migrants from Kano. The demand for local hired labour was limited because, in a mainly Maguzawa society, there was an abundant supply of women for work in family farming units.

From the mid-1960s, local men increasingly took to hired labouring as a source of income. This process was stimulated by the rise in the market demand for labour resulting from the withdrawal of women from heavy farm work, consequent upon Muslim conversion. Hired labour was also needed to meet the growing demand for grain in the interregional trade with northern Kano (chapter 1). Moreover, demand for hired labour rose because the postwar commodity boom in cotton continued to expand well into the 1970s (Williams 1981: 80, 81). As more local people became more involved in labouring, the levels of indebtedness declined. In the words of HH 48 (who had been a prominent labourer and still worked for others part-time): 'Labouring is better than credit because you buy guineacorn with your own money, and then at harvest, your crops are your own. Not one will ask you for money [as credit repayment].' According to HH 11, a prominent Maguzawa farmer: 'Bashi is not so common now. Before we all got credit but now we rest from it. People get more money from crop sales than before. People now get money by jingina [land pledging]. A strong man can get money from labouring to feed his family.' Thus, the change in labour relations had led to a change in credit. The consensus among the villagers whom I questioned was that needy farmers had benefited.

By the mid-1970s, the hired labour force consisted mainly of boys and young men sent out to work by their fathers, and young household heads. An important additional source of hired labour consisted of seasonally migrant workers from more northern regions. They, too, were usually young, in their twenties or early thirties. They normally came for weeding, returned home, and came again for harvesting. Farm labouring appeared to be a particular stage in the life cycle of local farmers, and in the annual work cycle of seasonal migrants.

During 1976–9, hired labourers were in a strong bargaining position. The demand for guineacorn and maize, the two major crops grown for sale, was rising in the rural and urban areas which were market outlets for Marmara (chapter 6; Clough and Williams 1987: 184–97). Because of high and rising pay rates, the profit margins of employers were small. Whichever village I visited, rural employers complained about the cost of hired labour. And it was a common topic of discussion among the grain traders whom I met in the various marketplaces of southern Katsina. My impression was confirmed when I calculated the costs and returns in farming guineacorn of some Large Farmers in Marmara (chapters 5 and 7).

In 1978, I followed a merchant-farmer of Kankara town as he toured his 600-acre holding. He had to supervize personally his entire workforce, which had been divided so as to weed individual sections on piece rates. They worked slowly, needed much cajoling, and were often granted extra money if they pressed. In December 1985, when I returned to Malumfashi for data on costs and returns in cotton production, I was introduced to a prominent farmer of Malumfashi District. He stressed that the main restriction on increased cotton cultivation was the high cost of labour in weeding and cotton picking. He emphasized that labourers who negotiated a payment of 'N400 would not finish the job until they had been paid N600'. During the 1985 guineacorn harvest, I observed the same tendency to bargain up agreed pay rates among hired labourers in Marmara.

An incident in 1978 revealed the bargaining power of hired labourers. The village head was deputed by a title holder in Katsina to engage a labour force on the large field which he had acquired to the west of Marmara. When the absentee owner demurred at the pay rate negotiated, the young men of Marmara downed tools and complained to the district head. He ensured that they were paid the rate which had been earlier agreed.

This chapter seeks to test my sense of labour relations by an analysis based on numerical evidence. In so doing, my main concerns will be the significance of hired labouring, and its effects on production using family labour.

Method

To make analysis clearer, I distinguish broadly between three groups during the 1978 farming season: (1) household heads who 'frequently' hired labour, (2) those who 'frequently' neither hired in labour nor hired out their own labour, and (3) those who 'frequently' hired out their labour. (There were no household heads who frequently both hired in and hired out labour.) Among those who 'frequently' hired labour, it was further possible to distinguish between those who used 'mainly' hired labour and those who used 'much supplementary' hired labour (Chart 4.1).[1]

These categories were developed from information provided by twenty-eight farmers in the 1978 farming season with respect to their total output and farm expenditure, and their labour use in the various farm operations. Of these, fifteen gave the information on the farm as part of a tour of their fields and a discussion of their farming practices; thirteen discussed their farming at home. For only seven farmers were the data complete and for one farmer (HH 20, a young entrepreneur) almost complete. Equally important, I spent much time

Chart 4.1. Categories used in analysing arrangements for labour hiring, Marmara, 1978

I.

FREQUENTLY HIRED LABOUR:

One-third or more of total weeding time was performed by hired labourers.

A. Used mainly hired labour: over one-half of total weeding time was performed by hired labourers.

B. Used much supplementary hired labour: one-third to one-half of weeding time was performed by hired labourers.

II.

FREQUENTLY NEITHER HIRED IN NOR HIRED OUT LABOUR:

A. Small supplementary hired labour: less than one-third of total weeding time was performed by hired labourers.

III.

FREQUENTLY HIRED OUT LABOUR:

One-third or more of the total time spent weeding was performed on the farms of employers.

Table 4.1. Key informants on farming expenditure and practices, Marmara, 1978

	Holding	Off-farm occupations(s)
Large Farmers:		
1. HH 6	35.0 acres	Kolanut wholesaler
2. HH 7	22.4 acres	Grain wholesaler
3. HH 20	12.0 acres	Maize trader, cotton buyer, bus owner
Middle Farmers:		
4. HH 32	8.5 acres	None
5. HH 43	6.3 acres	Migrant labourer
Small Farmers:		
6. HH 63	3.3 acres	Survey worker, part-time labourer
7. HH 65	3.2 acres	Butcher
8. HH 79	2.5 acres	Herbalist, part-time labourer

walking through the fields while farming was underway, observing general farming practices. From these different types of observation, I have constructed the scheme of labour use, and applied it to all 108 farming household heads.

I have chosen weeding as the farm operation from which to identify the extent of labour hiring among household heads because it was the farm operation that they associated most critically with yield. As a result, weeding was the operation in which the greatest number of household heads were likely to have been 'frequent employers'. In contrast, the heavy work of harvesting occurred long after the rains had finished. It was often performed in a more leisurely fashion than weeding. A 'frequent employer' of labourers for weeding sometimes relied on his own and family labour for planting and harvesting. Furthermore, it was easier for me to identify the extent of labour hiring with reference to weeding than with reference to all farm operations. This is clear from a look at the many operations performed on the two main crops grown in 1978 (Chart 4.2).

I cannot chart the extent of labour hiring for this plethora of activities, but I can do so for weeding, at least within the broad categories outlined. The sequence in Chart 4.2 was the ideal. If there were a cash shortage, 'frequent employers' during the first weeding dispensed with the second weeding and ridging on some of their fields.

Chart 4.2. Farm operations for the two main crops of the Marmara farming season*, 1978

Guineacorn and maize	**1.**	Clearing the ground before the rains (March, April).
	2.	Applying manure and/or artificial fertiliser before the rain (April).
	3.	First ridging after the rains begin (May).
	4.	Planting (May).
	5.	First weeding (June).
	6.	Second weeding (July).
	7.	Second ridging – banking up the ridges (July).
	8.	Cutting stalks – maize (September, October).
Guineacorn:	**9.**	Cutting and gathering the heads.
(December)	**10.**	Tying the heads in bundles for transporting and storage in granaries (*rumbuna*).
	11.	Transporting from the field.
	12.	Storage in granaries.
OR:	**9.**	Cutting and gathering the heads.
	10.	Threshing the heads.
	11.	Winnowing the field.
	12.	Measuring and filling sacks with kernels.
	13.	Transporting from the fields.
Maize	**9.**	Picking the cobs (October).
	10.	Transporting from the field.
	11.	Peeling the cobs.
	12.	Shucking the cobs.
	13.	Measuring and filling sacks with kernels.

* Neither cotton nor groundnuts were grown in significant quantities in 1978.

Patterns of Labour

Since there were so many combinations, I begin by summarising the main degrees of own, family and hired labour used by all 108 household heads with farmland during the 1978 farming season.[2] The largest single group farmed on their own – 43 per cent of household heads. They had in the main very small holdings. Those who farmed either on their own or with family labour only together formed 63 per cent of all household heads. These included twenty-three heads who *fre-*

quently hired out their own labour (21 per cent of all household heads). The remaining 37 per cent of household heads used some degree of hired labour. Ranging from HH 63 to HH 1, their holdings varied from 3 acres to 50 acres (see Appendix 6, Table 2 for a summary of the patterns of labour use among all household heads).

Mean and median sizes of holdings were, expectedly, larger for those who farmed using *mainly hired* labour, and for those who combined hired labour with their own and family work. Farmers who relied entirely on their own and hired labour tended to be distinctly younger than the other types of labour user. They also tended to have holdings only slightly larger than the hamlet mean of 8 acres (Appendix 6, Table 2).

Conspicuous were the five farmers who relied on *mainly hired* labour and at the same time had comparatively large family workforces. Together, they controlled 22 per cent of hamlet acreage. They comprised some of the largest land users – HH 2, HH 3–4, HH 6 and HH 9. Users of *much or small supplementary hired labour* – as a supplement to the family workforce – controlled 30 per cent of hamlet acreage. They, too, included some of the largest farmers – HH 1, HH 5, HH 7–8 and HH 10–11 (Appendix 6, Table 2).

Some of the frequent labourers were quite old and deployed large family workforces on their own fields. But seventeen of the twenty-three frequent labourers had no family workforce and tended to be among the youngest household heads (Appendix 6, Table 2).

Below, Table 4.2 shows that one-half of hamlet land was controlled by farmers who made frequent use of hired labour. So we must ask:

Table 4.2. Patterns of labour use among household heads in the weeding operation, Marmara, 1978

			Acreage				Age	
Categories	**No.**	**Per cent**	**Acres**	**Per cent**			**Mean**	**Median**
I. Hire labour	24	22%	408	50%	17	12	49	45
II. Neither hire in or out labour	61	57%	337	42%	5	4	48	50
III. Hire out own labour	23	21%	64	8%	3	2	42	40
Totals:	**108**	**100%**	**809**	**100%**	**8**	**4**	**47**	**45**

Acres: mean/median: (refers to the two unlabelled columns)

was production making frequent use of hired labour increasing its share of hamlet land at the expense of production based mainly on family labour? Clearly, it had done so in the recent past. Yet chapter 3 showed how farmers engaged in land accumulation were facing increasing constraints on the enlargement of their landholdings. This account shows that the labour supply was limited mainly to younger men. To further probe the impact of the labour market on forms of production, we must examine the group of employers and then, the nature of the hired workforce.

The Frequent Employers

The frequent employers formed a distinctly heterogeneous grouping – prominent landholders whose production was based on mainly hired labour; older farmers whose production was based primarily on the family but who employed much supplementary hired labour; older farmers without a family workforce whose farmland was too great for them to farm by themselves; and mainly young, enterprising farmers with no adult family workforce who invested in production using mainly hired labour. However, beyond underlining the heterogeneity of frequent employers as a group, we need to relate labour hiring to the changing nature of rural economy and society. In chapter 3, I showed that the causes of land transfer are usefully explained by invoking a process of 'long-term wealth acquisition', and the distinction between those engaged in it and those not so engaged. I now relate labour hiring to this process. Long-term wealth acquisition is a manifold social process involving the accumulation of wives, children, clients and other dependents, as well as things – farmland, cattle, equipment and money. The rural Hausa of southern Katsina conceive of 'wealth' (dukiya) as including both physical assets which are convertible into money and family members and other persons to whom there are varying ties of 'responsibility' (hidima). Thus, long-term wealth acquisition embraces various income sources and various sorts of moral obligation. It implies an interaction between agricultural and nonagricultural investment, the proceeds of each flowing into the other.

The amount of money generated by off-farm activity differentiates long-term wealth acquirers from other people. Lucrative off-farm occupations make possible accelerated investment in farmland and hired labour. There is a second criterion of long-term wealth acquisition: strategic intention. Those engaged in this process are seriously interested in acquiring 'wealth' (dukiya). In contrast, the majority of men and women are mainly concerned with achieving that limited surplus of income over expenditure which makes possible a higher standard of consumption of food and clothing, a higher quality of local housing, and a gradual expansion in the size of the household to which they belong. To a certain extent, the distinction between those who are and are not engaged in long-term wealth acquisition is a matter of degree. Both groups attempt to achieve material and social *expansion*. Nevertheless, it is crucial to isolate analytically those who continuously plan for wealth and who, because of the scale of their off-farm income, are able to translate plans into reality.

In analysing the frequent employers, my primary question will be: to what extent was labour hiring part of the process of long-term wealth acquisition? This raises subsidiary questions. How was frequent hiring related to the size of landholding? How was it related to the size of the family workforce? In these terms, three variables are essential to understanding frequent employers: (1) their involvement in long-term wealth acquisition; (2) the size of their adult family workforces; and (3) the size of their holding. In Table 4.3A, I introduce 'Very Large Farmers', with 25 acres or more.

Clearly, in Table 4.3A, frequent hiring was closely associated with long-term wealth acquisition. Among the wealth acquirers, we can distinguish between those using mainly hired labour (Subgroups I and II) and those who hired labour as a supplement to the family workforce (Subgroups III and IV). Users of mainly hired labour tended to be younger and have smaller family workforces than users of supplementary hired labour. Users of supplementary hired labour included HH 1, who was able to meet at least half of his weeding requirement by the intensive use of a family workforce of six (he alone constitutes Subgroup III).

The distinguishing feature of those frequent employers not engaged in long-term wealth acquisition (Subgroups V and VI) was that their off-farm occupations allowed of small savings and therefore, only small-scale investment in land and hired labour. In Subgroup V, HH 22 (12 acres) had no off-farm occupation. HH 42 (6 acres) was a small table retailer (*mai teburi*) of cigarettes, soap and sundry items. HH 45 (6 acres) was a house builder in nearby Malumfashi who had little time for farming. In Subgroup VI, HH 15 (13 acres) was a donkey transporter. HH 23 (11 acres) retailed the small amounts of cassava grown locally. HH 28 (10 acres) was a donkey transporter. The one exception to this pattern, HH 19 (12 acres), had the farm output and off-farm income (from oxen hire) to initiate a process of wealth acquisition. But as one of the few remaining Maguzawa (discussed below), he devoted unusual time to maximising the yield of his existing holding. He weeded his fields four times instead of the customary two. And part of his grain surplus was set aside for guineacorn beer.

Two of the farmers in Subgroup VI were older men but without adult sons who might have worked for them. In both their cases, it is truer to say that they hired labour to remedy a shortage of family workers, instead of hiring labour as a 'supplement to the family workforce'.

Table 4.3A charts a certain type of progression through the life-cycle of employers. Frequent employers who were young inevitably needed hired labour, since they lacked a family workforce. As they aged, their family workforces tended to increase. Thus, their reliance on hired labour tended to diminish. Older employers engaging in long-term wealth acquisition tended to rely less on hired and more on family

Table 4.3A. The frequent employers, Marmara, 1978

				Adult family workers		
	No.	Acres	Acres: mean/median	No.	Age (mean/median)	Total acres
A. Those engaged in long-term wealth aquisition						
I. Very Large Farmers						
Mainly hired labour	4	43–35	39/38	3/3	50/52	155 (38%)
II. Large to Small Farmers						
Mainly hired labour	8	19–3	11/11	1/1	39/40	85 (21%)
III. Very Large Farmers						
Supplementary hired labour	1	50	(50)	(6)	(65)	50 (12%)
IV. Large to Small Farmers						
Supplementary hired labour	4	22–6	12/10	3/2	52/55	48 (12%)
B. Those not engaged in long-term wealth acquisition:						
V. Mainly hired labour	3	12–6	8/6	1/1	48/40	24 (6%)
VI. Supplementary hired labour	4	13–10	11/11*1	3/1*1	55/55	46 (11%)
Total (A and B):	**24**	**50–3**	**17/12**	**2/2**	**49/45**	**408 (100%)**
Hamlet totals:	108	50–0.5	8/4	2/1	47/45	809*2

*1 Rounded to the nearest whole number.
*2 The total is different from Table 4.1 because the acreages of all farmers are rounded.

labour than younger ones. However, once farmers acquired very large holdings, they tended to use mainly hired labour even when they had large family workforces. Nevertheless, the largest landholder in the hamlet (Subgroup III) was still able to use family labour for at least half of his weeding requirement. Because of this progression through time, we can analyse the frequent employers into three groups (Table 4.3B).

The analysis shows why an expansion of landholding does not necessarily lead to production based on mainly hired labour. It is rather a question of the farmer's combined resources from farm and off-farm activity, and the rate at which his family workforce increases. In conclusion, most frequent employers were engaged in long-term wealth acquisition. The frequent employers were finely balanced between those who invested in hired labour as the primary source of labour (19 per cent of hamlet acreage) and those who employed hired labour to supplement, or remedy a shortage of, family labour (21 per cent of hamlet acreage). An intermediate category consisted of young men without family workers. These would divide with increasing age between the two main groups of frequent employer (Table 4.3B). The

Table 4.3B. The frequent employers, Marmara, 1978

	Farmers		Acreage		
Groups	**No.**		**Acres**		**Description:**
I. Invest in hired labour as primary source of labour *(Sub-group 1, Table 4.3A)*	4	4%	155	19%	*They had large family workforces but their holdings were usually too large to be farmed except through mainly hired labour.*
II. Invest in hired labour to supplement, or remedy a shortage of, family labour *(Sub-groups 3–6, Table 4.3A)*	12	11%	168	21%	*They include Very Large, Large, and Middle Farmers.*
III. Intermediate, youthful category *(Sub-group 2, Table 4.3A)*	8	7%	85	10%	*They will enter either I, or II, according as their family workers and landholding increase.*
Totals:	**24**	**22%**	**408**	**50%**	
		Per cent of all Farmers		**Per cent of all hamlet land**	

labour market had developed through, rather than in opposition to, the underlying demographic and acquisitive forces of rural society.

The Hired Labour Force

Like the group of frequent employers, the hired labour force was complex:

1. Household heads who frequently hired out their own labour
2. Male dependents sent out to labour frequently by household heads
3. Women employed in planting and in picking harvest produce
4. Seasonally migrant labourers from more northern regions
5. Occasional labourers – household heads and dependents who occasionally picked up cash through labouring when not engaged on their own farms.

My evidence is restricted to labourers from Marmara and seasonally migrant labourers who came to Marmara from more northern regions. But we must remember that Marmara employers were drawing labour from the surrounding hamlets – and that they were competing for it with employers in the surrounding hamlets as well.

Household Heads Who Labour Frequently

Frequent labourers were generally younger than the frequent employers and those who neither hired in nor hired out labour (Appendix 6, Table 2). Their relative youthfulness suggests that they would relinquish this work as they grew older. Compared with other household heads, they also had much smaller landholdings (Appendix 6, Table 3).

And yet, while those who laboured frequently were younger and had less land than those who did not, many household heads who were young or short of land were not frequent labourers (Table 4.4). Even among the thirteen household heads with 0.3 acres per capita or less, fewer than one half were frequent labourers (Table 4.4).

Why, then, did some household heads become frequent labourers? Most of them did not have any particular skill, trade or asset for earning off-farm income. Most were 'general or migrant labourers' in their off-farm activity (Appendix 6, Table 3). The four 'migrant labourers' toiled in Lagos in the postharvest dry season as building workers and porters, or in Yorubaland as kolanut pickers. The twelve 'general la-

Table 4.4. The connection between age, landholding and frequent labouring, Marmara, 1978

		All	50 or more	Under 50	35 or less
A.	**Age**	**All**	**50 or more**	**Under 50**	**35 or less**
	Labourers	23/21%	6/11%	17/31%	8/31%
	All farmers (100%)	108	53	55	26
B.	**Acres**		**4 or more**	**Under 4**	**Under 2**
	Labourers	23/21%	4/7%	19/36%	7/37%
	All farmers (100%)	108	55	53	19
C.	**Acres per capita*1**		**Over 0.6**	**0.6 or less**	**0.3 or less**
	Labourers	23/21%	6/11%	17/33%	6/46%
	All farmers (100%)	108	56	52	13

*1 The median among all households was 0.7 acres per capita.

bourers' were employed preparing and laying the mud balls used by house builders, making guineacorn fences, carrying water or working as grain porters and grain mill operators.

Was there a connection between frequent farm labouring and the lack of an income from a skill, trade or transport? These terms have broad meaning in rural life. 'Transporters' include both donkey and bus owners. 'Traders' include vegetable retailers who picked up one or two naira a day as well as commodity wholesalers. The term 'skill' is especially broad. It includes Western skills (e.g., bus driver, tailor), indigenous skills (e.g., house builder, butcher), those with esoteric knowledge (Qur'anic mallams) and praise singers. It also includes some who were not really 'skilled' at all – a Qur'anic beggar, and HH 82, a professional beggar who lucratively dangled the stump of his left arm at the central mosque in Lagos. But all had applied their minds to carving out an economic niche – an individual role in the supply of goods or services for which there was local or distant demand, and in which they could develop a reputation. While sana'a is translated as 'occupation, trade or profession' (Abraham 1962), in Marmara it had this special connotation of 'economic niche'.[3]

So let us distinguish between those whose off-farm occupation involved trade, transport or 'skill', on the one hand, and those who were semiskilled general labourers, on the other.[4] The results are striking. Far more than the rest of the population, the frequent farm labourers were semiskilled. There was a strong connection between lack of a sana'a and frequent farm labouring (Table 4.5).

Table 4.5. The connection between off-farm occupation, age and frequent farm labouring, Marmara, 1978

Off-farm occupation	Non-frequent farm labourers			Frequent farm labourers		
	Total:	Age:		Total:	Age:	
		+50	under 50		+50	under 50
1. Trade, transport, 'skill'	72/85%	39/83%	33/87%	5/22%	3/50%	2/12%
2. General labour	2/ 2%	1/ 2%	1/ 3%	15/65%	2/33%	13/76%
3. *1None	8/ 9%	6/12%	2/ 5%	1/ 4%	0	1/ 6%
4. Not known	3/ 3%	1/ 2%	2/ 5%	2/ 9%	1/17%	1/ 6%
Total:	85/99%	47/99%	38/100%	23/100%	6/100%	17/100%

85 [+] 23=108 landed household heads

*1 All eight had 6.4 acres or more.

As household heads increased in age, they acquired 'skills' in trade, transport or some other activity. As they increased in skill, the incidence of farm labouring sharply dropped. Therefore, as they increased in age, household heads tended to drop out of the agricultural labour market. Consequently, the supply of hired farm labour among household heads tended to be limited to younger men.

This helps explain why, despite their youthfulness, few of the landless household heads were frequent farm labourers. Six of the twelve landless household heads had skilled indigenous professions (as butchers or blacksmiths) or Western skills (as bus drivers). Three had year-round jobs with the local government (Table 4.6). It is not that the young tend to be farm labourers; it is rather that farm labourers generally lack skill, and so tend to be young.

Adult Male Dependents Frequently Hired Out by Household Heads

Another source of hired labour consisted of adult male dependents released by household heads from family farming to work frequently on the farms of employers. Of the 108 household heads, 42 had adult dependent workers, married or unmarried. Only 11 hired out their adult male dependents 'frequently', i.e., at least two long mornings of the week (Table 4.7). Among farmers with adult dependent workers, those who hired them out tended to have less land and land per capita, and fewer occupational skills, than those who did not (Table 4.8).

Table 4.6. Landlessness and frequent farm labouring, Marmara, 1978

Landless household heads	Age	Family size	Occupation(s)	
1. HH 109	35	3	Ploughman, farm labourer	I
2. HH 110	35	9	Local authority roadworker	I
3. HH 111	55	2	Local authority roadworker	I
4. HH 112	30	3	Bus driver	I
5. HH 113	55	2	Local authority roadworker	I
6. HH 114	30	4	Bus driver	I
7. HH 115	35	3	General and farm labourer	I
8. HH 116	40	8	Butcher	M
9. HH 117	55	2	Blacksmith	M
10. HH 118	40	3	Small retailer, farm labourer	M
11. HH 119	35	7	Butcher	M
12. HH 120	35	5	Butcher	M
Mean/Median	**39/35**	**4/3**		

Indigene 58% (I), or Immigrants 42% (M):

It is worth focusing on farmers with 4 to 9 acres – a broad range whose yields might well have suffered if they had frequently hired out their dependent workers. Only three of the thirteen farmers in this range frequently hired out their dependents (Table 4.7). This suggests that farmers with four or more acres were disinclined to hire out their family workforce because to do so would detract from the weeding of their own fields. Above relatively low acreages, farmers gave priority to their own farming.

Female Labour

The custom of wife-seclusion among the Muslims of Marmara was governed by certain conventions. Women were debarred from the heavier tasks – weeding, reaping and transporting crops from the field. As the tendency to acquire a sana'a limited the supply of male labour, so religious practice restricted the supply of female labour. Women were active in planting. They were the main source of hired

Table 4.7. Frequent labourers among adult dependents of household heads, Marmara, 1979

	Farm	Family size and dependent workers		
Farmer	Acres/*per capita*	Size	Dependent workforce	Off-farm occupation(s)
HH 1	49.9/*2.3*	22	5	Bus owner*[1]
HH 2	43.3/*2.2*	20	2	Bus owner*[1]
HH 3	41.5/*2.4*	17	2	Bus driver*[1]
HH 4	36.0/*4.0*	9	4*[2]	Oxen-cart transporter*[1]
HH 5	35.4/*2.7*	13	3	Oxen hire
HH 6	35.0/*2.5*	14	2	Kolanut trader
HH 7	22.4/*1.4*	16	4	Grain trader
HH 8	21.1/*2.6*	8	1	Oxen hire
HH 9	19.0/*1.1*	17	1	Corn miller, cotton buyer
HH 10	16.4/*1.2*	14	4	Shop keeper, cotton buyer
HH 11	16.3/*1.6*	10	7*[2]	*None*
HH 13	13.2/*0.9*	14	1	Grain trader, Oxen hire
HH 15	12.9/*3.2*	4	1	Donkey transporter
HH 16	12.6/*1.0*	13	5	Part time grain trader
HH 17	12.3/*1.4*	9	1	*None*
HH 19	12.0/*1.2*	10	7*[2]	Oxen hire
HH 21	11.8/*1.0*	12	1	Oxen hire, migrant labourer
HH 24	11.2/*1.1*	10	2	*None*
HH 32	8.5/*0.7*	12	2	*None*
HH 33	8.3/*1.0*	8	7*[2]	*None*
HH 34	7.7/*1.3*	6	2	Oxen hire
HH 35	7.4/*0.5*	16	2 X	House builder
HH 36	7.4/*1.1*	7	1 X	General labourer
HH 40	6.7/*1.1*	6	1	Goat trader, butcher
HH 43	6.3/*0.5*	12	2 X	Migrant labourer
HH 44	6.2/*0.6*	11	1	Grain trader
HH 46	5.9/*1.0*	6	1	Oxen hire
HH 49	5.1/*0.8*	6	2	Kolanut trader
HH 50	4.9/*0.4*	11	1	Chief of motor park
HH 52	4.5/*0.6*	7	1	General retailer

Table 4.7: continued on next page

Table 4.7: continued from previous page

HH 54	4.3/*0.7*	3	1	Vegetable retailer
HH 56	3.9/*0.5*	8	1	Retailer, tailor, smuggler
HH 62	3.3/*0.4*	9	1	Qu'ranic mallam, teacher
HH 64	3.3/*0.3*	10	3 X	Roof maker
HH 66	3.2/*0.5*	7	1 X	Tailor
HH 74	2.7/*0.3*	10	3 X	Hides and sugar trader
HH 75	2.7/*0.4*	7		Liman
HH 80	2.5/*0.6*	4	1 X	'General labourer
HH 82	2.3/*0.2*	13	1 X	Professional Lagos beggar
HH 83	2.3/*0.5*	5	1 X	Commission agent
HH 95	1.4/*0.2*	6	1 X	General labourer
HH 98	1.3/*0.2*	7	1 X	*not known*

Dependents labour frequently (X)

**1* Also Oxen hire.
*2 Maguzawa wives are part of the family workforce.

Table 4.8. Conditions of hiring-out adult dependents, factors which predispose household heads to hire-out dependents

	MORE THAN 3.3 ACRES		3.3 ACRES OR LESS		ALL	
A. Acreage						
Adult dependents labour	3	27%	8	73%	11	100%
Adult dependents do not labour	29	93%	2	7%	31	100%
Total with dependent workers	32	76%	10	24%	42	100%
B. *1Acres/capita	**Over 0.5**		**0.5 or less**		**All**	
Adult dependents labour	2	18%	9	82%	11	100%
Adult dependents do not labour	27	87%	4	13%	31	100%
Total with dependent workers	29	69%	13	31%	42	100%
C. Off-farm occupations	**Trade/transport/skill**		**General labour**		**None/n.k.**	
Adult dependents labour	6	54%	4	36%	1	9%
Adult dependents do not labour	22	71%	4	13%	5	16%
Total with dependent workers	28	67%	8	19%	6	14%

**1* The median among all households was 0.7 acres per capita.

and family labour for picking and shucking maize, picking cotton and winnowing rice and guineacorn. Within these limits, the supply of female labour was plentiful in relation to the demand for it.

Seasonally Migrant Labourers

Because the supply of hired labour from local households was inadequate to meet the demand, employers throughout Malumfashi and Kankara districts sought out seasonally migrant labourers. Ecological differences in Nigeria make this possible. The rainy season arrives later in more northern areas, where the rainy season is shorter. As a result, it is possible for seasonally migrant rural labour to move south. Most migrant labourers in Malumfashi and Kankara districts came from Daura and Danbatta, over 100 miles to the north, where the farming season was later and shorter. They returned home to plant and weed their own farms, and came back south for harvesting. During 1976–79, their movements were facilitated by good roads and plentiful transport. Thus, most migrant labourers performed this work as a complement to farming in their own home regions.

Marmara can be compared with Dan Marke, a village 10 miles to the north with lower population density and more bush land. The holdings of the largest farmers were bigger than any in Marmara. Frequent employers in Dan Marke relied much more on seasonally migrant labour. Among them was Alhaji Z, the biggest rural grain trader in Kankara District (chapter 7). In 1985 he told me: 'The majority (*yawanci*) of my labourers come from the north, for example, from Daura and Danbatta, where they do not plant until we have finished the first weeding in southern Katsina, and they harvest early, before the harvest in southern Katsina.'

Seasonally migrant labourers tended to fit their labouring into the cycle of their family farming. The same pattern was evident among Marmara farmers who were seasonally migrant labourers. Before the rainy season had begun in Marmara, they moved south to the kolanut farms of Yorubaland, or to plant grains in southern Zaria. They returned home for planting and weeding, and migrated south again during the interval before harvesting.

Two patterns were visible in 1978 among men who arrived in Marmara as seasonal migrant labourers. First, most of them were men in their twenties. Secondly, a minority of them looked for a permanent place in the community. Labourers who settled tended to acquire land, develop a sana'a and eventually give up frequent labouring. Among the nine immigrants aged under forty, five had arrived as labourers, four had acquired land, three were still frequent labourers in 1978 and one had acquired a sana'a in addition to working as a farm labourer.

Occasional Labourers

The hired labour force also included household heads who offered their services for a long morning or two but could not be relied on for more extended periods, and married male dependents available on afternoons and days off from family farming. Most of all, it was augmented by boys aged ten to fifteen released occasionally from family farming, for a long morning or an afternoon. Any walk through the fields during the farming season showed that younger boys were the single largest source of hired labour in weeding.

Labour Rates and Modes of Recruitment

There were two types of labour rate – daily rates and piece rates. They stemmed from the different availabilities of occasional and frequent labourers. Daily rates accommodated the labour force internal to the area, which was mainly available on an occasional basis. Piece rates applied mainly to frequent labourers who had the time to perform an operation from start to finish.

Daily rates included payment for the long morning and payment for the afternoon. There were two piece rates corresponding to different modes of recruitment. First, a well-known local labourer (*kongila*) could assemble a large labour force. They would then bargain as a group with the employer and, once the job was finished, the lump sum would be divided up equally. Secondly, an employer could assemble a small group and bargain over the lump sum to be paid; or he could divide a field into sections, assign each worker a section, and bargain with them individually over the payment (a procedure known as *debe*).

There was some variation in daily rates for weeding. But a narrow band quickly became established in the farming season. The most common rates for a long morning's work were N1.00 in 1977, N1.50 in 1978 and N3.50 in 1985. Rates for a long morning's work, and my evidence for piece rates, have been converted into their value for an eight-hour man day (Table 4.9). The piece rates given may be considered typical since the Large Farmers concerned were major employers by piece rate.

Table 4.9. Labour rates per man-day (N) for weeding offered by various employers, Marmara

Farmers	Rates of pay: 1977		Rates of pay: 1978		Rates of pay: 1985	
Large	**Daily**	**Piece**	**Daily**	**Piece**	**Daily**	**Piece**
HH 2	1.33					
HH 4	1.33, 1.60		2.67			
HH 7	1.33, 1.60		2.00	2.22, 5.20		7.47
HH 19			2.67			
HH 20	1.33, 1.87	2.20	2.00, 2.67,	2.17*3		
			3.33	5.33*4		
HH 24	1.33, 1.67					
*1LFNH					4.00	8.33*6
Middle						
HH 28			2.00		4.67	
HH 36			1.67	2.33*5		
HH 42	1.33					
HH 45			2.00			
Small						
HH 56	1.60	1.67*2				
HH 63			2.00			

*1 Large Farmer in neighbouring hamlet.
*2–6 The daily rates corresponding to piece rates on these particular fields were:
*2 1.60, *3 2.67, *4 2.00, *5 1.67, *6 4.00

There were two reasons why piece rates per man day were usually higher than daily rates. First, the *value* of frequent labourers was usually higher than that of occasional labourers, because they weeded more quickly. Occasional labourers had little incentive to work quickly. In contrast, frequent labourers wished to finish a job as quickly as possible in order to get on to the next one. Secondly, frequent labourers were in short and fluctuating supply relative to occasional labourers. Thus, piece rates incorporated a premium for their value and scarcity, and fluctuated greatly even within the narrow limits of the Marmara farming season.

If the supply from other household heads was insufficient, the supply of migrant labour was uncertain and, moreover, employers were competing with each other for the available supply. There were major consequences. First, the main rate paid to frequent labourers, the piece rate, was rising in real terms over the period 1977–85. Table

4.10 shows the change in high and low daily rates, and in known piece rates. While it only compares rates with guineacorn prices rather than with prices for a basket of goods, this is a relevant comparison. Labourers spent more of their pay on guineacorn for their families than on any other item. Moreover, guineacorn was the major crop on which labour was employed.

Looking more closely at Table 4.10, I examine daily rates separately from piece rates, since the former were paid mainly to occasional, and the later to frequent, labourers. July prices are crucial because they were the peak prices which labourers actually had to pay for guineacorn during the time when they were weeding. Daily and piece rates rose in real terms from 1977 to 1978; 1984 was exceptional, there being a severe drought, and guineacorn prices reached record levels in anticipation of a very poor harvest. Even so, it is interesting that from the weeding period of 1984 to that of 1985, daily pay rose in real terms since by the weeding period of 1985, guineacorn prices had dropped more sharply than daily rates. Over the period 1977–85, piece rates rose substantially in real terms.

Table 4.10. Labour rates for weeding and guineacorn prices per sack in nearby markets (N), Marmara, 1977–85

	DAILY RATES*1		KNOWN PIECE RATES		MARKET PRICES OF GUINEACORN*2	
	Low	**High**	**Low**	**High**	**Peak** (*July*)	**Harvest** (*December*)
1977	1.33	1.60	1.67	2.20	24	18
1978	2.00	2.67	2.17	5.33	30	18
Change:	**+50%**	**+67%**	**+30%**	**+141%**	**+25%**	**0**
*31984	5.60	6.40	*n.k.*	*n.k.*	135*4	80
1985	4.00	4.67	7.47	8.33	72*5	30
Change:	**–29%**	**–27%**	***n.k.***	***n.k.***	**–47%**	**–62.%**
Rise 1977–85:	**+200%**	**+192%**	**+347%**	**+279%**	**+157%**	**+67%**

The 1977 harvest was plentiful. The 1978 and 1985 harvests were even more abundant (chapter 6). The 1984 harvest was poor.

*1 This is the daily equivalent of a long morning's work weeding.

*2 See also chapter 6.

*3 These are the recollections of farmers interviewed in December 1985.

*4 The drought during the rainy-season of 1984 raised prices until the rainy season of 1985.

*5 Prices began to fall during the rainy-season of 1985 when farmers and traders judged that forward deliveries would be secure at harvest.

A second consequence of competition among employers was that they gave labourers 'nonwage' benefits. Normally, employers provided a midday meal of guineacorn porridge served with sauce, or money in lieu of food. They also offered seasonally migrant labourers free accommodation and an evening meal.

Thirdly, piece rates were paid mainly by frequent employers – most of whom were Large Farmers – while daily rates were paid by all strata. It follows that Large Farmers paid considerably more for labour than Small and Middle Farmers.

The fourth consequence affected the organization of the labour force. Frequent employers with large holdings sought out one or two client labourers (yara, sing. *yaro*), who could be relied on for most of the farming days when they were needed. They could be local household heads or seasonal migrants. In return, clients could expect special help from their employers, e.g., grain for their families in times of dearth, or money for ceremonial expenditures. Thus, the hired labour force was not only differentiated as I have described – between local frequent labourers, seasonal migrants, occasional labourers and women. It was also structured between a core of clients and the great majority who were not attached to employers by reciprocal ties of personal obligation.

Family Farming

We turn now to the form of production based on own and family labour. When adult dependents farm under the control of their household head, the common work unit is called a *gandu* (pl., *gandaye*) (chapter 1). In discussing the nature of gandu since the end of slavery, writers have concentrated on the practices linking household heads and their married dependents (Smith 1955: 20–21; Buntjer 1970a: 26–27; Hill 1972: 38; Goddard 1973: 207–8). But in Marmara, the term was used more broadly. If a man said he weeded 'with his gandu', he meant his unmarried adult dependents as well. Still, Marmara Muslims have clear ideas concerning the labour of married dependents, and the notions of mutual obligation which underlie it. I will focus discussion on the practices linking household heads and their married dependents. Abstractly stated, gandu among the Muslims of Marmara is a customary economic relationship based on kinship between two or more married men, in which they form a joint unit of production and consumption and accept the decisions of one with regard to the allocation of labour and other resources between different crops and fields on the land jointly used. It is a voluntary labour relationship in which the head controls the unpaid labour of married subordinates for recognized periods of the day and week during the farming season. In return, he is obliged to provide from the produce or proceeds of the land jointly used: tools, seed, at least two meals a day for all members of the joint household throughout the year, the expenses of at least the first marriage of all working dependents, all naming ceremony expenses and their head tax. He is also obliged to provide married subordinates with a plot or field (gayauna, pl. gayauni) – small in relation to the land jointly used – which they use on their periods away from gandu, and the produce of which they can dispose of as they wish.

There is a difference between gandaye linking fathers and married sons and gandaye linking married brothers or other male kin. In paternal gandaye, the land jointly used is regarded as belonging to the head, in the specific sense that local custom and the Alkali courts recognize his right to sell any of it. But at the same time, married subordinates have a claim on the land jointly used, in the limited sense that should any one of them choose to leave the joint unit with the consent of the head, and after having established a family of his own, he ought to be granted a small field, which is then recognized as his property. In other kinds of gandaye, ownership rights are more complex because the association of such people in a joint unit may signify the delayed partition of a common inheritance against which the members have different claims.

Among Muslims, there were three significant variations in gandu practices. First, the labour which married subordinates were obliged to give varied between four, or more commonly five or six, long mornings of the week during the farming season. Secondly, while gandu heads always had to pay the expenses of their male dependents' first marriages, there was no fixed rule concerning subsequent marriages. While a rich farmer would finance the subsequent marriages, a gandu head of restricted means was only expected to make a contribution. Thirdly, while year-round feeding of married subordinates and their wives and children was the ideal, in practice it was impossible for poorer gandu heads to meet this commitment. It was normal for married subordinates to help feed the joint household from their own plots and off-farm earnings.

Some married men remained in gandu as long as the head lived. Sometimes older married sons left paternal gandaye by mutual consent when they saw that their fathers had a sufficient workforce of younger sons. Sometimes a father amicably dismissed his older married sons to make their way with whatever gayauni and small parting gifts of land he was able to provide, because the strain on his resources of a large joint unit was too great. Very seldom did a married son leave gandu against his father's wish.

Twenty-nine of 108 household heads (27 per cent) used the labour of married male dependents – i.e., they were heads of 'gandu' conventionally so called. The low percentage is easily explained. Few farmers had living fathers, because of the early age at which most men die; and a high proportion of farmers had no adult sons.

Four kinds of gandu were discernible. Twenty-two farmers used the labour of married sons. Four used the labour of married junior brothers. Two had under their authority more distantly related junior kinsmen (a 'kin' gandu). One used the labour of a married son, a married brother and a more distantly related married kinsman (a 'composite' gandu). Of the seven gandaye which were not paternal, six were durable over many years. That 20 per cent of gandaye joined married men apart from fathers and sons in a long-term labour relationship shows the institution's flexibility. Ten of the twenty-nine gandaye included unmarried male dependents. In eight, unmarried sons or brothers made at least as great a labour contribution as married male dependents (Appendix 6, Table 4).

Three cases vividly illustrate the flexibility of gandu. HH 16 was a part-time grain trader with 12.6 acres. His two oldest sons had left gandu and become successful farmers and traders. They provided him with free ploughing services. He farmed with two married and three unmarried sons. During the dry season, the oldest son in gandu often took his place on long-distance trade journeys.

HH 32 farmed 8.5 acres with two married sons. He had no off-farm occupation. In 1977, he and his sons had to spend much time as hired labourers. The sons each gave him N1 for every long morning of hired labour performed in lieu of work on the gandu farms. Since his holding was quite large, their hired labouring prevented him from weeding it adequately. Yields dropped severely.

In 1978, his sons developed year-round off-farm occupations – one, as the hamlet's only bread seller; the other, as a motor boy. Instead of performing hired labour, they each gave him N1 every day from their off-farm earnings. At the same time, they continued farming with him. Yields improved. Whereas in 1977, the holding had yielded 12 sacks of maize, 13 bundles of guineacorn and a tiny amount of cotton, in 1978, it yielded 112 bundles of guineacorn, 8 sacks of sweet potatoes and a small amount of maize eaten by the family.

The case of HH 32 is significant. Strictly, the sons would only have been expected to either provide the equivalent of a long morning's wages or farm with the father during the weekly period of labour obligation. In 1978 these sons did both. Furthermore, the case shows how sons can be tied to the father by a sense of loyalty and mutual interest that transcends the weekly labour obligation.

HH 43 was a frequent farm labourer and a migrant labourer in the dry season. He had 6.3 acres and a household of twelve. He farmed with two sons, one of them married, and they fed as a single unit throughout the year. His married son was a hard-working farm and general labourer who had acquired a pledged field in addition to those given him by his father. He gave freely of the grain from his own fields. HH 43 was also given free ploughing by the husband of his niece. He was able to maintain the viability of his household through work as a labourer, the hard work and helpfulness of his married son, free ploughing from his kinsman and credit from his patron, repaid out of harvest earnings.[5]

In conclusion, we can see that gandu is an institution – an established set of practices based on ideas of mutual obligation. The institution is extensive, in that the obligations cover a wide range of social activity. It is flexible, allowing of variation in practice. And it defines a voluntary labour relationship. The mutual obligations continue only for as long as married men accept it.

We ought to distinguish between the 'contractual' and 'cooperative' aspects of gandu. Too much focus on structural features like paternal authority (e.g., Hill 1972: 43–46) or behavioural patterns like the 'name-avoidance and shame' which first-born sons display toward their fathers (e.g., Smith 1955: 43–44), can obscure the strong loyalty or affection which may link fathers and sons. In the light of this feeling, and the broader matrix of cooperation between kin in which the institution is embedded, we can visualize more clearly the outlook of many Muslims. They see themselves as building multipurpose family enterprises. Subordinate adult males tend to share the aspirations of their superiors for a mutual form of security and success in farm and off-farm enterprise. Thus, any discussion of the social relations of production and exchange which define 'family farming' should go beyond the internal characteristics of the farming unit. It should explore the broader framework of economic cooperation between adults closely related by kinship or marriage. In these wider terms, the family remains central to a society wherein hired labour has spread rapidly.

The Incidence of Gandu

There was a high incidence of paternal gandu in relation to the potential (Table 4.11). Thirty of thirty-nine resident married sons (77 per cent) were in gandu with their fathers in 1978. Of the nine resident

Table 4.11. The incidence of gandu, Marmara, 1978

*1Decile	Acreage Range	Gandaye totals: Paternal/composite gandaye	Gandaye totals: Fraternal/kin gandaye	Gandaye totals: Percentage incidence of gandu	Married sons: Total	Married sons: In gandu	Gandu heads: Mean age
I.	49.9–16.3	6	3	82%	8	7/ 87%	52
II.	14.4–11.6	4	1	45%	7	5/ 71%	54
III.	11.5–8.3	3	0	27%	8	5/ 62%	56
IV.	7.7–6.2	4	0	45%	7	5/ 71%	56
V.	6.0–4.0	1	1	18%	2	2/100%	55
VI.	3.9–3.2	2	1	27%	2	2/100%	57
VII.	3.1–2.6	1	0	9%	2	2/100%	(70)
VIII.	2.5–2.0	1	0	9%	1	1/100%	(55)
IX.	2.0–1.1	1	0	9%	5	1/ 20%	(60)
X.	1.1–0.5	0	0	0%	–	–	–
Totals:		23	6	27%	42	30/71%	55

*1 There are 11 farmers in Deciles I–X and 9 in Decile X.

married sons no longer in gandu, two were given permanent off-farm employment as drivers of their fathers' buses.

Two had left their father with five adult dependent workers, and had gone on to establish successful independent households. Two (the elder sons of HH 35) had left their father with several adult dependent workers and established successful households of their own, at a stage when the father's family size in relation to farming resources made their support no longer possible. Three left because of the poverty of their fathers.

Only three married sons of living fathers had emigrated. The two older sons of HH 24 may be said to have emigrated because of the 'relative success' of the father. For his gradually acquired acreage (11.2, excluding gayauna) and family size (fourteen) were much above the hamlet means (8 acres, seven persons). But gradually his family size had outstripped his economic capacity, so that the two eldest sons found urban employment, leaving him with the labour of one married and one unmarried son. The one married son of HH 94 found urban employment because of the poverty of his father.

More interesting than the incidence of paternal gandu in relation to the potential, was the variation in incidence through the landholding scale (Table 4.11). Among the bottom two deciles the incidence in relation to the potential was 1 out of 5. Poverty had forced the married sons of two fathers to seek work outside gandu. In deciles VIII through V the incidence in relation to the potential was 100 per cent. In the top four deciles, 73 per cent of married sons farmed under their fathers. All but the poorest household heads farmed with the assistance of all their married sons. The institution was strong through most of the landholding scale.

Though the incidence of gandu in relation to the potential was higher in the lower and middle deciles, the absolute incidence was highest in deciles I to IV (Table 4.11). 60 per cent of Large Farmers were gandu heads, in contrast 29 per cent of Middle Farmers and 12 per cent of Small Farmers headed gandaye. The concentration of gandaye among larger farmers reflected differences in age among household heads, and the process whereby wives and children were accumulated along with landholdings (Table 3.19).

Polly Hill has drawn a distinction between strong and weak gandaye, to the extent that a quarter of the gandaye in Batagawara were so weak because of poverty, that neither fathers nor sons could 'effectively exert their rights or meet their obligations' (Hill 1972: 46). Chart 4.3 lists the gandu heads in Marmara who were Small Farmers. Most were 'viable': i.e., they could meet household expenses without transferring land or going into debt. Off-farm skills were crucial to their viability. Also, one head hired out his sons as a large work team to generate considerable income. Thus, the viability of the gandu could actually be increased by hired labouring.

Farming for the Family versus Labouring for Others

An important question is raised by cases of gandaye hiring out their labour: do their own holdings suffer? Planting is done rapidly. Harvesting can be performed in a leisurely fashion. But timely weeding in June and July is essential to achieve normal yields by hamlet standards.[6] If hiring out dependents leaves the gandu inadequate labour-time to complete two weedings in these months, then its yields will fall. If yields fall, it is likely to become more economically dependent on employers. If the gandu becomes more dependent on the employers of its dependents, then the *substance* of production relations based on the family is undergoing critical change, even if the outward *forms* appear stable.

In Marmara, eleven household heads frequently hired out the labour of their adult dependents in 1978 (Table 4.7). Since there were

Chart 4.3. Likely financial position in 1978 of gandu heads among Small Farmers, Marmara

	Family size	Acreage per person	Adult family workers[*1]	OBSERVATIONS Off-farm work
HH 50	11	0.4	2	Chief of motor-park. This post provided him with commissions on all passengers and trucks loaded at Marmara. **Financial: Surplus**
HH 56	8	0.5	2	Shop keeper, tailor, smuggler. Had two lucrative sugar cane *fadama*. Married fourth wife in 1978. **Financial: Surplus**
HH 62	9	0.4	2	Mallam, school teacher. The most respected Qur'anic commentator (*mai tafsiri*). Drew salary as primary teacher. (Lent money in farming period of 1979.) **Financial: Balance**
HH 64	10	0.3	4	Roofmaker, labourer. He and his three sons earned good money as a team of farm labourers. Incurred expenses of oldest son's second marriage in 1978. **Financial: Moderate deficit**
HH 74	10	0.3	3[*2]	Hides trader, sugar cane retailer. His three sons were kerosene retailer, dry season migrant labour and butcher respectively. They were also farm labourers. **Financial: Balance**
HH 82	13	0.2	2	Professional Lagos beggar. He had lost his arm in a fight. He used his earnings as a beggar to marry his second wife and pay for his son's two marriages. **Financial: Moderate deficit**
HH 95	6	0.2	2	General and farm labourer. He and his son were general and farm labourers. **Financial: *n.k.***

*1 Includes the gandu head. *2 The gandu head was retired from farming.

many combinations of work-time spent on family and employers' farms, I consider each individual case (Chart 4.4). Only one of them is likely to have experienced 'requirement conflict' – between the time required on employers' fields to generate household income and the time required to adequately weed family farms. Underlying the variety of circumstances, we can analyse these farmers into two broad groups. Group 1 had large holdings in relation to the family workforce

Chart 4.4. Likely 'requirement conflict' among household heads in the weeding period, Marmara, 1978

Farmer	Age	Acres	Workers	Notes	Conflict likely:
1. **HH 35**	65	7.4	**2**	Very strong, he worked on his own fields. He and his sons gave his holding priority. He had achieved high yields in 1977 (Appendix 2, Table 1).	**No**
2. **HH 36**	45	7.4	**1**	He hired out his own labour on afternoons only. He hired out his son on 2–3 long mornings per week during weeding.	**No**
3. **HH 43**	60	6.3	**2**	He and his sons were frequent labourers. His own weeding of his fields was confined to afternoons.	**Yes**
4. **HH 64**	60	3.3	**3**	Both he and his sons were frequent labourers. But his acreage was small in relation to the family workforce.	**No**
5. **HH 66**	40	3.2	**1**	He himself was not a frequent labourer. Had time to weed his acreage on long mornings.	**No**
6. **HH 74**	70	2.7	**3**	He was a retired farmer. His sons were frequent labourers. But his acreage was small in relation to the family workforce.	**No**
7. **HH 80**	45	2.5	**1**	He gave his own holding priority on long mornings, hiring out his labour on afternoons. Son hired out most long mornings.	**No**
8. **HH 82**	55	2.3	**1**	He himself was not a frequent labourer. His son laboured frequently, and weeded his holding on afternoons.	**No**
9. **HH 83**	30	2.3	**1**	He himself was not a frequent labourer. His junior brother laboured frequently.	**No**
10. **HH 95**	60	1.4	**1**	Both he and his sons were frequent labourers. His acreage was tiny in relation to the family workforce.	**No**
11. **HH 98**	55	1.3	**1**	Both he and his son were frequent labourers. His acreage was tiny in relation to the family workforce.	**No**

– the first three farmers and HH 66. Group 2 had small holdings in relation to their workforce. Only Group 1 farmers would have been likely to experience conflict between time required for hired labour and time required to weed family holdings. But this was precisely the group who gave their own holdings priority. Hence the small proportion of labouring households falling into the 'low-yield trap' – not having the time to adequately weed their own farms.

These findings agree with those of Polly Hill. She organized two surveys in Batagawara, one of forty employers and one of eighteen known labourers. She concluded: 'The work of the regular labourers was seldom undertaken at the expense of their own, or their father's, farming' (Hill 1972: 108, 112, 117–18, 121).

HH 32, whom I used to demonstrate the flexibility of gandu arrangements toward the start of this section, is also an instructive case. Because his holding was large in relation to the family workforce, he did fall into the low-yield trap when he hired out his sons' labour in 1977. But in 1978, his sons developed remunerative off-farm jobs which removed the need for hired labouring. Thus, it is unwise to infer from 'requirement conflict' to a necessary cycle of impoverishment.

We have seen how the hired labour force is structured between a small core of client labourers and the majority of frequent and occasional labourers. But it would be mistaken to assume that client labourers are locked into long-term dependence on their employers. At least in one case, HH 66, the client labourer had developed tailoring as an off-farm occupation while still in his master's house, and he eventually became independent. In summary, the evidence from Marmara points away from the 'low yield trap' and a cycle of impoverishment: most labouring households had such small holdings that hired labour was actually a source of net additional income.

Gandu among Muslims and Maguzawa

The conversion of indigenous households to Islam, and the gradual influx of Muslim immigrants from Kano Emirate, have profoundly altered gandu. A comparison of Maguzawa with Muslim gandaye clarifies three interrelated changes – in religion, family farming and the growth of production using hired labour.

Writing about a Maguzawa area ten miles from Marmara, Last explains that the replacement of typically Maguzawa cultural habits with Muslim ones is a matter of several years (Last 1979: 243). In 1976–79, Islamic belief had prevailed in Marmara for almost twenty years. There was thus a perspective from which to view the cumulative effects of conversion on production systems.

The pattern of reciprocal obligations in Maguzawa gandaye was profoundly different from that among the Muslims. The first difference was the relative freedom of working dependents from the household head. Maguzawa gandu heads used the labour of wives, male dependents and dependents' wives for only three long mornings of the week. In return, these were free to cultivate the gayauni which had been given them, or their personally acquired holdings, for four days. The wives of the gandu head had greater freedom than the wives of male dependents. Whereas the gandu head's wives farmed their own holdings four days of the week, the wives of male dependents farmed their own holdings for one day and worked for their husbands three long mornings. The second difference was the special relationship linking wives of the gandu head with their married sons. They would often form a common granary from their gayauni. And mothers would purchase land for their sons, which was the sons' independent property.

The third difference was the close linkage between the household granary and family food provisioning. Gandu granaries were opened at the start of the farming period and closed between the millet and guineacorn harvests. During the farming period, some heads fed their dependents twice, other three times, a day from these granaries. At harvest, the head would give each of his wives and the wives of his male dependents three to four bundles of guineacorn (roughly equivalent to a sack in weight) which they would mix with the produce in their personal granaries. Then for six months, the wives of the head would feed him and his unmarried dependents from their own supplies, while the dependent married men, their wives and children would live off their gayauni. From the sale of gandu produce, the head paid the marriage and naming ceremony expenses of all dependents, and the head tax of adult males. Gandu grain was also sold to wives who brewed and sold beer.

Behind the hamlet lay an active Maguzawa culture. I spent much time drinking beer in a Maguzawa 'big house' three miles from Marmara. I rented a field from a gandu head, Sarkin Noma, and farmed it with the hired labour of his sons. Sarkin Noma was the matrilateral parallel cousin of HH 1 of Marmara. So it is possible to compare two closely related men – the one, a big Maguzawa farmer, implacably hostile to conversion; the other, Marmara's largest landholder, who had become a Muslim and made the pilgrimage to Mecca.

Sarkin Noma supervized a family workforce of 27 persons. The gandu assembled on three long mornings of the week. It included his

4 wives, 11 adult male dependents and their 12 wives. Three close kin of the gandu head, including his oldest son, had separated from the gandu.[7]

Over time, Sarkin Noma had acquired a composite gandu workforce, a large landholding, a herd of cattle, small livestock, three oxen and a plough. Lacking contacts in the local government or FADP, his fertilizer purchases were limited. He had specialized in farming. He had developed little influence beyond the Maguzawa hinterland in which was his own 'big house'. In contrast, HH 1 had been a grain trader for many years, before shifting his investment from trade to transport. Over time, he had developed one of the two largest gandaye among Marmara Muslims, a landholding of 50 acres, a herd of cattle, six oxen and three ploughs. He employed considerable supplementary hired labour. Moreover, he had developed contacts in the local bank, in the FADP and, through his brother, a successful farmer-trader who had moved to Malumfashi town, he had urban commercial contacts. In 1978, he obtained 100 bags of fertilizer from the FADP. In 1979, he received a bank loan to buy the first tractor in Yaba village area.

The contrast between these men, both highly successful in their separate cultural worlds, exemplifies the economic changes resulting from conversion to Islam. As Last demonstrates, beyond a certain level of commercial turnover, it is very difficult for a farmer to operate as a trader unless he converts to Islam. For Islam is the passport to larger trading networks and urban and political contacts (Last 1979: 240–42). Despite his success in long-term wealth acquisition, Sarkin Noma was confined by religious belief and cultural practice to a rural world. In contrast, HH 1 had many lines to the urban world of Islam, commerce and (to a lesser extent) of government.

Working three long mornings of the week, twenty-seven persons in gandu with Sarkin Noma provided him with the rough equivalent of a thirteen-man family workforce among Muslims working on six long mornings of the week. HH 1 headed a six-man workforce. Unlike Sarkin Noma, he needed to employ supplementary hired labour.

Sarkin Noma's oldest son had left gandu, acquired land, a team of oxen and a plough, and become a bicycle repairman. Sarkin Noma's third son, in gandu with him, was a moneylender and had become a seller of cooked fish. He had purchased or received as pledge seven fields. He had bought an ox which he added to his father's three, and used his father's ploughing services free of charge.

In comparison, HH 1's oldest son drove his father's bus, his second son the tractor. HH 1's two married sons in gandu had land, but smaller than the holding of Sarkin Noma's third son. They lived a more prestigious life, were better dressed than Sarkin Noma's sons, but had less real wealth and independence.

Using these case studies, let us compare the economic processes of Maguzawa and Muslim rural culture. In both cultures, we can distinguish between those who are and are not engaged in long-term wealth acquisition. Among the former, we can further distinguish between the *bases*, the *form* and the *focal point* of wealth acquisition. There are three *bases* to wealth acquisition among the Maguzawa:

1. Younger men still in gandu can use the six-month food-provision guarantee, the right to marriage expense out of gandu proceeds, and any surpluses which they produce during the four days of the week when they are free, as a basis for wealth acquisition. Depending on their intelligence and skill, and the prior success of their gandu head's enterprise, they are poised to accumulate land and, through marriage and procreation, family labour.
2. Once they become independent, their long-term prospects benefit from the fact that the claim of their subordinates on gandu food is limited to the farming period.
3. Through the exchange of gandu produce for the money and goods required in bridewealth, they will expand their female workforce and, through any offspring, their total workforce. However, the *form* of wealth acquisition remains narrow – agriculture, livestock and short-distance trade (Last 1979: 241). The *focal point* of wealth acquisition is the expansion of the household.

The rural Muslim engaged in wealth acquisition cannot use female labour in weeding or the heavy work of harvesting. If he is a dependent, he has less labour-time free from his gandu head than do the corresponding Maguzawa. If independent, he is committed to providing his household with food throughout the year. So there are three bases to wealth acquisition among Muslims:

1. By trading or through other off-farm activity, he earns the money to hire additional labour.
2. In the short term, he employs hired labour in lieu of female labour.
3. In the long term, he uses income to contract additional marriages and expand the number of his male dependents. Through

> religion, he has access to trading networks, and to urban as well as rural commercial contacts. Thus, the form of wealth acquisition is wide.

The rural Muslim is competing with other wealth acquirers for land and hired labour. He is confronted with a supply of hired labour which is variable, uncertain and limited by an in-built tendency to move out of labouring and into skilled off-farm occupations. Therefore, he is concerned to expand his family workforce through marriage and procreation. While the *bases* and *form* of wealth acquisition among Maguzawa and Muslims differ, the *focal point* remains the same – the expansion of the household. (HH 1 had the largest household as well as the largest gandu in Marmara.) Maguzawa culture and Muslim religious discourse both gave high value to big families and family responsibilities. The prestige which Muslims accorded polygyny itself created a tendency for the number of children to rise with the increasing age of the household head (Table 3.19).

Let us now compare the two cultures with respect to those who are not engaged in long-term wealth acquisition. Among Maguzawa, the gandu head's obligation to feed his household is limited to the farming period; in contrast, Muslim household heads are involved in a year-round commitment – and without the assistance of women's labour. Hence, there is much stronger pressure on Muslims to develop an off-farm occupation.[8]

We come to a misconception – that as a result of Muslim conversion, abstinence from beer unleashes a 'hidden surplus' of grain for long-term wealth acquisition. Some Maguzawa have this notion, and it can be part of the reasoning which leads a man to convert. A Maguzawa farmer told me: 'People *yin Sallah* (convert) because of money. One who drinks cannot save money.' As beer exchange is at the centre of their social life, it reinforces their generosity and sense of extended social obligation. To that extent, it does detract from wealth acquisition. Nevertheless, a man who converts and foregoes the expense of beer also foregoes the labour of his wives and their contribution to family food supply. While conversion may turn some beer into capital, most grain previously reserved for beer is probably turned into family food. For the majority of farmers not engaged in wealth acquisition, the main economic effect of conversion must be the development of an off-farm occupation (sana'a) to compensate for the loss of women's labour and food supply.

The spread of hired labour does not signify the breakdown of the household as the basis and focal point of production. Nor is it solely the result of increasing commodity exchange. In southern Katsina, it is as much a response to Islam.

A Comparison of Gandu in Marmara with Gandu in Other Areas

Before concluding, we ought to relate this account to the findings from other village studies. Since the late colonial period, several have measured the incidence of gandu. There is no sign of a tendency for its absolute incidence to decline (Table 4.12). A few have also measured the incidence of paternal gandu in relation to the potential. These showed that most married sons continued to farm with their fathers (Table 4.13).

All writers on Muslim gandaye have found that most were paternal. In northern Zaria, Smith found broad variations in their organization. The 'ideal' paternal gandu corresponded in respects to the practices in Marmara. However, six long mornings of work in gandu was the norm – in contrast to a range of four to six long mornings in Marmara

Table 4.12. The incidence of gandu in villages studied in Hausaland

	Year:	Gandaye:*6	Farm units:	Per cent:
*1 Northern Zaria	1950	15	59	25%
*2 Northern Katsina	1967	48	171	28%
*3 Northern Soroto	1967			17%
*4 Northern Zaria	1970			24%
*5 Southern Katsina	1979	29	108	27%

*1 Smith 1955: 20 *2 Hill 1972: 45 *3 Goddard 1973: 213 *4 Buntjer 1970a *5 Clough, above. *6 All types.

Table 4.13. Married sons in paternal gandu in Hausa villages studied

Year:	1967	1971	1979
Area:	*1 Northern Katsina	*2 Central Kano	*3 Southern Katsina
Resident married sons:	69	95	39
Married sons in gandu:	59	75	30
Per cent:	85%	79%	77%

*1 Hill 1972: 45 *2 Hill 1977: 140 *3 Clough, above.

(Smith 1955: 20). In northern Katsina, Hill found a similar pattern to Marmara. But whereas in Marmara fathers normally fed sons in gandu twice a day throughout the year, in Batagawara fathers were obliged to their married dependents for only the evening meal. As in Marmara, sons in gandu helped their fathers with grain (Hill 1972: 43–45, 50).

In northwestern Hausaland, Goddard found different processes at work. He surveyed three villages in the Sokoto Closely Settled Zone in 1967. The absolute incidence of gandu was considerably lower than in the other areas studied (Table 4.14). Moreover, Goddard distinguished three functional types:

1. the 'complete' gandu, in which the mutual obligations were similar to those found in Zaria and Katsina;
2. the 'land' gandu, in which married subordinates paid their own tax, although otherwise obligations were as in the 'complete' gandu;
3. the 'cooperative' gandu, in which the individual members controlled their respective shares of the land and provided their own food and tax payments, though they continued to farm together.

Under all three types, the gandu head 'contributed' to the expenses of childbirth and naming, and was responsible for financing the first marriages of younger men. In the three villages, only 18 per cent of gandaye were 'complete', 37 per cent were of the 'land' type and 45 per cent were merely 'cooperative'. Thus, the 'strength' of gandu had declined (Goddard 1973: 214–15).

Table 4.14. Iyalai in paternal gandu, Sokoto Closely Settled Zone, 1967

Village type	Iyalai in paternal gadu (as a percent of the total possible)	Type of gandu: complete/land	Co-operative
1. Riverine	81%	48%	52%
2. Accessible	74%	63%	37%
3. Remote	48%	73%	27%
Average	74%	55%	45%

Iyali, pl. Iyalai: the conjugal family, comprising a man, his wife or wives and children.
Source: Goddard 1973: Tables III and IV.

Goddard explained the low incidence of gandu by the particular circumstances of northern Sokoto. Before the colonial conquest, it was the centre of the caliphate, and so tribute and population flowed into it. After the conquest, Sokoto was thrown back on its own limited resources and became relatively remote and inaccessible, bypassed by the railway to the southeast. Inaccessibility has been an important factor inhibiting the development of cash crop farming, particularly of groundnuts and cotton (Goddard 1973: 216). This combination of high population density and declining agricultural opportunities led men to seek income from seasonal labour and off-farm occupations. The incidence of gandu had consequently declined.

Goddard's attempt to explain the shift from 'complete' to 'cooperative' gandu was less successful. The three villages had been chosen according to the criteria of accessibility to markets and to riverine land capable of cultivation in the dry season. Arranged in terms of decreasing market accessibility and riverine acreage, Goddard argued that both the incidence and the very 'strength' of gandu declined. In fact, his data shows that as riverine land and access to markets decreased, the incidence of gandu declined, but the 'strength' of gandu actually rose (Table 4.14). Only at a general level was Goddard clear: compared with the other areas, the Sokoto villages were weakly integrated in lucrative produce markets, and so both the incidence and functions of gandu had declined as men sought income outside of the gandu framework.

Goddard was of the opinion that rising population density and the 'spread of monetary economy' increased tension between members of the gandu and undermined the authority of the gandu head (Goddard 1973: 215–16). On the 'spread of monetary economy', his position was oddly contradictory, since his own comparisons showed that in regions where there was more market income from farming, the incidence of gandu was higher (Goddard 1973: 216). His views on rising population density have been undermined by the more recent research of Hill and Ross in the Closely Settled Zone near Kano city, with densities as high or higher than those which he had surveyed (Table 3.5).

Hill found that in Dorayi, few married sons left gandu. Fathers were reluctant to release married sons from gandu and seldom granted them gayauna. The 'abnormally close economic relationship between fathers and sons' (Hill 1977: 84) stemmed from extreme land scarcity in an area where the mean holding was 2.2 acres. Sons seldom migrated, because they lacked the resources to set up elsewhere. Also, their propensity to emigrate was limited because they were under great pressure to provide for ageing fathers (1977: 143–45).

Though Paul Ross was primarily interested in the nature of land transfers in his village, he provides insights into economic relationships between fathers, sons and other kin. Population density has been rising since the nineteenth century, when the area was a 'farming, marketing, and manufacturing centre' (Ross 1987: 225). This has had direct effects on gandu. In other areas, married sons may establish independent households with land given by their fathers. However, in Hurumi fathers were not required to grant land to sons if this jeopardized their land base (1987: 232). Married dependents' control over gayauni was highly restricted: they were obliged to hand over to the household head all grains and a portion of the legumes (1987: 231).

Fraternal units of production and consumption (Ross nowhere refers to gandu) were much more common than in other areas studied. After the death of the father, a senior brother continued to organize production – though with restricted authority, since his juniors also had claims on the inherited land. Nevertheless, junior brothers commonly delayed 'actualization of such claims', and used their legal claim on a portion of the land as leverage to assure 'continued support for life-cycle events, sponsorship of non-farm occupations, and the like' (1987: 232).

Women have been very active in asserting their claims to land under Maliki law as daughters or sisters of deceased owners. In consequence, they owned 21 per cent of land in 1975 and were the largest group offering temporary use rights. Ross comments that 'the emergence of female land ownership, to the extent that it fosters closer ties between off-spring and their mothers, is likely to strengthen the ties between full siblings' (1987: 242). Indeed, the trend in 1975 was for each son to receive his share on the father's death, and then full siblings recombined all of their allotments under the leadership of one of their number (1987: 234). Women who were related as full siblings then directed their land claims to the leader. Women's participation in land claims is an incentive for full brothers to farm together, making use of their sisters' portions while providing for their sisters' needs.

In chapter 3, we observed the flexibility of institutions governing land transfers in response to rising population density in Marmara. The research of Hill and Ross suggests that family labour also responds flexibly to increasing population pressure. But the essential reciprocity of gandu remains, whereby married dependents provide labour in return for the provision of an array of socially defined subsistence needs. And since gandu heads are less willing to part with land as it becomes more scarce, the incidence of gandu in relation to its potential is likely to rise.

Ross's outstanding study also shows how changes in land and labour institutions are interconnected. As women assert their legal land claims, full brothers are more willing to farm collectively after the death of their fathers in order to enjoy use rights over the land of mothers and full sisters. As I argued earlier, institutions of family farming must be understood in terms of the broader matrix of transfers between close kin.

The notion of 'custom' helps us understand how communities modify their institutions for the transfer of land and labour power. 'Custom' signifies the accretion of past wisdom and social habit. It also signifies the community's sense of a total and changing social reality. The customary is not a rigid set of ideas and practices which snaps under pressure. It is rather a 'consensus of practical knowledge' which enables individuals to revise their practices in virtue of their membership of particular communities. 'Custom' is the community's self-knowledge expressed in action. It is social praxis.

More deeply, 'custom' refers to the moral transfers between people – to the ways in which they negotiate in their minds and actions the claims of obligation which they make upon each other. In northern and southern Katsina, a similar balance prevailed in the obligations linking gandu heads and their subordinates. Near Kano city, the nature of mutual obligations had changed in response to rising land scarcity. Fathers persisted 'in clinging on to all their sons even when they themselves are landless and unable to provide them with farming work' (Hill 1977: 138). Few married sons migrated. Of those who did, 37 per cent 'vanished overnight, never to be seen again' (1977: 143). Hill's vivid description of 'disappearance' is a telling account of the effect of communally sanctioned ideas of moral obligation on individual behaviour:

> The young men who disappear under cover of night . . . are commonly known as *'yan duniya* (lit. 'children of the world' . . .) and are spoken as having adopted the world as their mother. The *dan duniya* may threaten departure . . . but more often no prior hint is given of an act which might even be un-premeditated. The relatives are aghast and humiliated . . . Great efforts are sometimes made to trace the migrant, and it is not unknown for his sons or brothers to vanish likewise in the course of their search. The hostile act of vanishing may be directed against the community at large rather than close kin . . . So much shame and misery attaches to these departures, which are often seen as inexplicable in terms of what is known of the humdrum circumstances of the case, that witchcraft is sometimes invoked as an explanation. (Hill 1977: 143–44)

Clearly, sons were so imbued by community consensus with a strong sense of obligation to provide for near-landless fathers, that migration often took the form of disappearance.

I have stressed the complexity of factors which influence land and labour institutions. This very complexity helps explain the personal adaptability and institutional flexibility of rural Hausa people. Their flexibility is further clarified if we view rural people as members of communities which collectively revise their 'custom' in the light of changing circumstances. A discernible moral unity gives coherence to variable patterns: the group of closely related kin, though variously defined, is the focal point for meeting human social needs through the cooperative adjustment of land entitlements and labour relationships.

Conclusions

This chapter has been concerned with interconnections between two forms of production – that characterized by the frequent use of hired labour, and that reliant on family labour. The wider aim behind this analysis has been a clearer understanding of the processes of individual enrichment in Marmara. I have continued to use the term 'long-term wealth acquisition' introduced in the previous chapter. I have found this term more appropriate than 'accumulation', because it can be easily related to a wide array of evidence, whereas 'accumulation' has become an analytic term with more general meanings. I have confined my own use of 'accumulation' to the augmentation by rural people of specific assets which can yield an increase, for example, land.

The processes of long-term wealth acquisition around Marmara are not timeless, sui generis features of local culture. They have changed as part of the broader changes in Hausa history. Islamic conversion and the development of communications have been central. Long-term wealth acquisition is now based on the two-generational male family workforce, participation in Muslim trading networks, and the use of earnings from farm and off-farm activity to expand landholdings and the employment of hired labour. Most frequent employers in Marmara were engaged in long-term wealth acquisition. But because earnings flowed partly into the enlargement of their households and family workforces, reliance on hired labour tended to diminish with increasing age. In Marmara, the acreage used by frequent employers was balanced between those who used hired labour as the primary source of labour (19 per cent of hamlet land) and those who used it to supplement their family workforces (21 per cent of hamlet land).

An intermediate group comprised young entrepreneurs without family workforces (10 per cent of hamlet land). They would divide with increasing age between the two main groups of employer.

In Marmara, the tendency for farmers to acquire, with increasing age, a skilled off-farm occupation, resulted in a youthful hired labour force. Most household heads were reluctant to release their male dependents for work as frequent labourers. Consequently, occasional labourers were the largest single element in the hired labour force. Frequent labourers – whether local farmers or seasonal migrants – were in short and fluctuating supply relative to the demand for them. In consequence, piece rates were rising in real terms from 1977 to 1985. In other words, employers were not just competing with each other for a reliable labour force. They were also competing with the tendency among all farmers to look for a skilled off-farm occupation – and the peripatetic tendency among young labourers to seek the most remunerative labouring opportunities in a national labour market.

The institutions of family farming were centred on, but not limited to, gandu. Gandu itself was part of a wider web of transfers between closely related kin. The actual incidence of gandu in relation to the potential was high except among farmers with less than two acres. It was highest among a broad range of Small and Middle Farmers with two to six acres. The withdrawal of women from a major role in food supply after conversion to Islam had increased the necessity of off-farm occupations. It had also increased the labour obligation of subordinate males in gandu. This intensified their economic dependence on gandu heads. Thus, conversion had accentuated the tendency of household heads and their male subordinates to think and act in terms of *multipurpose family enterprises*.

The preference of farmers for a skilled off-farm occupation, the existence of alternative opportunities, complementary with family farming, in a national labour market and the strength and flexibility of family farming institutions – these factors have placed hired labourers in a strong bargaining position. They have also affected the evolution of production relations. Firstly, the rising cost of hired labour has reinforced the high value placed on the enlargement of the family workforce through marriage and procreation, and secondly, employers seek out client labourers to whom they are bound by personal ties of reciprocal obligation. The organization of the workforce can be visualized as a series of concentric circles moving outward from the family farming unit: family labour, client labour, migrant labourers, local frequent labourers and most numerous of all, occasional labourers – especially unmarried boys.

In Marmara, hired labour had developed within a web of flexible production arrangements marked by three kinds of complementarity – between family farming and hired labouring; between production in the area and production in other ecological zones; between farming and off-farm occupations. The growth of hired labour reflects the development of a new form of production – but this form is compelled to adjust to the availabilities of labour provided by family-based production. As a result, the hired labour force is heterogeneous. Indeed, 'hired labour' is itself a heterogeneous concept in an economy marked by widespread land ownership. In Marmara, hired labouring provided additional income to most households who performed it. By increasing their viability, it reduced their need to sell land or go heavily into debt.

A comparison of gandu in central Hausaland and in Sokoto suggests that the impact of market economy on production relations will vary sharply with the nature of market integration. That impact will depend especially on the geographical situation of the locality, and its communications with the national centres of the market economy. Where an area is geographically remote and bypassed by rail or roads (e.g., rural northern Sokoto), production for the market is difficult and outward labour migration results. This tends to undermine the strength of cooperative production arrangements. In contrast, where an area is near market centres, or at least well linked to them (e.g., southern Katsina), producers can expand market output through existing relations of production. Moreover, two-way migration patterns can develop. Labour flows back and forth between ecological zones without undermining household production (Map 3).[9]

This chapter continues the discussion in chapter 3 of historical changes in the modes of organising rural labour. A comparison of writings on recent gandu with work on earlier periods suggests a further theme. Admittedly speculative, it is too exciting to be ignored. Through wars, jihad, colonial invasion and the insertion of Hausaland in the world market, the abolition of slave labour, population growth, Nigerian independence and the parade of regimes – changes at all levels of society – a certain idea of the subordinate worker has endured in the countryside. His labour ought to be requited with the goods needed for his continuation as a social person – land (where possible), food for himself and his family (at least in the farming season and often throughout the year), the payment of his marriage and naming ceremony expenses and dues to the political overlords. Moral obligations link master and labourer. Particular pressures at particular times and places lead to particular adjustments. But the core concept of moral reciprocity remains.

We can see this theme at work in the treatment of hired labourers as well as subordinates in gandu. When a rural employer approaches a potential labourer, and they bargain over rates of pay and other conditions, they share a certain concept of the person. Through employment, the hired labourer is seeking participation in the processes of rural society. The village employer respects his search because he can hardly do otherwise: they inhabit the same moral world. The bargaining power of hired labourers results not just from demographic determinants and relative supplies and demands. It arises as well from the Hausa view of the status of working persons, fashioned by the long sweep of Hausa history.

When foreign bodies invest in agriculture – be they urban merchants, army officers, or international companies – it might seem that they will not be checked by rural Hausa notions of moral reciprocity. But even large-scale organizations face constraints when they penetrate rural society. Big agricultural investments tend to be made in areas of low population density, where land is abundant, and so they must cope with relative labour scarcity. Equally important, urban investors will be confronting a rural labour force with a distinctive attitude to the rights of working persons.[10] As we saw at the beginning of the chapter, Marmara labourers went on strike and took political action to ensure that a 'foreign' investor fulfilled the terms of the labour agreement negotiated by local chiefs.

In conclusion, the development of hired labour has been integral to the continuance of production relations based on family, kinship and clientage. Two conceptual approaches help clarify the continuity. First, rural persons should be seen as total economic actors in search of income to provision and enlarge their households, not as farmers pure and simple. This approach is historically conditioned, for the widespread search for a sana'a is partly the result of historical change. Secondly, rural communities revise their collective understanding of land entitlements and labour obligations in order to preserve, through changing circumstances, the capacity of close kin to meet household needs.

A determinist approach might argue that as population density rises, a growing percentage of households will have no land. They will be separated from ownership of means of production and transformed into rural proletarians. That view neglects a cardinal fact. Rural people are adaptable and creative, not just as individuals, but also through their institutions and collective consciousness. Hausa agrarian studies can easily neglect this approach, because formal institutions (for example, sarauta power) seem imposed from above. But though their methods of self-determination are informal, communities flourish in rural Hausaland.

Notes

1. In this chapter, 'farmer' always refers to 'household head'.
2. See Appendix 3 for all farmers listed by labour use.
3. I am indebted to Mr Richard Bruce for first pointing out to me the essential importance of off-farm occupations in the rural economy of northern Nigeria, during his fieldwork on the Jos Plateau.
4. See Appendix 1 for a listing of all off-farm occupations of all household heads in the hamlet.
5. For credit, see chapter 5.
6. For typical yields in Marmara, see Appendix 2, Tables 1 and 2.
7. This arrangement was similar to that described by Greenberg in his classic study of Maguzawa in Kano Emirate. Succession to the leadership of the 'patrilineal group' and with it, the headship of the compound, was collateral, descending from older brothers to younger brothers (Greenberg 1946: 17). The cyclical break-up of the gandu, and from it, the emergence of new gandaye, was normal. The gandu assembled on four days of the week, three days being devoted to gayauni. The gandu granaries were used to feed all members during the rainy season; at other times they lived off their gayauni.
8. The distinction between Maguzawa as 'farmers' and Muslims as 'traders or craftsmen' can be pushed too far. Greenberg asserted that 'compared to farming, other economic activities play a minor role in the life of the maguzawa' – but then admitted that they traditionally pursued a variety of dry-season crafts (Greenberg 1946: 19).
9. See Iliffe 1971 (12–17, 26–67, 30–33) for a fascinating study of these processes in Tanzania.
10. On the constraints facing agri-business plantations in Nigeria, see Andrae and Beckman 1987 (48–51, 59–60) and Forrest 1993 (198–200).

Chapter 5

CREDIT RELATIONS AND SOCIAL CONSUMPTION

Introduction

This chapter describes the range of credit practices in Marmara. It is particularly concerned with the terms on which various types of credit are extended. But as in previous chapters, the deeper aim is a better understanding of the range of economic relations between richer and poorer villagers; the patterns of wealth acquisition; most generally, the evolution of production and exchange relations.

Since credit pays for spending, I relate credit to the patterns of expenditure in rural society. I show how different types of credit meet distinct social needs. Types of credit can be described straightforwardly in terms of the practices linking lender and borrower. They can also be analysed as institutions – patterns of behaviour followed by large numbers of people, which they explain and justify in terms of moral rules – commonly accepted notions of the dutiful and the forbidden. This chapter will show that *flexibility* underlies credit institutions.

In two ways, chapters 5 and 7 complement each other. First, both are concerned with money flows between rural people. This chapter focuses on the ways that rural people borrow money to finance basic household expenditures. Chapter 7 concentrates on the ways that they borrow in order to become rich. Secondly, their method of analysis differs from that in previous chapters. Previous chapters combined surveys of the total population, partial surveys and case studies to arrive at conclusions. But this chapter and chapter 7 rely on case studies to argue the existence of general patterns. There were six types of credit, or credit institutions, in Marmara:

1. *Adashi:* a revolving credit association organized by women, in which men also took part. Each member contributed fixed, equal sums weekly or biweekly, and a different member withdrew the total contribution each time, until all members had received their share.
2. *Biki:* a circulation of gifts between two persons, whereby each gave money, grain or cloth at the wedding or naming ceremonies of the other.
3. *Rance:* short-term money credit without interest.
4. *Bashi:* medium-term money credit with interest.
5. *Jali:* a medium-term loan without interest for the purpose of commercial investment. Jali also referred to the money which a person set aside for commercial investment in order to make a profit (*riba*). A person might acquire jali by saving, or setting aside a part of harvest or off-farm earnings. Jali loans were often acquired from senior traders in reward for services (see chapter 7).
6. *Jingina:* the pledging of farm land in return for a sum of money. The receiver enjoyed the use of the land until the money was repaid.

Before relating these credit types to the pattern of household expenditure, let us review the main studies of credit in rural Hausaland.

The Literature on Hausa Credit

There are two detailed studies of credit in Hausaland. Both date from the colonial period. The first, *Hausa Village and Cooperation,* 1937, is a report filed by a colonial touring officer, L.C. Giles (MS in Rhodes House, Oxford University). Giles spent a month visiting villages to the south of Zaria city, where plenty of bush land was available. Giles generalized broadly on the strength of individual examples described in detail. It is certainly the most vivid picture ever written of Hausa rural economy. Its main strengths are that Giles sought to understand credit in terms of the relations between men and women, and the conditions facing people at different times in their annual economic cycle.

> The most important feature in Hausa peasant economy is the position of the wife. She is usually as rich as her husband, often richer. Her finances are separate from his; easy divorce and polygamy emphasize this and help explain it ... Briefly, the wife is responsible for the preparation of food, for firewood, for water: and custom obliges her to help substantially at the marriages of her children, especially at her daughters'. The responsibility for everything else is the husband's. She is free to employ her spare time and all her property to her own profit. (Giles 1937: 21)

Wife-seclusion was 'rare and lax in the villages'. Women often had their own small farms. Most goats and fowl were owned by women (Giles 1937: 21, 23). Spinning was still the most profitable woman's craft. It involved women in a process of investment and savings. Typically, they sold spun cotton or woven cloth to buy grain, which they stored against a price rise, when they sold it to buy livestock or foodstuffs (Giles 1937: 25).

Women provided their husbands with interest-free loans in three situations. First, mothers were responsible for their daughters' dowries. They would also help their sons find the bridewealth for marriage. Secondly, women loaned their husbands money to purchase the 'eternal trinity' of pepper, salt and locust beans (soup ingredients), and at harvest husbands would repay with goats or cloth to the value of the debt. Thirdly, wives loaned their husbands money for tax payment, interest-free if repaid within two or three months (Giles 1937: 27, 28).

The three most common reasons for borrowing among ordinary farmers were lack of food grain, the need for money for their sons' marriages and the need to pay tax: 'For food, and for your son's marriage, you borrow without hesitation or impatience: an unmarried son in the compound is a horse which has not been tethered.' With regard to food grain, the most common credit transaction was grain to be repaid with grain. Women were the chief lenders. Rates of interest were variable. A woman might loan her husband one bundle in return for one; more commonly, wives would give husbands a goat to sell, worth (say) two bundles in the rainy season, and he would repay four to six bundles at harvest (an interest-free loan in money terms, since grain prices had dropped sharply in the meantime). Wives commonly lent grain to other men through their husbands. When the borrower was not a husband, the usual transaction was one bundle in return for two or three at harvest. Where grain was repaid with cash, interest rates also varied: bundles lent when the price was one shilling might be repaid at one shilling and six pence; if lent when the price was two shillings, repaid at three shillings and six pence (Giles 1937: 28, 30–32). In an area where a 'reasonable crop' for an ordinary farmer assisted by a young son was sixty to seventy bundles of guineacorn, millet and maize, some 30–40 per cent of farmers borrowed grain annually – usually five bundles or less (Giles 1937: 16, 31–32).

Merchants and rich farmers were the chief lenders of money for marriage expenses. They commonly gave goods to be repaid with cash. The borrower then sold the article (often at a discount). Again, rates of interest were variable. A gown worth 10 shillings would normally be repaid with 15–30 shillings. The total marriage expense for a poor man's son was in the range of 15–20 shillings; for a 'middle class' farmer's son, 20–40 shillings; for the son of a merchant or rich farmer, 40–60 shillings. The majority of farmers had to borrow for this purpose, the typical loan being around 10 shillings (Giles 1937: 34–35).

The sale of crop futures was common. Women were the main buyers of future grain, at 4d–6d a bundle for harvest delivery, when the price might be 8d. It was normal for farmers to sell unripe sugar cane to merchants and women:

> In fact all these speculations are dangerous ... the price of guineacorn is affected by the state of the markets in the other Provinces; it falls after the cotton is sold, since growers still needing money now have to sell corn; it falls if good early rains bring forward some of the plants which are used to eke out the food supply during the wet season; and falls again when the millet is near. So in 1936 corn hoarders lost their profits when millet was harvested a month early and corn slumped: the most astute moneylender in Zaria bought corn at 8/– and had to resell at 3/6. (Giles 1937: 45)

Firms bought cotton through an advance system. Licensed buyers distributed the advances to middlemen and to farmers, deducting the advances from the value of cotton sold. Some 75 per cent of the advances were in cash, 25 per cent in kind. Licensed buyers failed to recover 10–20 per cent of the advances in the same season, 5–10 per cent were never recovered: 'In the 1935/36 season the "advance" system reached its peak, but the loss by bad debts was so frightening that a good deal less was given this season.' In an area where 'average' cotton output was worth 12 shillings, advances to farmers ranged from 5 to 25 shillings (Giles 1937: 16, 45–48).

The Islamic prohibition of usury did not prevent widespread lending with interest, but it made moneylenders willing to sometimes extend the term of a loan, reduce the interest, forgive part of the debt or give the debtor more time to repay with interest, instead of taking him to court and thereby losing both interest and 10 per cent (court fees) of whatever was recovered (Giles 1937: 71, 72). Giles concluded:

> Broadly, one may say that village life is permeated with small-scale debt – and that it can never become a burden. It is essentially short-term debt, not carried forward from year to year, and the interest is fixed when the loan is taken up, and does not increase month by month ... Everyone borrows, from wife, friends, and moneylenders, usually at heavy interest ... But the peasant can never become seriously embarrassed by debt ... The peasant debtor is saved (1) because local sentiment is all against pressing a debtor hard, (2) by the weakness of Moslem judicial procedure, where the recovery of a debt is concerned ... [D]istraint is permitted, but unheard of; even if the Alkali orders the debtor to pay within (say) a month, his order is difficult to enforce, and will be forgotten unless the creditor re-appears; (3) above all, because there is no land shortage: the wits of the lender would be equal to fastening an injurious contract on land; but who would make a contract with land as its security when the debtor could borrow another farm for a bundle of corn, or clear a new farm for nothing? (1937: 69)

Giles stressed his debt to the local knowledge of A.H.S. Vigo, an agricultural officer. In 1957, Vigo organized a large-scale survey of rural credit during a food crisis (rains had been poor in the previous year).[1] The survey administered a questionnaire to 2,400 farmers.

The report covered four provinces – Katsina, Sokoto, Bauchi and Bornu. Katsina, the country's largest source of cotton and third largest source of groundnuts, was notably more prosperous than the other three provinces. The survey found that 68 per cent of all informants were in debt, ranging from 47 per cent in Katsina to 83 per cent in Bauchi. The average value of loans ranged from £13 in Katsina to £22 in Bauchi. Forty-seven per cent of informants said food was the major purpose of credit, 14 per cent cited payment of farm labour and 13 per cent said ceremonial expenditure. (In Katsina, the proportion in debt for food was only 22 per cent, and the largest proportion was indebted for 'unspecified' reasons – covering expenses for petty trade, local industry, medicine, alms and consumer goods.) Forty-nine per cent of all informants said that traders were the source of their credit, followed by 'relations' (20 per cent of informants) and friends (19 per cent). Most loans were said to attract interest rates of over 90 per cent if repaid with crops and 50–100 per cent if repaid with cash. Because the survey took the form of a questionnaire, there is no way of telling the extent to which loans were repaid.

Vigo also included detailed descriptive material. Most loans were apparently short-term, repayment being due at the groundnut and cotton harvests. The moneylenders were mainly Arab and Nigerian traders who arranged preseason loans of cash or kind in return for harvest groundnuts. They operated through agents who lived in the villages (especially hamlet heads). These were responsible for repayment of all advances. Cash loans, he observed, were advanced at 8–10 shillings in return for one bag of unthreshed groundnuts worth 18–20 shillings, or 25–30 shillings in return for one bag of threshed groundnuts worth 40–50 shillings. Cloth was to be repaid at double its value in cash, salt at slightly less than double. Court action to obtain repayment was unusual. Vigo made no comment on the extent of unrecovered loans.

Giles illustrated the variability of interest rates, and the difficulty of forcing debtors to pay them. He related these features of rural lending to the abundance of land, the local practice of Muslim law and the fact that married women were the major source of credit. Vigo showed a connection between rural credit and marketing but otherwise did not relate credit practices to the rural economy and culture.

The Structure of Social Consumption and Expenditure in Marmara

Most household heads were involved in a spending cycle so mandatory that we may speak of the structure of social consumption (Chart 5.1). Of course, there were other expenses. Farming expenditure varied with the wealth of the household head, the size of his holding and his use of hired labour. The majority of household heads made at least small investments in goats or sheep; as wealth increased, investment became larger and more sophisticated. Often, there might be additional heavy expenses – especially, visits to rural medicine men, the purchase of medicines from travelling salesmen, visits to the government hospitals or private clinics in the towns, the purchase of gifts for kin who came to stay during the postharvest dry season. However, the listed expenses were unavoidable.

Periodical Expenses – Zaka

There were two kinds of alms giving: *sadaka* and *zaka*. Sadaka was the informal and occasional distribution of gifts to those in need. More generally, it meant any gift given spontaneously in the name of God

Chart 5.1. The structure of social consumption among household heads, Marmara, 1978

Daily	Periodical	Occasional
Food grain, soup ingredients (*cefane*)	**Alms (*zaka*):** September–February **Head tax (*haraji*):** November (self and adult sons)*1 **Ceremonial gifts (*biki*):** December–March, and other times if necessary **House repair:** January–March **Salla:** Clothes for wife and children (*Id il Fitir*); ram, goat or special meat (*Id il Kebir*)	**Naming ceremony (*suna*)** **Marriage (*aure*)**

*1 Six Naira per adult male in 1978.

and for the sake of good will between giver and receiver. Thus, a man who bought a small portion of cooked meat from a butcher and gave it to his friends would call it sadaka. In contrast, zaka was a more formal obligation. All farmers would distribute a portion of their harvest among the mallams of their choice.[2] According to informants, a tenth of each crop ought to be given. Some mallams said that the obligation went further: a wealthy man who, after giving zaka, was able to store part of his crop until the following harvest, should pay a tenth of the stored crop as well.

In 1977, HH 63 gave two of his five bundles of guineacorn, and four of his forty sacks of maize. He distributed it among ten mallams and a household head who was a Qur'anic beggar. Information from four other farmers showed zaka declining with landholding from 9 to 6 per cent.

Occasional Expenses – *Suna* and *Aure*

When a woman gave birth to her first child, she returned to her parents' home for some months before and after the delivery. Her husband (or her husband's household head, if he were a subordinate in gandu) provided wood for forty days of hot baths after the delivery. He presented her with at least one length of cloth. Also, to her parents he presented *kauri*, the head and legs of a goat or sheep, used to prepare a special dish.

In Marmara, the expenses borne by the husband after the delivery of first-born and later children were the same. He bought his wife *kayan yaji,* consisting of *citta* (a pepper), ginger, salt, black pepper and other pungent and fragrant condiments. He gave a number of *tiya* (measures) of grain. On the sixth evening after birth, the hamlet praise singer announced the naming ceremony (suna) for the morrow. At the naming ceremony, the husband gave money to the liman and other mallams who said the prayers, and kolanuts to all who came. He slaughtered a ram or goat, special portions going to the midwife and the liman; the remainder to the guests. The senior male relative of the wife (her father, if he were alive) gave similar gifts. Total expenses were fairly standard (N30–35) varying somewhat with the means of the husband and of the wife's parents.

In the cycle of necessary social spending, by far the most burdensome expenditure was likely to be marriage. To see how various credit practices meet different social needs, we must understand the nature of and variation in total marriage expense. Young women normally married for the first time from the age of 15 to the age of 20; young men, from 18 to 25. There was a strong propensity among household heads to marry a second wife: 48 per cent of all household heads had more than one wife. Seventy per cent of the wives of household heads had co-wives (chapter 1). Divorced women usually remarried soon after the compulsory period of waiting between marriages required by Muslim law. Men usually remarried or took a second wife from among divorcees. Household heads considered it a duty to ensure that their previously unmarried male dependents marry a girl who had never been married before. Thus, the distinction between the two major types of marriage expenditure – that for a previously unmarried girl (*budurwa*), and that for a divorced girl or woman (*bazawara*). Budurwa marriage expenses were greater than those for a bazawara.

A household head was unlikely to take a second wife unless he had the means or could borrow them without great difficulty of repayment. He usually limited the number of his wives according to his income – more generally, his sense of responsibility for existing household needs. As we saw in chapter 4, the average number of wives rose from 1.1 in the bottom decile of landholders to 2.4 in the top decile; 84 per cent of Large Farmers had two or more wives; 71 per cent of Middle Farmers but only 29 per cent of Small Farmers had two or more wives.

While a household head could postpone indefinitely his marriage to a second wife, he could not easily postpone his responsibility to secure the first stable marriage of his unmarried dependents. If he failed to provide for a daughter, her mother would divorce him. If he continued to plead patience to a son, the son would eventually leave his household.

For a budurwa marriage, the expenditure of the boy's parents was much greater than that of the girl's parents. Since the spending of the boy's parents was greater, and necessary for cementing the gandu, I will focus on the patterns among the parents of young men. Often, a boy would court a girl for a year or more. Using earnings from his gayauna and off-farm work, he would frequently give her and her mother small money gifts. But the major expenditure consisted of a formal inventory of gifts mainly provided by the boy's parents. Negotiations between the two families usually began before the December guineacorn harvest, and were always conducted by an intermediary. At each stage, the appropriate gifts would be presented during the harvest and postharvest periods. The marriage ceremony would take place after harvest, usually in January or February. The first stage might be *Toshi*, or *Na gani-Ina so* ('I definitely desire her'), consisting of cosmetics, jewellery, head-ties and scarves given at Id il Fitir before the harvest; however, this was not essential. In sequence, the main stages were:

1. *Ji magana:* The boy's parents greet the girl's parents.
2. *Dukiya,* or *baiko:* Bridewealth. The boy's parents give the girl's parents a lump sum to buy her: a large decorated metal pot for storage, a number of smaller flowered pots for decorating her bridal room, cotton mattress, pillows, floor mats, kerosene lamp, bags of sugar and salt, calabashes of kola nut, lengths of cloth.
3. *Sa rana:* The boy's parents give money to set the marriage day – distributed among mallams, the girl's parents and grandparents, and women of the girl's house.
4. *Lefe:* The boy's parents present the girl with clothing, shoes, cosmetics, jewellery and lengths of cloth stored in a metal chest.
5. *Dauren aure:* The marriage ceremony. The boy's parents give money to the mallams who perform the ceremony, the representative of the girl and her parents, and the village head, and kolanuts to all who attend. Sadaki is presented – the small money gift to the bride required in Muslim law.
6. *Kudin kunshe:* Before the wedding, the boy's parents give money for the girl's hair-dressing and preparing her legs and hands with henna.
7. *Biki:* The wedding feast. Many tiya of guineacorn, peppers, okra and other ingredients are used in cooking, a goat is slaughtered and further small money gifts distributed.

The girl's parents buy the bed. At the wedding feast, their other presents are paraded by women from the girl's house and village – mortar and pestle, at least one sack each of grain, dry pepper and other soup ingredients, several large enamelled metal pots and dozens of small brass bowls. Also, they present the boy's parents with a handsome money gift.

The mother of the girl was the arbiter of her choice. Sometimes, a boy and his parents would spend heavily only to find that the mother at the last hour had switched her favour to another suitor. Then, the boy and his parents would attempt to recover at least their spending on the main gifts, first through the village head, then the Alkali court. The wrangling and anxiety was often very intense. As the postharvest dry season is the season of marriages, so also it is the season of marriage litigation.

I recorded the details of five budurwa marriages in four households (Table 5.2). Two other farmers also gave me estimates of their total marriage expenses in the course of many discussions of other matters. The marriages are presented in order of increasing ability to spend from farm and off-farm income (Table 5.3). There was great variation in spending at each stage. Total expenditure was most influenced by the costliness of two stages – bridewealth (dukiya) and the ensemble of the girl's personal adornments (lefe).

Villagers stressed that total spending on a budurwa depended, firstly, on the character (hali) of the girl's father – especially his willingness to help the bridegroom avoid financial hardship. For example, one farmer, HH 33, set bridewealth for his daughter's marriage at only N30 in 1978, when it was often N100; another set it at N60 in 1979, when it was often N100–200. The extreme example of 'helpfulness' is thought to be a particular kind of marriage – auren sadaka. A girl's father tells her he will give her as sadaka, spends a sizable sum on her clothing and other personal effects, calls the liman to perform the marriage ceremony and at night gives the name of the bridegroom to the mother, who leads the girl to the bridegroom's house.

Secondly, total expense depended on the degree of competition for the girl. A young man might find that the girl's parents would insist on a higher bridewealth if he were competing with a rich man or his son. Thirdly, it could vary with the wealth of the suitor and his parents, rising sharply with their total income (Table 5.3). Lastly, the range of marriage spending varied between years with the range of money income in the community (Table 5.1). From 1976 through 1979, the typical range of expense for a budurwa marriage doubled, because farmers forsook cotton as a cash crop for the more lucrative guineacorn and high-yielding yellow maize. By 1985, yellow maize

Table 5.1. Changes in budurwa marriage expense (N), Marmara, 1976–85

	Villagers' estimates of total expense for:	
	1. Ordinary farmer	**2. Rich farmer**
Year: 1976	150–200	300–400
1978	300–400	600
1979	300–500	600–1000
1985	400–500	1000

Table 5.2. Detailed spending on a marriage to a previously unmarried girl (budurwa), Marmara, 1978–79*1

	1978			1979	
	Sample 1.	**Sample 2.**	**Sample 3.**	**Sample 4.**	**Sample 5.**
	HH 36	HH 49	HH 21	HH 49	HH 55
Age	45	55	35	59	30
Holding	7.4 acres	5.1 acres	11.8 acres	5.1 acres	4.0 acres
Off-farm work	*General labour*	*Retail: kolanut, sugar cane*	*Labour, Ox ploughing*	*Retail, kolanut, sugar cane*	*Bus driver*
Bridegroom	**Son**	**Son**	**Brother**	**Son**	**Self**
Toshi	–	70	–	82	–
Ji magana	20	50	18	70	40
Dukiya	100	40	178	120	60
Sa rana	6	6	6	34	40
Lefe	94	100	100	130	300
Dauren aure	14	18	14	*2	30
Kudin kitso	4	4	4	10	10
Biki	31	25	38	*2	90
Total:	**269**	**313**	**358**	**446**	**570**

**1 These are in order of increasing ability to spend.*

*2 Marriage plans were broken off before the ceremony, and the boy and his parents had to go to the Alkali court to recover part of their expenditure.

had been absorbed into the local production pattern, fertilizer for yellow maize was more difficult to obtain, and drought in 1984 had reduced income. Even after the good harvest of 1985, the expense of a budurwa marriage was little more than it had been in 1979.

Table 5.3. Recorded range of total expenditure (N) on marriage to a previously unmarried girl (budurwa)*1

Sample 1.	Sample 2.	Sample 3.	Sample 4.	Sample 5.	Sample 6.
HH 36	HH 49	HH 21	HH 55	HH 7	HH 19*2
7.4 acres	5.1 acres	11.8 acres	4.0 acres	22.3 acres	12.0 acres
Labourer	*Kolanut, sugar cane retailer*	*Migrant labour, Ox ploughing*	*Bus driver*	*Grain trader*	*Ploughing*
COST:	COST:	COST:	COST:	COST:	COST:
1978: **269**	1978: **313**	1978: **358**		1978: **600**	
	1979: **446**		1979: **570**	1979: **600**	1979: **1,000**

Samples 1–6 are presented in order of increasing money income from all sources.
**1* All are marriages of sons of household heads, except in 1979, sample 4, the household head, and sample 5, a younger brother.
*2 His son was taking a third wife, and had more land – 19.6 acres – than himself. The son and his mother paid over half of the expenses.

Table 5.4. Recorded range of total expenditure on marriage to a divorced girl or woman (bazawara)*1

	1.	2.	3.	4.	5.	6.	7.
	HH 108	HH 79	HH 65	HH 66	Son of HH 32	HH 112	HH 7
Age:	35	55	55	40	25	30	55
Holding size: (acres)	0.5	2.5	3.2	3.2	2.3	0	22.3
Off-farm work	Butcher	Herbalist	Butcher	Tailor	Bread seller	Bus driver	Grain trader
1978				N171		N265	N200
1979	N60	N84	N36*2		*N300*[3]		

**1* These are presented in order of increasing ability to spend.
*2 Payment of lefe was postponed until the following harvest.
*3 The mother provided N200, the father N50 and the son N50.
Note: Expenditure on bazawara marriages was extremely variable, and depended on: the age of the girl or woman, the degree of competition for her and the wealth of the bridegroom

The Contribution of Women to their Children's Marriage Expenses

In a society where divorce is common, and both men and women are likely to have several different marriage partners in the course of their lives, the bond of affection between mothers and their offspring can be closer than that between spouses. When a woman is between marriages, or old and no longer interested in having a husband, she can rely on her adult sons and daughters for support.

The long-term effect of Muslim conversion has been to make household heads responsible for the year-round feeding of their dependents (chapter 4). Muslim men who are Small or Middle Farmers find that most of their annual income goes to defray the cycle of necessary expenses. Muslim women have the specific responsibility of clothing their daughters; otherwise, their earnings from house trade, farming and other work are largely free from daily commitments. Therefore, the wives often have greater savings than their husbands. They invest in goats and sheep; if they are wealthy, in cattle. In Marmara, women owned many more goats and sheep than men did.

Mothers make a large contribution to the marriages of their children. Among the four budurwa marriages for which I have evidence, the mother's share of the son's marriage expense varied from 22 per cent to 67 per cent (Table 5.5).

In summary, budurwa marriage expenses varied greatly. Mothers made a large contribution to the marriage expenses of their sons. They thus reduced this burden on household heads. I will now consider different credit practices which helped defray marriage expenses – adashi, biki, rance and jingina. Then, I will develop a model in order

Table 5.5. A mother's contribution to her son's marriage expenses, Marmara, 1978–79

1978							
Example A.	Stage	Cost	%	**Example B.**	Stage	Cost	%
HH 49				HH 21			
Mother's share	*Toshi*	70N	22	Mother's share	*Lefe*	100N	28
Total:		**313N**	**100**	**Total:**		**358N**	**100**
1979							
Example C.				**Example D.**			
HH 49	Stage	Cost	%	HH 32	Stage	Cost	%
Mother's share	*Toshi, Lefe*	212N	47	Mother's share	*Lefe*	200N	67
Total:		**446N**	**100**	**Total:**		**300N**	**100**

See Tables 5.2 and 5.4 for further details on these marriages.

to relate the elements in the cycle of necessary spending to each other and to the various types of credit.

Adashi Groups

In saving, women were helped by their membership in rotating savings and credit associations. Most women belonged to at least one adashi. The members contributed a fixed, usually small sum of money weekly or biweekly, a different member receiving the total contribution on each occasion, until each member had had her share. Each group was run by a woman (*uwar adashi*) responsible for organising contributions and the schedule of withdrawals. Men also belonged to adashi. For example, HH 108, a butcher, belonged to a group which included both men and women. In 1979, he gave one naira every Monday and Thursday, and after 14 weeks collected 28 naira – equivalent to the price of a large goat.

Adashi served two purposes. By committing members to a relationship of trust, they made it possible for most women and men to avoid the frittering away of farm and off-farm earnings. Secondly, they made it easier for people to consolidate small capital sums and so acquire an asset, especially small livestock.

Biki Partnerships

Biki partners were any two persons who agreed to make donations of money, grain or other goods at each other's naming and wedding ceremonies. *Biki* means feast, especially a wedding feast. But in this context, biki refers to the contribution which a person made at the ceremonies of others to help defray the cost. In 1978 and 1979, contributions ranged from 30 kobo to 5 naira, from two to six tiya of grain, or might involve one or two lengths of cloth.

Every man and woman had a number of biki partners. Two people established a partnership very informally, by one simply making a donation at the ceremony of the other. Donations were usually given at the gathering (*tarewa*) on the evening of the ceremony, but might be given privately.

The principles of biki are clear. If one makes a donation in cash or kind at the partner's ceremony, the partner doubles the donation at one's own next ceremony. This process of doubling continues until one of the partners has reached the limit of his means. At his partner's next ceremony, he then gives half of his partner's previous contribution. Gift and countergift then proceed from the new, lower level of donation. The practice was more flexible. Partners did not always double the previous contribution, but simply gave a larger sum. As described by the butcher, HH 108: 'If I give 50 kobo, he will give one naira. I will then give N1.50, and he will give me N2.50. When the money becomes too much – for example, N3.00 – I will give N1.50 and keep N1.50. I give half of what he gave and keep half for myself. Then we begin again.'

Biki partnerships commonly occurred between friends, close kin (though not parents and their children), women (including co-wives), richer and poorer household heads and members of the same profession. For example, butchers or traders, who worked in the same markets, gave each other biki. The sum which a person gave to a partner might become considerable over a number of years, but when a ceremony occurred in his own household, he was assured a generous return contribution from his biki partners.

Biki was a form of saving to meet the cost of expensive naming and wedding ceremonies. It revealed an important similarity with adashi. Instead of saving individually – by putting away money or investing it in a personal possession – the participants saved socially, by giving to others. Biki and adashi were but two forms of a more general tendency to save money by binding it up in long-term social relationships (chapter 7).

Biki partnerships were a valuable relationship between richer and poorer men. In the short term, the relationship was likely to be asymmetrical, favouring the richer partner. Men who were rich by village standards tended to have much larger households than poorer men. Therefore, a rich man was likely to have several ceremonies, and to receive a flow of gifts from his poorer partner before the partner had a ceremony of his own. But in the long term, the relationship was likely to affect more beneficially the poorer partner. Since the poorer partner was likely to be giving at several ceremonies of the richer partner before he had the chance of a return gift, the eventual return gift would more than compensate for his own previous donations.

Many men of limited means would form biki partnerships with a rich man. In the sense of cash and kind flows from 'those with more' to 'those with less', such partnerships facilitated the marriages of poorer men which would otherwise have been difficult to finance. For example, HH 108 spent N60 in 1978 on his marriage to a divorcee. His biki totalled N43. Of eighteen named contributors, nine were much better off than himself.

Chart 5.2. Total biki donations (N) to particular farmers at their wedding ceremonies, Marmara, 1978–79

Farmer:	Age	Acreage	Cost*1	*Biki**2	%	Notes
HH 21	35	11.8	358	70	19%	His younger brother's first marriage to a *budurwa*. He was in *gandu* with HH21.
HH 36	45	7.4	269	200	74%	His son's first marriage to a *budurwa*. The *biki* was so large because he and his wife had given biki at many weddings but this was the first wedding of their oldest child.
HH 55	30	4.0	570	58	10%	His marriage to his third wife, a *budurwa*.
HH 108	35	0.5	60	43	72%	His marriage to a *bazawra*.

***Biki* as a % of marriage expenses:** (the % column)

*1 This includes the expenses paid by the mother of the bridegroom.
*2 Part of the biki was given to the mother of the bridegroom.
Note: Biki listed are money sums only: total biki was actually a higher percentage of marriage expenses because much biki was given as grain.

Rance

In terms of the total volume of money borrowed annually, the most important single type of credit was rance, a money sum borrowed without interest for a short period – generally supposed to be a week or less. Sums borrowed ranged from tiny to very large (e.g., N200). Long-standing friends in trade might even borrow up to N1,000. People were continually borrowing small amounts from each other. During 1977–79, sums above N5 were usually borrowed from one of the richer household heads.

People borrowed for many reasons. Among the most prevalent were: to meet daily or periodical expenses for a few days, fund wedding and naming ceremonies, complete a purchase or finance trading activities for a short period. We can distinguish six common situations:

1. *Among traders in the same line of trade.* Traders or butchers who operated regularly in the same markets obtained rance from each other.
2. *Among traders in different lines.* If traders in different lines had different periods of cash flow, because the markets in which

they traded occurred at different times of the week, they would often borrow from each other. For example, HH 7, the largest grain wholesaler, sold Marmara grain every Sunday in a distant market. Every week in 1978, he would give N60 to a kolanut retailer, HH 97, who purchased on a Monday, and had usually sold enough kolanuts by Friday to repay the loan.

3. *A medium-term credit 'on call'.* Similar in form, but different in substance, was the situation wherein two traders in the same or different lines had a long-standing friendship. One would use the other's money; it was considered rance and could be called in at any time without objection; but in fact, the borrower knew he could rely on its use for several months. In this way, HH 7, the grain wholesaler, used N200 every week as rance which had been loaned by the hamlet chicken trader, HH 12, in May 1978 and was not repaid until July.
4. *Having loaned as rance his weekly earnings, the lender would need to borrow rance.* For example, on Sunday 16 April 1978, HH 7 earned N620 from the sale of grain.

   On Monday–Wednesday, he spent the money:

Rance:	to HH 97, to buy kolanuts at a Monday market	N 60
	to A in another village, to buy kolanuts	100
	to HH 52, a shopkeeper, to buy palmnut oil	10
	to a Malumfashi trader, to complete the purchase of a bus	200
	Total given:	370
	Grain purchases:	232
	Household expenses	10
	Remaining cash income:	8

   On the Wednesday, he borrowed rance to complete the purchase of grain and buy household food. He repaid this on the Friday, by which time N300 of the N370 he had loaned had been repaid.

   HH 20 bought maize in Marmara, and sold it weekly or stored it against short-term price rises in the more northern markets. During November 1978, he had lent his entire trade earnings of the previous week as rance, and himself required it to buy family food.
5. *Instead of selling an asset between market days, the seller took rance to meet his needs until the following market day.* For exam-

ple, a farmer borrowed N60 from me on the Saturday to meet marriage expenses, on the grounds that there was greater demand for his goats at a Tuesday market than in Marmara. On Wednesday he repaid the loan.

6. *For marriage.* There was a crucial connection between rance and biki. Every household head had a certain 'credit limit' for marriage expenses, because potential creditors had a rough idea, not only of his material assets, but also of the extent of his participation in biki networks. Therefore, it was common to borrow rance for naming ceremonies and weddings, and repay with biki donations.

It was also common to repay part of the rance with biki donations while defraying part until the following harvest. In December 1978, HH 53, a tailor, borrowed N20 from me for his marriage. As of the following July, he had still not repaid it. In September 1978, HH 66, also a tailor, borrowed N30 from me for his marriage (Table 5.4). He repaid N25 out of his maize earnings in October. N5 was still not repaid as of the following July. In both cases, it was clear that the balance of the loan would not be paid until the 1979 harvest.

Situations one through four may be distinguished from five and six because they involved credit transactions between traders. In these four there were two kinds of risk. (1) Some of the lender's money might not be repaid within the period promised. Thus, the lender would be deprived of commercial opportunities in his own trading activity. Given this opportunity cost, there was often a negative interest rate attached to rance between traders. (2) The lender could never be wholly sure whether the borrower's venture would falter or collapse.

Situation five is revealing. Marmara was integrated in a grid of periodic marketplaces. Traders from distant rural areas and cities attended, raising prices above those set by local rural demand. People accepted that they should help each other obtain these price benefits by lending between markets. The six situations illustrate general features of rance:

1. Lenders are borrowers.
2. Credit is often triangular. A lends to B because A has borrowed (or can borrow) from C.
3. Rance involves the ebb and flow of subsistence funds as well as surplus funds, because creditors, too, can borrow short term.
4. Rance is a form of mutual self-help in a small community.

5. There are two situations in which short-term credit is converted into medium-term credit: (a) a relationship of trust and friendship develops; (b) the high cost of marriage in relation to income makes it likely that part of the repayment will be delayed.
6. Rules are clear in principle but flexible in practice.

Biki and Rance – Two Case Studies of Very Small Farmers

HH 93 was a Small Farmer who relied on farm labouring as his major source of income. He came landless to Marmara in 1976. HH 43 gave him a section of his large compound in which to live with his family, and loaned him (*aro*) 0.4 acres inside one of his fields. By 1978, HH 93 had acquired aro a total of 1.5 acres, including a half acre from HH 43's next-door neighbour and kinsman. In 1979, he had to return one field but received a larger field from another villager. His hold on land was thus based on interweaving ties of friendship, kinship and co-residence, and on the availability of aro tenures.

From his own account, I have reconstructed his likely income and expenditure for the year after the 1978 harvests (Chart 5.3). In 1978, he borrowed N20 of 'high-interest credit' – bashi (discussed below). After the maize harvest, he repaid N12 with maize having a market value of N30. He repaid N8 with N10. Thus, his total repayments included 100 per cent interest, six months after taking the loans. In 1978, he gave little biki, since 'I was in the circumstances and character of a stranger.' In 1979, he gave 20 tiya of biki worth N10. However, he received total biki worth N35 at his child's naming ceremony. This covered his spending on the ceremony.

He and his family spent little beyond essentials. Like many households, they reduced their grain consumption over August and September, the months before the maize harvest. Consequently, their daily food grain averaged less than the recorded tiya (about 6 lbs., 2.7 kg.) for a family of five. Still, HH 93 would have needed a small amount of 'high-interest credit' before the 1979 harvest.

HH 108, also an immigrant, farmed a half acre in 1978. A young butcher, he traded or butchered a few goats each week, operating with his own and borrowed money. Net earnings were not more than 1–3 naira per animal, or N4–18 per week. He had no wife or family.

He borrowed from me rance of N40 for goats in October, N100 in November, each time repaying after a week. Thereafter, he borrowed rance of N95 – N50 for marriage expenses to a bazawara and N45 for butchering. He later borrowed further rance of N20. His total debt had risen to N115. His total marriage expenses were N60. At the wed-

Chart 5.3. HH 93: Income and expenditure (N), Marmara, October 1978–September 1979

Age: 35, Family size: 5 (*self, one wife, three small children*),
Holding in 1978: 1.5 acres

INCOME	*N*	*N*	EXPENDITURE
Crops			**Daily**
Maize: 1.5 sacks*1	30	182	Food grain at 1 tiya*1 per day
Guineacorn: 3.0 sacks*1	60	412	*Cefane* at 1.13 per day, as:
Cowpeas: 0.5 sacks*2	20		0.17: Groundnut oil
Post harvest season			0.08: Palm oil
labour:			0.03: Salt
Well-digging and house building	120		0.10: Pepper
(*part day-rate, part piece-rate*)			0.20: Locust beancakes (*daddawa*)
Farm labour:			0.10: Maggi cubes
(*part day-rate, part piece-rate*)			0.45: Millet flour and milk (*lunch*)
May: Planting		18	Kolanut: 0.05 per-day
26 days at 1.5 per-day	39	30	Credit re-payment, 'high interest' 1978*3
June-July Wedding			**Periodical**
52 days at 4.0 per-day:	208	6	Tax:
September-December Harvesting		6	*Zaka:* 0.3 sacks *1 of guineacorn
104 days at 2.0 per-day:	208	10	*Biki:* 20 tiya*1 of grain
Other		18	Face cream for wife/1.5 per month
Biki at child's naming ceremony:		20	*Salla:* clothing for his family
(*N20 & 30 tiya*1 of Guineacorn*)			**Occasional**
	35	30	Naming ceremony of child
Total income:		30	Repayment of *bashi* loan
	715	732	**Total expenditure:**

Balance: (–) 17

*1 From January through July, Maize and Guineacorn prices remained fairly constant at 50 kobo per tiya or N20 per sack.
*2 From January to July Cowpeas rose from N20 to N44 per sack.
*3 See text below.

ding, he received biki of N43. At the end of December, he combined his biki with earnings from trade and repaid N60.

With the N55 still owing, he continued to trade and butcher. He sank N38 of the money into acquiring four small farms, one jingina, and three aro. His intention was to 'farm well so as to earn capital [*jali*]', and repay my N55 at the harvest. He also borrowed money from others – including N280 for a cow which he sold at N320 after four months. Even after acquiring farmland, he was still able to trade or butcher 2–3 goats weekly. He exemplifies (besides boldness and cunning) how

1. rance is essential for a poor man building a household and an enterprise;
2. a borrower, by gradually developing a credit relationship with a particular lender, manoeuvres a short-term loan into a medium-term one; and
3. biki relations make it possible to borrow and repay a considerable sum for marriage.

Stages in Financing a Budurwa Marriage – Small and Middle Farmers

I pause now to consider in more depth the financing of a critical expenditure in the lives of household heads – the marriage of their sons to previously unmarried girls (budurwai, sing. budurwa). Were household heads with relatively small landholdings caught up in a 'squeeze of social reproduction', so that they needed to sell land in order to meet the marriage expenses of their children? My evidence suggests that a general category like 'Small Farmer' does not provide the specificity needed to answer this question. Rather, we need to locate 'Small Farmers' in their likely position in the life cycle when the marriages of their children occur, and recall that both landholdings (chapter 3) and off-farm income (chapter 4) vary with age. If a man had his first marriage in the age range of twenty to twenty-five, and his oldest son likewise, then he would likely be forty to fifty at the time of his oldest son's first marriage. Because of the high rates of divorce and remarriage and infant mortality, he might well be in his fifties. We have already noted the tendency for landholding to increase with age: the mean landholding rose from 4.4 acres (median, 3.3) among those in their thirties to 9 acres (median, 4.5) among those in their fifties (Table 3.18). Thus, a man having to finance the first marriage of his oldest son was likely to have more land than younger men. In this chapter, we have seen that women provided crucial financial support in their children's marriages. Moreover, there was an important connection between short-term credit (rance) and marriage-gift exchange (biki), so that a part of the borrowing undertaken to meet marriage expenses was later répaid from the money donated as biki.

I narrow the analysis further by concentrating on that group of farmers who had one unmarried adult dependent worker in 1978. Among these household heads, age tended to be about 55, with a family size around six people, and a holding of approximately 4.5 acres (Table 5.6). Moreover, they tended to have skilled off-farm occupations.

To compare the items in the cycle of necessary expenses, I have constructed a model budget for a household head with a family of six, becoming seven at the start of the year after the marriage of his oldest son to a budurwa (Chart 5.4A).[3] In the model, he farmed 4.5 acres – about the median among household heads having one, unmarried dependent worker (Yields, crop prices and off-farm earnings are typical of 1978–79).

Table 5.6. HHs with one adult, unmarried, dependent worker, Marmara, 1978

Household	Age	Family size	Acreage	Off farm occupations:
HH 15	60	4	12.9	Donkey transporter
HH 44	55	11	6.2	Grain trader, plough owner
HH 46	45	6	5.9	Plough owner
HH 52	55	5	4.5	General retailer
HH 54	60	3	4.3	Vegetable retailer
HH 66	40	7	3.2	Tailor
HH 80	45	5	2.5	General / farm labourer
HH 98	55	7	1.3	General / farm labourer
mean:	**52**	**6**	**5.1 acres**	
median:	**55**	**5.5**	**4.4 acres**	

Chart 5.4A. A model: The cycle of necessary expenses (N), Marmara, October 1978–September 1979

Household head age: 55. Family size: 7 (*self, two wives, one adult son and his new wife, two children*). Holding: 4.5 acres, and off farm occupation as tailor.

Current income:	N	N	Current Expenditures:
Farm Output:			**Daily:**
Guineacorn, 3.5 acres			Food grain at 1.5 tiya*2 per-day
(*3.5 sacks/acre*1: 12.2 sacks*):	245	288	(*38 tiya per sack*):
Maize, 1.0 acres		365	*Cefane**3 at 1.0 per-day:
(*6 sacks/acre*1: 6.0 sacks*):	120		0.10: Palm oil

Chart 5.4A continued on next page

Chart 5.4A continued

	365		0.10: Salt
(Daily Consumption: 1.5 tiya[*2]			0.05: Pepper
(*38 tiya/sack: 14.4 sacks*):			0.10: Locust bean cakes
Surplus: 3.8 sacks:	76		0.10: Maggi cubes[*4]
Tree products:			0.10: baobab leaf (*kuka*)
(1 sack of kalwa at 40[*1])	40		0.05: okro (*kubewa*)
Guineacorn chaff:			0.25: lunch/millet flour (*fura*)
(*12 sacks at 1 per sack*)	12		0.15: lunch/milk
Tailoring:	400		**Periodical:**
Son's hired-out labour[A]:		12	Tax for two at 6 per person
May: Planting		25	*Zaka* at 7% of output
(*22 mornings at 1/day*)		45	Biki: at 30 and 30 tiya
June–July: Weeding		23	House repair[*5]:
(*43 mornings at 2/day*)			10.00: earth
September–December: Harvesting			4.00: 10 bundles of grass
(*65 mornings at 1.5*)	205		2.50: labour for earth mixing
			6:00: Plasterer
			Salla[*6]:
		44	cosmetics at 5:00
			three lengths of cloth at 7:00
			clothing for children at 2:00
			special cow meat at 4:00
			kolanuts (20 kobo)
			Basic farm expenses:
		73	4 per sack of ourput[*7]
		8	Yellow Maize fertiliser[*8] (4 bags)
Total income	**1022**	**833**	**Total expenditure**

Notional Balance: + 139

A. In gandu with him, his son was at his service five long mornings a week.

**1* For typical yields of guineacorn and maize, see Appendix 2. The price of guineacorn and maize was fairly constant at N20 per sack from January–July 1979.

**2* For the range of recorded consumption of food grain, see Appendix 4.

**3* Strictly speaking, this refers to 'soup ingredients', but farmers usually included all daily money costs of feeding. See Appendix 4.

**4* Maggie cubes for flavouring soup were almost universally purchased.

**5* Expenditure was very variable. The model uses the expenses of HH 63 for building two walls for his compound, minus expenditure on water carriers – a job performed in this case by the son.

**6* Also derived from HH 63, his spending was on three women and five children.

**7* The only money costs for a farmer reliant on family labour would have been ploughing, transport of produce from the field, threshing, winnowing and bagging.

**8* For fertilizer consumption and prices, see Appendix 2, Table 2.

He planted 3.5 acres with guineacorn, the preferred food crop, and one acre with yellow maize, achieving typical yields.[4,5] He had small additional incomes from selling his tree products and the chaff after winnowing his guineacorn (in reality, tree products could be a much larger source of income; and money from the sale of the bran left after pounding guineacorn also would need to be considered).

He relied on his own labour for weeding and harvesting while hiring out his son's farm labour.[6] His off-farm income, N400, is that estimated by a tailor. (In comparison, a small general retailer would have earned N370–510 annually – net daily earnings of N2–4 during and after harvest; around N1 in June–July, when farm labourers spent cash, and 50 kobo in the late dry and late rainy seasons, when cash was scarce).

Concerning his expenses, the estimates for daily food grain and soup ingredients (*cefane*) are based on discussions with many farmers (a household of seven generally ate 1–1.5 tiya of grain daily [2.7–4 kg.]; see Appendix 4).[7] The model significantly exaggerates average daily food grain, because the majority of households curtailed grain consumption in the two months before the maize harvest.

At 1979 market prices, this farmer had an annual notional financial balance of nearly N140 with respect to the cycle of daily, periodical and basic farm expenses. Normally, he would have invested part of this in goats and sheep, and spent most of it on visitors, clothing and medicines. But in a year of budurwa marriage he would focus his surplus on the marriage.

This farmer's ability to finance the budurwa marriage of his son depended critically on three factors – the contribution which the boy's mother was able to make, the scale of biki donations at his son's wedding and the level of his savings. For Small and Middle Farmers, long-term saving took two main forms. First, acquiring land was itself a form of saving. It made possible a larger current income and therefore a larger capacity to finance marriage. Quite separately, farmers regarded land as a form of wealth which could be pledged in order to pay for the marriages of their sons – and thus cement the household unit of production (chapter 3).

Secondly, smaller farmers purchased young goats and sheep which could be bought for as little as N6–8, sold for N20–30 after a year, and when fully grown, sold for N40–50. As a form of savings and investment, goats and sheep involved small capital sums with high rates of capital growth. They were ideal for people trying to save a large amount in relation to current income, out of small annual balances on current income. Because female livestock gave birth to more livestock; because livestock were able to graze freely in the postharvest dry season; and because household heads were normally in or approaching middle age before they had to sell livestock for their children's marriages, purchasing young goats or sheep was an efficient form of long-term saving. Like grain, livestock was sold for many reasons. But like grain, it was looked on as ideally circulating within a sphere of exchange related to the preservation or expansion (through marriage) of the household.

For his son's marriage, the farmer in the model would begin by selling grain at the October maize and December guineacorn harvests[8] (Chart 5.4B). He would sell livestock at the guineacorn harvest or in the postharvest dry season. If he still needed funds, he would borrow short-term credit (rance). After the wedding, he would repay as much as possible of the rance from marriage donations (biki). Finally, he might pledge land in the postharvest dry season in order to complete expenses. While some Small and Middle Farmers pledged land for marriage, my land transfer record suggests that this was not common (Table 3.31).

Later, in the rainy season, if he exhausted his grain and the ability to buy it, he would take 'high-interest credit' – bashi. It was difficult to obtain bashi earlier than the rainy season, because lenders suspected that a borrower would need still more credit in the rainy season, and so be unable to repay the total amount borrowed. Thus, the financing of a marriage went through stages related to particular times of year and specific periods in the agricultural marketing cycle.

Regarding marriage expense, the model posits a total of N450 – toward the upper limit of marriage expenses for an ordinary farmer in 1979 (Chart 5.4B). Regarding marriage finance, the model makes two assumptions, reflecting the typical circumstances of household economy: first, this Small Farmer would have had perhaps four animals for which he could fetch moderate prices; secondly, he would have been willing to sell up to half of his grain output (in this case, 44 per cent). Then, it considers two possibilities:

(A) he could rely on the boy's mother to finance a fifth of marriage expense;
(B) he could rely on her for two-fifths.

In both situations, the farmer would have needed rance to finance the marriage, repaid partly or wholly out of biki donations at the wedding feast. But whereas under (A), the relatively small contribution of the mother would have required him to pledge an acre of his smallholding, under (B), the large contribution of the mother rendered land pledging unnecessary. Yet even if he had to pledge land, the main conclusion that I draw from the model is that the range of this Small

Chart 5.4B. A model: The financing of a budurwa marriage (N), Marmara, 1978–79

October 1978 to September 1979: total income = N1022. The cycle of daily, periodical, and farm expenses – total expenditures = N883. Annual balance = +N139.

A.		B.	
Marriage expenses:	*N*450	Marriage expenses:	*N*450
Marriage finance:	450	Marriage finance:	450
Mother's share (*20%*)	90	**Mother's share (*40%*)**	180
Grain sales (8 sacks at 20):	160	Grain sales (8 sacks at 20):	160
Livestock sales (4 goats at 20):	80	Livestock sales (4 goats at 20):	80
Rance:	70	*Rance:*	30
Pledge of one acre:	*1 50		
	450		**450**
Biki (50 cash & 1 sack of grain):	70	*Biki:*	70
Rance repayments:	(–)50	*Rance* repayments:	(–)30
Remaining *Biki* donations	20	Remaining *Biki* donations:	40
Remaining current income:	862	Remaining current income:	862
Cyle of expenses:	(–)883	Cycle of expenses:	(–)883
Notional annual balance:	**(–)1**	**Notional annual balance:**	**19**
*Bashi**2, two loans			
@N5 for 1 harvest sack of grain	10		
Year two: *October 1979 to September 1980*			
Current income:	**948**	**Current income**	**1022**
Reduced guineacorn acreage, 2.5 acres:	175		
Maize, 1.0 acres:	120		
Other (Chart 5.4A):	653		
Current expenditure:	**899/909**	**Current expenditure:**	**883**
Rance repayment for marriage:	(–)20		
Actual repayment of *bashi*:	*2(–)10–20		
Cyle of expenses:	*3(–)869	Cyle of expenses:	(–)883
Notional annual balance:	**39/49**	**Notional annual balance:**	**139**
Year three: *October 1980 to September 1981*			
Current income:	948		
Current expenditure:	933		
Pledged acre recovered:	(–)50		
Cycle of expenses:	(–)883		
Notional annual balance:	**15**		

*1 For values of pledged fields, see note 7, chapter 3.
*2 For bashi, and actual repayment rates, see text below.
*3 883N (-) the farm expenses on the pledged acre.

Farmer's income sources was wide enough to enable him to reclaim the pledged land several years after his son's marriage (Chart 5.4B).

The model abstracts from a variety of possible situations. However, it brings together all of the evidence hitherto discussed – the comparative pressures to pledge land on the different categories of farmer (chapter 3), the contribution of hired labour to the domestic economy of smaller farmers (chapter 4), typical household expenditures in a structure of social consumption (this chapter), and the modes of financing the cycle of necessary expenses. Because it is comprehensive with respect to the evidence, it demonstrates cardinal themes:

1. Underlying changes in the rural economy were unlikely to have forced smaller farmers into selling land or borrowing heavily in order to give their sons a budurwa marriage.
2. The ability of smaller farmers to afford budurwa marriages resulted from: the significant contribution of women to their children's marriages; a prior, indigenous process of saving by *both* men and women; credit-without-interest (rance); and participation in the networks of marriage-gift exchange (biki).

Overcoming the Obstacles to Marriage Finance among Poor Farmers

Wedding a budurwa was the preferred form of marriage for previously unmarried men. But marriage institutions were sufficiently flexible to enable poor farmers to overcome the difference between the desirable and the possible. A young man could marry a divorced girl (bazawara) if his father had such little land that there was no possibility of pledging it. Marrying a bazawara set in motion two devices for reducing the burden of wedding expenditure. A major element, the provision of clothes and jewellery for the bride (lefe), could be postponed until the following harvest; and the gathering of biki partners (tarewa), could also be postponed, in order to solicit greater contributions at the following harvest. For example, HH 74 had only 2.7 acres. His three adult sons farmed together in gandu. The youngest son was still unmarried, and in the dry season of 1979, he met his own expenses in marrying a divorced girl. Both lefe and the tarewa were postponed until the 1979 harvest.

High-Interest Credit: Bashi

This account has shown how three credit institutions (adashi, biki and rance) enabled most Small and Middle Farmers to meet occasional expenditures essential to the preservation and expansion of their households. But as a result of meeting a variety of expenses, yearly financial deficits often occurred. I turn now to consider the credit practice through which annual deficits were met – high-interest credit, or bashi.

Villagers said that in the distant past (before World War II), bashi consisted mainly of bundles of grain, repaid with twice as many bundles at harvest. In the more recent past (circa 1940–1960), bashi mainly took the form of money borrowed before harvest and repaid with money at 100 per cent interest. According to HH 48, this reflected the old principle that 'a cowrie draws a cowrie' (*wuri ya jawo wuri*). According to informants, the rising opportunities to earn money from hired labouring since the mid-1960s had reduced the need for bashi.

In 1976–79, by far the most common form of bashi consisted of loans known as *kudun buhu* ('the price of a sack') or *falle*. Lenders advanced money to half of the expected harvest value of the crop with which they were to be repaid. Loan agreements were made for repayment with crops, mainly with guineacorn or maize. Under falle (pronounced **pul**'lai, with the accent on the first syllable), during the rainy season, from May through August, lenders considered the yearly price peak (or likely peak) for the crop, and the general quality and quantity of the crop growing on the land. They then speculated on the harvest price per sack. They calculated around half of the speculative harvest price, and gave this to borrowers in return for a sack at harvest. For example, in 1977 the peak July price for guineacorn was N24 per sack. Lenders speculated that the price would drop by one-third, to around N16 at harvest in December. Then they gave N6 to N8 in return for a sack of guineacorn at harvest. The actual harvest price was N18. The nominal money return to this form of lending was thus 125–200 per cent after five to seven months. In referring to the returns, people

Table 5.7. Falle loans and guineacorn prices (N per sack), Marmara, 1975–79

	1975	1976	1977	1978	1979
Peak July prices		16	24	30	20
May–July estimate of harvest prices:		12	16	16–20	16
Falle loan:		6	6–10	8–12	8–10
Lowest December prices:	8	12	18	18	14

Table 5.8. Known falle lenders in Marmara, Marmara, 1978–79

	Size of holding	Off-farm occupations
Lender: 1. HH 1	49.9 acres	Bus owner, oxen hire
2. HH 2	43.3 acres	Bus owner, cloth trader, oxen hire
3. HH 3	41.5 acres	Oxen hire
4. HH 5	35.4 acres	Oxen hire
5. HH 6	35.0 acres	Kolanut trader
6. HH 7	22.4 acres	Grain trader
7. HH 12	14.4 acres	Chicken trader
8. HH 14	13.2 acres	Oxen hire, part-time grain trader
9. HH 25	10.2 acres	Maize trader, oxen hire
10. HH 27	9.9 acres	Bus owner, cotton buyer, hamet head
11. HH 39	6.8 acres	Donkey transporter
12. HH 62	3.3 acres	Qur'anic mallam
13. HH 83	2.3 acres	Commission agent

Table 5.9. Informants on the nature and incidence of falle loans, Marmara, 1978

Informant	Size of holding	Off-farm occupation	Credit status
HH 7	22.4 acres	Grain trader	Lender
HH 11	16.3 acres	*None*	*Neither*
HH 20	12.0 acres	Maize trader, cotton buyer, bus owner	Borrower
HH 28	9.6 acres	Donkey transporter	Borrower
*1MFNH	8.0 acres	*None*	Lender
*2HH 39	6.8 acres	Donkey transporter	Lender
HH 62	3.3 acres	Qur'anic mallam and school teacher	Lender
HH 63	3.3 acres	Cotton buyer, survey worker	Borrower
HH 89	2.0 acres	Qur'anic mallam	Borrower
HH 92	1.5 acres	Cotton buyer, marijuana seller	Borrower
A	–	Qur'anic mallam	Borrower
B	–	Hamlet praise-singer	Borrower

*1 Middle Farmer, neighbouring hamlet.
*2 Informant 2 of land survey.

used the word for 'money profit' (riba) and never used any separate or special term denoting 'interest'. In order to show the lender's profit, people often explained falle simply by saying 'one sack is repaid with two', but in fact loans were in money and involved speculation as to the harvest price.

In any year, there was a range of rates for one falle 'loan', i.e., a range of prices were offered for one sack at harvest. The rate offered by lenders depended on their speculative judgement, their caution, their assessment as to whether a relatively high advance would result in a higher rate of repayment at harvest, and the strength and duration of their personal relationship with particular borrowers. Everyone insisted that falle agreements were enforced by the Alkali court in Malumfashi. But most lenders were afraid to employ this sanction because of ill-will from kin and neighbours. The major sanction was the borrower's expectation that he would need credit from the same lender in the following year.

Lenders approached falle as a technique for purchasing grain futures and storing them against a future price rise. Grain repayments might be sold anywhere between six and eighteen months after receiving the grain. Lenders aimed to establish a long-term relationship with the borrower. In this way, credit would be extended in the second and subsequent years out of the lender's profit from the first year of the relationship. And so, having given credit in July or August of Year 1, they had to set aside grain or money from loan repayments which they would give to the same borrower in July/August of Year 2. One lender explained it thus: 'This year, you give one sack and get two sacks. You store them. One sack is profit, one you give again next year. Next year, you get two sacks. But one is to be given again in the third year. So after two years, you have given one sack and made two sacks profit.'

Hence, grain repayments were treated as including an element for reinvestment in the relationship between lender and borrower. Falle loans were given by a range of persons, from urban merchants operating through hamlet agents, to rich hamlet farmers, to small farmers with a financial surplus. Household heads were as likely to borrow from lenders in other hamlets as from those in Marmara.

There were many reasons why an annual deficit requiring bashi might arise. According to HH 28: 'Farmers have many responsibilities [*hidimomi,* sing. *hidima*]. Some will marry or pay for their children's marriages; some will give N1–3 at the biki of others – at some biki they will have to give N5; some have no grain to eat or even to plant, so to farm, they must take bashi.' According to HH 6: 'One does not have food. Another is not well and needs medicine. Another needs money because his wife went to the Alkali for a divorce and he must pay the money of two or three or four sacks of guineacorn to get her back.' Discussing the matter together, the hamlet praise singer and HH 11 said:

> The majority [*yawanci*] of household heads [*masu gida*] get bashi. Those who give bashi do it in order to store guineacorn until the price doubles. That is why they do it. [HH 11: 'Storing guineacorn is better than storing money, because it becomes dearer.'] Even those with guineacorn, or those without it but with an occupation, will need some bashi because of Salla responsibilities.

Underlying the variety of circumstances, four situations made it necessary for the majority of household heads to take falle loans. First, some men who were normally in yearly financial surplus sold so much grain to finance a marriage that they later needed credit to meet daily or farm expenses. Thus, HH 53, a tailor, at the beginning of the farming season:

> If it were not for my marriage, I would have trading capital [jali] to go to Kano, buy cloth and sell it here. In the rainy season, there is no money in tailoring. Because of my marriage responsibilities, I have no guineacorn left, except a small amount to feed my family. I will ask my senior brother for bashi to buy fertilizer for maize.

Secondly, the limited acreages and off-farm incomes of many farmers meant that, selling grain after harvest to meet various needs, they had exhausted their grain supply and their capacity to buy it before the following harvest. Thirdly, there was a particular timing to bashi. Most falle loans were given in late July and August. By then, weeding had been completed. There were no opportunities to earn cash from farm labour until the rice harvest in September. There was a lull in off-farm activity, since most farmers no longer had cash to buy goods and services. Fourthly, farmers had formerly grown small quantities of early millet, harvested in August as a stop-gap food, but it had been replaced by the higher yielding yellow maize. Maize was not dry enough to bag and sell until October. Thus, the replacement of early millet by yellow maize had increased farmers' annual grain supply but reduced their supply in August.

According to informants, the combination of these situations meant that by August, some two-thirds of all household heads had finished their grain. One-half had to remedy grain shortage by taking falle loans. This type of credit was so related to the seasonality of economic life that the English word 'August' was commonly used to describe the month of 'trouble' (*wahala*).

According to HH 20: 'Seventy out of one hundred household heads will finish their grain by "August".' HH 28 stated, '"August" is the month of suffering. Grain is finished. Farm labour does not provide enough money to buy food. *Cefane* [ingredients for daily food, more generally, daily household needs] eat up money.' According to HH 63: 'I do not "think", I know, that half of the household heads get bashi. The time for receiving is the rainy season, but mainly "August".' The hamlet's most learned mallam, HH 62, put it this way:

> Only a small number now have grain [22 July]. The remainder can be divided into two parts. One part will make ends meet until the maize harvest by poor men's skills [*sana'a na talauci*]. For example, people who are strong enough can be grain porters. The other part must get bashi. This is over half of the household heads in the town.

In chapter 3, I broadly distinguished Small Farmers (with less than 5 acres) from the rest on the grounds that those farming less than five acres were likely to be in annual financial deficit. 'Those with less than five acres' (55 per cent of landholders) appears to correspond neatly with the 'half' reported as needing bashi. But it would be wrong to think that all Small Farmers needed bashi – or that all Middle or Large Farmers did not. Some Middle Farmers followed a cautionary policy of borrowing during the two months before the maize harvest rather than risking their remaining grain supply. Some Large Farmers had sold all of their crops in the course of paying for hired labour. Very importantly, Large Farmers had such big families that the drain of farm and off-farm income sometimes required them to take bashi before harvest.

Rates of Repayment of Bashi

Secrecy shrouded bashi. People were only willing to discuss it when they were alone or with close friends. Lenders were extremely reluctant to divulge details. Grain traders were on their guard when being questioned lest the subject of bashi were broached. Borrowers approached very privately the business of finding a lender and making an agreement. It was very difficult to obtain reliable information from lenders on the rate of repayment. I could only collect the information from the lenders after spending much time with them. HH 7, the major hamlet grain trader, finally disclosed details after ten months of daily collaboration. HH 39, the donkey transporter who was my assistant in the land survey, was at first evasive. After two months working together, he suddenly decided to discuss the subject – behind closed doors. HH 83 described his lending in a whisper.

The case studies show that the practice was very different from the express terms of falle agreements (Table 5.10). Most lenders were unable to obtain anything like full repayment of their loans. Different lenders experienced very different repayment rates. There was great variability among borrowers in their repayment rates. Furthermore, borrowers treated variably the notion of a 'sack' of grain. Of the 78 loans given by the four lenders in return for one sack at harvest, 64 per cent were repaid with the cash advance only, 23 per cent were

Table 5.10. Rates of repayments of falle loans: case studies (N), Marmara, 1977–78

1977:	Description	No. of loans	Repayments	*1Repayment Rate
HH 7	The major hamlet grain trader	42 at 10	16 loans – full sacks	61%
			1 loan – 20	
			1 loan – 12	
			21 loans – advances of 10	
1978			3 loans – defaults	
*4MF, NH	No off-farming skill, (*8 acre holding*)	20 at 10	20 loans – advances of 10	37%
*5HH 39	Donkey transporter	11 at 8	2 loans – incomplete sacks*2	44%
			9 loans – advances of 8	
HH 83	Commission agent	5 at 12	2 loans – full sacks	86%
			3 loans – incomplete sacks*3	

Total loans: 78

- 50 repaid with cash advance
- 18 repaid with full sacks
- 5 repaid with incomplete sacks
- 3 defaulted
- 1 repaid with 20
- 1 repaid with 12

**1* Repayments of all loans with sacks of 40 tiya is taken as 100 per cent repayment. In practice, 'full' sacks usually contained 38–39 tiya – except for two sacks of 40 tiya repaid to HH 83. Where loans were repaid with the cash advance only, the number of tiya of grain which could be bought with the advance at the time of repayment has been used to calculate the repayment rate.

**2* One contained 35 tiya and one 30 tiya.

**3* One borrower repaid one loan with 33 tiya, and another repaid two loans with 60.

**4* Middle Farmer, neighbouring hamlet – Informant 1 of the land survey in chapter 3.

**5* Informant 2 of the land survey.

repaid with 'full' sacks of 38–40 tiya, 6 per cent with sacks of 30–35 tiya, 3 per cent with various money sums and 4 per cent were defaults. Moreover, lenders had to exert themselves to recover their cash advances, and these were often not repaid until the postharvest dry season. In consequence, lenders could not use them to buy guineacorn at low harvest prices.

Anecdotes reinforce the case studies. Two mallams told me that the biggest lenders were HH 1, HH 2, HH 3 and HH 6, and that HH 2 – considered the wealthiest man – would give up to 20 loans for a sack at harvest. But they insisted it would be impossible for him to receive more than 10 sacks in repayment. 'Those with wickedness [*mugunta*] or without either the right character or the means [hali] will only repay the money they had been given.' HH 6 told me that during the 1973 Sahel drought [*Busau*], he had given 80 loans and had not recovered either money or grain in repayment. He had recently scaled down the extent of his lending, because 'if you give N12, you get N14; if you give N14, you get N16.' Together, case studies and anecdotes suggest that bashi could not be used to impoverish the borrower.

I explore the case studies in reverse order. The lender with a high repayment rate was HH 83. Young, indigenous, but with only 2.3 acres of land, he was an all-purpose dealer who made small commissions (*la'ada*) by bringing buyers and sellers together. Though not rich, he was known for his generosity. His few borrowers could rely on him every year for bashi.

HH 39 was a donkey transporter who in 1978 used part of his off-farm earnings to add two acres to his holding and part to loan out as bashi. He saw his attempt to profit from 'high-interest credit' as a complete failure and swore he would never give loans again.

The farmer in a neighbouring hamlet who distributed N200 as falle loans managed to retrieve only his cash advances. The failure to obtain full repayments, he believed, was due to his unwillingness to sue people before the village head or take them to court. 'I know if I sue [*kara*] people, they will not speak to me again.'

In terms of relations between the richer and the poorer villagers of the hamlet and the connections between credit and grain marketing, the most interesting case is HH 7. He bought and sold annually at least twice as much grain as any other hamlet grain trader (chapter 7). An immigrant who had lived in Marmara for almost twenty years, he was not linked by ties of kinship or marriage to other hamlet households. In July and August of 1977, he distributed 42 loans to 18 persons, at a rate of N8–10 in return for a sack of guineacorn at harvest time. Sixteen loans were repaid with sacks of guineacorn at the December harvest or at various times in the postharvest dry season – sacks containing 38–39 tiya. Twenty-one loans were repaid with the cash advance of N10 only, one with N12, one with N20 and three loans were defaults. In terms of the money value of all cash and kind repayments at the various times of repayment, his investment of N418 in falle loans generated N571 – a gross return of 37 per cent between five and ten months after lending the money (Chart 5.5).

Chart 5.5. The 1977 falle loans of HH 7

TERMS: N8–10 IN JULY – AUGUST IN RETURN FOR A SACK OF GUINEACORN

		Loans		Actual repayments in sacks and in money (N)			
Borrower	Acreage	Loans	Value (N)	Amount	Month	Hamlet prce	Value
HH 16	12.6	4	40	3 sacks + 20	JAN. 1978	0.55 / tiya	*1 83
HH 20	12.0	8	80	7 sacks + 12	MAR. 1978	0.60 / tiya	*1 172
HH 35	7.4	3	30	1 sack	JAN. 1978	0.55 / tiya	*1 21
HH 46	5.9	3	30	2 sacks	DEC. 1977	0.45 / tiya	*1 34
HH 52	4.5	3	30	30	JUNE 1978		30
HH 59	3.6	1	10	10	JAN. 1978		10
HH 63	3.3	2	20	20	JAN. 1978		20
HH 68	3.1	1	8	1 sack	DEC. 1977	0.45 / tiya	*1 17
HH 72	2.8	1	10	10	JAN. 1978		10
HH 76	2.6	1	10	10	JAN. 1978		10
HH 79	2.5	2	20	2 sacks	DEC. 1977	0.45 / tiya	*1 34
A*3		2	20	20	JAN. 1978		20
B*4		1	10	10	JAN. 1978		10
*5 C, NH*2		1	10	10	JAN. 1978		10
D, NH*2		4	40	40	JAN. 1978		40
E, NH*2		3	30	30	JAN. 1978		30
F, NH*2		1	10	10	JAN. 1978		10
G, NH*2		1	10	10	JAN. 1978		10
Total:		**42**	**418**				**571**

*1 Sacks are calculated to contain 38 tiya. *2 Neighbouring hamlets.
*3 The hamlet praise-singer. *4 Client labourer of HH 7.
*5 A kinsman and member of his gandu

HH 7 was bitter: '[In August of 1977] I had four hundred naira and all was spoiled [*lalace*] because of bashi. In the rainy season people have nothing to sell, then they have Salla responsibilities, but at harvest they forget you helped them. At harvest everyone becomes a "rich man" and refuses to repay with guineacorn.' Notwithstanding his anger, we can analyse his returns differently. HH 7 firstly approached falle as a technique for purchasing grain futures and storing them against a price rise. Cash repayments were used to buy guineacorn at postharvest prices and store it alongside kind repayments. Moreover, in advancing money to numerous persons, he could not be certain who would repay, or at what rate. Therefore, we can analyse his falle lending as part of a marketing strategy involving inherent uncertainty as to the rate of repayment, and the final price received for stored produce. And since lenders sought a long-term relationship with borrowers such that advances in the second and subsequent years were financed out of gains in the first year of the relationship, we can subtract credit re-extended to borrowers in order to calculate the net returns from one year of falle lending.

As we have seen, 16 loans were repaid with sacks of grain. Eighteen loans were repaid with the cash advance of N10, and one with N20, in January 1978. By that time, the price of guineacorn had already risen from its harvest low. Moreover, he had overhead costs for the purchase of empty sacks and for donkey transport from the place of sale to his storeroom. At prevailing prices and overhead costs, he used the N200 to buy and store 8 sacks. One loan was repaid with N12 in March and three were each repaid with N10 in June. At prevailing prices and overhead costs, he bought and stored 1 sack. In return for his initial advance of N418, he recovered or bought 25 sacks of guineacorn.

He stored the 25 sacks until 2 July 1978. Then, he sold them at his main outlet market, 120 miles away from Marmara. He sold them at a wholesale price of N33.50 per sack. After deducting motor transport and porterage, his earnings were N783. For an initial investment of N418, his gross return was N365 – 87 per cent after approximately eleven months. In August of 1978 he extended N72 in falle loans to three borrowers from the previous year. Thus, the net return on his original outlay was N293 – 70 per cent after approximately one year.

In 1978, HH 7 reduced the scale of his lending – 16 loans to six persons. He did so partly because of the low repayment rate on 1977 loans. Also, he observed that almost all farmers had stopped planting cotton and had planted grains instead. So he suspected that the markets would be flooded with grain in 1979, thus removing the interseasonal price rise. His judgement was correct (Table 5.7 above). Of his six borrowers in 1978, three were borrowers from the previous year. Two of them had repaid all of their 1977 loans with sacks of guineacorn. However, HH 7 also gave 2 loans to one borrower (HH 35) despite the fact that he had failed to repay most of his 1977 credit. As of January 1979, 5 of 16 loans had been repaid with sacks of guineacorn, none with money.

His lending of N418 in 1977 may be compared with the possible alternative investments. First, he could have purchased cattle at N200–250 in July of 1977. The maximum he would have obtained would have been N400–500 per animal in the dry season of 1978 – less feeding and watering costs. Secondly, had he used the money to buy guineacorn at a market price of N24 in July 1977 and store it until July 1978, his gross return, after deducting total overhead costs of N2.17 per sack to his outlet market, would have been N127, or 30 per cent. Thirdly, had he continually reinvested N418 with profits in the weekly grain trade to his outlet market, the return after one year would have been far higher than 100 per cent. But there was no way he could guarantee the continual reinvestment of this sum in weekly trading. For the claims on his income of household and farming expenditure, and of requests for short-term credit (rance) from other traders, varied sharply and were often great (chapter 7). As a result, his participation in the weekly turnover trade varied from three sacks to thirty-eight sacks.

In the light of the alternatives, lending on a large scale was a rational strategy. It was also a risky one. Large-scale lenders could not rely on a postharvest increase in grain prices. While Marmara prices rose substantially after the 1977 harvest, there have been several years in which recorded prices in various parts of Hausaland hardly rose from harvest to the subsequent rainy season – 1936, 1964, 1968 and 1979 (Giles 1937: 56; Williams 1981: 112; Table 5.7 above). From harvest 1984 to the rainy season of 1985, the price actually dropped from N80 to N72 in Marmara, and from N90 to N52 in the Funtua interregional grain market.[9] Entrepreneurs in this society were juggling with various types of risk. To store produce risked the possibility that produce prices would stagnate, and denied the investor the accumulated gains of weekly trading. To loan out funds risked a low repayment rate. To keep them in highly liquid form by trading in periodic markets invited the constant claims of household, friends and kin. Achieving profitable balance between social risks was part of the skill of the accumulator.

According to Marmara mallams, the correct Muslim practice in cases where an exchange of money for grain involved delayed payment, was for the 'creditor' to give a measured quantity of grain, to ask the current market price for it, and at harvest the 'debtor' would pay for the grain at the price when it was given. Their understanding of Muslim law may be compared with Giles's summary (following Ruxton 1916) that Muslim law 'abhors uncertain terms in a contract' (Giles 1937: 73), and with Hill's statement (following Meek 1949) that Qur'anic prohibitions against usury and gambling included the taking of risks in forward contracts (Hill 1972: 329). Local Muslim practice was followed in the credit relationship between HH 5 and HH 45:

> For five years, I went to Alhaji at night and received ten tiya of guineacorn. When this was finished, I went for another ten. I would come and go by the back road behind HH 76's house. Alhaji would say, 'I want to help you. I will not give you twenty tiya and ask for one sack at harvest.' But what is the price of guineacorn now? That is what you will pay me in cash at harvest. If we saw each other in the day, Alhaji would just stop and say, 'How are things?'.

Since grain prices dropped between the rainy season and harvest, HH 5 was receiving the equivalent of 'interest' in kind from HH 45 when the loan of grain was repaid with money – but at a rate much less than that expressed in falle agreements. Note, once again, the secrecy surrounding credit.

Apart from the annual borrowing of grain, HH 45 would go to HH 5 for short-term loans without interest (rance). HH 5 was a strict Muslim who maintained a Qur'anic mallam. This example shows how the local understanding of Muslim law influenced some of his credit relationships. It also illustrates how a variant form of annual lending can be embedded in a wider friendship.

Among the Marmara borrowers in these case studies, borrowing increased with the size of landholding. There was also a distinct tendency for the repayment rate to increase with the size of landholding (Table 5.11).

Explaining the Low Repayment Rate of 'High-Interest' Credit

Case studies, anecdotes and individual examples reveal the variety of credit relationships. They show that in annual credit agreements: the *incidence* of indebtedness was high; the *average levels of debt* tended to be low; and the *rate of repayment* of debt tended to be very low. Because of the variety of credit relationships, a full explanation of the

Table 5.11. Marmara borrowers in four case studies (N), Marmara, 1977–79

Loan terms: *N*8–12 in return for one sack of Maize or Guineacorn at harvest time.

Category	Number	Mean no. of loans	Repayment rates
Large Farmers	3	4.3	11 loans: 10.7 sacks of grain 2 loans of 20*N*, 12*N*.
Middle Farmers	4	2.2	6 loans: 5.2 sacks of grain, 3 loans: defaults.
Small Farmers	8	1.5	4 loans: 3.8 sacks of grain, 8 loans: cash advances only.

Source: Chart 5.5 for HH 7, and fieldnote tables for the other three lenders.

low repayment rate is bound to be complex. Moreover, rather different considerations were likely to have affected borrowers in their relations with small-scale and large-scale lenders. I will move from the simple to the complex, from the narrowly economic to the social.

The two obvious sanctions which might have enforced a higher repayment rate were legal and economic. Concerning the legal sanction, most creditors were afraid to sue because of ill-will in a small community. However, where large sums were involved by hamlet standards, creditors occasionally sued debtors before the village head in Yaba, and obtained repayment in produce, or at least recovered their cash advances. For example, HH 21 received from the father of HH 3 a falle loan to be repaid with ten sacks of groundnuts. When his groundnut crop failed, he offered money as repayment in lieu of produce, but was sued before the village head, and so borrowed from other sources in order to repay with groundnuts. HH 97 borrowed a large sum from Alhaji D, the main grain trader and falle lender in Yaba village, and repaid the money only after Alhaji D arraigned him before the village head. These examples suggest that the legal sanction sometimes applied in cases of large-scale default but that the majority of small-scale borrowers could not have felt threatened.

For small borrowers, the main sanction was economic – the expectation that they would need credit from the same lender in subsequent years. However, people often had a number of possible lenders to whom they could apply, in Marmara or nearby hamlets. For example, HH 79 received bashi not only from HH 7 (Chart 5.5) but also from his own junior kinsman, HH 25, and Alhaji I, the largest landholder in a nearby hamlet. HH 28 used to receive falle from his patron, HH 2, but in 1978 he also obtained it from HH 39. Thus, the effectiveness of the economic sanction was influenced by the number of social and economic ties which any particular borrower had developed with alternative lenders.

The sense of rising prosperity during 1977–79 reduced the effectiveness of the economic sanction. The rise in the market value of grain also made borrowers less willing to repay loans with grain. This was the explanation offered by HH 7. According to a borrower, HH 45:

> Before, people used to give bashi openly. Everyone knew. Now, you have to come in the night. For example, ten years ago [circa 1968] we were all in the midst of trouble. He who got bashi would definitely repay because next year he would need again. Now, people are difficult because it is possible to make wealth [*wadata*]. A man will not repay because he thinks next year he will not need a loan.

That the repayment rate had dropped in recent times was expressed lugubriously by Alhaji D of Yaba village: 'I want to stop giving bashi. Before, people were afraid of death. For seven days, there was silence if a man died. Now, as soon as he is buried, he is forgotten. Only money is considered now. The heart of men has dried up [*zuciyar mutane ya bushe*].'

However, the sheer pervasiveness of low repayment rates, combined with the tendency of Large Farmers to repay more of their loans than Small Farmers, show that more complex social factors were at work than a purely economic explanation would suggest. Taken together, the data suggest that it was accepted locally that bashi could not be used to impoverish the debtor; and that there had always been variation in repayment rates, related to the income of borrowers. In other words, the high formal rate of interest expressed perennial risks for lenders.

In this society, the relationship between borrower and lender is very often personal. Of equal importance, the specific credit link is affected by the whole range of economic exchanges between them. The result is an intricate array of actions and reactions. In consequence, the outcome of many credit agreements is unpredictable.

One of the borrowers of HH 83 was an immigrant mallam to whom, with his family, he gave room in his own compound. This man's repayment rate was high. But at the same time, he could expect help from HH 83 in various ways, especially rance repaid from his earnings as a Qur'anic teacher and provider of charms. HH 39 obtained his highest repayment rate from his full-brother, HH 18. But then, he and his full-brother were involved in close daily cooperation across various spheres of household and agricultural life. They jointly purchased, used and rented out a plough in 1979. HH 39 obtained 'interest' from his full-brother in a context of close economic cooperation yielding mutual benefits.

HH 7 achieved his highest repayment rate from HH 20 (Chart 5.5). Their personal relationship was both angry and intimate. Many years before, HH 7 had spent a large sum as the negotiator (*abokin ango*) in HH 20's wedding. At various times HH 20 had borrowed small sums which he had never repaid. As an entrepreneur in cotton buying, maize trading, farming and eventually, in transport, HH 20 took far greater risks, made more, lived in greater style and lost more than HH 7. HH 7 resented both his greater flair as a man and money maker, and his extravagance. HH 20 tried to repay his falle loan of N80 with N100. They quarrelled, HH 7 refused the money, and only later from earnings as a cotton buyer did HH 20 repay seven of the eight sacks of guineacorn originally promised.

HH 35 repaid HH 7 only one of the three sacks owing under his 1977 credit agreement, and none of the sacks owing in 1978. In HH 7's words, 'He has eaten up [*ya cinye*] the money.' Nevertheless, HH 35 was the skilled house builder whom HH 7 chose to rebuild and extend his compound in 1979.

HH 79 repaid both of the sacks owing to HH 7 in 1977 (Chart 5.5). But at the same time, HH 79 could expect various kinds of help from HH 7. He received 20 tiya of guineacorn in 1978, with which he paid his tax. He sought rance of N60 from HH 7 in order to marry in 1979.

B repaid HH 7 only his cash advance in 1977 (Chart 5.5). But then, B was his client labourer (yaro). HH 7 could rely on B for farm labour, paid at the daily rate, in a situation of labour scarcity and rising labour costs. In May 1978 he gave B a bag of fertilizer and in August, one sack of guineacorn with which to feed his family. Likewise, C repaid only HH 7's cash advance. At the same time, C was a junior kinsman and a member of his gandu labour force.

In these instances, lenders and borrowers were linked in a wider exchange of goods and services, wherein each made claims on the other's resources. From these examples, I conclude that a wider field of exchange, flowing through various kinds of personal relationship, creates an area of manoeuvre in credit agreements. Furthermore, this wider exchange forges personal bonds between borrower and lender which allow for various possible solutions to the question of loan repayment. It therefore leads to a form of moral questioning. A borrower asks himself whether it is 'right' or 'obligatory' to repay loans to a particular lender – and on what terms. A lender asks whether it is right to extend new credit to, or otherwise help, a particular borrower who has defaulted or failed to repay in full. The main sanction behind many credit agreements is moral, and the morality is situational.

The language of villagers revealed that they were wrestling mentally with two contrasting viewpoints. On the one hand, they had a clear notion of the 'exploitative' rich. Many informants spoke of falle using this sentence: 'They make profit, we suffer [*sun ci riba, mun sha wahalla*].' Two mallams, in describing the lending of the rich, said forcefully: 'It is not "help" [*taimako*]. May God root it out from us [*Allah ya tsine mana*].' On the other hand, these same mallams preserved a notion of *mutumci* – the treating of every man with respect, more deeply, of according him his humanity: 'You should show *mutumci* to those who helped you when you had no guineacorn.' Failure to abide by a loan agreement was a sign of dishonesty (*rashin gaskiya*) or wickedness (*mugunta*). The solution to this apparent contradiction depended on the context, on the assessment by lender and borrower of the sum total of claims which they made upon each other.

Villagers' assessments of particular credit agreements were also related to their varying moral evaluations of individual rich men. These turned on the question of generosity. A rich man who invested his money in other people through a range of economic relationships – biki, rance, falle, and labour hiring – was regarded as generous. He who carefully conserved his wealth was mean. For example, the hamlet bread seller described the late father of HH 3 in terms with which HH 21 – whom HH 3 had sued – might well have disagreed:

> Alhaji was a man of great kindness. People would chat with him until late at night. If he gave you N200 and you spoiled it, he would be concerned to give you more. HH 103 ate N600 of Alhaji's money. There was not a single person with whom he quarrelled in Marmara. It was to him that labourers would go for work.

The hamlet praise singer offered a comparison of HH 2 with Alhaji U in a nearby hamlet. (He was the youngest brother of Alhaji U and a political opponent of HH 2, but that does not detract from its interest.)

> Alhaji U helps people. He gives plenty of credit – the money of one sack in return for two sacks at harvest. He gives labourers pay without a lot of talk. Because of this, he always has hired labourers – even if he doesn't call them. But HH 2 disagrees with his labourers and has to be argued into giving more pay. As for kudun buhu – only if absolutely necessary [*sai dai 'lalle, ya kamata'*].

> Even now, HH 2 wants to buy another bus but he doesn't lest people say he has used his salary as a local government councillor to buy it. And people say that he is taking his salary and not giving people even kolanut!

Considering language and situational ethics leads us to the most general question – the extent to which low repayment rates reflected the people's consciousness of social change. Villagers were keenly aware that three changes had resulted in a more unequal rural society – increasing population pressure, the expansion of interregional markets for grain and Muslim conversion. Rising demographic pressure had subdivided the land. The involvement of some farmers in long-distance trading networks had given them the means to acquire land (especially from departing pastoralists) and hire labour. Muslim conversion had deprived household heads of women's farm work. It had opened up inequality between farmers based on differences in the number of sons and the ability to hire labour. These changes had concentrated economic power in the hands of farmer-traders.

The expansion of grain markets since the late colonial era had changed credit relationships. In the distant past, grain marketing by donkey transport had been confined to the harvest and postharvest periods. Grain had been sold to pay tax and meet marriage payments, and had been exchanged reciprocally at the ceremonies of friends and kin. It had been borrowed in return for twice as much grain at harvest. Thus, to a large extent it had circulated within the spatial confines of the community, and a sphere of exchange intimately concerned with the reproduction of the household. But the development of year-round grain marketing, increasingly integrated with other regions, had given grain a permanent and rising money value. It had become difficult to borrow grain. Instead, loans were in money, and grain repayments were stored by lenders against a price rise. In the eyes of villagers, their grain was now 'leaving the village', and the gains from this process were accruing disproportionately to farmer-traders. Together, HH 15, HH 99 and the hamlet blacksmith discussed the changes from an almost mythical past:

> Long ago, many farmers could produce one hundred bundles of guineacorn. Now, only the Alhazai or, for example, HH 9 [a corn miller with nineteen acres] can do this. The reason was that everyone worked harder, from six or seven o'clock to sunset. Women worked as well, and when they worked, they were stronger than men. People had not repented [*tuba*]. They believed that what they did was in proportion to their strength. Now that they have repented, they know that Allah

> alone brings or denies, so they rest more! Since Islam, women don't farm. Then, guineacorn and groundnuts were more plentiful than they are now. There was very little hired labour. People lived in mental darkness [*duhun kai*], and did not know the value of money. They used food as money. A man would labour all day and be given one or two bundles of guineacorn, which would last his family for two weeks. Now, only the rich can afford hired labour. [HH 15: For example, 'I have the land but I lack the labour, as I can't afford hired labour.'] Then, people truly lived together and helped each other. People kept secrets among themselves. If a man needed grain, he could get it from his neighbours and friends. 'A tiya draws a tiya': one tiya would be repaid with two. But now, it is difficult to get grain. Now, the big men prefer to sell their grain outside, and make money. Then, it was different, and grain was kept inside the community [gari].

In the forceful account of HH 83, borrowing from the rich entangled poor farmers in a debt trap and other ties of dependence:

> The reason why people don't pay back the big farmers [*manya manoma*] is that they know the intention of those men. For example, of ten sacks at harvest, you have to give two to the lender, two for tax, and one is for your wife and self for buying things. This leaves five and you eat a sack each month. By the rainy season you have none. The money given to you by the same big farmer, you use to buy back the guineacorn which you gave him at harvest to repay your loan. Then he is willing to give you rance to keep you working on his farms and finally you must go back to him for more credit. In this way he removes your crops every year – from one year to the next. This is the wish of the rich men in our village. It is not 'giving help' but 'giving credit'. It is called falle.

HH 83's summary exaggerates: for example, the tax of one person was worth a third of a sack in 1978, not two sacks. Moreover, it oversimplifies by neglecting the contribution of off-farm income to grain purchase. However, the most interesting points are explicit. First, the low rate of repayment was part of a situation of struggle and manoeuvre between rich and poor over the extent to which rich villagers appropriate the resources of poor farmers. Secondly, borrowers were able to resist the pressures from the rich!

Villagers saw credit institutions as evolving, and losing some of their moral value, because of changes in the rural economy. Historical consciousness conditioned their response as debtors. Repayment of loans with the cash advances only, was one way of limiting the demands made by the rich on poorer villagers.

In chapter 4, I used the evidence of changing gandu arrangements to argue that Hausa rural communities collectively yet informally revise their 'custom' in the light of changing circumstances. 'Custom' refers not only to the 'consensus of practical knowledge' of a changing social reality, but also to the 'pattern of moral transfers' between people – the ways in which they negotiate the claims of obligation which they make upon each other. Beneath the diverse adjustments of different communities is a unity of value: the proper purpose of economic endeavour is the preservation of the group of closely related kin as the focal point for meeting human social needs. Though the core group is the household, it cannot be understood without referring to its marriage and kinship ties with other households.

The low repayment rate in falle agreements was not just resistance to the demands of rich individuals. More deeply, it revealed an informal capacity to revise credit relationships, and the mutual obligations expressed in them, in line with people's view of the proper purpose behind all transfers – the provisioning of the household and its expansion through marriage and procreation. The power of rich villagers to appropriate the labour, or the products of labour, of poorer households was mediated by changing 'custom'. Custom was effective because rich and poor inhabit the same moral world.

In summary, the explanation of low overall and variable individual repayment rates is complex because falle was a complex and changing institution. It combined the elements of credit (bashi) and help (taimako) with elements of trading (*ciniki*) and profit taking (riba). It functioned as a relationship between the parties in which each established claims on the other's resources; as a mechanism through which creditors extracted resources from debtors; and as a marketing strategy in which creditors speculated in grain futures and then stored grain for a price rise. Lenders who stored cash and kind repayments in the form of produce made profits that were subject to uncertainty and risk. Repayment rates in the past had been higher than they were under the dynamic economic conditions of 1977–79. But the very complexity of factors affecting the institution imply that repayment rates had always been variable, and seldom such as to throw debtors into a downward cycle of economic decline. Repayment rates were low and variable because creditors and debtors were often linked in relationships through which they exchanged goods and services over a wider field than credit alone. Because they were aware of increased inequality, Small Farmers in the period 1977–79 lowered their repayment rates. This reflected the community's capacity to revise customary behaviour in order to protect ultimate values.

Informants differed as to whether secrecy had always been a concomitant of credit relations. But by 1977–79, it was vital to lenders. If all loans had been known, then lenders would have been under pressure to accept more liberal terms in extending credit. Secrecy functioned to prevent the dissipation of wealth through the pressures of public knowledge. To a certain extent, of course, the 'secret' was public: stories circulated of creditors' 'cruelty' and debtors' 'irresponsibility'. But this did not undermine the rule that both sides benefited from mutual confidence because both stood in need of the other.

Returns to Lending and Returns to Commercial Farming

Informants were agreed that the levels and incidence of falle indebtedness had declined as crop prices, hired labour and land pledging (jingina) had increased. Under certain conditions, jingina had become the alternative to falle. A comparison of the returns to falle lending with the profitability of farming pledged land increases our understanding of changing credit relations.

Jingina was a complex institution. For jingina givers, it was a way of avoiding the sale of land when they needed a large sum of money. For receivers, it was a way of acquiring land in conditions of increasing land scarcity. For both, it was a form of credit. The receiver enjoyed the use of the land until the jingina sum was repaid. Thus, the land was collateral for a money loan, such that the creditor made his 'interest' in the form of returns to farming before the 'principal' was repaid. Jingina should be related to key features of Hausa rural economy: villagers' experience of improvements in the means of production (chapter 1), and the search among most farmers for an off-farm occupation (sana'a) (chapter 4). Under these circumstances, jingina was primarily a countercyclical mechanism whereby farmers financed big expenditures in times of need, with the reasonable expectation of reclaiming the land when their income increased (Table 3.31).

Land was pledged from harvest through the postharvest dry season. Once farming was underway, it was difficult to pledge land, and farmers needing credit would take falle loans. Thus, receiving pledged land and falle lending involved overlapping but rather different periods and so, to a certain extent, were not substitutable for each other as forms of credit.

How did the returns to farming pledged land compare with the returns to falle lending? To explore these questions, I will concentrate on that substratum of hamlet farmers who invested both in agriculture for profit and in falle lending. My evidence comprises case studies of two such farmers. I will examine profit margins on all of their fields for which I have evidence, not just pledged land, during the 1978 farming season. They sold their maize in October–November 1978, for the demand among interregional rural traders was concentrated in that brief period. They stored most of their guineacorn until May–June 1979, when they sold it to pay for farming operations.

HH 6 was the lender who had failed to recover eighty loans given during the 1973 drought. He was the only wholesaler of kolanuts in the hamlet. He expanded his holding from 22 acres to 35 acres in 1978. He had one unmarried son and a young farm servant (*bara*) who lived in the household. Hired labourers performed most farm work. HH 7 was the main wholesale buyer of guineacorn, selling in distant market places (chapters 6 and 7). He expanded his holding dramatically, from 6.2 acres to 22.4 acres in 1978. He deployed a four-man gandu supplemented by hired labour. Both men achieved their 1978 farm size mainly by acquiring pledged land.

HH 7's lending has been treated in detail. I was closely involved with him throughout my fieldwork. I lived in the compound where he stored his grain, followed his marketing operations and came to know his gandu well. At first reluctantly, later with greater interest (as it gave him the chance to describe his business problems), he let me join him as he toured his fields during the farming season, when he related his production costs for each farming operation. While these costs covered only half of his total acreage, I summarize them here because he recounted them in detail. I became friendly with HH 6 much later. At the harvest of 1978, he volunteered to show his fields to me, and volubly discussed the cost of each farming operation. The survey covered all but four acres of his holding – two acres which he gave to his dependents, and two unaccounted for.

On 31 acres, HH 6's investment in inputs and all farm operations yielded him a return of 15 per cent. However, most of this return was generated by the two acres on which he planted yellow maize. On the 29 acres planted to guineacorn, his return to investment in production was only 2.5 per cent (Table 5.12). On 11.4 acres of his holding, HH 7's investment in all inputs and operations yielded a return of 61 per cent, given Marmara selling prices at the times that he sold his output.[10] Yellow maize planted on 1.7 acres generated three-quarters of the return. On the 9.7 acres planted to guineacorn, his return was 21 per cent (Table 5.12). HH 7 achieved a higher return to farming guineacorn than did HH 6 because on his largest field, production was based on gandu labour. It is not costed here. This field (No. 8) provided all his profit from guineacorn. In contrast, HH 6 relied mainly on hired labour.

Table 5.12. The returns to farming using hired labour (N): two case studies, Marmara, 1978–79

		Size of field	Total cost*1 (*1978 fertilizer prices*)	Revenue	Margin	Return
Farmer: HH 6						
Field: 1.	Maize	2.0 acres	192	483	291	**152%**
2.	Guineacorn	2.2 acres	148	320	172	
3.	Guineacorn	1.9 acres	98	138	40	(fields 2–6)
4.	Guineacorn	9.5 acres	719	780	61	**2.5%**
5.	Guineacorn	8.0 acres	600	500	(–)100	
6.	Guineacorn	7.4 acres	478	360	(–)118	
	Total:	**31.0 acres**	**2235**	**2581**	**346**	**15%**
	Holding:	35.0 acres				
Farmer: HH 7						
7.	Maize	1.7 acres	168	462	294	**178%**
8.	Guineacorn	4.9 acres	194	340	146	(fields 8–10)
9.	Guineacorn	1.8 acres	110	100	(–)10	**21%**
10.	Guineacorn	3.0 acres	183	150	(–)33	
	Total:	**11.4 acres**	**655**	**1052**	**397**	**61%**
	Holding:	**22.4 acres**				

*1 Total operating cost: from field clearing through harvest and off-farm transport. It excludes the cost of acquiring pledged fields (no. 1, 2 and 6–10). Jingina sums would increase the annual cost of production, though by an amount which declines in proportion as the number of years the field is pledged rises.

Note: Fields 7 and 8 were farmed with gandu labour, supplemented by hired labour. The remaining fields were farmed mainly with hired labour.

Were these two men typical of commercial farmers in Marmara? They exemplify the two main types of frequent farm employer – those who relied on hired labour as their primary source of labour, and those who combined family and hired labour (chapter 4). Their fertilizer use and yields were consistent with the range of farming practices and yields of other farmers (Appendix 2).

They bought their fertilizer at N3–5 per 50 kg. bag from FADP village warehouses or indirectly from those who had. However, the economic price per bag ex-Funtua (the FADP headquarters) was N13 per bag.[11] Like other rich hamlet farmers, HH 6 and HH 7 used fertilizer on yellow maize but also applied large amounts to guineacorn. Without the fertilizer subsidy, their return to maize would have been more than halved, and they would have been making a small loss on guineacorn. In the absence of a subsidy, their investment decisions might well have been different. But at least we can say that the profitability of the decisions they did make was conditioned by the existence of the subsidy.

Since their only cash inputs apart from fertilizer were maize seed and hemp sacks for bagging produce, the negligible returns to guineacorn resulted from the convergence of low yields with the high cost of hired labour. Because of high labour costs, both men contracted their farmed areas significantly in the following season.

Returns to farming 1978 guineacorn were also small because there was little interseasonal price rise in 1979. In many years, however, the rise has been substantial. Table 5.13 shows the years for which I have evidence. In Table 5.14, I examine returns under hypothetical conditions of a big price rise, but no fertilizer subsidy. If the guineacorn price had risen 67 per cent from harvest to the rainy season, then their returns would have been much higher – between 58 to 64 per cent. Their returns under these conditions would have been close to the 70 per cent return which HH 7 made to falle lending in 1977–78, when the interseasonal price rise had in fact been 67 per cent. Falle loans are distributed roughly a year before the grain accruing from loan repayments is actually sold. Outputs of guineacorn in commer-

Table 5.13. Interseasonal price rises for guineacorn (N), Marmara, 1975–85

	December		July:	Percentage change:
Year: 1975	8 per sack	**Year: 1976**	16 per sack	**100%**
1976	12 per sack	**1977**	24 per sack	**100%**
1977	18 per sack	**1978**	30 per sack	**67%**
1978	18 per sack	**1979**	20 per sack	**11%**
***1 1984**	80 per sack	**1985**	72 per sack	**(–)10%**
***1 1985**	32 per sack			

**1* Data collected in Marmara in December 1985.

Table 5.14. The returns to selling crops (N): Two case studies, Marmara, 1978–79

Farmer: HH 6	Acres	Tenure	Labour	Fertilizer	ROUGH YIELD kg/ha	sacks per acre
1. Maize	2.0 acres	Pledge	HL	741 kg/ha	*1 2,698	*1 11.5
2. Guineacorn	2.2 acres	Pledge	HL	*2 0 kg/ha	1,875	7.3
3. Guineacorn	19 acres	Loan*3	HL	195 kg/ha	933	3.6
4. Guineacorn	9.5 acres	Purchase	HL	0 kg/ha	1055	4.1
5. Guineacorn	8.0 acres	Purchase	HL	0 kg/ha	803	3.1
6. Guineacorn	7.4 acres	Pledge	HL	133 kg/ha	622	2.4
Farmer: HH7						
7. Maize	1.7 acres	Pledge	*G*	726 kg/ha	3,027	12.9
8. Guineacorn	*1 4.9 acres	Pledge	*G*	202 kg/ha	899	3.5
9. Guineacorn	1.8 acres	Pledge	HL	343 kg/ha	719	2.8
10. Guineacorn	3.0 acres	Pledge	HL	82 kg/ha	642	2.5

RETURNS:

Farmer HH 6	1978–9	
1. Maize	152%	
2. Guineacorn	116%	261%
3. Guineacorn	41%	80%
4. Guineacorn	8%	81%
5. Guineacorn	(–)17%	39%
6. Guineacorn	(–)25%	10%
		2–6:*A 64%

RETURNS:

Farmer HH 7	1978–9	
7. Maize	178%	
8. Guineacorn	*4 75%	117%
9. Guineacorn	(–)9%	5%
10. Guineacorn	(–)18%	26%
		8–10:*A 58%

*A Return if no fertilizer subsidy and a 67 per cent post-harvest price rise in guineacorn.
HL: hired labour
G: gandu (with supplementary hired labour)
*1 One weeding only.
*2 Cattle manure – pastoralists corralled on the field.
*3 Aro: one year.
*4 One weeding and one ridging only, which reduced costs in relation to returns.

cial farming are stored until peak annual prices in the following farming season, i.e., roughly a year after most of the expenditure on inputs and farm labour. With both kinds of investment, there is therefore a similar time period before the returns are fully realized. In conditions of a large interseasonal price rise, the returns to farming guineacorn appear similar to those from large-scale falle lending.

In summary, three circumstances led to convergence between the returns to farming jingina land and the returns to large-scale falle lending. First, farmers planted a much larger proportion of their land to guineacorn than to high-yielding yellow maize, because market demand for guineacorn was much larger than for maize (chapter 6). Secondly, the returns to farming guineacorn were squeezed between relatively low yields (Table 5.14) and the high cost of hired labour. Thirdly, both guineacorn farming and falle lending were integrated in a marketing strategy whereby grain was stored for sale after the interseasonal price rise. Under these conditions, the returns to jingina and large-scale falle lending were similar. Moneylending had the advantage that it involved a tiny fraction of the time and energy absorbed in farming pledged land. Farming pledged land had the advantage, relative to moneylending, that risk was confined to uncertainty over the interseasonal price rise, whereas lending involved additional uncertainty about the rates of repayment.

We can thus understand why a rich village farmer, when asked for a large loan from a single borrower, would prefer receiving pledged land to moneylending. The risk of losing any return would be much greater with a single borrower than it would across the spectrum of borrowers. Moreover, in a land-scarce community, land-acquisition as a *long-term* strategy was more highly valued than maximising money returns as a *short-term* strategy. But these considerations would not stop him from lending unsecured money across a spectrum of borrowers, knowing that with money as with land, his ability to profit depended on the size of the interseasonal price rise.

There is a further connection between farming pledged land and moneylending. If the returns to farming guineacorn had been higher and more consistent, then it is likely that real rates of interest on unsecured money loans would have been higher than they were. This does not undermine my social analysis of falle repayment rates, with its emphasis on the personal or obligatory features in many credit relationships. But it is consistent with a social analysis to say that rates of return in one sphere of economic life are influenced by the returns in other spheres. The variable and often low returns to farming pledged land are one of the factors which explain the low and variable rates of 'interest' common in credit agreements.

The two case studies enable us to integrate the analysis of land transfers, labour and credit. As land became more scarce, jingina sums paid per acre had risen sharply and converged with selling prices. The high and rising cost of labour (Table 5.11) limited the profitability of farming. More generally, the social bargaining power of the various kinds of hired labourer lowered the money returns to commercial agriculture, and thus influenced in a downward direction the real interest rate in credit relationships.

Conclusions

In retrospect, Giles captured with remarkable clarity the quality of rural Hausa economic relations in his 1937 report. This is an exaggerated way of making a more accurate statement: there are surprising similarities in the general conduct of credit between the villages he surveyed in the mid-1930s and Marmara in the late 1970s – the contribution of women to household savings and thus to the household's ability to contract marriages for its younger members, and the variety of terms on which credit was given and repaid.

Comparing Giles's with this report, there had been two great changes between 1937 and 1977. First, large interregional grain markets had developed. As a result, loans of grain had been largely replaced by loans of money in return for grain. The greater infusion of grain into commodity exchange had accelerated the monetization of credit relations. Secondly, rising population density had resulted in land scarcity, and so increasing land values had led to land pledging as a credit practice. But the fascinating point is that credit continued to exhibit key features found by Giles: (1) there was a variety of terms on which credit was given and repaid; (2) credit did not proceed in a way to impoverish debtors.

This chapter has related the range of credit institutions to the cycle of necessary expenses. It has done so in order to show how different types of credit meet distinct social needs. Demonstrating the connection between credit and social expenditure has been necessary in order to address broader questions. Were the majority of Small and Middle Farmers viable – i.e., able to finance the cycle of necessary expenses without alienating land or going heavily into debt? What was the nature of economic relations between villagers engaged in long-term wealth acquisition and the majority of poorer villagers?

Three conclusions emerge from an exploration of case studies:

1. Credit institutions fell into three groups. First, adashi, biki and rance were characterized by 'simple' reciprocity – exchange in equal measure. Secondly, falle was characterized by what I term *moral reciprocity*. While large-scale lenders profited by lending, their returns were limited by a moral consensus: credit relations

ought to enable borrowers to provision their households and expand them through marriage and procreation. Thirdly, jingina was the one credit practice entailing the transfer of land from money borrower to moneylender. However, Large Farmers, not Small or Middle, were the main borrowers of money through jingina, and very often, they eventually repaid the loans and reclaimed pledged land (chapter 3). The main lenders of money under jingina were rich farmers, but the returns to farming pledged land were limited by the social bargaining power of the various kinds of hired labourer.

2. The range of credit institutions made it possible for most Small and Middle Farmers to finance the cycle of necessary expenses without alienating land or going deeply into debt. It enabled them to meet the heaviest expense of middle age – the marriage of their adult dependents.
3. While villagers expressed formal rules for items in the cycle of expenses and for credit practices, actual behaviour diverged from the rules in variable, sharp and unpredictable ways. Flexibility of practice meant that many poorer household heads were able to slip through the barriers expressed in formal rules. They were able to meet the cycle of expenses by operating in the interstices between the ideal and the possible.

This chapter has focused on the contribution of credit practices to the fulfilment of socially defined patterns of spending. The reverse analysis is equally essential. By exploring the cycle of expenses, we more clearly appreciate the factors influencing credit relations. Gifts – especially marriage gifts – circulated in the community. The flow of gift and countergift resulted from and reinforced a myriad of ties: kinship, marriage, friendship or simply the bond created by the face-to-face exchange of goods and services. It also arose from the local practice of Islam. While the rural practice of Islam did not enforce a ban on usury, it did fashion a social ethos which emphasized the importance of zaka and sadaka (chapter 1). Reciprocal and redistributive exchanges of money and grain linked people of similar and of very different income.

I briefly review the influence of credit institutions on each other. Adashi associations reveal women organising to consolidate their individual savings and those of poorer men. Resources saved and invested by women enlarged the capacity of households to expand through marriage, reduced the need to pledge land in financing marriage and, ultimately, reduced the annual levels of debt of the poorer household heads. Participation in biki networks increased the ability of men and women to obtain interest-free loans (rance) for marriages and naming ceremonies. The circulation of interest-free loans involved the ebb and flow of men's subsistence funds as well as their investment funds. Borrowers of rance then lent it out. The combination of these credit forms reduced the annual need for 'high-interest' credit (bashi).

Richer and poorer villagers were locked together in a complex arena of struggle (over labour rates), competition (over land acquisition), manoeuvre (in credit relations) and cooperation (through biki exchanges). We can visualize this complexity more clearly by abstracting from it a 'Small Farmer' and a 'Large Farmer' and then observing the various guises in which they appeared to each other. The Small Farmer might at different times be a labourer, a borrower, a giver of pledged land and a giver of gifts at the richer man's weddings. He might even be competing with the richer man to acquire pledged land. The Large Farmer could be the poorer man's benefactor at weddings and naming ceremonies, and his exploiter in a credit agreement. The same Large Farmer who was harshly castigated for his meanness would give alms scrupulously out of his harvest output.

This alternation of conflictual with cooperative images reinforces the general picture of Hausa rural economy that emerges from a study of land, labour and credit. Smaller landholders had a range of means for self-advancement and for resisting the pressures of the rich. The rich shared with smaller landholders a basic moral value: the household ought to be preserved as the focal point for meeting social needs.

Notes

1. *Survey of Rural Credit, Northern Region*, 1965 (mircrofilm in the Institute of Agriculture Library, Samaru, Nigeria).
2. Household heads who were mallamai or Qur'anic beggars (almajirai) were recipients rather than givers of zaka.
3. Estimates are made easier because market prices for maize and guineacorn were stable at N20 per sack through January–July 1979.
4. For typical yields, see Appendix 2, Tables 1 and 2.
5. He would have intercropped a small amount of cowpeas and groundnuts – enough cowpeas to add variety to the diet. Groundnuts did very poorly over 1976–79.
6. Eight of the fourteen household heads with dependent workers and less than 5 acres hired out their dependents frequently (Table 5.8).
7. A heaped tiya of guineacorn weighed slightly more than 2.7 kg., a sack of 40 tiya about 109 kg. A heaped tiya of maize weighed about 2.5 kg., a sack of 40 tiya, 100

kg. (weights in chapter 7, Case Study III, under *Market Outlet Retailer,* and Appendix 2, Table 2).

8. In a year of plentiful cotton, he would postpone grain sales as much as possible until the end of February, after cotton marketing, in order to benefit from post-harvest rises in grain prices.
9. Farmers and traders provided this information in December 1985.
10. This is for comparison with HH 6. In fact, he sold at higher prices in distant markets, but the extra return is attributable to trading. See chapter 7.
11. This information was given by the deputy manager, FADP, 1979.

Chapter 6

Interregional Produce Markets

Introduction

The previous chapters have analysed economic relationships within the hamlet of Marmara during the period 1977–79. This chapter goes beyond the hamlet. It examines the agricultural marketing during the same period, whereby the farmers of Marmara were linked to the much wider regional economy. Its focus is on the marketing of grains, which were the main source of income throughout 1977–79.

To understand agricultural marketing, we must broaden the scale of analysis in order to describe the trade linkages between Malumfashi Division, of which Marmara hamlet forms a part, and other areas. This chapter describes the main marketplaces for grains inside the division, and the major destinations of those grains beyond it. Since agricultural marketing linked Malumfashi Division with other regions, the chapter also looks at the pattern of interregional demand for grains from this division, and how that demand affected prices in the hamlet of Marmara and nearby marketplaces.

This chapter addresses an important question: to what extent did farmers in Malumfashi Division sell their grain within their hamlets, and to what extent was grain transported and sold in distant marketplaces? It also examines the types of trader who bought and sold their grain.

Primarily, however, it serves as a descriptive prelude to chapter 7 (*Rural Produce Traders and Wealth Acquisition*). That chapter will analyse the economic relations into which traders entered, and the impact of those relations on rural patterns of wealth acquisition.

Malumfashi Division in the Economic Region of Southern Katsina

The basic unit of analysis in this chapter will be one part of southern Katsina – Malumfashi Division, comprising the administrative districts of Malumfashi and Kankara. The reason for its choice is that Marmara had strong traditional and cultural ties with Malumfashi and Kankara Districts, but not with the other districts of southern Katsina.

Marmara hamlet is on the border between Malumfashi and Kankara Districts. It is well linked by road with both Malumfashi and Kankara towns. Politically, as a part of Yaba village, it is subject to the Malumfashi District Head. Economically, hamlet cotton buyers during 1976–79 operated with advances provided by licensed agents from the Nigerian Cotton Board who were based in Malumfashi town, and they sold their cotton at its buying station (*flotti*). Hamlet people attended the biweekly market in Malumfashi town and in its shops they made their bigger purchases (chapter 1). But economically, their ties with Kankara District were at least as strong as those with Malumfashi District. They attended Yargoje and Kankara markets more frequently than Malumfashi market. It was at Yargoje and Kankara that they sold grains and livestock, and purchased cloth. Moreover, hamlet traders often borrowed funds from traders in the villages and hamlets of Kankara District.

The main food and cash crop in Malumfashi Division during 1976–79 was a type of yellow guineacorn called kaura. Though groundnut production had sharply declined since the 1973 drought, it was still important in the north of Kankara District. Introduced by the FADP in 1975, yellow maize was planted widely in Malumfashi District. In both districts, the widespread production of cotton declined in 1977 and almost disappeared in 1978 (chapter 1).

Agricultural Marketing: Malumfashi Division

Farmers and traders distinguished four main periods in the annual agricultural marketing cycle:

1. Guineacorn Harvest: mid-November through December
2. Postharvest Dry Season: January through April
3. Farming Season: May to early August
4. Minor Harvests: mid-August to early November[1]

Harvesting usually began as early as August, with the reaping of millet. It was grown in small quantities by a minority of farmers, having been largely supplanted by the higher-yielding yellow maize. In September, many farmers harvested small quantities of rain-fed rice, which they grew on low-lying land where water gathered. Apart from its use as special food in marriage and naming ceremonies, rice was treated as a cash crop. Its sale was mainly confined to September and October. In October, yellow maize was harvested. Maize was an important stop-gap food which carried families through until the guineacorn harvest. Farmers across the spectrum of landholding sold most of their marketed maize in October and November, because the market, in northern Katsina, was confined mainly to those months. In late October and early November, farmers harvested groundnuts. Because of the high demand for it throughout northern Nigeria, larger producers were able to store some groundnuts against a price rise. The harvest of the main crop, guineacorn, began in November and reached a peak in December. Smaller landholders sold most of their marketed output of guineacorn from December through March. Larger landholders sold some guineacorn in December and January, but stored most of their marketed output until May, June and July, when they sold it in order to pay agricultural labourers. In the years when it was planted, cotton was harvested from December through January, and marketed in January and February.

Apart from January and February, therefore, agricultural marketing concerned the various grains, and groundnuts. From September through November, it was based on rice, maize and groundnuts. In December, and from March through August, it mainly consisted of guineacorn. In 1979, because of the sharp fall in cotton production in the previous farming season, guineacorn was the main crop marketed over a nine-month period, from December through August.

The Major Marketplaces for the Grains and Groundnuts of Malumfashi Division

A number of periodic marketplaces, meeting once or twice weekly, were frequently attended by the farmers of Malumfashi Division. All of these marketplaces offered a range of goods and services, including sections devoted to grains, small livestock and cloth. But in volume of grains and groundnuts, Kankara and Yargoje markets were far bigger than any of the others. The major reason for their size was that long-distance grain traders linked them to a vast market of two sorts: the grain-deficit area to the north of Malumfashi Division, and urban areas. Kankara and Yargoje were almost at the northern edge of the Northern Guinea Savannah (Map 3). They were strategically placed for traders to and from the Sudan and Sahel ecological zones. Both were on the Katsina-Funtua road feeding directly into the main highway system of Nigeria. For the farmers and small-scale hamlet traders in the division, the two marketplaces were the focal points of supply and interregional demand.

To the north, the market demand for the grains and groundnuts of Malumfashi Division extended deep into the Niger Republic. Traders from Niger entered Nigeria through Illela, north of Sokoto, and Jibiya, north of Katsina. The former was more than 250 miles, and the latter more than 100 miles, from Kankara and Yargoje. From northwest to northeast, market demand extended more than 200 miles, from the environs of Sokoto city to the hinterland of Danbatta in northern Kano State.

Throughout this grain-deficit area, the Fulani pastoral population was much greater, and the ownership of livestock by the farming population was more widespread, than in southern Katsina. Millet was the dominant food crop. Millet yields were lower than the guineacorn yields of southern Katsina, thus encouraging big demand for guineacorn from Kankara and Yargoje. Otherwise, the nature of production varied from west to east. To the north of Sokoto in Niger, floodplains extending eastwards from Birnin Konni provided large amounts of onions. In the Sokoto Closely Settled Zone, the floodplains of the Sokoto and Rima Rivers supported a dense population which grew rice and sugar cane as cash crops. In the hinterland of Danbatta, the floodplains of the Gari and Tomas Rivers supplied the market with large amounts of tomatoes and peppers, while upland farms yielded sweet potatoes and cowpeas. Before the 1973 drought, Kaura Namoda in northern Sokoto State, and Danbatta in northern Kano State, had been major producers of groundnuts but since the drought, they had purchased these from Kankara. Thus, the essential pattern of interregional exchange was guineacorn and groundnuts from Malumfashi Division in return for money from the sale of livestock and riverain produce.

Four marketplaces outside the division were also important in linking its farmers to the northern grain-deficit area – Funtua, Sokoto,

Mai Aduwa and Danbatta (Chart 6.1 and Map 3). Much of the grain and groundnuts carried to these destinations did not flow through Kankara and Yargoje. They were transported by traders who had purchased them directly from hamlet farmers.

Funtua was the principal commercial town of southern Katsina. Its marketplace brought together wholesale sellers from southern Katsina with wholesale buyers from Niger, Sokoto State and the cities of Zaria and Kaduna. Buyers from Kaduna and Zaria came mainly during the harvest periods, whereas buyers from Niger and Sokoto came throughout the year. In Sokoto marketplace, the majority of grain was purchased wholesale by rural traders who sold it in nearby hamlets. Mai Aduwa was a small village on the border with Niger near the town of Daura. It mushroomed weekly into one of the largest marketplaces (in area) in northern Nigeria (Map 3). The size of this marketplace stemmed from its position on the border between two countries. This enabled it to provision the wholesale market in Niger as well as wholesale and retail markets around Daura town. Danbatta marketplace served the rural consumers of Danbatta District. The eastern and southern parts of Danbatta District were in the Kano Closely Settled Zone, with population densities of over 350 per square mile, rising steeply with proximity to Kano city (Mortimore 1968: 298).

Agricultural marketing between Malumfashi Division and the cities was concentrated in the months of the Guineacorn Harvest, and January. Although Malumfashi Division was only 75 miles north of Zaria and 60 miles west of Kano, wholesale buyers in those cities had developed long-standing contacts with different areas of supply. According to the traders whom I studied, Kano city obtained most of its guineacorn from southern and eastern Kano State, Gwarzo (west of Kano city), and Sundu marketplace on the marches of Zaria and Kano Emirates; most grain flowed to Zaria city from Sundu marketplace and southern Zaria (see Hays 1975 for a study of grain marketing between Sundu and Zaria).

Chart 6.1. Major marketplaces buying grain and groundnuts from Malumfashi Division

Marketplace:	Market day:	Distance from Kankara:
Funtua	Monday, Thursday	48 miles
Sokoto	Thursday	254 miles
Danbatta	Sunday	140 miles
Mai Aduwa	Sunday	135 miles

The Organization of Wholesale Trading in the Major Marketplaces

Kankara and Yargoje

Farmers used donkeys and buses to transport grain and groundnuts to the market; produce from more distant off-road hamlets was often brought by small-scale traders who had purchased it from the farmers and transported it by donkey. In Kankara and Yargoje marketplaces, most grain was purchased by three types of buyer: (1) farmers, in the Post-harvest Dry Season, using off-farm earnings; and the middle/late Farming Season, using earnings from farm labour, and credit; (2) government contractors, in the Minor and Guineacorn Harvests; (3) private traders, throughout the year.

Produce was sold and bought through market measurers (*masu auna,* sing., *mai awo*) who would rent a stall or simply a space from the local authority. They did not normally buy in their own right, but merely performed an intermediary service. They were paid by sellers, at the rate of one tiya per forty tiya sold, or its money equivalent. There might be a small price variation between measurers, and a change in market conditions could affect prices during the market day. Wholesale traders used market measurers to buy the bulk of their produce. Thus, the 'market' price was the same for retail and wholesale buyers.

At Kankara and Yargoje, we can distinguish between *contractors and private traders.* Contractors bought on behalf of state and local governments. Their purchases were limited to the harvest periods, when market prices were lowest. Private traders operated throughout the year. They bought with their own money and that of patrons. Sometimes, the bigger private traders were contractors as well. Secondly, we can distinguish between *local* and *external* traders. (For case-studies, see chapter 7.)

Two specializations were noticeable among produce traders. While grain traders bought some groundnuts, they tended to leave groundnuts to its own specialists because supply was concentrated in the northern part of Kankara District. Yellow maize also had its own specialists because the area of demand was limited mainly to the marketplaces of northern Katsina Emirate.

Funtua

The wholesale produce trade was transacted through substantial dealers, called *masu rumfa* (sing., *mai rumfa*). Traders would gather in the shed (*rumfa*) of the dealer, who also bought and sold in his own right and on contract. The mai rumfa would receive a small commission (la'ada) of 20 kobo per sack transacted. Moreover, he would undertake to store large volumes for several days until sellers had found a buyer, or the buyers had found transport. Furthermore, he would store produce for several months for trading friends. He found buyers for big farmers who were seeking to unload large volumes of output.

In the Post-harvest Dry Season of 1979, traders from Niger bought through one mai rumfa alone 400–600 sacks of kaura. I followed two Nigeriens to their home village of Galmi, east of Birnin Konni. Their long-distance trading benefited from good roads and plentiful transport. Leaving Galmi on Saturday, they arrived in Funtua on Sunday, did business on Monday and were back in Galmi by Tuesday evening. On Wednesday, they sold their grain in Galmi market. In 1979 in Funtua, these two traders purchased 300 sacks per week in the Post-harvest Dry Season; during the Farming Season, considerably less, as farmers in Galmi were eating from their own granaries. In the Farming Season, their more regular source of supply was in the Sahel northeast of Zinder, almost 300 miles from Galmi (Map 2).

Sokoto

Wealthier produce traders from southern Katsina had private arrangements for storing produce for several months. Ordinarily, however, a long-distance trader wished to sell quickly and return home without tying up his capital, in order to continue weekly trading. The intermediaries who expedited wholesale transactions were the market commission agents (*dillalai*, sing., *dillali*). They brokered wholesale sellers' grain for a commission of 20 kobo per sack.

Mai Aduwa

Private traders from Malumfashi Division sold guineacorn wholesale as long as interregional price differences allowed a profit margin – January through July in 1978, January through March in 1979. They paid dillalai 20 kobo per sack to broker their guineacorn. They sold to different kinds of wholesale buyer – contractors for the Government of Niger, private traders from the towns and rural areas of southern Niger, private traders provisioning nearby villages, and retailers in Mai Aduwa marketplace.

Danbatta

Unlike the preceding three markets, there was no physical distinction between the wholesale and retail produce sections. Traders from southern Katsina piled their sacks in the sand beside the retail stalls. They sold through commission agents (dillalai), the commission being 20 kobo per sack. There were three main types of wholesale buyer –

market retailers, who bought and sold in their own right; small-scale traders who bought to provision outlying villages; and contractors from the adjacent district of Minjibur and Emirate of Kazaure. A further type of wholesale buyer made Danbatta an interesting place. Camel caravans from the region of Agades purchased grain during the rainy season and again at harvest time. In the rainy season, they sold dates, their original load, at Magaria in southern Niger, where they purchased dum-palm fronds (*kaba*) for sale in Danbatta marketplace and the surrounding villages. At harvest time, they came with potash and salt from the desert.

Between these four marketplaces there were differences in the structure of total demand for wholesale produce. The four formed a spectrum in terms of the volume sold retail in comparison with that transacted only between wholesale traders. At one end, in Sokoto and Funtua, retail marketing was relatively unimportant. At the other, in Danbatta, the majority of sacks transacted wholesale flowed immediately into retail trading. Mai Aduwa occupied an intermediate position on the spectrum. Differences in the structure of demand had three consequences for the organization of wholesale marketing:

1. *The payment of brokerage fees.* In Sokoto, traders from southern Katsina were competing to find a wholesale buyer. Consequently, sellers customarily paid the commission (*la'ada a ciki,* or inside the wholesale price). In Funtua, both parties had usually travelled some distance to the place of transaction. As a result, either buyer or seller might pay the commission. Indeed, this was a bargaining point in negotiating the wholesale price. In Danbatta, traders from southern Katsina were selling to the full range of wholesale buyers, among whom market retailers were the largest single category. Given the strength of retail demand, wholesale buyers were competing for the supply to a greater extent than at Sokoto or Funtua. Consequently, buyers tended to pay the commission (*la'ada a waje,* or outside the wholesale price).

2. *Periodicity of trading.* In Sokoto, wholesale buyers bought large amounts at harvest-time and in the Post-harvest Dry Season for storage and sale during the Farming Season.[2] In Danbatta, traders from southern Katsina were selling to a vast retail marketplace which flourished throughout the year. In Sokoto, wholesale demand was more concentrated in the months of December–April than it was in Danbatta, where it was always strong, fluctuating with the rhythms of the annual marketing cycle.

3. *The structure of supply.* Traders from southern Katsina to Sokoto tended to be wealthier or to have access to larger patron funds than traders to Danbatta. In consequence, they tended to carry larger vol-

umes per journey (50–100 sacks), and to accept greater risks of delay in selling. They travelled less frequently in the Farming Season. Traders to Danbatta tended to be smaller actors, carrying in the range of 10–50 sacks per journey, but they travelled weekly in all seasons. Danbatta was a more secure outlet market for the smaller trader.

Produce Outflows from Kankara and Yargoje Marketplaces in 1978–79

My research assistant from Marmara collected statistics of produce outflows by lorry at Yargoje and Kankara marketplaces. They covered most of the Guineacorn Harvest and Post-harvest Dry Season at Yargoje; and these two seasons plus the most intensive part of the Farming Season at Kankara.[3] During this period, guineacorn accounted for almost all of the produce outflow by lorry.[4] The relative importance of different months was strongly affected by the fact that in the previous farming season, farmers had given up cotton and planted grains instead. Lacking cotton, they marketed an unusual amount of guineacorn in the Post-harvest Dry Season of 1979. From Yargoje, the major destination was Danbatta marketplace, which accounted for 40 per cent of the produce outflow by lorry. Kankara was a much larger marketplace than Yargoje. From Kankara, the principal destination was the Republic of Niger, accounting for nearly two-thirds of the total (Table 6.1).

Since Kankara and Yargoje were the major marketplaces for grain in Malumfashi Division, I analyse them together for the data period

Table 6.1. Summary: Produce outflows Kankara Market, weeks ending 5 December 1978–19 June 1979

All quantities are in number of sacks

Month	Nigeria	Niger	Unknown	Total:	Nigeria %	Niger %
December	6,977	4,250	130	11,357	61%	37%
January	11,131	5,680	374	17,185	65%	33%
February	3,069	7,430		10,499	29%	71%
March	3,508	9,820	276	13,604	26%	72%
April	2,389	10,742		13,131	18%	82%
May	2,221	14,655		16,876	13%	87%
*1June	933	6,989		7,922	12%	88%
Total:	**30,228**	**59,566**	**780**	**90,574**	**33%**	**66%**

*1 First three weeks only.

common to both (Chart 6.2 and Table 6.2). From 10 December through 8 April, almost 71,000 sacks were transported from Kankara and Yargoje marketplaces – approximately 7,300 tons.[5] At least 42 per cent went to the Republic of Niger. If we combine Niger with grain-deficit regions inside Nigeria, then at least 61 per cent of the total produce outflow was transported to the grain-deficit area north of Malumfashi Division. Only 26 per cent went to cities in Nigeria. Moreover, almost two-thirds of the total produce was carried in long-distance trade – to destinations over 100 miles from these marketplaces.

The grain-surplus regions referred to in Chart 6.2 (eastern Sokoto and southern Katsina) had large agricultural projects funded jointly by the federal government and the World Bank. Contractors taking grain to destinations in those areas delivered it to government warehouses; private traders stored it against a price rise. It is likely that some of this grain was ultimately sold in grain-deficit regions. Thus, the total produce outflow to the grain-deficit area north of Malumfashi Division was probably greater than 61 per cent.

This complex picture is very different from Hays's findings in his big study of Sundu rural marketplace in northern Zaria in 1970–1. In his research, 'rural assemblers' – the only traders to transport grain

Chart 6.2. Kankara and Yargoje markets: Destinations, outflows by lorry from the market, 10 December 1978–8 April 1979

A. Niger	
1. Cities	Kano, Kaduna, Zaria, Katsina
2. Grain-deficit regions	Towns: Daura
	Periodic marketplaces:
	1. *Central Katsina:* Dutsinma, Masawa, Jikamshi, Dan Gani
	2. *Northern Katsina:* Caranci
	3. *Northern Kano:* Danbatta, Badumi, Bichi, Babura, Tofa
	4. *Northern Sokoto:* Sokoto marketplace
3. Grain-surplus regions	Towns: Malumfashi, Gusau
	Periodic marketplaces:
	1. *Eastern Sokoto:* Chafe, Rimin Gado
	2. *Southern Katsina:* Bakori, Yankara
4. Funtua entepot market	
B. Niger	

Table 6.2. Kankara and Yargoje markets: Destinations, outflows by lorry from the market, 10 December 1978–8 April 1979

I. Immediate destination	Volume	Per cent	Volume	Per cent
A. Nigeria:			**38,057 sacks**	54%
1. Cities	18,265 sacks	26%		
2. Grain-deficit regions	13,733 sacks	19%		
3. Grain-surplus regions	3,895 sacks	5%		
4. Funtua entepot market	2,164 sacks	3%		
B. Niger			**30,006 sacks**	42%
5. Through Illela	16,676 sacks	24%		
6. Through Jibiya	13,330 sacks	19%		
C. *Not known*	2,730 sacks	4%	2,730 sacks	4%
Total:	**70,793 sacks**	**100%**	**70,793 sacks**	**100%**
II. Distances by road:				
A. Less than 70 miles	4,684 sacks	7%		
B. 70–100 miles	17,738 sacks	25%		
C. More than 100 miles	45,641 sacks	64%		
D. *Not known*	2,730 sacks	4%		
Total:	**70,793 sacks**	**100%**		

from Sundu – sold all grain in cities, the farthest being 85 miles away (Hays 1975: 41, 52–53).

The amount shipped to Niger through the border at Illela – 280 miles distant – was considerably greater than that shipped across the border at Jibiya, 100 miles away (Table 6.2). Malumfashi Division was linked by traders to a truly vast, and international, grain market. In 1979, the incomes of farmers in the division were powerfully sustained by demand for grain from Niger.

Produce Marketing Outside Marketplaces – The Example of Marmara

I have focussed on the marketplaces where farmers in this division sold their produce, and the sorts of trader who bought there. Now, I return to Marmara to consider more basic questions. To what extent did farmers sell produce directly to traders in the hamlets rather than at marketplaces? Then, what did hamlet traders do with the produce purchased?

The roadside settlement of Marmara was only seven miles south of Yargoje, fourteen miles south of Kankara, and eight miles west of Malumfashi, on an excellent road system served by dozens of small passenger buses (four of which were owned by farmers in the hamlet). Though it was much closer to Yargoje and Malumfashi, its traffic to Kankara was much heavier. Kankara marketplace joined a larger number of buyers and sellers than the other two marketplaces combined. In 1977–79, grain prices tended to be higher at Kankara than at Yargoje. Even after paying the higher transport fare to Kankara, farmers still made a net gain compared with Yargoje.

From December 1977 through March 1979, average monthly prices for a sack of kaura guineacorn sold to traders in Marmara hamlet were never more than 9 per cent less than the average monthly price in Kankara marketplace (Table 6.3). For a farmer taking one to three sacks from Marmara roadside to Kankara, there were few months when the price difference between Marmara and Kankara was greater than the marketing cost (Table 6.3). If he lived beyond the roadside settlement, he had to hire a donkey to carry his grain from homestead to roadside, reducing still further the months when there was a net price advantage at Kankara. For a farmer marketing a large number of sacks, two factors were usually sufficient to prevent him from transporting his produce to market: uncertainty on the morning of the market day as to the market price; and the time involved in arranging transport or waiting at Kankara market for buyers. Thus, most of the marketed output of grains and groundnuts was sold to hamlet traders, not at marketplaces.

The price difference between hamlet and marketplace was so small because hamlet traders were directly involved in long-distance produce trading. If the difference between the price which they offered farmers and the Kankara market price had been consistently greater than the marketing cost to Kankara, they would have failed to attract produce.

Who were the hamlet farmer-traders? Four farmers bought guineacorn, groundnuts and rice, and transported them over 125 miles to the weekly marketplace of Danbatta. Four others specialized in purchasing yellow maize and carried it to a circuit of marketplaces in central and northern Katsina. Of these eight, six lived in the roadside settlement of Marmara and two in homesteads a mile behind the roadside. The eight purchased over a radius of about two miles, buying from individual homesteads as well as larger settlements, from Maguzawa as well as Muslims. The landholdings of farmer-traders, or their ownership of other assets, made them richer than the average. They

Table 6.3. Price differentials and marketing costs for the farmer from Marmara to Kankara for *kaura* guineacorn

A. Costs of marketing Guineacorn from Marmara to Kankara, 14 miles

0.20N per sack transport fee

0.10N per sack loading at Marmara

0.20N per sack unloading at Kankara grain sheds

0.65N average fee to the market measurer (*one tiya per 40 sold*)

Total: 1.15*N*

Fixed cost: 0.60 personal return fare

B. Average marketing cost in 1978 per sack of *kaura* guineacorn on:

One sack: 1.75, Two sacks: 1.45, Three sacks: 1.35

C. Average monthly price per sack of *kaura* guineacorn of 40 Tiya:

	Marmara	**Kankara**	**Price difference**	**Marketing costs** (*on 1–3 sacks*)
1977: December	18.00	19.00	1.00	1.57 – 1.17
1978: January	22.50	24.00	1.50	1.70 – 1.30
February	28.00	28.50	0.50	1.81 – 1.41
March	*unk.*	*unk.*	*unk.*	*unk.*
April	27.60	28.20	0.60	1.80 – 1.40
May	28.25	28.80	0.55	1.82 – 1.42
June	30.00	31.50	1.50	1.89 – 1.49
July	29.20	30.50	1.30	1.86 – 1.46
August	26.00	26.40	0.40	1.77 – 1.37
September	22.50	24.50	2.00	1.71 – 1.31
October	25.60	25.60	0.00	1.74 – 1.34
November	21.00	20.00	(–)1.00	1.60 – 1.20
December	18.40	19.50	1.10	1.59 – 1.19
Average:	**25.37**	**26.14**	**0.77**	**1.75 – 1.35**
1979: January	18.00	19.60	1.60	1.59 – 1.19
February	17.50	19.20	1.70	1.58 – 1.18
March	20.25	21.90	1.65	1.65 – 1.25

Table 6.4. Grain traders in the Marmara hamlet area, Marmara, 1977–79

Trader:	Acres	Other Assets	Age	Family size
		A. TRADERS IN GUINEACORN, GROUNDNUTS AND RICE		
HH 7	22.4	Cattle	55	16
HH 13	13.2	Two oxen and plough	40	14
HH 14	13.2	Two oxen, plough and groundnut decorticator	45	11
HH 44	6.2	Two oxen and plough	55	11
		B. TRADERS IN YELLOW MAIZE		
HH 16	12.6	None	65	5
HH 20	12.0	Bus (1979)	40	7
HH 25	10.0	Two oxen and plough	35	5
Son, *1LFNS	*unk.*	*unk.*	25	*n.k.*
		C. MEANS, ROADSIDE SETTLEMENT:		
	7.8		47	

**1* Large farmer, neighbouring settlement (in the hamlet area).

had families much larger than the mean (Table 6.4). From March 1978 to February 1979, these traders carried almost 1,500 sacks of grain and produce to Danbatta. This was equivalent to 175 tons of produce per year, or nearly 3.5 tons per week[6,7] (Table 6.5).

Hamlet traders stored only a small proportion of guineacorn purchased at harvest until the peak prices of the Farming Season (chapter 7). They sold most guineacorn within the week of purchase at their final outlet market. Table 6.5 shows that some farmers stored guineacorn and sold much more in the Farming Season than during or just after harvest. Farmers sold a high proportion of their minor crops at harvest. The evidence for guineacorn and the minor crops complement each other and the evidence for credit practices (chapter 5). From July until December, the majority of farmers met cash needs, first by taking money credit repayable at harvest, and then by sales of minor crops.

The tendency of farmers to delay guineacorn sales until after harvest may be compared with the figures in Hays's marketing study of villages in northern Zaria in 1970–1. Hays surveyed eighteen households in each of three villages, stratified by landholding into 'large' and 'small' farm units.[8] Unlike Marmara, guineacorn was intercropped with millet. Large and small farmers averaged half of their guineacorn

Table 6.5. Produce outflow from Marmara to Danbatta, weeks ending 26 March 1978–18 February 1979 (figures in sacks)

A: Periods	G'corn	G'nuts	Rice	Maize	Locust Beans	Average share per week: volume	Average share per week: per cent
26 March–30 April	172						
Post-harvest Dry Season							
1 May–6 August	601	54	6		2		
Farming Season							
7 Aug.–5 Nov.	147	52	74	5			
Minor Harvests							
6 Nov.–*1 31 Dec.	159	14		1			
Guineacorn Harvest							
1 Jan.–18 Feb.	169	13	4				
Post-harvest Dry Season							
Total, 45 weeks:	**1,248**	**133**	**84**	**6**	**2**		
B: Traders' Shares							
HH 7	667	16	59			16	50
HH 44	291	16	16	2	2	7	22
HH 13	247	83	9	4		8	25
HH 14	34	18				1	3
Son, HH 1	9						
Total:	**1,248**	**133**	**84**	**6**	**2**	**32**	**100**
C. Estimate, 52 weeks:	1,435	153	97	7	2	33	
D. *2 tons per week: (*Metric tons*)	149	13	12	0.7	0.2	3.4	

*1 Two weeks missing – ending 12 November and 19 December.
*2 For weights of sacks of the different crops, see Appendix 2, Table 2.

crop still in storage six months after harvest. Small farmers averaged 14 per cent of their guineacorn in store eleven months after harvest (Hays 1975: 19–20, 23–24, 34–37). In Marmara, two-thirds of farmers had exhausted their guineacorn nine months after harvest (chapter 5).[9]

Marmara, only seven miles on a road from the nearest big marketplace, was 'exporting' directly some three tons of produce per week in long-distance trade. How typical was this pattern of other hamlets in the region? To what extent did farmers in other hamlets sell directly to long-distance traders, as opposed to selling their produce at marketplaces? In Marmara, all farmers lived within two miles of a roadside. Thus, Marmara was a hamlet where grain traders had the special advantage of low overhead costs in transporting grain by donkey from the farmer to the roadside; more generally, facility in making arrangements with lorry transporters. The question therefore becomes: to what extent did other hamlets have access to long-distance traders?

In other hamlets of the division, this question resolves itself into three issues. How did the returns to long-distance trading compare with the returns on short-distance trading to the nearest marketplace? Did traders have, or could they borrow, funds for long-distance trading? Were traders able to make arrangements with lorry transporters for regular pick-up to distant destinations?

Comparative Returns to Long-Distance and Short-Distance Trading

The price paid to the farmer by traders in a hamlet was usually less than the price at the nearest produce marketplace. It was considerably less than the price at long-distance market outlets. For traders in any part of Malumfashi Division, the question would be the return to long-distance trade, after deducting donkey transport costs to the roadside, compared with the return to short-distance trade, after deducting the greater transport costs to the produce marketplace. Given the greater difference between 'farm' price and long-distance market price, compared with the difference between 'farm' price and nearby market price, the net returns to long-distance trading were usually greater than those to short-distance trading.

The Distribution of Trading Capital and Borrowing Facilities in the Rural Areas

Case studies will later show the range of relationships through which rural traders borrowed money for trade (chapter 7). Here, it is enough to clear up a possible misconception – that hinterland traders were poorer than roadside traders and so dependent on them for loan money. In fact, traders behind the road could be more wealthy than roadside traders, and loan the latter trading funds. For example, a little over three miles behind Marmara roadside lived MGT in an isolated homestead. He transported thirty to fifty sacks of guineacorn weekly to the market in Sokoto. He kept his guineacorn in HH 1's storeroom in Marmara, and had useful contacts with other farmers up and down the road. When he was becoming too old to trade, he married his only daughter to the senior son of HH 7, Marmara's main grain trader, and continued to trade through him. He gave his son-in-law a long-term loan with which to trade on his own account, and HH 7 short-term trading loans.

Two miles behind the Marmara roadside was Unguwa Makau. This settlement contained many traders in different lines. One of them was the patron of Marmara's oldest maize trader. Another maize trader, HH 25, obtained loans from a farmer whose hamlet was three miles behind the Marmara roadside. It had a markedly higher proportion of plough owners than Marmara. Since cattle are one of the more liquid forms of rural wealth, there are good grounds for believing that long-distance traders in the hinterland would actually have had access to more money than traders near the roadside, where the population was more dense and the traditional cattle trails were continually encroached upon by farmers expanding their acreages. Funds for long-distance trading were at least as available in the hinterland as in roadside hamlets.

The Maguzawa beyond Marmara sold large amounts of grain to Muslim traders from the roadside settlement. Among the Maguzawa, I observed no long-distance grain traders. Concerning the Maguzawa, Last has argued that conversion to Islam is essential for trading beyond a narrow financial limit. According to Last, the scale of trading in Hausa society depends on the network of friends who give goods on credit or money loans with which to buy produce. A non-Muslim can expand a network within a narrow limit of turnover. To maintain the pace of expansion beyond that limit, he must convert. The other economic factor favouring conversion is the need to accumulate trading capital. In Maguzawa society, agricultural wealth circulates in the form of gifts. This limits the accumulation of trading funds (Last 1979: 239–40).

If the relative number of traders is less among the Maguzawa, they will have greater need of marketplaces than Muslims. This explains a curious fact: that Yargoje marketplace flourished so near to Kankara marketplace. Yargoje was at the centre of the largest concentration of Maguzawa in Malumfashi Division.

Ease of Arrangements with Lorry Transporters

This is the issue which separated hinterland hamlets from roadside hamlets. In practice it was more difficult for traders living at distances of (say) five to ten miles from a roadside to remain in continuous contact with lorry transporters or farmers in roadside hamlets who could offer them storage facilities and act as their agents.

Considering the three issues, it becomes possible to compare trade movements in Marmara with those likely in other parts of the division. Farmers had little need of produce marketplaces where they had access to long-distance traders. Long-distance traders normally lived on or near a roadside. They used their own funds and tapped the resources of wealthy farmers in the hinterland. As distance from a roadside increased, it became more difficult for farmers to maintain regular contact with traders. The proportion of produce sold to long-distance traders diminished, and the proportion sold at nearby marketplaces, or to short-distance traders using those marketplaces, increased.

This analysis explains why the two big marketplaces for produce were in Kankara District. Kankara District was more poorly served by roads than Malumfashi District. As a result, a higher proportion of farmers in Kankara District were beyond regular contact with long-distance traders. Moreover, a higher ratio of produce traders in Kankara District found it difficult to make regular arrangements with lorry transporters. Therefore, they engaged in short-distance trade to Kankara and Yargoje marketplaces.

Farmers in Malumfashi Division must have sold a considerable share of their produce directly to long-distance traders. It came mainly from hamlets on or close to the roadside. A higher proportion of farmers in Malumfashi District, with its more ramified system of secondary roads, sold their produce to long-distance traders than in Kankara District.

Interregional Exchange between Malumfashi Division and Danbatta District

Long-distance traders linked hamlets and marketplaces in Malumfashi Division primarily with the grain-deficit area to the north. Let us now explore the pattern of exchange with one part of that area, Danbatta District in northern Kano State. As guineacorn was the main product traded between Malumfashi Division and Danbatta District, I begin by comparing their guineacorn prices. I then explain the price pattern for guineacorn in terms of the annual agricultural marketing cycles in the two areas, and the ways that these cycles intermeshed.

Relative Prices of Guineacorn

Table 6.6 compares producer prices in Marmara with the price in Kankara Tuesday market and the retail price in Danbatta Sunday market. Prices at each level are monthly averages of the prevailing price per week for a sack of kaura guineacorn. Since most guineacorn pur-

Table 6.6. Guineacorn prices (N), 1977–79

		Producer price	Measurer's price	Retail price	Price: percent difference Marmara - Danbatta
	Month:	**Marmara**	**Kankara**	**Danbatta**	
1977:	December	18.00	19.00	27.28	**34%**
1978:	January	22.50	24.00	30.80	**27%**
	February	28.00	28.50	34.76	**21%**
	March	*unk.*	*unk.*	*unk.*	***unk.***
	April	27.60	28.20	34.76	**21%**
	May	28.25	28.80	34.10	**17%**
	June	30.00	31.50	36.96	**19%**
	July	29.00	30.50	36.96	**21%**
	August	26.00	26.40	30.80	**16%**
	September	22.50	24.50	29.04	**22%**
	October	25.60	25.60	29.92	**14%**
	November	21.00	20.00	30.36	**31%**
	Average	**25.33**	**26.09**	**32.34**	**22%**
	December	18.40	19.50	25.52	**28%**
1979:	January	18.00	19.60	24.64	**27%**
	February	17.50	19.20	23.76	**26%**
	March	20.25	21.90		
	April		21.80		
	May		21.20		
	June		21.50		

chased by traders in Marmara was going to Danbatta, the comparison summarizes the degree of linkage between prices in areas of supply and demand. It covers fifteen months from the Guineacorn Harvest of 1977. Producer prices are those paid by HH 7, the leading grain trader in Marmara, for a measured sack containing 40 tiya.[10] Kankara prices are those paid per tiya by grain measurers in the market, multiplied by 40. The final retail price in Danbatta market is the retail price per tiya, multiplied by 44 (see the discussion below).[11]

Marmara traders bought grain from producers by the sack and in variable tiya quantities. HH 7 bought most by the sack. In the Postharvest Dry Season, women and sons of household heads would sell him 5–20 tiya from their gayauna output, to get money for biki donations. Prices paid to tiya sellers – multiplied by 40 to obtain their sack equivalent – could be less than, or the same as, prices paid to sack sellers, but the difference was small.[12] When demand in relation to supply was showing a steady upward trend, HH 7 would quickly settle on the same price to tiya and sack sellers. When demand in relation to supply was stagnant or falling (as in early 1979), he would try (sometimes unsuccessfully) to buy at a discount from tiya sellers.

Through most of 1978, the difference between Marmara producer prices and those in nearby Kankara marketplace was usually smaller than the cost to the farmer of marketing a sack from Marmara to Kankara. In October 1978, the price gap shrank to nothing and in November, the price was actually higher in the hamlet than in the marketplace. In early 1979, the price gap slightly favoured Kankara marketplace (Table 6.6).

For the hamlet trader, the price in Kankara marketplace was neither a buying nor a selling price. It was a *price indicator* – a kind of benchmark – enabling him to visualize market forces. When, as in early and mid-1978, prices were rising in the nearby marketplace, this indicated to him that demand was continuing strong in relation to supply. He would try to pay a producer price not higher than the nearby market price. When, as in October–November 1978, prices in the nearby marketplace were tumbling as harvest supplies came in, he was unable to 'keep up with' the fall in prices, and ended up paying producers as much as, or more than, they would have got in the nearby market. When, as in early 1979, the nearby market price was stable, he was able to offer a producer price lower than the nearby market price (Table 6.6).

Danbatta market retailers normally bought grain in their own right from southern Katsina traders. Though they used the word tiya, they manipulated bowls of various sizes in selling guineacorn. They measured guineacorn using a bowl of the same size as the standard Katsina tiya for three types of customer – purchasers who were bulk buyers, personal friends and trading friends of long standing. But for the many anonymous buyers of small quantities, the most commonly used bowl allowed 44 measures to be sold from a sack of 40 standard Katsina tiya. The use of a smaller bowl than the tiya guarded retailers against wholesalers from southern Katsina who sold them sacks containing less than 40 tiya. It also protected their profit margins from downward price fluctuations during the market day (see chapter 7, Case Study III under *Market Outlet Retailer*).

The interseasonal price rise was almost twice as sharp in the area supplying Kankara marketplace as it was in Danbatta marketplace (Table 6.6). In the agricultural year beginning December 1977, Kankara market prices rose from December to June by 66 per cent whereas retail prices in Danbatta rose over the same period by 35 per cent. The difference between the mean monthly producer price in Marmara and the mean monthly retail price in Danbatta was much greater during and immediately after harvest (November–January) than it was during the rest of the year. Prices in Marmara and Kankara were very close. Prices in all three markets tended to change in the same direction. There were some small, but revealing, differences between price trends in the supply area and the demand area, particularly in November.

In looking more closely at price changes, I note that Table 6.6 averages weekly market prices over a month. This tends to smooth out price variations within each market as well as between markets. In summary, the difference between mean monthly producer prices in Marmara and mean monthly retail prices in Danbatta averaged 22 per cent for the agricultural year beginning with the Guineacorn Harvest of 1977. The price gap tended to be greatest at harvest. Thereafter, the gap narrowed until the preharvest months of the following year. It averaged 26 per cent from December through February – when smaller farmers sold most of their marketed output. It averaged 19 per cent from May through July – when larger farmers sold most of theirs. Long-distance traders found their profit margins squeezed at the very time when larger farmers were selling most of their marketed output.

Agricultural Marketing Cycles in Malumfashi and Danbatta

We have already outlined the agricultural seasons. Let us now examine them more closely in the two areas. By examining particular supplies and demands in different seasons, we will better understand the shape of the price curve for guineacorn (Figure 6.1). We will also see how exchange between the two areas was rooted in their culture, work patterns and social relations of production. Five features of rural economy affected the supply of and demand for guineacorn:

1. Marriage expenditure;
2. The production and marketing of other agricultural products (including livestock);
3. The importance to household income of off-farm occupations;
4. The essential role of hired labour in agriculture;
5. Inequality in landholding and hence, in the capacity of farmers to feed their families.

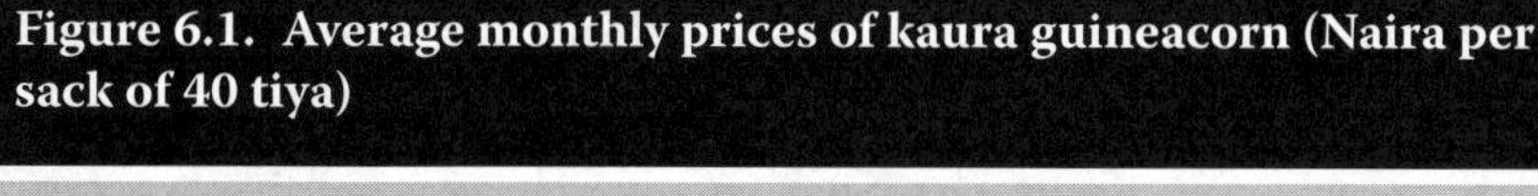

Figure 6.1. Average monthly prices of kaura guineacorn (Naira per sack of 40 tiya)

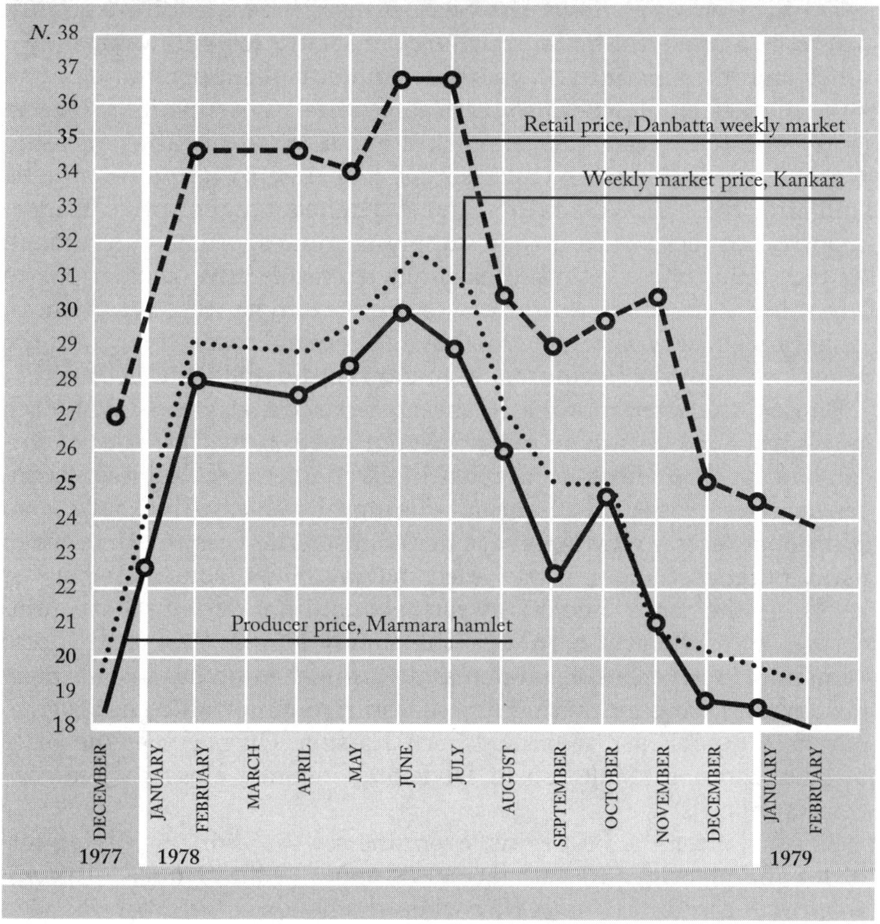

The impact of any one of these features on the market for guineacorn varied greatly with the season. For clarity, I consider separately the annual marketing cycle in each area. Yet necessarily, I note the seasonal impacts of external demand from Danbatta on prices in Malumfashi, and of external supply from Malumfashi on prices in Danbatta.

I begin with the marketing cycle in Malumfashi Division. During the Guineacorn Harvest, the main feature to influence supply was expenditure on marriage. Farmers across the spectrum of landholding sold large quantities to defray marriage expenses. Demand was at its lowest because rural households were eating the newly harvested grain crop. Supply rose in relation to demand. Therefore, the price fell from preharvest levels.

During the Post-harvest Dry Season, marriage expenditure continued to be a powerful force impelling farmers to sell guineacorn. Two other factors came into play as determinants of supply and demand – the marketing of other products, and off-farm occupations. During January and February, farmers picked and sold cotton. They also sold goats, sheep and cattle, which earlier had time to fatten on stubble land after the various harvests, and so fetched a higher price. Consequently, farmers reduced their supply of guineacorn to the market. At the same time, they used earnings from off-farm occupations to buy it for their families, in order to preserve their stores of grain. In January–February, the supply fell, while demand rose. As a result, the price rose from the beginning of January to the middle of February.

During the later months of the Post-harvest Dry Season, March and April, expenditure on marriage continued. However, sales of cotton had finished and sales of most kinds of livestock declined. Farmers therefore returned to the marketing of guineacorn. There is an additional reason why larger farmers did so. This was the time when many purchased oxen, cattle prices having fallen from their harvest levels. At the same time, many farmers continued to purchase guineacorn with off-farm earnings. The supply rose in relation to local demand. However, external demand was pushed up because farmers in Danbatta were marketing dry-season riverain produce in order to purchase guineacorn from southern Katsina. On balance, the price of guineacorn in Malumfashi Division remained close to January–February levels.

In May, after the first rains, everyone set to ridging, applying fertilizer and planting. Smaller farmers stopped selling guineacorn until *yabanya* – the time in late May when the newly sown crop was high enough for them to gauge the size of the next harvest. Moreover, they harvested and sold their main tree crop, locust beans (*kalwa*). Supply of guineacorn from smaller farmers therefore fell. Supply from larger farmers increased, to acquire funds for ploughing services and chemical fertilizer. Overall, supply rose marginally.

Many farmers who had earlier been buying grain with off-farm earnings now opened their granaries to feed their families. At the same time, many used earnings from hired labour, others from the sale of locust beans, to buy guineacorn. Overall, demand rose marginally. Guineacorn prices fluctuated weekly, but remained close to April levels.

In the mid–Farming Season (June and most of July), marketing was dominated by the important role of hired labour in agriculture. It was also affected by inequalities in landholding and hence, in family food supply. Larger farmers increased their sales in order to pay hired labourers for weeding. Many smaller farmers experienced difficulties in grain provisioning. Some bought guineacorn with earnings as labourers. Others obtained credit repayable at harvest (chapter 5). Demand rose in relation to supply, and so did price. In Marmara, the price reached its highest annual level (N32) in the first week of July, but fell to N24 by the last week. In Kankara, the price fluctuated between N30 and N32 in June, stabilized at N32 in the first three weeks of July, before falling to N26 in the last week.

By late July and August, larger farmers had completed weeding and ridging, and therefore did not need to sell grain to pay hired labour. Farmers with sufficient grain to meet household needs were eating it rather than selling it. Smaller farmers who had exhausted their grain met family needs by obtaining cash loans repayable at harvest (chapter 5). August was the 'hungry month', not only because grain stores were at their lowest annual levels, but also because there was less opportunity to earn the wherewithal to buy it. This was the month of restricted grain consumption. Many households substituted vegetable dishes. The supply of guineacorn was limited to those farmers with a surplus over household needs. They unloaded part of this on the market, anticipating price falls during the upcoming harvest. Demand fell in relation to supply. The price fell.

During the Minor Harvests, farmers in this division harvested and sold small amounts of millet (August), larger amounts of rice (September) and considerable quantities of yellow maize (October and November). In November, those in the northern parts of Kankara harvested large amounts of groundnuts. Larger farmers increased their sales of old guineacorn (from the previous year) to pay for the harvesting of the minor crops.

Millet, rice and maize were substitute foods for guineacorn. Demand for guineacorn fell while supply rose. The price fell. However, the price of guineacorn temporarily increased in October because many labourers employed in harvesting yellow maize bought guineacorn, the preferred staple. As the agricultural year drew to a close, newly harvested guineacorn began to enter household granaries and the market, raising supply, lowering demand and so lessening the price.

In the model of a 'simple' rural economy, characterized by broad equality in landholding and guineacorn as the single crop, a small and gradual price rise would be expected over the year. At harvest, many farmers would sell guineacorn to finance marriages, and before the end of the agricultural year, some would need to buy it. In contrast, the complex circumstances of Malumfashi Division generated a sharp interseasonal price rise. We can, moreover, sort out their relative impact on the price. In a year after a farming season in which much cotton has been planted, the sharpest increase is likely to occur in January and February, when farmers withdraw from the guineacorn market while they sell their cotton. The next price rise, in the Farming Season, will be much less steep. For, although demand increases from smaller farmers, supply rises from larger farmers in order to pay hired labourers. Further, the planting of a large area to a nonfood crop, cotton, is bound to increase the difficulties of smaller farmers in food provisioning. Thus, the planting of cotton is the single most important factor generating a sharp price rise during the year.

This argument is borne out by the evidence from Kankara marketplace for the three years in which fieldwork was conducted (Chart 6.3). All three were years of good harvests.[13] The major difference was between the first two years and the third. In 1975–6 and 1977–8, cotton was plentiful, but in 1978–9 cotton production was negligible. In the first two years, most of the annual increases in the price of guineacorn occurred from December to the end of February, when cotton was being sold. The subsequent price rises, in the Farming Season, were gentle. In 1978–9, however, farmers marketed guineacorn continuously from harvest through the Post-harvest Dry Season. The price of guineacorn actually fell from December through February, and the price rise in the Farming Season was less than it had been in 1975–6 and 1977–8. In all three years, larger farmers had to sell such large amounts of guineacorn in order to finance farm labour that the price rise in the Farming Season was slight.

* * * * *

The pattern of rural economy in Danbatta District, fifteen to forty miles north of Kano city, was very different from that in Malumfashi Division. The sandy soil is much less fertile than the clay soil of southern Katsina (Map 3). In sharp contrast to southern Katsina, where farmers usually grew their various crops in separate fields (some cowpeas being interplanted), farmers in Danbatta everywhere practiced mixed cropping of grains, groundnuts and cowpeas. At Danbatta Sunday market, thousands of sacks of guineacorn from southern Katsina were purchased by farmers, and by traders provisioning hamlets in the district. Since the 1973 drought, and the consequent onset of Ro-

Chart 6.3. Percentage changes in guineacorn prices, Kankara market, 1975–79*1

1975–76	Price fluctuations: Naira per sack	Per cent change
December to February	8.00 – 12.00	50.0%
March to April	12.00 – 14.80	23.0%
May to August	15.20 – 16.00	5.0%
*2August to December	16.00 – 12.00	(–) 25.0%
Inter-seasonal rise (*Dec.–August*)		100.0%
End 1975 to end 1976		50.0%
1977–78		
December to February	19.00 – 28.50	50%
March to April	28.50 – 28.20	(–) 1.0%
May to August	28.80 – 31.50	9.0%
June to December	31.50 – 19.50	(–) 38.0%
Inter-seasonal rise (*Dec.–June*)		66.0%
End 1977 to end 1978		3.0%
1978–79		
December to February	19.50 – 19.20	(–) 1.5%
March to April	21.90 – 21.80	(–) 0.5%
May to June	21.20 – 21.50	1.4%
*2June to December	21.50 – 14.00	(–) 35.0%
Inter-seasonal rise (*Dec.–June*)		10.0%
End 1978 to end 1979		(–) 28.0%

**1* Monthly averages of weekly marketplace prices, e.g. from the first Tuesday of December to the last Tuesday of February.

*2 Information supplied by Marmara villagers.

sette disease, groundnuts from southern Katsina were also much in demand.

The district stretched twenty-five miles north–south and thirty miles east–west at its greatest extent. Cattle ownership was much more widespread among sedentary farmers, and the number of small livestock much greater, than in Malumfashi. There was also a much larger Fulani pastoral population, mainly in the northern part of the district. Two rivers, the Gari and the Tomas, run along the western and northern boundaries and through the southern parts. Farmers there produced irrigated vegetables and sugar cane for sale. As in southern Katsina, land was unequally distributed and the demand for hired labour was high.

The retailer whom I studied in Danbatta market introduced me to a hamlet near Danbatta. Unguwa Heru was located in the midst of extremely sandy soil. The majority of farmers owned cattle. From harvest through the Post-harvest Dry Season, they kept their cattle in the hamlet, herded by small children. Farmers had long-standing agreements with pastoralists. At the start of the rains, they divided their herds into three parts, keeping some at home, sending a part with Fulani to graze in the open country north of Danbatta town, and the largest part to the bush. These cattle returned at the millet or guineacorn harvests. The Fulani were not paid for herding but had the free use of the milk and manure in the Farming Season.

Farmers had to supplement their own grain supply with purchases of guineacorn, selling cattle in return. Bulls were not sold until their seventh year, cows until their fourteenth year, when they had ceased delivering. The ideal was to sell cattle in October–November or December–January, after they had fattened on the stalks after the millet or guineacorn harvests. Thus, Unguwa Heru maintained an integrated livestock and crop economy. In contrast to southern Katsina, where the primary forms of material wealth among farmers were land and grain, in Unguwa Heru it was cattle. Ecological differences between Danbatta and southern Katsina made it possible for many farmers in Danbatta to buy guineacorn by selling livestock.

In Danbatta District, the demand for guineacorn in relation to local supply and external supply from southern Katsina was least at the December harvest. The price of guineacorn was at its lowest annual level. But demand itself was much stronger than in Malumfashi Division at the same time of year. The reason is that in Danbatta, farmers were selling an increasing number of livestock from the millet harvest in September onwards through the guineacorn harvest in December, in order to buy and store guineacorn until the following farming season, when there was a shortage of local grain. Thus, the price gap between Malumfashi Division and Danbatta District tended to be relatively wide in December (Table 6.6). Though in both areas demand in relation to supply was at its lowest annual level, in Danbatta, demand was sustained by livestock sales. This explains why the rise in prices from harvest into the subsequent farming season was much less steep in Danbatta than in Malumfashi.

In January–February, farmers and pastoralists continued to sell increasing numbers of livestock, which fetched higher prices than in December, having had time to fatten on stubble land after harvest.

They used part of the proceeds to buy guineacorn. At the same time, farmers in Malumfashi Division were withdrawing from guineacorn marketing while they sold their cotton. In Danbatta, demand for guineacorn in relation to local and external supply increased, and so did the price.

In March, April and May, sales of livestock abated. Sales of dry-season irrigated produce greatly increased. Demand for guineacorn increased. But external supply from southern Katsina also rose, since farmers there had finished selling cotton and returned to marketing guineacorn. The price of guineacorn fluctuated around February levels.

The Farming Season began later around Danbatta than in Malumfashi. In June and July, farmers and pastoralists sold cattle to pay their hired labourers. Large farmers sold grains for the same reason. Demand for guineacorn, from smaller farmers and hired labourers, rose in relation to local and external supply. The price of guineacorn reached its highest annual level. Danbatta retail prices reached a peak of N39.60 in the first week of June, at the same time as in Kankara, and then fluctuated around N37.40 until the fourth week of July, when they dropped to N35.20.

August was the month of restricted grain consumption in Danbatta as in southern Katsina. Demand for guineacorn fell in relation to supply. The price fell. In September, farmers harvested millet, their main crop. This lowered demand for guineacorn. In October and November, farmers increasingly sold cattle in order to buy and store guineacorn from southern Katsina against the next Farming Season. The price rose somewhat, before falling at the Guineacorn Harvest in December.

Guineacorn prices at Danbatta closely followed a similar pattern to those in Malumfashi Division, but at a higher level (Figure 6.1). In both markets, there was an inverse relation between guineacorn and livestock price changes. Prices of livestock were highest at harvest and in the Post-harvest Dry Season, lowest during the Farming Season. They were highest in December–February because supply consisted of livestock fattened on stubble land; there was great demand from farmers with harvest money to spend. Prices were at their lowest in June–August because Fulani sold much livestock in order to pay hired labourers farming for them; there was little demand for livestock from Hausa farmers concentrating their resources on agriculture.

Differences in the pattern of guineacorn price changes between the two areas resulted from differences in their agronomic systems. In November 1978, the price fell sharply in Malumfashi while rising slightly in Danbatta. In the former, harvested yellow maize and early varieties of guineacorn depressed the price. In the latter, farmers were selling livestock to buy guineacorn. The contrast in price changes shows that local conditions do not vary in the same ways in all months. However, the interaction of supplies and demands limited the scope and variation of price differences between the two areas.

Traders moving between the two areas transmitted demand for guineacorn from Danbatta District to Malumfashi Division. This raised producer prices in Malumfashi above the level they would have been without interregional trade. Traders carried supply throughout the year to Danbatta marketplace, thus reducing prices there. In the year beginning with the Guineacorn Harvest of 1977, the average monthly gap between Marmara producer and Danbatta retail prices only exceeded the average annual divergence of 22 per cent around harvest time, or immediately thereafter (Table 6.6).

Summary

During the period 1977–79, produce traders linked Malumfashi Division with two sorts of market – the immense grain-deficit area to the north, including Niger, and the cities of northern Nigeria. Trade to the grain-deficit area north of the division absorbed a much higher proportion of total produce outflows than did trade to Nigerian cities. Most produce flowing out of the division was carried in the long-distance trade. Produce prices in Malumfashi Division depended on external demand in other economic regions, transmitted by long-distance traders. In consequence, the income of farmers was governed by a market which stretched into Niger.

The wholesale produce trade was well organized. Inside the division, produce was bulked either in marketplaces or in the hamlets themselves. Beyond the division, four marketplaces were major centres for breaking bulk or trans-shipping produce – Funtua, Sokoto, Mai Aduwa and Danbatta. Brokers in those marketplaces played a crucial role in bringing together wholesale sellers and buyers. By negotiating decisions over produce prices, they helped clear stocks and assisted the process of price formation.

There were two types of wholesale marketing – government contracting and private trading. Sometimes, a man was involved in both types of trade. Purchases on government contract were concentrated in the harvest periods, whereas those of private traders continued throughout the year. Consequently, the flow of produce through private traders was much greater than the flow to government agencies.

From a case study of one hamlet, Marmara, I have argued that there was a very considerable outflow of produce directly from the hamlets in long-distance trade. Moreover, this outflow was carried by hamlet farmers who specialized in produce trading as an off-farm occupation. They used their own funds and borrowed funds from wealthier farmers.

Three main points emerge from a study of the market for guineacorn in Malumfashi Division and Danbatta District. First, trade in guineacorn from Malumfashi to Danbatta was rural–rural, not rural–urban. Long-distance traders were linking large rural populations. Secondly, trade limited the price difference between the two areas. Thirdly, their rural economies were well integrated with each other, in the specific sense that guineacorn prices in each area were determined by supplies and demands over both.

Because traders constantly linked Malumfashi and Danbatta, we should approach their marketing cycles in an integrated fashion. In both areas, inequality in landholding and hence, in food supply, caused an increasing number of households to buy guineacorn as the agricultural year progressed – consequently, a rise in the price of guineacorn. But we can distinguish between years in which an important nonfood crop (cotton) was available in the area of supply, and years when it was not. In years when cotton was plentiful, guineacorn prices rose sharply in both areas in the Post-harvest Dry Season, because farmers in the area of supply withdrew guineacorn from the market while they sold their cotton. In years when cotton was not plentiful, prices rose little after harvest because farmers in the area of supply sold guineacorn continuously. Within any year, we can further distinguish between the Post-harvest Dry Season and the Farming Season. During the Farming Season, the need to finance hired labour impelled rural employers to market large amounts of guineacorn. Although both areas were marked by inequality and hired labouring, in the absence of a nonfood crop, there was not a sharp rise in food prices over the agricultural year.

Notes

1. Seasonal dates used below reflect conditions around Marmara in 1978.
2. In May 1978 I counted over 8,000 sacks of grains in the wholesale section of Sokoto marketplace, for sale or awaiting collection.

3. Spending each market day at the motor parks, he was helped at Yargoje by a local lorry commission agent and at Kankara by the chief of the motor park (*Sarkin Tasha*).
4. Research done earlier showed that in October–November, groundnuts and yellow maize were the chief exports by lorry.
5. The number of tiya measures per sack varied with the trader and his market outlet, from 38 to 40. 38 tiya of guineacorn weighed 104 kg. (Appendix 2, Table 2 endnote 3).
6. In addition, the leading maize trader (HH 20) bought and sold 220 sacks over September–November, each of the other maize traders somewhat less, for a total of 600 sacks of maize, or 60 tons.
7. The period during which this information was collected cuts across two agricultural years, from the Guineacorn Harvest of 1978 and that of 1979. Normally, hamlet traders bought a small amount at harvest for storage until the farming season. Thus, the figures include a small amount carried to Danbatta in the Farming Season of 1978 but actually purchased at the previous harvest; they exclude a small quantity bought in the 1978 harvest but not sold until the subsequent Farming Season. Still, they indicate broadly the volume of guineacorn, groundnuts and rice sold by all farmers to hamlet traders over the period.
8. The 'small' farm units averaged 5 acres (2.1 ha.), the 'large' farm units, 19.5 acres (7.9 ha.).
9. The difference in findings is great. His 'small farmers' tended to have more land than most farmers in Marmara. The nine sampled small farmers in each of his three villages averaged 1.4, 2.0 and 3.0 ha., respectively. In Marmara, 50 per cent of landholding household heads had 1.7 ha. or less; 40 per cent had 1.3 ha. or less.
10. For weights of a tiya and sack of guineacorn, see chapter 7, Case Study III under *Market Outlet Retailer*, and Appendix 2, Table 2, note d.
11. In Marmara and Kankara, I collected the information. In Danbatta marketplace, I collected prices for nine weeks in the four agricultural seasons of 1978; for all other weeks, prices were provided by a lorry commission agent from Marmara who travelled weekly to Danbatta, and by HH 7. (The market days when I collected prices were: 15 January, 26 February, 23 April, 21 May, 4 June, 6 August, 24 September and 17 December.)
12. The reduction for tiya sellers was in the order of 80 kobo on a sack valued at N27–30 in 1978, and N1–2 on a sack valued at N18 in 1979.
13. Late rains in the summer of 1977 reduced yields in comparison with the summers of 1975 and 1978.

Chapter 7

Rural Produce Traders and Wealth Acquisition

Introduction

In chapters 3 to 5 I analysed the economic relationships between richer and poorer villagers of Marmara hamlet. Through studies of land, labour and credit, we observed various constraints on the acquisition of wealth. This chapter addresses a final question: how do some people overcome the constraints in order to become rich?

I consider wealth in two senses – the specific accumulation of farmland (and the labour power to work it), and the more general, many-faceted process of acquiring 'wealth' as the rural Hausa understand it. Already, we have discussed avenues to wealth. A number of villagers in Marmara began with an historical advantage: their families had been in the area longer and had therefore acquired more land over the years. Others through their conversion to Islam were able to enter Muslim trading networks, and hence, to acquire trading funds, sources of supply, and markets. Most widely, trading in one line or another generated profits which could be invested in land, and in family and hired labour power. By 'trading', I mean either the bulk purchase of commodities for resale in smaller amounts (e.g., cloth), or the purchase of small amounts for bulking and wholesale transfer (e.g., grains or cotton). I also include shopkeeping, but completely exclude the small-scale vending from wooden tables (*teburi*). In Marmara, trading was certainly connected with success in the expansion of landholding (Table 7.1).

This chapter examines trading in a particular group of commodities – grains and groundnuts – in order to explore how rural people acquired and augmented investment funds for commerce and agriculture. Through case studies, it describes how rural traders borrowed investment funds. Moreover, it shows how they distributed their income and expenditure between various ends.

As chapter 6 went far beyond Marmara to outline the system of produce marketing in which the hamlet was embedded, so, too, this chapter moves beyond Marmara to study the range of social relationships which rural traders entered in the course of pursuing wealth.

Why case studies in produce trading? Studies in grain trading are particularly apposite, because in the grain-surplus region of southern Katsina, guineacorn was the major source of agricultural income for most farmers during 1976–79. Groundnuts remained the second largest source of farm income for farmers in Kankara District. Case studies of grain and groundnut trading are likely to throw more light on the general processes of wealth acquisition in this economic region than are studies of, for example, the cotton or cloth trade.

The three cases concern, firstly, a *large-scale marketplace trader* in grains and groundnuts; secondly, a *wealthy rural intervillage wholesaler* of grain; and thirdly, a *hamlet grain wholesaler*. In each case, different types of social relationship were dominant – for the Market-

Table 7.1. Landholding and participation in trade, Marmara, 1978

Landholding	Household heads	Acreage range	No. of traders or former traders
Deciles: I	HH 1 – HH 11	49.9 – 16.3	6
II	HH 12 – HH 22	14.4 – 11.6	4
III	HH 23 – HH 33	11.5 – 8.3	1
IV	HH 34 – HH 44	7.7 – 6.2	3
V	HH 45 – HH 55	6.0 – 4.0	3
VI	HH 56 – HH 66	3.9 – 3.2	2
VII	HH 67 – HH 77	3.1 – 2.6	1
VIII	HH 78 – HH 88	2.5 – 2.0	0
IX	HH 89 – HH 99	2.0 – 1.1	2
X	HH 100 – HH 108	1.1–0.5	0

place Trader, his ties to a local ruler; for the Intervillage Wholesaler, his links with private urban merchants and government contractors on the one hand, and hamlet wholesalers on the other; for the Hamlet Wholesaler, his links upward to the intervillage wholesaler, and outward to other hamlet traders. Each of these traders occupied different *niches* in the marketing system of the region.[1]

In the conclusions to this chapter, I compare the three studies in order to delineate a model of the local rural Hausa process of wealth acquisition. In the Conclusion of the book, I connect these cases to the different kinds of evidence in the earlier chapters, in order to advance a more general model of the pattern of accumulation characteristic of rural southern Katsina. Therefore, readers will ask to what extent these three cases are 'representative' of other farmer-traders.

The cases grew out of fieldwork. Nothing was preplanned about my selection of traders. Chronologically, knowledge of the Hamlet Wholesaler led me to the Intervillage Wholesaler, and later but separately, to the Marketplace Trader. A result of fieldwork is that I was living in a specific village. Consequently, I have a deeper knowledge of the main produce trader of that village – the Hamlet Wholesaler – than I do of the Intervillage Wholesaler or Marketplace Trader, who lived and worked in other places. However, a second result of fieldwork is that my work with the Hamlet Wholesaler led directly to my work with his rural patron, the Intervillage Wholesaler. Thus, the case studies of both of these men should be read as an *example of a relationship* – between an important rural patron and his numerous clients in many villages.

A third result of fieldwork is that my investigation of marketplaces and trading networks in Malumfashi and Kankara districts revealed that the Intervillage Wholesaler was exceptional in his wide range of activities and clients. Moreover, the Marketplace Trader was one of the largest traders in the Kankara grain market. In other words, these two men were significant examples of influential produce traders during the period 1976–85. A further consequence of fieldwork is my discovery that the Intervillage Wholesaler and Marketplace Trader were, in the whole area, *much discussed as models of material success*. The fact that they were discussed widely in the community as examples of 'success' gives us insight into the local interpretation of 'wealth' and the paths toward it.

Put differently, the reasons for researching these three traders in the first place – a product of the limitations and opportunities of the fieldwork method – must be somewhat different from the reasons for presenting them in the analysis below. For analysis, I offer four reasons for taking them to be 'significant'. First, the case studies of the Hamlet Wholesaler and Intervillage Wholesaler are examples of the patron-client relationship, and for this purpose, I was fortunate that the patron concerned was locally important. Secondly, the case study of the Marketplace Trader is significant for understanding the possible bonds which could develop between a rural trader and a powerful member of the local ruling class, precisely because he had become so successful in fashioning the bond. Thirdly, the local discussions in which I engaged in trying to unravel the actions of these traders furnished me with an entrance into the collective mentality of the produce marketing system. Finally, because these traders occupied different marketing niches, they provide a perspective from which to search for similarities and differences in local forms of wealth acquisition.

My argument for the 'representativeness' of these case studies in no way stems from an assumption that, as particular individuals with discrete characteristics, they were demonstrably typical. Rather, they were 'typical' in a very different sense: they illustrate the tissue of relationships between persons on which the trading system depended. From this standpoint, the crucial necessity in any case study approach is not a procedure for determining the extent to which the specific attributes of the individuals studied are widely shared by others. Rather, the need is for a density of evidence on relationships through which the activities being studied occur. If I am correct below in my presentation of complex relationships, then it is difficult to see how other case studies from the same region could present a radically different picture; that would imply a different system of trading and farming, and a different set of local understandings of economic life.

Part I: The Marketplace Trader

R. was an immigrant in Kankara town from Daura, in the far north of Kaduna State. Around forty-five years old in 1978, he had started his career as a young waterboy in the house of the *mai gari,* the ruler of Kankara town. R. was described by other traders as the mai gari's 'servant' (*bara*, pl. *barori*).

By 1978, R. had become the mai gari's most trusted retainer. As his *sarkin gandu,* he was responsible for managing the farms of the mai gari and paying the farm labourers. At first, the mai gari had given him a gayauna field, a plot granted to a son or other dependent for his own use. But with time and success as a trader, R. had purchased many farms of his own. Eventually, he had called members of his family from Daura. By 1978, his own household was very large, numbering over twenty.

R. traded in grains and groundnuts on the private market. He bought and sold in marketplaces, not in hamlets. Two sorts of transaction marked his commercial relationship with the mai gari. In 1978, R. received N2,000 during the groundnut and guineacorn harvests, and bought these products for storage against a price rise, the proceeds of any sale being handed over to his master. Secondly, R. received N2,000 as a trading loan at harvest. This money was his to work with for one year, until the following harvest. Then, the mai gari called him to 'balance' (the word was used in Hausa). Upon producing the N2,000, it was returned to him as an annual trading loan. No interest was charged. The relationship between the two men was so close that, during the intervening months, the master did not call his servant to inquire about the loan, or ask for its return. R. distributed his loan among various productive investments and family expenditures. The mai gari recognized that if R. lost money (*fadi,* or 'fell down') in trade, he would sell his own farm output in order to repay the loan, and thus renew the commercial association with his master.

R. never divided trading profit (riba) with the mai gari. The idea seemed absurd to the produce traders with whom this was discussed: 'How can the boy [yaro] give the master of the house [mai gida] profit?' Furthermore: 'R. is in the house of the mai gari. So how can he go to him with profit?' However, before receiving an interest-free trading loan, R. spent much time buying, storing and selling for his master. Essentially, the superior was purchasing the all-purpose labour time of the inferior with many sorts of 'help' – household security for himself and his family, farmland and commercial credit.

The mai gari kept his keen commercial nose close to the ground. He could often be observed gliding through the Tuesday market, watching produce movements and produce prices. But he gave R. freedom to establish what contacts he chose among his fellow traders. R. had developed two kinds of trading association – 'in-market' and 'external'.

With regard to his in-market associations, R. assembled many produce measurers and porters at Kankara weekly marketplace, purchased grains and groundnuts from farmers, and stored them in his warehouse. During the Postharvest Dry Season, he made friends with traders who came from the north to buy produce while it was relatively cheap – from Sokoto, Katsina, Daura and the Republic of Niger. He helped them find produce in the highly competitive buyers' market which then prevailed. When produce prices had risen during the subsequent farming season, R. himself entered the market as a seller of stored produce. He then tapped his northern friends who were still buying in Kankara marketplace, in the competitive sellers' market which had emerged.

The context of these transactions was the circulation of price, demand and supply information among the traders who congregated in Kankara Tuesday marketplace from the wide area of northern Nigeria and southern Niger. Much of their intercourse aimed to forge links of trust, through friendly discussion and communal Muslim prayer. Traders sat in groups of friends on top of or beside their sacks of grain, joking and talking politics. They prayed together in the various praying grounds at the edge of the marketplace. They arranged the potential sale of crops which they had retained in their home storerooms or warehouses. And all asked those known to them from distant parts about the speed of their sales, the quantity of crops growing on the land, the proportions of different crops planted by producers, seeking anxiously to pry intelligence about present and future market conditions.

In Kankara marketplace, I was never aware of any deal to pay cash for future produce at a discounted price. Rather, traders purchased future produce by extending *falle* loans before harvest to farmers in their home villages (chapter 5). Secondly, some types of produce, for example groundnuts, varied greatly in quality and needed to be closely inspected before a price could be agreed upon. Thirdly, most traders lacked the money to commit to futures trading. Most importantly, personal associations were themselves developed in order to guarantee the participants secure forward positions. This point becomes much clearer when we consider R.'s external associations.

On most Saturdays, R. travelled in a lorry full of produce to Danbatta marketplace. On Sunday mornings, he would negotiate the sale of his supplies to three sorts of buyer: wholesalers operating with their own and contract money, small traders buying several sacks each for sale in the outlying villages and retailers selling by the measure. Sometimes he would travel instead to the Sunday marketplace of Mai Aduwa on the border with Niger. There, he sold to private traders and government contractors from Niger. At Mai Aduwa, he was in a favoured position because he had developed many contacts among the Nigerien traders who came regularly to Kankara. Occasionally, R. also took produce to Sokoto, when price differences between marketplaces made this worthwhile.

From 9 April 1978 through 4 February 1979, R. carried to Danbatta an average of 48 sacks of produce per week (about 4 metric tons)

(Table 7.2). The scale of his trading was thus much greater than that of the four Marmara hamlet traders (Table 6.5). Not all of this was R.'s own produce. Some belonged to the mai gari, some he had purchased for traders in Danbatta.

R. had developed a reputation for regularity in coming to Danbatta, and reliability in handling other people's money. One wealthy trader had become his patron (*uban gida*). Each week, he advanced R. money to buy him produce at Kankara. At the 1978 harvest, he also used R. to buy groundnuts, which he stored for a price rise. In return, he gave R. cowpeas and rice from Danbatta market to sell in Kankara, which R. only paid for after selling them. He also gave R. short-term trading loans (*rance*). He had even offered to buy R. a lorry to manage from R.'s home base in Kankara (an offer which R. had refused).

Table 7.2. Produce carried by R. to Danbatta marketplace (sacks), 9 April 1978–4 February 1979

Date	Groundnuts*[1]	Guineacorn*[1]	Locust beans	Date	Groundnuts*[1]	Guineacorn*[1]	Locust beans	Date	Groundnuts*[1]	Guineacorn*[1]	Locust beans
9 April	*[1]33	*[1]22		23 July	31			5 Nov.			
16 April	10	41		30 July		*unk.*		12 Nov.	110		
23 April	42	*unk.*		6 Aug.	18			19 Nov.		*unk.*	
30 April				13 Aug.	18			26 Nov.	140		
7 May	73			20 Aug.	17			3 Dec.	156		
14 May	52			27 Aug.	17			10 Dec.	93		
21 May	62			3 Sept.				17 Dec.	50		
28 May	52		2	10 Sept.	12		3	24 Dec.	94		
4 June	30	7		17 Sept.	17			31 Dec.	22		
11 June	17	16		24 Sept.	11			7 Jan.	121		
18 June	33			1 Oct.	21		2	14 Jan.	95	15	
25 June	40	4		8 Oct.	20		6	21 Jan.	63		
2 July		*unk.*		15 Oct.	17			28 Jan.	97		
9 July	40			22 Oct.	18			4 Feb.	120		
16 July	50			29 Oct.		*unk.*					

Average: 47 sacks (4 tons) of groundnuts.

*[1] At 86 kg. per sack of groundnuts, 104 kg. per sack of guineacorn (Appendix 2, Table 2 note d).

Marketing Relations between a Wholesaler and his Retailer

R. normally sold the greater part of his produce at Danbatta through particular retailers to whom he gave preference. The day began when wholesalers and retailers met each other by the thousands of sacks carried overnight by lorry, piled high in the sand beside the market sheds. In the early morning (7–9 A.M.), wholesalers and retailers negotiated the wholesale prices per sack that retailers would hand over at the close of the market day. During mid-morning (9–11 A.M.), retail selling occurred on the basis of fluctuating retail prices because the market had not yet stabilized. During late morning and afternoon (11 A.M.–5 P.M.), prices normally settled (*kasuwa ta kwanta:* 'the market has settled down'). More accurately, each retailer had decided on a spectrum of retail prices within a narrow range across the market (during 1977–79, the maximum difference observed among retailers was 5 kobo per measure on any market day). In the late afternoon and early evening (5–7 P.M.), retailers sometimes lowered their prices to clear part of their remaining stocks. Retailers kept unsold sacks to sell at the Friday market in nearby Kazaure, and handed over the money owing to their wholesalers at the following Sunday market in Danbatta.

At the start of the market day, the notional price around which negotiation revolved was that for a sack containing 40 *tiya,* or large measures. In fact, wholesalers brought sacks containing from 37 to 40 tiya. It was common practice – considered 'acceptable but not strictly ethical' – for a bulk seller to state that a sack contained x number of tiya when in fact there were several fewer. If his statement were accepted, then he could meet his overhead marketing costs with the payment for the nonexistent tiya. The difficulty facing the wholesaler was that, to the extent that his sacks contained fewer than 40 tiya, his produce was accepted less readily and sold less quickly than the produce of wholesalers who had a reputation for bringing sacks containing 40 tiya. An experienced retailer could see that a sack contained less than 40 tiya, and subtract the price of one or two tiya in making an offer to the bulk seller. His problem was his inability to judge the exact degree to which the volume fell short of 40 tiya. In consequence, there was a range of wholesale prices in the market. Moreover, retailers scaled down their offers for sacks which were less than 'full' (by N1.00–2.00 in 1978, when wholesale prices averaged N31 for sacks of 40 tiya [Appendix 5, Table 1]).

Retailers aimed at the very least for minimum net earnings which would allow them to meet a series of household needs in the coming week. But if demand did not meet expectations, retail prices might drop during the day, or retailers might be left with a large number of unsold sacks. Retailers would then be left with net earnings which were lower than anticipated.

Under conditions of flexibility in trading behaviour, competition, and uncertainty over retail prices, R.'s practice of selling his stocks through particular retailers was of mutual benefit. R. benefited because when there was excessive supply, his stocks were given preference by retailers. His reputation for selling sacks containing 40 tiya increased the speed with which retailers sold his stocks. Even so, there were occasions when part of his stocks remained unsold. For example, on 19 February 1978, R. left thirteen sacks wholly or partly unsold. The retailers undertook to sell them at a nearby marketplace before the following Sunday. His retailers benefited from their association, because when retail prices dropped unexpectedly, or large stocks remained unsold, they could protect their minimum earnings by asking R. to defer payment on some, or even all, of the stocks that had been sold. For example, on 26 February 1978, when for the second week running there was excessive supply, one of R.'s retailers did not pay him anything for sacks which had been sold. Thus, R. was able to offer his retailers some regularity in their market income. On their part, his retailers gave R. access to bulk buyers and regular customers who purchased part of his supply, and access to other marketplaces as an outlet for unsold supplies.

Commentary

R. was successful in acquiring 'wealth' (*dukiya*), as this was understood in rural Hausa society. He had gradually developed a trading operation which was large in scale by local standards. He had used loans and trading profits to expand his landholding and the scale of farming. He managed the farms of an important title-holder, which gave him a respected social position. Also, he had greatly enlarged his household. In the words of a trader, R. was a man of great 'responsibilities' (*hidimomi,* sing. *hidima*).

R. had acquired wealth through successfully entering a series of distinct personal relationships. Through the *master-servant relation,* R. received interest-free loans from the ruler of Kankara at one harvest which were not due until the next. R.'s case exemplifies a connection between agriculture and borrowing for trade: *the size of the long-term loan was determined by the lender's assessment of the borrower's scale of farming.* Secondly, R. had developed a *patron-client relationship* at his main outlet market. Through this relationship, he was advanced produce for sale in his home marketplace, received short-term trading loans, and had even been offered freedom to manage transport for the patron. Thirdly, R. had developed *trading friendships with external traders* who came to Kankara. In return for helping them find produce when prices were relatively low, they purchased his stored supplies when prices had risen. Fourthly, he had developed *trading friendships in the distant outlet markets* which he supplied. His long-standing relationships with a number of retailers were a form of trading friendship. These gave him a degree of security in competitive selling under conditions of market uncertainty. In return, he allowed his retailers to postpone payment for his produce when markets were oversupplied and their anticipated income jeopardized. Effectively, R. was granting his retailers interest-free short-term credit.

Each of these types of relationship differed and involved a diverse set of obligations and rewards. Other traders stressed that R.'s good fortune stemmed from his good 'character' (*hali*). They saw his material success in moral terms. R. was involved in two interconnected investment cycles – material investment and investment in personal ties. He reinvested trading profit in the expansion of his trade turnover, landholding and farm output. By accepting a series of obligations based on personal knowledge and trust, he generated an increase in the number of his trading friends – and hence, in his capacity to trade and borrow money in the future.

Part II: The Intervillage Wholesaler

Alhaji Z. was at least seventy years old. He was a *batalaka*, or commoner, who dealt with local rulers like the mai gari of Kankara but, unlike R., kept a certain distance. He lived in a roadside hamlet several miles from Kankara. Like many of the farmers and all of the traders in his hamlet, Alhaji Z. was an immigrant from Kano Emirate. A local farmer told me, 'our traders are Kanawa because they save their money, but we Katsinawa spend ours.' Newcomers are only partly embedded in local commitments. This gives them an advantage over native-born villagers in saving money for investment.

Alhaji Z.'s hamlet of origin was near Kano city. In the 1920s he entered the trade in potash (*kanwa,* used as a salt supplement in food and for animals, and formerly in soap making) and the trade in locally woven cloth. Then, the commerce was conducted by *fatauci,* long-distance trading donkey caravans. He traded over an area with a north-south axis of 200 miles. He bought potash along the northern frontier of Nigeria, and sold it in villages near Kano, and around the town of Gwarzo, west of Kano city. He bought locally woven cloth in the villages of western Kano, and those of Kankara and Malumfashi in southern Katsina, selling it along the northern frontier.

Around 1930, he decided to settle and farm in southern Katsina on the site of his present hamlet. At the same time, he continued his trading expeditions. Z. became the leader or *madugu* of caravans with over fifty donkeys. Eventually, he was joined by his younger brothers. Together, they exploited a chalk mine near the hamlet. They worked alongside their employees and head-loaded the chalk south along a route of villages to Zaria city, where they sold it locally and to colonial firms. Later, they transported the chalk by donkey.

In 1945, Z. stopped trading in potash and local cloth. He continued in chalk, but transferred much of his energy and resources to the produce trade. At first, he traded guineacorn by fatauci from southern Katsina to Zaria city. He gradually built up a widening circle of mercantile and aristocratic contacts in Zaria and other towns and cities. Operating with advances provided by urban merchants and the native authorities, he bought and stored grain on their behalf and received commissions in return. The geographical expansion of his trading routes and associations was aided by the development of roads and lorry transport. Around 1970, Alhaji Z. discontinued chalk mining and concentrated entirely on the grain and groundnut trade.

Over 1975–79, Alhaji Z. was involved in three types of produce trading:

1. He engaged in turnover trading. Using his own investment funds (*jali*) and short-term loans (*rance*) from trading friends, he bought grains and groundnuts at the Kankara and Yargoje markets and resold them at various northern marketplaces.
2. He combined lending to farmers with futures trading, through the distribution of *falle* loans to farmers (for falle, see chapter 5). Lending money at a rate of half the speculative harvest price per sack of guineacorn, in return for a sack at harvest, he stored repayments in guineacorn for a price rise in the subsequent farming season. Repayments in money were used to buy grain in the postharvest dry season, and also stored for a price rise.
3. He bought harvest produce and stored it for a price rise. He used his own trading capital to buy harvest produce, either directly or through rural clients. Further, he used advances from urban merchants in Kano, Sokoto, Katsina, Zaria, Kaduna and Jos, and

from the local government authorities, to buy and store grains on their behalf.

The transactions between Z. and his urban contacts were different in kind from those between R. and the mai gari. First, R. was involved in all-purpose subordination to the mai gari. In contrast, Z.'s connections with his urban backers were more strictly commercial. They were friends-in-trade (*abokanan ciniki,* sing. *abokin ciniki*) rather than patrons (*ubannin gida,* sing. *uban gida*). Secondly, because Z.'s trading friends were urban and therefore far away, Z. had more freedom of manoeuvre than did R. For the mai gari as a rural lord was always aware of the prices which R. paid for his produce, whereas the urban friends of Z. were not. And for that matter, they did not much care.

In the agricultural year 1975–76, Alhaji Z. quoted to his urban trading friends a harvest price for guineacorn of N10 per sack of 40 tiya. In fact, harvest prices in December fluctuated around N8 per sack. Therefore, Alhaji was able to turn over the urban advances several times in weekly trading before late January. Then, he used them to buy grain for his trading friends at the current market price of N10. This practice was acceptable to his trading friends. For they benefited in two ways. Firstly, they were able to use Z.'s storage facilities and, secondly, tap the rural stores of Z.'s circle of clients. Their objective in advancing money was to profit from the difference between the rural harvest price and the urban midyear rainy season price. From June through August, merchants sent their lorries to collect the stored produce from Z. or his rural clients.

According to his client trader in Marmara ('M.' below, Case Study III), Z. had five kinsmen and twelve clients (*yara,* or boys) spread through eleven hamlets and villages. He advanced them money at harvest to buy produce for him and store it in their own warehouses. Moreover, he would occasionally give them money to effect a major purchase from a farmer in their areas of supply. In return, he gave them medium-term, interest-free credit – loaned at harvest for trading in the postharvest dry season, and due for repayment before the onset of the farming season. Maintaining and expanding a group of client traders required him to exercise patience or forbearance (*hakuri*) in lending money – a prized attribute among the rural Hausa. According to M., some of Z.'s clients only repaid these loans after two years had elapsed. One absconded with the money. I was present at the hearing of a complaint that Z. brought before the village head of Yaba. In 1975, he had loaned N600 to a trader in the village. Only N400 was repaid, and in 1979, he sued him before the village head for the remaining money.

Thus, a lifetime of trade had involved Alhaji Z. in seven main types of entrepreneurial activity:

1. Exploiting the opportunities for making money in different commodities, and shifting between them as their earning potential changed.
2. Exploiting the possibilities for profit making from the price differentials in space and time.
3. Lending money to farmers and storing the cash and kind repayments as produce against a price rise.
4. Working in partnership with his close kinsmen to combine their resources.
5. Tapping the resources of wealthier men in the city to become wealthy himself in the countryside.
6. Tapping the local knowledge, areas of supply and storage facilities of client traders.
7. Saving and reinvestment. Profit (riba) from the sale of any commodity was invested in expanding the volume he carried, and thus the total level of profits.

The process of reinvestment was connected with the austerity of Z.'s life. Like most rural traders in this region, he was a devout Muslim. He had built onto the side of his house the biggest mosque in his hamlet. He ate and dressed simply. He talked sparingly, with frequent references to God and the Qur'an. In Hausa society, these qualities aided Alhaji in expanding his enterprise, for his probity attracted others to him. An insight was provided by M.:

> Alhaji is a senior man of the old type (*dattijo irin na da*). He doesn't spend money on motorcycles, buses, women or his house. He spends it on farms. He stores food. Because of this, his house never suffers from lack of food. He gives a lot of food to his kinsmen in times of food shortage. He is not a boy like Alhaji Q [Z.'s younger brother], or our Mallam N [HH 20, the young entrepreneur]. They spend money on houses, motorcycles and clothes. Alhaji Z. is like our Alhaji I [HH 1 of Marmara]. He is not to be seen around the town. He does not waste time in talk.

The annual volume of his purchases was a trade secret which he refused to divulge. My own estimate is that Alhaji Z. purchased perhaps 15,000 sacks of various types of produce for himself and others in the agricultural year 1975–76.[2] What proportion of his total purchases was bought at harvest and then stored until the peak prices of the following year? My informant discovered that in March 1976, Z. was storing in his Kankara warehouse 1,000 sacks for urban merchants,

500 sacks for local government authorities, and 250 sacks for himself.[3] To this we should add some 850 sacks which would have been stored for him by seventeen subordinate traders – altogether, some 2,600 sacks, or about 17 per cent of his annual purchases. Moreover, he had use of the warehouses of trading friends at Funtua, Sokoto and Kano – as much for transhipment as for long-term storage. Perhaps a fifth of his total annual purchases was stored from harvest against a midyear price rise. Most of this was for others.[4]

Alhaji Z. had also invested in agriculture. Slowly, he had acquired thirteen fields of different sizes. His landholding included three fields located over ten miles from his hamlet. Based on the six fields which he asked me to measure (34 acres, including a distant field), his total holding could not have exceeded 100 acres in 1978. Most of his acreage was planted to guineacorn, either sole cropped or intercropped with millet, groundnuts and cowpeas. He employed many seasonal migrant labourers. They were mainly boys and young men from the drier parts of the north around Daura.[5] Apart from their pay, he gave them food and sleeping space in his compound.

In 1979, he reduced his total farmed area to eight fields, because of the high cost of hired labour in the previous year. Moreover, he planted five of these with yellow maize. He increased his use of fertilizer from 16 tons the previous year to over 20 tons. His primary concern was to lower labour cost by reducing total acreage, and compensate by increasing total yield through planting yellow maize. In his own words: 'I am planting eight farms and preparing them very well, since preparing a farm is as important as fertilizer. I want less work and more fertilizer because the money for hired labourers is too much.'

Z. owned three teams of oxen. In 1978, he made the down payment for a tractor to be purchased from the FADP. Apart from agricultural investments, he had five grain-grinding machines operating in four hamlets, and a Ford passenger van. (His younger brother, also a produce trader, owned a lorry.)

The expansion of his trading and farming had led to the expansion of his household. Alhaji Z. had three wives and ten children. His oldest son transported his produce to different markets. His second son drove the bus. Three younger sons formed a permanent labour force. There were also five daughters. Very old relatives, and several Qur'anic mallams, were also kept by Alhaji Z. Living in separate compounds but working full time for his enterprise were three men – a younger brother, the younger brother of his father and his sister's son. The first supervized the purchase and storage of produce at Kankara and Yargoje. The second was his all-purpose assistant, supervising farm labour and running messages to and from Z.'s clients in the hamlets. The third handled his trade to Kano city and Sokoto marketplace.

Thus, we may also speak of Z.'s investment in his male kin. They formed a management team who could be trusted to handle his money. They supplied him with reliable information. They helped supervise his expanding operations. Each received N400 as a personal trading loan in 1978, apart from advances to buy and store grain on Alhaji's behalf. They also received rance, supposedly short-term loans which in fact had very flexible periods of repayment. Z. also paid the head tax (*haraji*) of his sons, provided their families with food and financed the many marriages of his sons and daughters.

An example illustrates how, even with close kin, Z. had to show extreme patience before retrieving some loans. His half-brother had wanted to sell Alhaji Z. a grain mill, but Z. had refused. Instead, Z. had loaned him N600. Later, he increased the loan to N1,200. At the following harvest, Z. had asked for the N1,200, only to be told by his half-brother that they had agreed on the sale of the grain mill. When the half-brother sought a wife for his son, he named Z. as the go-between and gave him N600 for the girl's family. The marriage plan collapsed, but Z. refused to return the N600.

The half-brother sued him before the Alkali. On hearing of the size of the un-repaid loan, the Alkali arrested the half-brother. However, Alhaji had him released. At the next harvest, his half-brother repaid N400. But N200 remained unpaid.

The costs of supporting a large family enterprise were heavy. The commitments were sometimes uncertain. But as much as his urban trading friends above and his clients below, investment in close kin was at the heart of the success and scale of Z.'s trading and farming.

I end with a brief comparison of R. and Z. Due to his close association with a ruler, R. had greater economic security than Z. But Z. had greater economic power and social prestige in the world of the rural *talakawa*. The intervillage wholesaler occupied a different sort of social space from the big servant of a rural aristocrat. A hierarch among his own rural clients, he was their nexus with the towns and political authority. He was the conduit of city money to fuel their affairs. Conversely, he was the channel through which rural produce was funnelled from producers to merchants and contractors at profitable rates.

Analysis

In one way, Alhaji Z. is the most interesting case study in this chapter: here, we have a whole life-time surveyed. In brief, fifty years of activity had led to a household of over twenty members, a core management-and-labour team of eight closely related kinsmen, a large number of trading friends and clients, a bus, six oxen, five grain mills, an annual trading volume of some 1,500 tons of produce and a landholding around 100 acres. In the introduction, I distinguished between two different notions – the processes of long-term wealth acquisition characteristic of this society, and the more specific accumulation of farmland and labour power. In terms of land and farm labour, the major point to emerge is that the results of a lifetime were actually quite limited. His holding could not compare with those established by foreign or local companies (Andrae and Beckman 1987: 37–51).

The case study indicates the reasons for limited accumulation. The various types of personal relationship through which Z. conducted his trading-and-farming enterprise prevented a more concentrated reinvestment of profits in the purchase of land and the employment of hired labour. Local hired labour and seasonally migrant labour were costly relative to Alhaji's capacity to pay them.

However, by the criteria used among the rural Hausa, Alhaji Z. was a very wealthy man. His life had been well rewarded by God. They construed the size of his household and the scale of his trading associations as essential indices of wealth. In this society, the entrepreneur did not take risks just in commodity markets, but also in the cultivation of trading friends and clients upon whom he relied for investment funds and access to supplies and information. Such risks favour a certain type of person. On the one hand, he is able to assess a complex flow of information in his head, without the benefit of reading or writing, and relate it to a shrewd judgement of prospective trading associates standing in front of him. On the other, he surmounts losses with forbearance (*hakuri*), and submission to the will of God (*ikwan Alla*).

The basic processes in the organization of Z.'s enterprise are illustrated in Figure 7.1. Analytically, Figure 7.1 distinguishes between inner and outer circles of activity. The inner circle contained the complex of personal relationships through which Z. traded and sold produce, and managed his land. The outer circle comprised the market porters whom he hired to load and carry produce, and the local and seasonally migrant labourers deployed among his fields. Inside the inner circle, it distinguishes between 'superior' and 'lateral' friends-in-trade. The former were private city merchants and well-placed persons in local authority from whom Alhaji received advances and contracts. The latter were rich traders like himself, upon whom he could depend for short-term trading loans or storage facilities. Lateral friendships

Figure 7.1. Organization of Z's enterprise

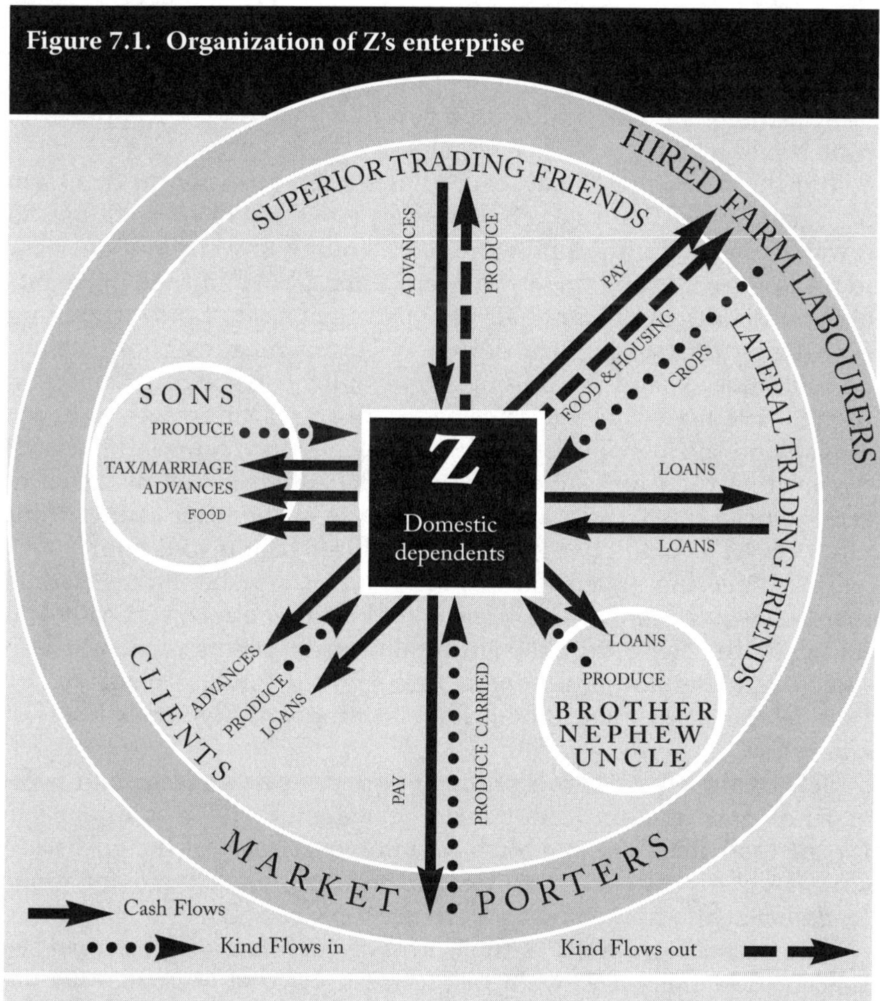

increased his ability to respond to weekly or monthly changes in market conditions.

The model in Figure 7.1 illustrates three crucial facets of his organization. First, it was intrinsically different from a 'household model', based on the gandu of father and adult sons as the unit of enterprise (chapter 4). The complex labyrinth of personal relationships through which Z. worked enabled him to break through the limits of economic scale set by his own investment funds and the human resources of his immediate household. Secondly, it reveals that over time, trade and not farming was the primary causative force in the expansion of the total enterprise. It was through friendships in trade that he obtained his investment funds. Produce advances, commissions and short-term trading loans generated trading profit greater than that possible with his own funds. The expansion of trading profit made possible a level of investment in land and labour power which were exceptional in rural society.

Thirdly, the model illustrates the limits to expansion in this form of organization. The inner circle reveals a pattern of obligations and rewards, centred on Z.'s household, extending upward and outward to trading friends and downward to clients. Cash and kind payments of various sorts to the inner circle constituted a set of prior claims on Z.'s trading funds and farm output. Without meeting those claims, he could not expand the trading sector of his enterprise, or maintain the team of managers and supervisors in the farming sector. Funds available for hiring labour logically can be seen as 'sums left over' after meeting the claims of the inner circle. Alhaji Z. had managed to acquire near 100 acres of land. But because of the prior claims of his inner circle, he could not guarantee the hired labour to farm it.

The increasing expansion in the volume and value of Z.'s trading sector depended upon the expansion of his inner circle, vertically and horizontally. Therefore, the sum total of prior claims on Z. was also increasing. Therefore, the general limits on the funds available to pay farm labour continued to hold force at progressively larger levels of enterprise.

Behind the organization of his enterprise was Z.'s large and ever-expanding household of domestic dependents. He was responsible for the food, marriage and birth ceremony expenses of the wives and children of his sons. Furthermore, he regularly made large donations (*gudummawa*) when working kinsmen took new wives or had more children. Looking closely at the centre of Z.'s inner circle, we can see that prior claims on Z. were rising irrespective of expansion in the trading sector of his enterprise.

Part III: The Hamlet Wholesaler

The final case study brings us back to Marmara. In much more detail than with R. or Z., we look at the economic activities of its leading produce trader, HH 7 (hereafter 'M.'). M. bought and sold twice as much produce as any other trader in Marmara (Table 6.5). But, unlike R. and Z., M. was not rich. In the crucial year 1978 he made enormous efforts to acquire wealth. Thus, M. gives us the opportunity to explore the difficulties which a farmer-trader must overcome in acquiring wealth.

Like R. and Z., M. was an immigrant in southern Katsina. He still made visits to his home village in the closely settled zone near Kano city. M. kept a certain distance from the other people in Marmara. He had built his family compound a mile from Marmara rather than on its edge, like other immigrants. His first language was Fulani. He had close kinsmen with herds of cattle scattered through western Kano and southern Katsina. He was also particularly conscious that his paternal lineage had aristocratic connections: his father's sister was the mother of the *dagaci*, or village head, of his home village. He and the dagaci were *abokin wasa*, or 'joking relatives', a close relationship between cross-cousins among the Hausa or Fulani.

In 1978 M. was around fifty-five years old and had lived in Marmara since 1960. For a number of years, he pursued produce and livestock trading, but did not farm. He would return to his home village every few months to greet his parents. In his own words, he did not buy farms in Marmara because he was planning to return home finally to 'embrace' (*rungume*) his parents. When they died within four months of each other, there was nothing to carry him back home. Thereafter, he began to buy farms in Marmara – 'but from behind, the price of farms had already risen'. M. exemplifies both the advantages and disadvantages which can result from immigrant status. Like R. and Z., his original efforts to save money had not been reduced by local obligations of kinship. Unlike them, his close associations with his village of origin had detracted from the ability to accumulate land in his new home.

Since 1963, he had carried guineacorn and rice northward to Danbatta and to Sokoto. Like Alhaji Z., he engaged in three forms of grain trading – turnover trade, storage against a price rise and a combination of money lending with futures trading (falle). He had also combined grain trading with livestock trading. Whereas grain prices were higher around Danbatta than in southern Katsina, cattle prices were lower. He used part of his earnings from the sale of grains in Danbatta market to buy cattle, which he transported by lorry to Marmara. There, he paid Fulani to herd the cattle to Kankara market or to Sheme, an important cattle centre attended by Hausa traders who were active in the cattle trade by rail to Lagos (Map 1). By using part of his earnings from the turnover trade in grains to buy cattle, for resale in other markets, he augmented his total trading funds for grain trading.

In 1976, M. had two main objectives: to store grain for sale in the farming season, in order to pay hired farm labourers ; and to use earnings from the sale of stored grain to buy cattle – which he also sold in order to pay labourers. Thus, long-distance grain and cattle trading were intimately linked to a strategy of agricultural expansion through the use of hired labour.

The scale of M.'s trading and hence, of his farming, had expanded slowly over the years. He had limited funds to set aside on the purchase of harvest grain for storage. Moreover, he had to balance the gains from trading across time through interseasonal grain storage, with the gains from trading across space in grain and cattle markets. Furthermore, a large part of his trade earnings and farm output had been reserved for the expansion of his household. In 1977, M. headed a five-man gandu – one of the largest in Marmara – which provided much of his farm labour (HH 7 in Appendix 6, Table 4). He maintained a household of fourteen – twice the average size in Marmara.

We can view the results of M.'s seventeen years of economic activity by looking closely at the farming season of 1977. He had just 6.2 acres of farmland – less than the mean holding in Marmara. Secondly, he had a few head of cattle which he reserved as long-term investment. Thirdly, he had a large household and a big family labour force.

Finally, he had accumulated over his working life investment funds of around N2,000. Part he kept as cash and part as grain stocks in trade. M. referred to this sum as his jali. Both Abraham (1962) and Hill (1972) translate jali as 'trading-capital'. Robinson (1925) defined it more broadly, as 'property, power' or 'something with which to trade [*abin jali*]'. M. used the term to denote the liquid assets available for investment in all economic or social spheres which contributed to the growth of his wealth (dukiya). As we have seen, rural Hausa in this part of southern Katsina conceived of 'wealth' or 'riches' as including not just physical assets which could be converted into money, but also family members and other persons to whom there were varying ties of 'responsibility' (hidima). For M., marriage payments and expenditures on house building – i.e., expenditures which enabled his household to grow – were appropriate uses of jali, as were his everyday expenditures on trading and farming.

At the end of 1977, M. was poised to set in motion major changes in his life. His oldest son needed to be married. M. himself had been unsuccessful in keeping a second wife, and was intent on having one, and he planned a dramatic expansion of his landholding, to be farmed by both his family and hired labour. So he abandoned livestock trading, and focused his energies on produce trading and farming. This study shows how, in 1978, he achieved his objectives. But first, we must explore the types of social relationship into which M. entered in the course of pursuing wealth.

Socioeconomic Relationships

Clientage

M. had been a client (*yaro*) of Alhaji Z. (Case Study II) since 1972. He referred to Alhaji Z. as his *uban gida* (literally, 'father of the house'). Defined by Abraham (1962) as the 'master of a servant', uban gida was used by rural Hausa in southern Katsina to denote the person upon whom a man could rely for loan money in trade or other money-creating enterprise. In return, the borrower regularly provided his uban gida with services in trade, agriculture or both. Moreover, he displayed the sort of deference in public that he would show to his father (*uba*). In December 1975, Alhaji Z. gave M. money to buy and store 30 sacks of guineacorn, which he collected in April. In January 1977, he gave M. N1,600 to buy 100 sacks, which he collected in July and sold for N3,000, when prices were much higher. In January 1978, he gave M. N1,200 to buy and store 50 sacks, which were collected in August by one of Z.'s trading friends and transported to Jos.

Although Z.'s village was twelve miles from Marmara, Z. and M. met each other frequently at marketplaces. M. would keep Z. informed of the market prices for grain supplies around Marmara. From time to time, Z. would give him money to effect a large purchase from a local farmer, sell it in Danbatta and give him the earnings. For other purposes, M. also acted as Z.'s local intermediary. For example, in 1976 Z. gave him N620 to purchase a second-hand grain mill in Marmara.

In return for his services, Z. gave M. a trading loan of N400 at the guineacorn harvest of 1977. According to M., this money was to be returned before the following farming season. He called it jali as he did his own investment funds. When I asked HH 20 (the maize trader and bus owner), to define jali, he explained it thus: 'Alhaji Z. gives M. money, and M. trades with it until the rainy season, when he returns it without interest or profit. But if Alhaji Z. wishes to sell grain at Danbatta he can give M. money for the purpose, and ask him to store the grain before selling it in the rainy season.'

In fact, after trading with the N400, M. sank it into farming, and did not repay it until the following harvest. Every few months, Z. would inquire after the money. In the middle of the farming season, he called M. and asked for the money. The following conversation took place:

Z.: I gave you money so that you would turn it over [*juya shi*]. What have you done with it?

M.: Farming has eaten it all.

Z.: It is not thus that we arranged with you. Why did you not tell me this?

M.: Why should I tell you what you already know?

This manoeuvring between patron and client was based on a mutual assessment of the other's dependability. M. compared his relationship to Z. with that between R. (Case Study I) and the mai gari: 'If Alhaji hears that I have spent his money on buying farms, he is happy. Or if he hears that I am on my farm, he will bring out more money and give it to me. But if he hears that I am in my house, he will send his younger brother to get the jali from me.'

Nevertheless, M. suffered much anxiety before the 1978 maize harvest enabled him to completely repay the N400 loan from Z. He was aware that one of Z.'s wealthy brothers had a client-trader arrested, and then forced him to sell his house, in order to recover a loan. Furthermore, the situation of clientage leads to conflicting perceptions and feelings in the client. On the one hand, M. was grateful to Z. for allowing him to convert his trading loan into a farming loan. On the other, M. was aware that his labour time in buying, storing and selling grain enabled the patron to make large profits.

Under the patron-client relation, the granting of a 'long-term' interest-free loan (jali) in return for economic services opened up a wider social interaction. For a number of years, M. had an uban gida, Alhaji Q, who lived in a village near Danbatta. M. would buy guineacorn for Q. in Marmara, and he would go to Q. for jali. By 1978, Q. no longer regularly required M.'s services, nor did he give him jali. Occasionally, however, M. would receive a short-term loan (rance), repaid at the next Sunday market. But though their economic connection was almost dormant, M. would still attend when Q. had a naming or wedding ceremony. And when M. sought a wife in Danbatta, he used Alhaji Q. as the intermediary with the woman's family.

The patron-client relation was a flexible arrangement to mutual advantage. It allowed changes in the degree of independence of each from the claims of the other. In the long-term M. was seeking greater freedom from the claims which Z. could make upon his labour time – and greater social equality with Z. in the eyes of other people. As we have seen, M. repaid Z. the N400 out of his 1978 maize output. Before doing so, he borrowed N200 from another source, to be repaid at the 1978 guineacorn harvest. Then, he increased this loan to N400 and obtained an extension of the repayment period. Thus, he had less need of Z. for credit. He told me that he did not ask Z. anymore for jali in 1979 because Z.'s son had shown him 'disrespect' (*rashin kunya*) in the marketplace. When Z. actually offered him N400, M. carefully refused. But this did not sever a broader relationship of mutual need – and respect. M. still received from Z. short-term loans of N20–30, repayable after a week or two (rance). And Z. was still concerned to avail himself of M.'s area for regular grain supply. In 1979, Z. purchased 100 sacks of guineacorn through M.

The notions behind the terms uban gida and yaro were not strictly complementary. A man's uban gida remained so, as long as he and his uban gida were on good terms, and he exchanged his labour time for various forms of commercial help. But once he discontinued receiving jali, or providing his skill and labour time regularly, he was no longer considered to be the yaro. It was much like the continuing, but looser, relationship between a father and the son who had parted amicably from his gandu labour force (chapter 4).

Trading Friendships

In order to increase his investment funds, M. cultivated 'trading friends' (abokanan ciniki). These were traders and farmers from whom he borrowed short-term loans without interest (rance). 'Trading' friendships were understood to be commercial. People usually distinguished between their abokanan ciniki and their close friends (*abokanai*). However, sometimes trading friendships developed out of close friendship. In a society centred on the rites of marriage, childbirth and family, a prospective borrower would often try to initiate a trading friendship by making a *biki* donation at the potential lender's ceremonies (for biki, see chapter 5).

Traders, in developing new trading friendships, were endeavouring not just to increase the total credit available, but also to extend the period over which they could use it. Since traders operated mainly in weekly marketplaces, the first step was to increase the period of the loan from one to two weeks. The next step was to borrow the same sum for several, then many, weeks running. If a trading friendship became a bond marked by sympathy, the borrower might obtain a large sum which would be 'on call' but not actually demanded for several months. Flexibility, based on trust, was the central feature of rance in a society marked by the personal, face-to-face nature of most economic transactions. Nevertheless, flexibility was anchored in the creditor's knowledge of the borrower's position in the annual marketing cycle.

If a trader were storing produce against a price rise, his creditor knew that he would have extra income to repay rance in the months of peak produce prices. Thereafter, the next peak in his economic cycle would be the period of harvests. Lenders in a trading friendship made it their business to know the borrower's state of affairs.

As a trader sought to obtain rance, he found himself under pressure to give it. And as he was seeking to lengthen repayment periods with his creditors, so, too, were his borrowers with him. He knew, in borrowing, that part of his credit would be loaned out again.

During 1978, M. had a 'core' group of trading friends from whom he could borrow over N1,000 in most weeks of the year. At the same time, he was the trading friend of several borrowers to whom he loaned over N200 in most weeks (Chart 7.1). M. was also continually borrowing from and loaning to a shifting group of other trading friends. Occasionally, he borrowed N200 from his patron in Danbatta. His net weekly credit fluctuated with the amounts he borrowed and lent. It reached N1,200 in July 1978.

Of M.'s core creditors (Chart 7.1), the first four were richer than himself, the last two of similar income. Of his core debtors, the first had an income similar to M., but the remaining three were much

Chart 7.1. M.'s core group of trading friends (N), Marmara, 1978

Weekly Short-Term Rance Creditors and Debtors			
Rance Creditors:			**Usual Credit**
	HH 27	Bus-owner, cotton trader, local politician	300
	HH 12	The hamlet long distance trader in fowl	200
	A.	Large farmer, neighbouring hamlet	200
	B.	Large farmer, neighbouring hamlet	200
	HH 10	The main shopkeeper	80
	HH 25	Maize trader, goat trader, oxen/plough hirer	60
Rance Debtors:			**1,040**
	N.	Kolanut trader, adjoining village	100
	HH 97	Kolanut retailer	100
	HH 65	Butcher	30
	P.	Landless butcher	30
			260
		Usual net weekly rance credit:	**780**

poorer than he. Among the core group, only A. and B. were close personal friends.

Loans were given as part of a developing commercial friendship. But from M.'s core group of trading friends, we can see that many such loans were given without hope of any financial gain. Overall there was an ethic of mutual help among traders. Although M.'s individual loans involved a dyadic relationship, the total flow of his rance moved from richer persons through the intermediate borrower to poorer ones.

A person's success in accumulating investment funds depended on his character (hali). A person with hali had many men (*mutane*) from whom he attracted loan money. Hali implied truthfulness and trustworthiness (*gaskiya*). But it also incorporated the ideas of redistribution and of reciprocal justice. Since the success of most traders depended on the willingness of others to loan them money, reciprocal justice required that they lend to those who were on the first steps of the credit ladder and struggling to succeed.

In the short run, a person only became wealthy if he was able to borrow, use profitably and repay more money than he loaned out. At the same time, the pattern of credit flows implied an ethic of diffuse generosity. Equally, this ethic expressed people's understanding of the actual process of wealth acquisition. People expressed both this ethic and their sense of social process through the belief that God materially rewarded the generous.

Falle Debtors

Having considered the social relations through which M. acquired investment funds, we turn to those through which he obtained his produce. M. treated falle credit as a technique for purchasing grain futures which were stored against the inter-seasonal price rise and then sold at a profit (chapter 5).

In 1977, M. gave twenty-seven loans to people with whom he had various personal ties, fifteen to those with whom he had no known tie. The rate of repayment was higher among those with whom he had personal ties. Among debtors who were small farmers or landless, those with personal ties to M. repaid at twice the rate of those who had no such tie. In the following year, 1978, M. reduced the scale of his lending, giving almost all loans to people with whom he had personal ties (Chart 7.2). This form of credit was embedded in and influenced by the personal relations between creditor and farmer.

We can now compare and contrast the three kinds of credit relationship into which M. entered. Through jali and rance, the creditor loaned money without interest. He hoped to generate either financial

Chart 7.2. M.'s falle debtors, debtor relationship (number of loans), 1977–78

			Repayments: Sacks	Repayments: Cash advances	Repayments: Defaults
		A. 1977: Various personal ties with M.			
LF	HH 20	Trading friend: borrower of rance (8)	7	1	
MF	HH 35	M's housebuilder (3)	1		2
MF	HH 46	Friend of M.'s personal friend, HH 63 (3)	2		1
SF	HH 52	Trading friend: borrower of rance (3)		3	
SF	HH 79	Recipient of M.'s help for tax and marriage (2)	2		
	*B.	Client laborer (1)		1	
	*C.	Kinsman and *gandu* member (1)		1	
	*D.	Personal and trading friend (4)		4	
		Total: 27	**12**	**12**	**3**
		B. 1977: No known personal tie with M.			
LF	HH 16	4	4		
SF	HH 59	1		1	
SF	HH 68	1	1		
SF	HH 72	1		1	
SF	HH 76	1		1	
Ls	*1A.	2		2	
	*E.	3		3	
	*F.	1		1	
	*G.	1		1	
		15	**5**	**10**	
		A. 1978: Various personal ties with M.*2			
	HH 35	M.'s housebuilder (2)			
	HH 79	Recipient of M.'s help for tax and marriage payments (3)			
	HH 97	Trading friend: borrower of rance (8)			
	H.	Trading friend: borrower of rance (1)			
		B. 1978: No known personal tie with M			
	HH 43	1			
	HH 68	1			

* Neighbouring hamlet. *1 Landless Marmara household head (hamlet praise singer).

*2 Rate of repayment only known to January 1979.

LF: large farmer MF: medium farmer SF: small farmer Ls: landless

Source: Chart 5.5

returns when the borrower bought and stored grain on his behalf, or reciprocal loans when needed. Or he gave for the sake of giving – because of God (*saboda Alla*), in the hope of God's favour in this life or the next. Through falle, he gave money loans in the hopes of generating a large financial increment from the money value of grain repayments. But beneath the differences, all three kinds of credit were pervaded by a quality of reciprocity: the unspoken sense of a long-term, mutually beneficial relationship was required before the lender could generate a financial increment from the borrower.

Grain Sellers

M. obtained small amounts of grain through falle lending. He bought most produce at the prevailing market price in Marmara. M. was operating in a competitive market: there were alternative traders to whom farmers could sell, and nearby marketplaces. As a result, the price which he offered hamlet sellers was very near the Kankara marketplace price; the difference was usually smaller than the marketing cost to the farmer of taking grain to market (Table 6.3). The price he offered could be higher than the Kankara price. As a long-distance produce trader, M. was mainly interested in the difference between the hamlet price and that in his final outlet market, Danbatta.

M. developed a growing circle of regular customers because he needed to guarantee a weekly flow of grain in long-distance trade. His regular suppliers benefited because they avoided the time spent travelling to a distant town with their produce and waiting for a buyer, and the uncertainty as to the behaviour of prices during the day at the marketplace.

Market Outlet Retailer

We turn now to the person through whom M. wholesaled at Danbatta. Unlike R., with his large turnover (Case Study I), M. sold most of his produce through one retailer, L., who relied on M. for most of his supplies (Table 7.3). M. had been dealing with L. since 1973.

In the early morning of the market day, M. would negotiate wholesale prices with L. Their agreement was witnessed by the market commission agent (*dillali*). At the close of the market day, L. counted the money owed to M. into the hands of the dillali, who handed it over to M. It consisted of the agreed wholesale prices multiplied by the number of sacks sold. The dillali then took note of any sacks unsold. L. would sell these at the Friday market in Kazaure and hand over the agreed wholesale amounts to M. on the following Sunday, using the dillali as intermediary. In reaching wholesale agreements, L. took title

Table 7.3. Wholesaler M. and retailer L., sales at Danbatta Sunday market, selected dates, 1978

	Wholesaler M.:			Retailer L.:			
Date	*M. Carries to:* **Danbatta**[*1]	*Retailers Sell* **Danbatta**[*1]	*Retailers Sell* **Kazaure**	**Buys from M.**	**Buys in total**	*Retailer Sells* **Danbatta**[*1]	*Retailer Sells* **Kazaure**
Jan. 15	22 sacks	22 sacks			*(23)*[*2]	23 sacks	
Feb. 19	23 sacks	13 sacks	10 sacks	23 sacks	*(23)*	13 sacks	10 sacks
Feb. 26	7 sacks	7 sacks		4 sacks	*(19)*	16 sacks	3 sacks
April 23	25 sacks	25 sacks		22 sacks	*(29)*[*3]	27 sacks	2 sacks
May 21	21 sacks	21 sacks		15 sacks	*(21)*	15 sacks	6 sacks
July 23	[4*]53 sacks	35 sacks	18 sacks	35 sacks	*(39)*	35 sacks	4 sacks
Aug. 6	20 sacks	20 sacks		20 sacks	*(26)*	26 sacks	
Dec. 17	7 sacks	7 sacks		7 sacks	*(12)*	12 sacks	

*1 All were guineacorn unless otherwise stated. See Appendix 6 for volumes carried by M. throughout 1978.
*2 22 guineacorn, 1 millet. *3 22 guineacorn, 7 groundnuts. *4 47 guineacorn, 6 groundnuts.

to the hemp sacks as well as to the produce. L. sold back to M. all used hemp sacks from which he had completed sales.

During the market day, L. sold by the tiya measure or the sack. His marketing costs were small – paying a commission of only 20 kobo to the dillali on every sack sold, and a small sum at the end of the market day to any assistants who helped him retail.

Like other retailers, L. faced a marketing situation which was simple on the surface but in reality peculiarly complex. First, L. was competing, not just for the wholesale produce on offer, but also for the flow of produce over time from wholesalers who came regularly to Danbatta. Secondly, wholesalers were selling him sacks which contained from 37 to 40 tiya. While L. could tell that sacks contained less than 40 tiya, he could never be sure by how much. Thirdly, he was selling to different types of buyer: anonymous buyers of several measures; customers of long standing, purchasing by the measure or by the full sack; bulk buyers who would buy several sacks for resale in outlying villages or on contract from the local government authorities. Finally, in making price agreements with wholesalers in the morning, he was uncertain about the behaviour of market prices through the rest of the day.

In consequence, he agreed wholesale prices for sacks believed to contain 40 tiya which were normally N1–2 more than the price for sacks believed to contain between 37 to 39 tiya. Furthermore, the price per sack which he offered to bulk buyers was negotiable. And in retailing by the measure, he manipulated bowls of various sizes. He had a large bowl for groundnuts and cowpeas. But for guineacorn, millet and maize, he used two bowls – a large bowl of the same size as the Katsina tiya, and a smaller bowl. The larger bowl, or 'tiya', contained slightly more than 2.7 kg. of guineacorn, the smaller bowl (here called 'measure') slightly less than 2.5 kg. He retailed guineacorn to customers of long standing using the tiya. He retailed to the many anonymous buyers using the 'measure'. From a sack containing 40 tiya, he could retail 44 'measures'. By using the smaller bowl, he protected his profit margin against wholesalers selling sacks containing less than 40 tiya, and against a drop in retail prices during the market day.

Wholesalers were competing for a supply outlet in Danbatta marketplace. Those who came regularly were given preference by retailers. And those who brought sacks containing 40 tiya were given preference over those whose sacks contained less. According to L., M. always sold him sacks with 40 tiya. On 6 August 1978, only 6 of M.'s 20 sacks arrived in time for the opening of the market. The remaining 14 were transported late from Marmara and only arrived midday. During the morning, L. resisted the efforts of other wholesalers to sell him their supplies. When M.'s 14 remaining sacks arrived, L. undertook to sell all of them, and succeeded in doing so.

L. bought and sold twenty to thirty sacks per market day (Table 7.3). He aimed by doing so to cover a series of domestic and farming expenses during the week. If L. did not know a wholesaler well, he would pay him the agreed price for all sacks sold. This could leave him with lower absolute earnings than he had anticipated. But if L. were well known to a wholesaler, he could ask that payment be deferred for some of the sacks which had been sold. On 6 August, L. asked M. to allow him 20 per cent of the total owed, because of expenses for special food and gifts during the Muslim fast of Ramadan (*hiduman azumi*) and the ensuing festival of Id el Fitr (Salla). M. agreed.

At the same time, retailers were competing for a regular flow of wholesale produce over time. This led to flexible marketing arrangements. On 23 April 1978, L. agreed to sell twenty-two sacks of M.'s supply, but only managed to sell twenty. Nevertheless, he still paid M. for the entire consignment, storing the remainder for sale at Kazaure market. Where they knew and trusted each other, the wholesaler's willingness to defer payment for stocks was balanced by the retailer's willingness to pay for some stocks in advance of sale.

A wholesaler like M. needed to dispose of produce weekly, in order to replenish his investment funds, continue buying in his area of supply and repay short-term credits (rance) to trading friends. A retailer like L. was seeking a degree of stability in his market income. Marketing through an established relationship reduced the uncertainty for both. Moreover, it enabled their social needs, grounded in a common religion and sense of social obligation, to be taken into account in economic transactions.

Relationships between wholesaler and retailer, such as between M. and L., were a form of *lateral trading friendship* between social equals. It was limited to the economic activity which joined them. They knew nothing about each other's families. At the same time, their relationship was based on a willingness to make allowance for the other's social as well as economic needs.

There was an interplay between 'personal marketing relationships' and 'market forces'. Wholesalers were not locked into personal ties at their normal outlet regardless of market conditions in other places. In 1978, M.'s trade was concentrated on Danbatta. In 1979, when it became clear that the supply to Danbatta had risen in relation to demand, M. diversified his trade. From 7 January through 1 April, he carried an average of 9 sacks to Danbatta on eight occasions, 12 sacks to Funtua on nine and 22 sacks to Sokoto on six. M.'s marketing in the new destinations itself proceeded through personal ties. At Funtua, his patron, Alhaji Z., introduced him to a wealthy dealer (*mai rumfa*), to whom he sold sacks wholesale. According to traders in Funtua, M. always sold more quickly, and at slightly higher prices, because of his reputation for full sacks of 40 tiya. At Sokoto, he sold wholesale through his son, whose father-in-law was a wealthy rural trader well known to the market commission agents. But according to his son, in the Sokoto trade M. always 'lifted two tiya from each sack in order to increase his profit'. Although diversifying, M. continued to transport grain to Danbatta. In June 1979, with more favourable conditions in Danbatta, he ceased trading elsewhere and increased his shipments there to over twenty sacks per week. Personal relationships never set rigid limits on the way market forces affected prices or produce movements, nor guaranteed profit margins. The wide range of personal relations actually facilitated the diversification of produce movements over a huge area.

Trade earnings revolved around units of measurement which were inherently flexible. Flexibility in manipulating these units was based on a commonly accepted notion of the 'correct' measure and the 'full' sack. These were the volumes from which buyers and sellers argued their respective ideas of a base price. A wholesaler, after considering the competition, might adopt different strategies in different marketplaces. M. decided to offer 'full' sacks in Funtua in order to cultivate a reputation for 'honesty' and sell his produce quickly; while 'underfilling' his sacks in Sokoto, in order to increase his profit margin. A retailer used measuring bowls of different sizes: he could thus discriminate between 'friends' and 'strangers'. Through experience, skill, personal relationships and flexible units of measurement, wholesalers and retailers sought to achieve *riba,* or profit. This complex effort was grounded in a common notion of social obligation inside and outside the marketplace.

Pastoral Kinsmen

M. never lost touch with the pastoral Fulani with whom he shared agnatic or affinal bonds and a common area of origin. At least once a year, he would journey fourteen miles from Marmara to the base camp of Raffa, the younger brother of M.'s mother. Twenty years before, Raffa had emigrated from their childhood village to southern Katsina in search of pasture for his cattle. One of his brothers was a Qur'anic mallam, who spent Ramadan at his base camp and the rest of the year with M. in Marmara. Similarly, M. journeyed to greet Alhaji Habu, whose base camp was in western Kano near the border with Katsina. Alhaji Habu's mother and M.'s father were senior and junior siblings.

The cattle which M. reserved as long-term savings, he kept with Alhaji Audu, whose base camp was twelve miles from Marmara. M. had given to Alhaji Audu in marriage the daughter of his late senior sister. Alhaji honoured M. as his father-in-law (*suruki*).

Household

In 1978, M. headed the only composite gandu in Marmara (Appendix 6, Table 4). It included his unmarried oldest son, a younger married full-brother, a still younger unmarried full-brother and a distantly related married kinsman. The large number of gandu workers enabled M. to concentrate on trade during the farming season – one of the busiest periods of the trading year. In return, he provided them, their wives and children with two meals a day throughout the year. He paid their annual head tax, covered their marriage expenses and made a large contribution at the naming ceremonies of their children.

M.'s senior wife (*uwar gida*) had been with him all his married life. She had given birth to his two surviving offspring. Apart from their son in gandu, they had a younger son whom M. had sent to the far northeast of Nigeria to study the Qur'an. He returned in 1979 to join the gandu. M.'s senior wife also kept as her child the unmarried daughter of M.'s younger sister. For most of the year, his household also included a Qur'anic mallam, his maternal kinsman. M.'s two junior wives (*amare,* sing. *amarya*) had left him in 1976.

At the beginning of 1978, M.'s household numbered fourteen. At the 1977 harvest, M. stored most of his output for sale after a price rise. Through 1978, he relied on current earnings from the turnover trade to buy food for his family. His household consumed two tiya of guineacorn daily (about 5.5 kg.), which came to an annual cost of N428. He spent N2.00 daily on *cefane* (soup ingredients) – N730 throughout 1978. With N6 as the annual head tax for himself and each of his adult male dependents, his basic annual household expenditure was N1,188.

His gandu and their dependents comprised ten out of his household of fourteen. The expense of their food and tax alone was around N850. This can be regarded as the recurrent cost of the family workforce. The funding of their marriages and naming ceremonies will be treated as a capital cost, and discussed below.

Client Labourer

M. had a client farm labourer, whom he called his yaro. B. was a young married man who cultivated a landholding in a settlement near Marmara. He headed a three-man fraternal gandu of his own. M. paid B. at the same rate as occasional daily labourers. However, he could always rely on B., in a situation of competition among employers for labour (chapter 4). In 1977, he gave B. one falle loan in return for harvest guineacorn, but B. only repaid the cash advance (Chart 5.2). In 1978, he gave B. a free bag of fertilizer and a free sack of guineacorn.

Summary

M. bought most of his produce at a market price, in competition with other rural traders. While he gave preference to certain farmers in order to encourage a reliable flow, he could not always guarantee to purchase all of their produce on offer because his investment funds were restricted and fluctuating. Within the framework of market pricing and competition, M.'s trading and farming proceeded through a variety of social relationships. Each had an economic function or range of functions – the provision of credit, supplies, market outlets or labour. Each committed M. to definite obligations. These made possible gain, but at the same time preempted some of the gain.

The 1978 Trading Year

In 1978, M. pursued two strategies in produce trading. He bought and sold produce weekly in the long-distance trade to Danbatta: I call this *turnover trading*. Secondly, he built up his stock of stored grain. During the Postharvest Dry Season, from January through March, he purchased mainly from small and middle farmers selling guineacorn to finance marriages. In April, he purchased mainly from large farmers selling it to buy oxen and fertilizer. Throughout the Farming Season, from May through July, he purchased mainly from large farmers selling guineacorn to finance farming expenses. In May and July, he sold his stock of stored grain at Danbatta. In August, the volume of his turnover trade slackened considerably. In Marmara, there was less supply, and in Danbatta, less demand. M. therefore turned his accumulated earnings to other uses. He distributed falle loans in return for harvest guineacorn. In September, the volume of M.'s turnover trade picked up, as he bought and sold newly harvested rice. In October, his turnover of guineacorn increased, mainly from large farmers who were selling it to pay farm labourers for their work harvesting the yellow maize. In November, he purchased and resold a small quantity of groundnuts from the local harvest. In December, he bought and sold the newly harvested guineacorn. The months of peak volume in M.'s turnover trade in 1978 were March–April, when many farmers across the spectrum of landholding marketed guineacorn after the close of the cotton-buying season, and May–July, when large farmers sold guineacorn to finance hired labour.

Chart 7.3. M.'s household, January 1978

Adult males	Age	Wives	Children	Subtotal:
Self	55 years	1		2
Younger brother	45 years	1	2	4
Younger brother	25 years			1
Son	22 years			1
Kinsman	40 years	1	2	4
Other dependents				
Daughter of M.'s younger sister	12 years			1
Qur'anic mallam	50 years			1
Total:				**14**

M.'s unit overhead costs varied with changes in the purchase price of new hemp sacks, of used sacks repurchased from his retailer in Danbatta and of motor transport rates (Appendix 5, Table 4).[6] Donkey transport rates varied with the distance from the grain seller to Marmara roadside. In 1978, total overheads were 6.7 per cent of the value of all sales (Table 7.4).

In 1978, M.'s profit margin on all sales was 6 per cent. Produce stored for sale after the interseasonal price rise accounted for only 4 per cent of his annual sales volume. However, it contributed 29 per cent of his annual profits (Table 7.4).

Table 7.5 relates M.'s trade expenditure to his revenue over 1978, to develop a picture of his seasonal and annual cash balances. Since expenditure on produce stored for a price rise was actually incurred in 1977, his 1978 cash balance was much higher than his annual profit

Table 7.4. M.'s profit margin on sales, 1978

All prices in N, all weights and quantities in sacks.

	Purchases		Storage		Sales					
*1Season	Sacks	Naira	Sacks	Naira	Sacks	Naira	Overheads	Cost of sales	Margin (N)	Margin per cent
(end 1977)			11	144						
*2Post harvest	237	6,044	30	430	218	6,492	428	6,186	306	5
Farming season	403	11,954			433	14,288	914	13,298	990	7
Minor harvests	132	3,146			132	3,648	283	3,249	219	6
G'corn harvest	57	1,265			57	1,536	122	1,387	149	10
Total:	**829**	**22,409**			**840**	**25,964**	**1,747**	**24,300**	**1,664**	**6**
Storage for price rise:	***331**	**460**			**31**	**1,006**	**66**	**526**	**480**	**48**
per cent of all sales										**4**
per cent of total margin:										**29**
Falle grain only:	*416	158			16	536	35	193	343	**64**
per cent of all sales:										**2**
per cent of total margin:										**21**

*1 Post harvest dry season: 1 January–30 April; Farming season 1 May–6 August; Minor harvest: 7 August–5 November; Guineacorn harvest: 6 November–31 December.
*2 Four weeks not known – ending 29 January, and 12–26 March.
*3 25 guineacorn, 6 rice. *4 chapter 5, Chart 5.5 et seq.
Source: Appendix 5, Tables 1–3.

Table 7.5. M.'s cash flow in trade and balance (N), 1978

Post harvest dry season				Farming season			
Date	**Spend**	**Earn**	**Balance**	**Date**	**Spend**	**Earn**	**Balance**
8 Jan.	*[1]189	135	(–) 54	7 May	987	*1,133	146
15 Jan.	537	729	192	14 May	869	*1,036	167
22 Jan.	416	432	16	21 May	679	*763	84
29 Jan.	*n.k.*	*n.k.*	*n.k.*	28 May	863	891	28
5 Feb.	569	570	1	4 June	897	952	55
12 Feb.	0	0	0	11 June	902	896	(–) 6
19 Feb.	*[1]670	403	(–) 267	18 June	1,160	1,188	28
26 Feb.	229	510	281	25 June	1,029	1,056	27
5 March	899	900	1	2 July	*[1]890	**1,240	350
12 March	*n.k.*	*n.k.*	*n.k.*	9 July	1,229	1,700	471
19 March	*n.k.*	*n.k.*	*n.k.*	16 July	965	1,020	55
26 March	*n.k.*	*n.k.*	*n.k.*	23 July	*[1]1,765	1,173	(–) 592
2 April	*[2]1,409	930	(–) 479	30 July	0	600	600
9 April	284	488	204	6 Aug.	603	640	37
16 April	235	620	385	**Total:**	**12,838**	**14,288**	**1,450**
23 April	749	775	26				
30 April	0	0	0				
Total:	**6,186**	**6,492**	**306**				
Minor harvests				**Guineacorn harvest**			
13 Aug.	559	544	(–) 15	12 Nov.	385	432	47
20 Aug.	335	364	29	19 Nov.	257	288	31
27 Aug.	145	168	23	26 Nov.	*[3]411	115	(–) 296
3 Sept.	0	0	0	3 Dec.	4	40	36
10 Sept.	*[1]372	364	(–) 8	10 Dec.	15	154	139
17 Sept.	59	172	113	17 Dec.	34	154	120
24 Sept.	262	276	14	24 Dec.	241	308	67
1 Oct.	224	232	8	31 Dec.	40	45	5
8 Oct.	235	260	25	**Total:**	**1,387**	**1,536**	**149**
15 Oct.	426	436	10	PHDS:	6,186	6,492	306
22 Oct.	652	656	4	FS:	12,838	14,288	1,450
29 Oct.	160	176	16	MH:	3,429	3,648	219
5 Nov.	0	0	0	GCH:	1,387	1,536	149
Total:	**3,429**	**3,648**	**219**	**Total:**	**23,840**	**25,964**	**2,124**

1, *2, *3* Produce bought this week was sold over: 2 weeks (1*), 3 weeks (**2*), or 4 weeks (**3*).

* Trade revenue includes sale of rice stored from 1977.

** Trade revenue includes sale of guineacorn stored from December 1977–June 1978.

Notes: 1. Trade expenditure figures are slightly distorted since, apart from the week ending 30 July, overhead costs are always included in the week of sale. For produce sold over several weeks or stored against a price rise, overhead costs were spread between the weeks of acquisition and sale. 2. N2,124 (Trade Balance) – 158 (16 sacks of falle grain paid for in 1977) – 176 (8 sacks bought week ending 15 January with recovered cash advances given in 1977) – 30 (1 sack bought in week ending 4 June with recovered cash advances given in 1977) – 96 (6 sacks of rice paid for in 1977) = 1,664 (profit margin on sales, Table 7.4).

margin on sales. Extrapolating from the weeks for which data is known, his cash balance for the Post-harvest Dry Season was in the region of N400, and for the year, N2,200. This was the net income from his trading activity. As we have seen, M. had to meet out of current trade revenues annual food and tax payments of N1,188. This left only about N1,000 for other uses.

Weekly trade expenditure tended to rise from the postharvest into the farming season, and fall sharply thereafter. Nevertheless, there was great fluctuation from week to week. In fact, there was no tendency for the trade revenue of one week to be invested in the trade expenditure of the subsequent week. Rather, the money available to M. for weekly trade fluctuated with the amounts he borrowed from, and loaned out to, trading friends. The claims on M.'s trade revenue arising out of his various social relationships made it difficult for him to simply reinvest weekly revenue in the expansion of trade expenditure. An important reason for the lack of congruence between weekly revenue and subsequent weekly expenditure, was that M. was investing part of his weekly trade revenue in other spheres. To these we now turn.

Agricultural Investments in 1978

In the Post-harvest Dry Season, M. embarked on a dramatic expansion of his farmed acreage (Table 7.6). He acquired most of the additional acreage by pledge (*jingina*). And in the harvests of 1978 M. more than quadrupled his output over the preceding season, from twenty sacks of guineacorn and shelled groundnuts to ninety-three sacks of all produce (Table 7.9).[7,8]

M. spent an enormous amount on artificial fertilizer, purchased from the FADP and the private market at rates which reflected the high degree of subsidy in Nigeria at the time. His fertilizer use on yellow maize approached, and on other crops far exceeded, the ideal recommendations of the FADP (Table 7.7).

Before planting, M. hired oxen teams to ridge his fields. After he had finished planting and weeding, he hired them again to bank up the crops. Except for one field ridged freely by a trading friend, M. paid high ploughing fees because he had no kinsmen among the plough owners of Marmara. On the biggest field which he owned, he intercropped guineacorn with millet and cowpeas. Most of the remaining fields were sole cropped with guineacorn (Table 7.7).

His greatest single expense was the employment of hired labourers – 36 per cent of money expenditure. If we include the cost of lunchtime food for family and hired labourers, then the money cost

Table 7.6. M.'s farm holdings, 1977 and 1978, Marmara, 1978

	1977: Field size and mode of acquisition		1978: Field size and mode of acquisition:		
Field no.	**size**	**mode**	**size**	**mode**	**cost**
1.	0.8 acres	Purchase			
2.	0.3 acres	Purchase			
3.	3.6 acres	Purchase			
4.	1.5 acres	Pledge			
5.			1.5 acres	Purchase	62
6.			4.9 acres	Pledge	100
7.			3.5 acres	Pledge	100
8.			3.0 acres	Pledge	14
9.			2.5 acres	Pledge	100
10.			0.8 acres	Pledge	30
Totals:	**6.2 acres**		**22.4 acres**		**N406**
Owned	4.7 acres		6.2 acres		
Pledged:	1.4 acres		16.2 acres		

of labour was 46 per cent of expenditure (Table 7.8). To appreciate M.'s spending on hired labour, we must survey the extent to which he combined it with his gandu. Before the rains fell, he relied on hired labourers to clear the fields. Once the rains had begun, after ridging by oxen, he relied mainly on his gandu for planting (M.'s four gandu members provided him weekly with six long mornings of work of about six hours each). The first weeding was the crucial farm operation because timely weeding facilitated the growth of young plants and therefore had a big impact on yield. To speed up the first weeding, he placed hired labourers alongside his gandu workforce while hired labourers worked on other fields. The second weeding was less crucial. To save money, he did not perform it on eight acres and across the remaining holding, his gandu performed it. At the maize harvest, M. employed women to pick and peel the cobs. He joined with other big farmers in the hamlet to hire a machine to shuck the maize. For his small groundnut harvest, he used his gandu. On the land planted to guineacorn, hired labourers reaped 9.7 acres, his gandu 11 acres. He relied entirely on his gandu to cut, gather, thresh and sack the grain.

Table 7.7. M.'s total estimated farm expenditure for 1978 (N), Marmara, 1978

	Maize	Guineacorn	Total
	1.7 acres	**20.7 acres**	**22.4 acres**
		1.6: with groundnuts, 3.6 with millet and cowpeas, 15.5: sole-cropped.	
Fertilizer use	**10 bags at 50 kg**	**50 bags at 50 kg**	**60 bags**
Fertilizer rate	726 kg/ha.	298 kg/ha.	
Farm clearing	3.00	38.00	41.00
*1Fertilizer	40.40	179.00	219.40
Maize seed	9.00		9.00
First ridging	1.50	121.00	122.50
Planting	0	17.50	17.50
First weeding	9.00	204.50	213.50
Lunch	0	47.25	47.25
Second weeding	9.00	*238.00	47.00
Lunch	0	*228.00	28.00
Second ridging	12.00	*2119.00	131.00
Harvesting	*344.50	*283.75	128.25
Lunch	0	*233.00	33.00
Hemp snacks	22.00	72.00	94.00
Off farm transport	18.00	23.20	41.20
Total:	**168.40**	**1,004.20**	**1,172.60**

*1 Part applied after first ridging, part between second weeding and second ridging.
*2 Estimated for 11 acres.
*3 N24.00 = 60 sacks of peeled cobs at 40 kobo per sack; N20.50 = fee to shuck cobs into 22 sacks of maize kernels.
Note: This does not include the annual costs of maintaining family labour.

He employed women to winnow it. M. used far more hired labour for the first weeding than he did for any other operation (Table 7.7).

M. sold his maize and groundnut output at harvest while his household consumed the millet and cowpeas. He stored most guineacorn and sold it in the farming season of 1979 to pay for farming. Yellow maize took only 8 per cent of acreage and 14 per cent of farm expenditure, but contributed 36 per cent of farm profit (Table 7.8). Had the family workforce not been available, the cost of labour would have more than doubled. The money profit from guineacorn would have

Table 7.8. M.'s estimated profit margins in agriculture (N), Marmara, 1978

Output and Marmara prices at time of sale		
Crop:	**Quantity**	**Price**
1. Guineacorn:	50.0 sacks of *kaura*	**20** *(May – June 1979)*
2. Guineacorn:	15.5 sacks of *mori**	**22** *(May – June 1979)*
Maize:	22.0 sacks	**21** *(November 1978)*
Groundnuts:	4.0 sacks	**30** *(November 1978)*
Millet:	1.0 sack	**24** *(August 1978)*
Cowpeas:	1.0 sack	**36** *(December 1978)*

	Maize	**Guineacorn**	**Guineacorn with intercrops**	**Total**
	1.7 acres	**20.7 acres**	**20.7 acres**	**22.4 acres**
Cash inputs	71.40	245.00	251.00	322.4 *27%*
Oxen ploughing fees	13.50	240.00	240.00	253.5 *22%*
Labour cost	45.00	490.00	490.00	535.0 *46%*
Machinery cost	20.50	–	–	20.5 *2%*
Off-farm donkey transport	18.00	21.40	23.20	41.2 *3%*
Total operating cost	**168.40**	**996.40**	**1,004.20**	**1,172.6** ***100%***
Total revenue	**462.00**	**1,341.00**	**1,521.00**	**1,983.00**
Margin	**293.60**	**344.60**	**516.80**	**810.40**
Percentage margin	**63%**	**26%**	**34%**	**41%**

*1 A type of guineacorn considered superior in taste.

been eliminated. The profitability of guineacorn depended entirely on the deployment of a large family workforce.

Apart from lunch expenses on the field, the social costs of maintaining a gandu have not been included in farm expenditure. In fact, M. met these costs from his earnings in the produce trade. Since gandu services were mainly confined to farm work, these costs ought theoretically to be included in farm expenditure. The expense in 1978 of their food and tax alone – some N850 – was sufficient to eliminate his money profits from farming (Table 7.8).

But M. did not look at it that way. For the alternative – hired labour – was expensive and its supply uncertain (chapter 4). More deeply, M. *assumed* the situation of a large household. It was the unquestioned basis from which he reflected on the comparative returns of different endeavours. Thus, Table 7.8 presents farming 'profit' as M. construed it.

In 1978, M.'s agricultural investment occurred when there was highly subsidized fertilizer, and the following year, guineacorn prices stagnated (chapter 6). Had the subsidy been eliminated, his profit margin on maize would have fallen and his margin on guineacorn would have evaporated. We should also consider his profits in a situation without fertilizer subsidy, and a considerable inter-seasonal price rise in guineacorn. Then, the profitability of maize would have fallen and that of guineacorn would have risen (Table 5.14).

The problem with yellow maize was that it required much more fertilizer than the other crops. Also, market demand for yellow maize

Table 7.9. M.'s farm output and yield, Marmara, 1978

Field	Size	Acquisition	Crop	Output	Per acre	kg/ha.*1
1.	0.8 acres	Purchase	Groundnuts	2.0 sacks	2.5 sacks	531
			Guineacorn	3.5 sacks	4.4 sacks	899
2.	0.3 acres	Purchase	Guineacorn	3.0 sacks	10.0 sacks	2,569
3.	3.6 acres	Purchase	Guineacorn	12.0 sacks	3.3 sacks	848
			Millet	1.0 sacks	*2 3.6 sacks	*2 924
			Cowpeas	1.0 sacks		
4.	1.5 acres	Pledge	Guineacorn	2.0 sacks	1.3 sacks	334
5.	1.5 acres	Purchase *(1978)*	Guineacorn	5.5 sacks	3.7 sacks	950
6.	4.9 acres	Pledge *(1978)*	Guineacorn	17.0 sacks	3.5 sacks	899
7a.	1.7 acres	Pledge *(1978)*	Maize	22.0 sacks	12.9 sacks	3,027
7b.	1.8 acres	Pledge *(1978)*	Guineacorn	5.0 sacks	2.8 sacks	719
8.	3.0 acres	Pledge *(1978)*	Guineacorn	7.5 sacks	2.5 sacks	642
9.	2.5 acres	Pledge *(1978)*	Guineacorn	8.5 sacks	3.4 sacks	873
10.	0.8 acres	Pledge *(1978)*	Groundnuts	2.0 sacks	2.5 sacks	531
			Guineacorn	1.5 sacks	1.9 sacks	488
		Average:			**3.2 sacks** *(Guineacorn)*	**813** *(Guineacorn)*
		Total:	**Guineacorn:**	**65.5 sacks**		
			Maize:	**22.0 sacks**		
			Groundnuts:	**4.0 sacks**		
			Millet:	**1.0 sacks**		
			Cowpeas:	**1.0 sacks**		

*1 For the weights per sack used in the conversion of yields into kg/ha. See Appendix 2, Table 2.
*2 Guineacorn and millet combined.

was much smaller than that for guineacorn. The advantage to M. of planting a small part of his guineacorn acreage with traditional inter-crops, was that it boosted considerably his farm revenue with only a slight increase in farm expenditure! Thus, M. rationally distributed his acreage between maize, guineacorn and inter-crops.

Other Commercial Investments

Though focussing his energies on trading and farming, M. responded to other commercial opportunities. In the Postharvest Dry Season, he purchased a plot of land in nearby Malumfashi, and laid the foundations for a compound. He said that 'the rest would have to wait until next year'. Aware of the expansion in Malumfashi town, he intended to build a compound and sell it at a profit. Later in the year, he bought a bull and added it to the herd maintained by his kinsman.

M.'s investments ranged from short -term (e.g., weekly expenditure in the turnover trade) to the long -term (e.g., investment in cattle). We should also remark on the geographical and social range of his planning. Until 1978, M. was integrating produce and livestock markets as distant as Sokoto, Danbatta and Kaduna. During 1978, his investments straddled long-distance trading, urban property, livestock and agriculture. M. naturally thought in long-distance and socially eclectic terms. He was aided in this by his dual identity as a Fulani with pastoral kinsmen and a 'Hausa' farmer: Hausa was his business language. Though he remained a rural person, long-distance trading had opened his eyes to social manners and commercial prospects in towns and cities. The expanding transport system helped his efforts to develop trading friendships over a vast area. In a diverse country like Nigeria, M.'s involvement in a variety of social settings was unremarkable. The distinguishing feature of farmer-traders like M. was their willingness to take risks concurrently in many milieux.

Social Investments and Expenditures

We turn finally to M.'s social investments. In 1978 M. undertook a major expansion of his household. In the Postharvest Dry Season, M.'s oldest son, Halilu, married the only daughter of a wealthy grain trader in the hinterland behind Marmara. MGT had long been M.'s trading friend. Having no male child, MGT treated Halilu like a son. He gave him farmland and after the guineacorn harvest, he sent Halilu on trading expeditions to the distant market of Sokoto. After several weeks of trading, he gave Halilu jali, which Halilu returned before the farming season of 1979, when he farmed for his father. Sometimes, Halilu would carry to Sokoto 80 sacks – 20 of his own, 10–20 for his father and 40–50 for his father-in-law. Halilu's marriage made him the most fortunate young man of the hamlet, with more farmland than many household heads, trading capital and a large trade turnover. M. benefited because through his son, he made use of MGT's brokers and wholesale buyers.

In August, M.'s young unmarried brother in gandu began courting a daughter of HH 10. M. fully supported the courtship. HH 10 had the largest shop in Marmara. Besides opening opportunities for Gambo, the marriage would have strengthened M.'s tie to HH 10 as a trading friend (Chart 7.1). It would have also deepened M.'s relationship with the oldest and richest kinship group in Marmara. HH 10 was one of those household heads who traced their residence through several generations and, consequently, tended to have much larger landholdings than farmers whose families had arrived more recently (chapter 3).

By the time of the marriage in 1979, M. had spent N600 (as much as he had spent on the marriage of his son) and over N300 on a room for the couple. In hamlet terms, these were expensive marriages (Tables 5.1 and 5.3). But if M. had failed in this regard, the young men would soon have left him. Equally, M. saw these marriages as strategic alliances with successful families. His spending was social investment.

In the midst of investments on trading, farming and household, M. was steadily pursuing a second wife for himself. On his weekly journeys to Danbatta, he courted a young divorcee, the daughter of a market seller of bows and arrows, knives and hunting guns. At the end of the post-harvest dry season of 1978, he married her. Six weeks later, she fled in the night, taking all her goods, he said, 'except the bed'. Touring his fields, he told an old farming woman his woes: 'My only fault [*laifi*] is that she was to pound one tiya of corn a day. She didn't like this. But did I do wrong, since I gave her no other work? She has disappeared. Perhaps she is still in Marmara, but I do not know.'

Soon after the flight of his second wife, he began courting another young divorcee at Danbatta. M.'s desire for another wife filled his conversation with close friends. He said to HH 63: 'Isa, there are beautiful women in Danbatta, as many as you could possibly want to see.' On a journey home from Danbatta, he and I went ten miles off the road to a hamlet near the old walled town of Jalli, to consult a mallam who divined in the sand that a man in his household was hostile, but that the marriage would take place – if God willed it. The mallam wrote a Qur'anic verse on a wooden board, washed it off, and gave the liquid to M. to drink at the end of the day's Ramadan fasting. The following week, M. returned to get a perfume for the marriage, to sprinkle around the woman's room, so that she would 'see' no other man. And he bought charms from farmers in Marmara. The marriage took place in September. M. made arrangements for her daughter from a previous marriage to join and later her younger brother.

The new wife was soon threatening to leave if he did not mend a leaking roof. Household repairs focussed M.'s mind on a lavish scheme. He planned a large room for his younger brother and a set of rooms, one for his senior, one for his junior wife. At the guineacorn harvest, he engaged HH 35 (his frequent falle debtor) as the master builder. The rooms were spacious, with high ceilings and cemented floors, the roofs finished and decorated with white chalk. M.'s marriages and the rebuilding of his compound revealed a willingness to spend on beauty, and a capacity for extravagance, which I had not earlier suspected.

In 1978, his combined spending on marriages and house building was N1,732. (Chart 7.4) This was considerably more than his farming expenditure. It was also greater than the value of his average weekly turnover trade (N500) and the grain he was storing for a price rise (N460). The importance of household expansion remained at the centre of his thinking about wealth.

Chart 7.4. M.'s social investments and expenditures (N), Marmara, 1978

	Social Investments	
January:	The marriage of his son to a previously unmarried girl (budurwa).	600
September–December:	Initial spending on his junior brother's marriage*[1]	151
November–December:	Building his junior brother's marriage room	311
	Social Expenditures	
April:	M.'s marriage to a divorcee	200
September:	M.'s second marriage to a divorcee	200
November–December:	Building materials for his wives' new rooms	270
Total:		**1,732**

**1* N107: Na gani ina so (toshin Salla). N44: Sa rana (cf. chapter 4).

Integrating the Spheres of a Farmer-Trader's Economic Activity: The Role of Savings, Borrowing, and Lending in the Expansion of M.'s Enterprise

We have seen how M. pursued a wide range of purposes in his social and economic life. They were guided by a clear goal of expansion. This required heavy borrowing as well as the use of savings. It also required a sense of timing, careful calculation and the ability and wisdom to manage a variety of human relationships. The fascinating question is: how does a farmer-trader schedule his spending and borrowing in order to balance a complex array of actions? Consequently, this part of the case study is concerned with practical finance. By integrating the different kinds of evidence about M., I seek to reconstruct a purposive man through one year of his life.

We will see that the seasons of the annual agricultural and marketing cycle controlled, to a degree, his plans and actions. Thus, I have constructed a narrative based on the seasons. For brevity, my descriptions only refer to the season being treated. To reduce tedium, I have confined numerical evidence as much as possible to the table for each season. Each table presents a summary of the stream of income and expenditure for that season. The End-of Season Balance refers to the actual cash which M. had in hand as a result. The last entry in each table, Average Weekly Trade Expenditure, is not a result of the previous numbers, but an average taken from Table 7.5, M.'s Cash Flow in Trade, to help the reader compare his average cash requirement in trade with his cash flow in other spheres.

Postharvest Dry Season (January–April)

In the summer of 1977, M. had distributed over N400 of his accumulated savings as falle loans. He entered 1978 with jali of about N2,000 – his own funds of N1,600, and the trading loan of his patron of N400. He gradually spent all of his own funds on the marriage of his son and his own first marriage, acquiring farmland and investment in an urban house plot. Thus, his weekly trade expenditure became increasingly dependent on his patron's loan.

During the Postharvest Dry Season, his balance of trade revenue over trade expenditure was about N400. But over the course of the season, household food purchases, paid for out of weekly trade revenues, absorbed most of the trade balance. There were other drains on his income. He enlarged his storeroom. To one of his trading friends, he loaned N100 for trading, but it was never repaid. Later, M. gave the same man N96 in the form of falle loans, to be repaid with grain at

Table 7.10A. M.'s income and nontrade expenditure (N), Marmara, January–April 1978

Income		Nontrade Expenditure	
Own investment funds	1,600	Marriages	800
		Son: 600*N*	
		Self: 200*N*	
		Farm acquisition	406
		Town plot	400
			1,606
Patron loans	400	Enlarged storeroom	100
		Loans given/outstanding	196
		Farm clearing	41
			337
Total balance	400	Food grain/cefane	394
	2,400		**2,337**
Seasonal balance:			**63**

Average weekly trade expenditure: 476

met out of own investment funds (jali) at the beginning, patron loan (jali) in the middle, and short-term credits (rance) at the end of the season.

harvest. At the end of the season, he paid labourers to clear his fields. Thus, various expenditures absorbed his loan. Before the end of the season, he was completely dependent on short-term credits (rance) from trading friends to engage in produce trading.

Farming Season (May–6 August)

In the months of May and June, M. was entirely dependent on short-term credits to finance his turnover trading. However, he had guineacorn and rice in storage. In May, he sold the stock of stored rice. Through turnover trading with short-term credits, and the sale of the rice, he generated a large trade balance. His closest trading friend, HH 12, allowed him to postpone repayment of a weekly credit of N200 until the middle of the farming season when he would sell his stored guineacorn. This gave M. additional funds to work with in May and June, the period of heaviest expenditure on farming.

M. usually spent his weekly trade balance on fertilizer and farm operations. Over the entire period under examination, he could not

Table 7.10B. M.'s income and nontrade expenditure (N), Marmara, May–June 1978

Income		Nontrade Expenditure	
May 1: Cash in hand	63	Farming	629
Loan from trading friend	200	Foodgrain/cefane	193
Trade balance	529		
Sale of stored rice: 156			
Turnover trade: 373			
	792		**822**
Sub-seasonal balance:			**(–) 30**
Average weekly trade expenditure: 923 *met out of short-term credits throughout the period.*			

cover the combined expenditure on agriculture and household food and, by the end of June, he was using trading credit to pay for household food.

The period from the end of June to the beginning of August was for M. the crucial part of the trading year. He sold all of his stored guineacorn in Danbatta, and he brought his turnover trading to its highest annual volume (Table 7.5). His balance in the turnover trade was small because of the narrow difference between prices in Marmara and Danbatta (Table 6.6).

Much of his income from the sale of stored guineacorn was committed to repaying debts which he had incurred in May and June, or to meeting nontrade expenditures. He repaid the N200 'medium-term' loan given in May by HH 12, and N30 borrowed at the end of June to buy food. He invested further money on farm operations. He then began to spend money on a prospective bride, and distributed new falle loans against the Guineacorn Harvest. Thus, the net income available from the sale of stored grain to plough back into turnover trading, was small. As for his balance in turnover trading, this was absorbed in the purchase of food. Consequently, he depended on short-term credits for weekly trading. In the week ending 30 July, the only produce which he carried to Danbatta consisted of five sacks of his own output, stored from the previous harvest. He moaned: 'I poured five sacks of guineacorn from my house into my jali, but it made little difference.' In the words of his friend, HH 63: 'M. has no jali now. He spent it all on farming and marriages. Here, there, he gets his money for trade.'

Table 7.10C. M.'s income and nontrade expenditure (N), Marmara, 2 July–6 August 1978

INCOME		NONTRADE EXPENDITURE	
Trade balance:	921	**Settlement of debts:**	230
Stored guineacorn: 783		Short-term: 30	
Turnover trade: 138		Medium-term: 200	
		Farming	206
		Courting a potential bride	100
		Falle loans	96
			632
Sale of own output:	139	Foodgrain/cefane	145
	1,060		777
Sub-seasonal balance:			**283**
Average weekly trade expenditure: 909			
met partly from sale of stored Guineacorn (2 July), and sale of own Guineacorn (30 July), but mainly from short-term credits.			

The Minor Harvests (7 August–5 November)

M. entered the season with cash of N283. In addition, he had four sacks of guineacorn output from the previous year. He transferred these to his trading stocks and sold them in Danbatta, realising N103. Thus, he had total investment funds of N386 from the beginning of the season.

This was a season of slack trade for M. N386 was usually more than sufficient to cover his weekly trade expenditure (Table 7.5). However, he knew from the start that nontrade expenses would be considerable: he was planning to marry; he had to meet the initial marriage payments of his younger brother; and the maize harvest was imminent. These burdens were bound to erode his investment funds, making trade difficult. Consequently, M. went to HH 12 and borrowed N200 for a month. At the same time, he began to cultivate closer ties with me, borrowing small sums for a week repaid out of trade revenue. After he repaid HH 12 the N200 from his weekly trading revenue, he borrowed the same amount from me, repayable at the Guineacorn Harvest. These loans allowed M. to spend on marriage and farming in the knowledge that he had sufficient cash for trade.

His balance from turnover trading was spent on family food. As in previous seasons, borrowing enabled M. to divert his investment funds and trade balance to nontrade expenditures.

Table 7.10D. M.'s income and nontrade expenditure (N), Marmara, 7 August–5 November 1978

Income		Nontrade Expenditure	
August 7, cash in hand	283	**Marriage payments**	207
Medium-term loan from		Self: 100	
trading friends	200	Junior brother: 107	
Sale of own output:	103	Farming	91
		Maize*1: 84.5	
		Millet/groundnuts: *2 6.5	
		Tax	30
Turnover trade balance	219	Foodgrain/cefane	293
	805		**621**
Seasonal balance:			**184**

Average weekly trade expenditure: 264

met at the beginning, from his cash reserve but increasingly thereafter, from a medium-term loan of 200N, occasionally supplemented by short-term credits.

*1 Harvesting and off-farm transport – Table 7.7.
*2 Off-farm transport and hemp sacks – Table 7.7.

The Guineacorn Harvest (6 November–31 December)

The last season of the year was normally a period of heavy trading for M. But since he had earlier used up his investment funds, he traded on a much smaller scale than in previous seasons (Table 7.5).

He had to repay the loan of N400 given by his patron a year before. To do this, M. sold his maize and groundnut produce. He reserved the sale of his major crop, guineacorn, until the postharvest and farming seasons of 1979. Most of his balance in turnover trading was spent purchasing family food. Given these priorities, M. had little cash and continued to rely on credit.

M.'s nontrade expenditure greatly increased. He embarked on the rebuilding of his compound (Chart 7.4). Harvesting guineacorn, he hired labour to supplement his gandu workforce. He made standing arrangements with trading friends in the hinterland of Marmara to store some of his grain purchases, and in return, he loaned them N200 which was not repayable until after harvest.

M.'s nontrade expenditure greatly exceeded his income from crop sales and turnover trading. To finance the deficit, he doubled the size of the medium-term loan from me, from N200 to N400, and when it became due in December, he rescheduled its repayment for March. Secondly, he borrowed much more from his core group of trading friends (Chart 7.1), and only repaid these 'short-term' loans in the last week of the season. Because they were aware of the large size of his guineacorn harvest, they allowed him to extend the period of repayment from a week to a month or more. Thirdly, he engaged in 'serial borrowing': whenever he repaid one loan after returning from his outlet market, he replaced it with a new loan from another trading friend. By the week ending 24 December, he had amassed short-term debts of N800. He paid off part of these from his trade earnings at Danbatta (Table 7.5). But most he repaid by contracting new loans from other trading friends. In this way, he managed to postpone any sales from his guineacorn output until after harvest.

Comparing M.'s income with his nontrade expenditure, we can see that the deficit was broadly equivalent to his house-building expenses (Table 7.10E). Essentially, M. increased his credit to push forward with house building.

Table 7.10E. M.'s income and nontrade expenditure (N), Marmara, 6 November–31 December 1978

Income		Nontrade Expenditure	
6 November, cash in hand	184	Patron's loan (jali) repayment	400
Additional medium-term loan		Purchase of a bull:	232
from trading friends:	200	Farming:	205
		Housebuilding:	581
Sale of own output:	688	Junior brother's marriage	
		payments:	44
Maize, 8 Nov.: *1552		Medium-term loan from	
Groundnuts, 12 Nov.: *1136		trading friends:	200
Turnover trade balance:	149	*2Foodgrain/cefane	133
	1,221		**1,795**
Seasonal balance:			**(–) 574**

Average weekly trade expenditure: 174

met at the beginning, from his cash reserve; in the middle, from a medium-term loan from his trading friend; and toward the end from short-term credits.

*1 22 sacks of maize sold at Dutsinma at 26N (–) O.90 overheads; 4 sacks of groundnuts sold at Danbatta at 36N (–) 2.10 overheads.

*2 During harvest, his household ate newly harvested guineacorn, thus reducing the weekly expenses of purchasing foodgrain.

Economic Analysis

Reviewing 1978, M. followed a particular strategy of borrowing, lending and investment. It can only be understood in terms of the bonds of obligation, and the opportunities arising, between himself and his household, patrons and trading friends. Apart from the first three months, M.'s turnover trading was completely or largely reliant on borrowed funds. And, since he also bought family food from his balance in turnover trading, household provisions were ultimately dependent on credit.

Credit was also important to his farming activities. He used part of his patron's loan for farm clearing, a medium-term loan for weeding and short-term credits to complete the harvesting process. Indirectly, borrowing generated his balance in the May–June turnover trade, which went into agriculture. There was an intimate connection between, on the one hand, his borrowing, and on the other, his money lending for harvest grain. Short-term borrowing for trade enabled him to accumulate 'high-interest' credit repayments from 1977 as stored grain. He sold these grains at peak prices, rather than dissipate them on weekly trading or family food purchases.

During 1978, credit made it possible for him to:

1. divert his own investment funds from trade to farmland and household marriages,
2. store the repayments of his debtors as grain until prices reached their peak, when it was sold for farming and further marriages,
3. expand the scale of his turnover trade, and thus, the profit available for farming and
4. finance family food purchase.

Patronage and trading friendships enabled him to shift his own capital into agriculture and marriage while maintaining the scale of his trading. This strategy entailed a sharp fall in his 'working capital', the commercial value of his liquid assets (Abbott 1987: 204–5).

In the light of the transformation which M. had accomplished, how are we to assess his 'working capital' at the end of 1978? One approach would be to treat the value of M.'s liquid assets at that time as a guide to his trading and farming capacity in the following year. At the end of 1978, his liquid assets consisted almost entirely of his own large output of guineacorn (Table 7.11). We would project into 1979 by considering only those expenditures which were necessary for the maintenance and expansion of an enterprise based on household labour and supplementary hired labour. These expenses would

Table 7.11. The growth of M.'s wealth: Expansion of M.'s enterprise, from late 1977 to late 1978, Marmara

A. Physical summary	Late 1977	Late 1978
Farmland:	**6.2 acres**	**22.4 acres**
Owned:	4.7 acres	6.2 acres
By pledge:	1.5 acres	16.2 acres
Harvest output:	**10 sacks guineacorn**	**65 sacks guineacorn**
	10 sacks groundnuts	**4 sacks groundnuts**
		22 sacks yellow maize
Average weekly:		
Stocks in trade:	26 sacks	9 sacks
Family size:	14	18
Additions to house:	–	Brother's room
Other fixed investments:		Storeroom, town plot
	1 January 1978 (N)	31 December 1978 (N)
B. Liquid Assets:	**212**	**1,279**
Own crops:	*10 sacks of guineacorn at *1 21.23*	*63 sacks guineacorn at 20.30*3*
Stored grain purchases:	**239**	**101**
	*5 sacks of guineacorn at *1 21.23*	*5 sacks guineacorn at 20.3*3*
	*6 sacks rice at *2 22.23*	
Loans recoverable:	**370**	**132*4**
	38 unrepaid falle loans at 8–10 'face value'	*11 unrepaid falle loans at 12 'face value'*
Investment funds:	**1,600**	**41**
a. Cash:	**1,154**	**0**
b. Traded stocks:	**446**	**41**
Current assets:	**2,421**	**1,553**
Short-term debt:	–	574
Net current assets: (*working capital*)	**2,421**	**979**

**1* Wholesale price, Danbatta: 23.00, Overheads: 1.77, 1 January 1978.
*2 Wholesale price, Danbatta: 24.00, Overheads: 1.77, 1 January 1978.
**3* Wholesale price, Danbatta: 22.50, Overheads: 2.20, 31 December 1978.
**4* Excluded is 100 in bad debt from post-harvest dry season.
Note: This table excludes additions to livestock – one calf, one bull – as the size of herd is unknown as of 1 January 1978.

be deducted, either from working capital, or from the trade revenue generated by that capital. Net trade earnings would be treated as reinvested in commerce during the Postharvest Dry Season, and in commerce or agriculture during the Farming Season.

On these assumptions, the first deduction from M.'s liquid assets would be the large remaining payments for the marriage of his younger brother at the start of 1979. These payments would have reduced his liquid assets to N550. In March, he repaid the N400 owing to myself, and recovered the N200 which he had loaned to trading friends. M. purchased hardly any grain for storage against a price rise during 1979, because he could see that guineacorn prices were stagnant (Table 6.6). Even allowing for a certain amount of capital growth from weekly trading, his commitments would have greatly reduced his liquid assets. This approach would predict a substantial drop in his capacity to farm in 1979.

However, it does not do justice to the complex social relations through which M. pursued his diverse objectives. His net liquid assets at the end of 1978 did correspond to his jali. But M. treated jali as investible in a range of social relations. As a result, he saw his brother's marriage payments, his house building, and the requests for loans of trading friends, as charges on his jali. At the same time, he was able to make claims on the jali of others. Quite separately, M.'s intention as the year opened was to reserve his harvest output as much as possible until the next Farming Season, when he would sell it to meet farming expenses.

These facets of his thinking were intimately connected. Because he gave short-term credit, he was in a good position to receive it. And though harvest grain was convertible into cash, at least partly they were classified as belonging to separate spheres which were subject to different claims. Money was more liable to diffuse social claims than was harvest grain. It made sense to reserve grain and generate funds for trading through the web of credit relationships.

Although his jali was quickly reduced by his brother's marriage payments, only part of it was invested in trading. Most was set aside as grain for sale and use in the Farming Season. As in 1978, so in 1979. The quantity of grain which M. traded weekly fluctuated with the difference between the amount of short-term credit which he borrowed and that which he loaned out (Table 7.12). Over the Farming Season, credit generated a positive trade balance, which he applied to farming. True, M. had to reduce production in 1979, but by combining trading credits with the sale of his stored output, M. was able to farm almost nineteen acres – nearly as much as in 1978.

Table 7.12. M's grain trading, Marmara, January–March 1979

Week ending	Purchases	TRADE Expenditure (N)	Sales	TRADE Revenue (N)	Difference (N)	Storage balance
31 December						*5 sacks
7 January	36 sacks	720	31 sacks	692	(–) 28	10 sacks
14 January	18 sacks	364	18 sacks	432	68	10 sacks
21 January	21 sacks	396	8 sacks	180	(–) 216	23 sacks
28 January	0 sacks	*[1]9	4 sacks	88	79	19 sacks
4 February	15 sacks	305	15 sacks	330	25	19 sacks
11 February	12 sacks	260	19 sacks	409	149	12 sacks
18 February	*[2]5 sacks	124	6 sacks	146	22	11 sacks
25 February	56 sacks	1,101	33 sacks	801	(–) 300	34 sacks
4 March	4 sacks	142	27 sacks	618	476	11 sacks
11 March	52 sacks	1,137	40 sacks	960	(–) 177	23 sacks
18 March	32 sacks	713	32 sacks	761	48	23 sacks
25 March	41 sacks	946	36 sacks	921	(–) 25	28 sacks
1 April	19 sacks	480	35 sacks	880	400	**13 sacks
Total:	**311 sacks**	**6,697**	**304 sacks**	**7,218**	**521**	**13 sacks**
Average:	**24 sacks**	**515**	**23 sacks**	**555**	**40**	

* Five sacks of guineacorn, repaid falle loans.
** Includes one sack of guineacorn, a repaid falle loan.
*1 Overheads from the previous week. *2 Rice.
Note: All sacks are guineacorn unless otherwise indicated.

The value of M.'s liquid assets at harvest provides only a suggestive guide to his trading-and-farming capacity. Its real measure was his ability to borrow. The readiness of others to lend him money stemmed from their complex assessment of his trustworthiness, trading skill, and willingness to take on responsibilities for others – in a word, his hali. If anything, spending on marriages and house building increased his moral stature as a 'man of responsibilities' (*mai hidima*) – and therefore, the sympathetic attraction of potential creditors.

The problem with the first approach is that it assessed M.'s liquid assets in terms of a 'household model' of his total enterprise. On the contrary, we must say of M. what we said earlier of Alhaji Z.: 'The complex of personal relationships through which [he] worked enabled him to break through the limits of economic scale set by his own investment funds and by the human resources of his immediate household.'

Financial Analysis

How did the interaction of M.'s income and expenditure lead to increased borrowing? Table 7.13 breaks down his income and expenditure into the main farming seasons. It shows his borrowing requirement at the end of each season, and the actual debt carried to cover his cumulative seasonal borrowing requirement.

Trade income (the Trade Balance in rows 4 and 6) is broken down into net earnings from weekly trading ('turnover') and those from the sale of produce stored against a price rise ('storage'). M.'s weekly trade expenditure fluctuated sharply, averaging N495 over the year. From this, he earned two and a half times as much – N1,279.[9]

We can see that, before the Guineacorn Harvest, M. kept his *seasonal* debt burdens low and long term (Row 26). By that time, he had ample harvest stocks to cover his debts. Once he had committed his

Table 7.13. M's money income and expenditure (HH 7) (N), Marmara, 1978

	Trade:	**Post-harvest Dry season**	**Faming season**	**Minor harvests**	**Guineacorn harvest**	**1978**
1.	Average weekly expenditure:	476	917	264	173	495
2.	Total expenditure:	*[1]8,089	12,838	3,429	1,387	25,743
3.	Total income:	*[1]8,489	14,288	3,648	1,536	27,961
4.	Trade balance:	***[1]400**	**1,450**	**219**	**149**	**2,218**
	Income:					
5.	Savings:	1,600	–	–	–	1,600
6.	Trade balance:	*turnover* 400	*turnover* 511	*turnover* 219	*turnover* 149	1,279
			storage 939			939
7.	Own crop sales:	–	*Guineacorn* 139	*Guineacorn* 103	*Groundnuts* 136	930
	:				*Maize* 552	

Table 7.13 continued on next page.

Table 7.13 continued from previous page.

8.	Periodic total:	**2,000**	**1,589**	**322**	**837**	**4,748**
9.	Cumulative income:	2,000	3,589	3,911	4,748	
	Expenditure					
10.	Food grain/cefane:	394	338	293	133	1,158
11.	Marriages:	800	100	207	44	1,151
12.	Housebuilding:	–	–	–	581	581
13.	*[2]Farming:	41	835	91	205	1,172
14.	Fixed investments:	farms 406 town plot 400 storeroom 100				906
15.	Loans, not repaid:	*[3]196	*[4]96		*[5]200	492
16.	Livestock:	–	–	–	232	232
17.	Tax:		–	*[6]30	–	30
18.	Periodic total:	**2,337**	**1,369**	**621**	**1,395**	**5,722**
19.	Cumulative Expenditure:	2,337	3,706	4,327	5,722	
20.	Periodic balance:	−337	+220	−229	−558	
21.	Cumulative borrowing: requirements:	337	117	416	974	974
22.	Credits not repaid:	400		200	774	
23.	Credits repaid:				400	
24.	Cash in hand:	63	283	184	0	
25.	Cumulative debt:	**400**	**400**	**600**	**974**	**974**
26.	**Debt composition:**					
	Long-term:	400 (*patron*)	400 (*patron*)	400 (*patron*)		
	Medium-term:	–		(*due*) 200	(*due*) 400	
	Short-term:	–			574	

**1 Estimate for 17 weeks extrapolated from 13 weeks evidence. See Table 7.5.*

**2 For 11 out of 22.4 acres, costs estimated for the second weeding through harvesting.*

**3* 100N in short term credit to trading friend (unrepaid at year's end) and 96N in eight falle loans to the same man, of which three repaid in grain and stored at year's end.

**4* Eight falle loans to five men, of which two repaid in grain and stored as of March 1979.

**5* Medium-term loans to two trading friends, to be repaid before the end of the 1979 post-harvest dry season.

**6* Head-tax (haraji) for five men in his household.

Note: Biki gifts and return gifts at marriage ceremonies are not included, as unknown.

savings to marriages and fixed investments, M. tended to operate with very small cash reserves (Row 24). Furthermore, if we combine his house building (N581) with his own personal marriage expenses (N400), we can gauge the extent of 'nonessential spending' – only 17 per cent of annual expenditure. This leads to an obvious but crucial point in understanding his strategy for borrowing: his life was austere. Like his patron, Alhaji Z., M.'s spending and, by implication, his borrowing was intensely oriented toward production, investment and household responsibilities.

Thus, we can extend the perspective with which we concluded our discussion of his working capital. M.'s ability to borrow stemmed not only from his creditors' assessment of his honesty, skill and social responsibility, but also from their knowledge that loans were not frittered away on a motorcycle here, a radio there or new clothing. Borrowers' austerity helps explain why the extraordinary circulation of credit-without-interest continued to function.

Table 7.14 measures the change over one year in the estimated commercial value of his wealth. In 1978, M.'s net worth rose by 9 per cent.[10] He achieved this by running down his cash reserve, shifting his investment funds from trade to agriculture and doubling his debt burden from 13 per cent to 25 per cent of his gross asset value.

But we should recognize the difficulties in the path of further wealth acquisition. In 1979, there was little opportunity to benefit from grain storage, because the interseasonal price rise was small. Furthermore, M.'s funds were subjected to a particular squeeze: from the farming season of 1978 to that of 1979, labour rates for a long morning of weeding rose by a third while the price of guineacorn fell by a third. And after all his efforts to secure the marriage of his younger brother, the bride ran back to her paternal home. The failed marriage had drained his money – and committed him to further expenses when Gambo searched for a new bride. The path to long-term wealth acquisition was strewn with risks.

M.'s Self-Assessment

M. was too preoccupied to be other than terse in satisfying my demands for exact information. Still, my constant questions did not erode his humour. He used to tease 'this European! Questions, always questions!' I was grateful whenever he invited me to join him in *kewaya* – the habit of doing a circuit of land under cultivation. On those occasions, he volunteered information less grudgingly. They were also occasions for 'overhearing'. Together, we would come across old

Table 7.14. Change in net worth, 'M' (HH 7) (N), Marmara, 1978

	1 January 1978	31 December 1978
A. Fixed assets		
House with land:	300	300
Additions to house:	–	581
Storeroom with compound	200	200
Additional storeroom:	–	100
Farmland:	218	218
(6.2 acres – 4.7 owned at 40, 1.5 by pledge for 30)	–	
Additonal farmland:		406
(16.2 acres – 1.5 purchased for 62, 14.7 by pledge for 344)	–	
Town plot:		400
	718	**2,205**
B. *Liquid assets		
Own crops:	212	1,279
Grain purchase in store:	239	101
Loans recoverable:	370	132
Investment funds:	1,600	41
A. Cash:	1,154	*nil.*
B. Traded stocks:	446	41
Current assets	**2,421**	**1,553**
C. Medium-term loans recoverable	–	200
D. Gross asset value (A+B+C)	3,139	3,958
E. Debt	400	974
	(long-term from patron)	*(400 med.-term. 574 short-term)*
F. Net worth (D – E)	**2,739**	**2,984**
Change in net-worth:		9%
1. Current (liquid) assets:	2,421	1,553
2. Short-term debt:	–	574
3. Net curent assets:	2,421	979
4. Current assets / Short-term debt		2.71

* See Table 7.11 for details.

Notes: 1. Excluded are additions to livestock, as size of herd was unknown on 1 January. 2. The value of M.'s original house and storeroom are estimated. So, too, is the farmland which he owned at the beginning of the year. These estimates take into account my limited evidence for the range of land prices (chapter 3, endnote 7); and the fact that M. had owned his original farmland for some time, improving it annually with manure. No allowance is made for inflation in the value of buildings and land held at the beginning of the year, because my evidence does not suggest that their value would necessarily have risen over the year. Fixed assets acquired during the year are valued at their cost of acquisition (farmland) or development (buildings) women weeding their small plots. M. would kneel in deference and then launch into a monologue designed to justify his treatment of his wives. The women would follow his harangues with sympathetic noises – designed to elicit further nuggets of information. And from time to time, M. seemed to want a listener like myself, from outside his personal circle, with whom he could survey his efforts. Then, he would review his career in a way that lit up successes, failures and motives.

Let the last words be with himself. His reflections revealed his strategic purposes. They gave shape to his basic notions of the desirable and the dutiful – in short, his sense of 'value'. While touring his fields in the farming season of 1978, he insisted: 'He who has money will add to it. For example, to farm it is necessary to spend. If I did not trade in guineacorn at N800 a week, I could not obtain the money I need to farm.'

Later, in August, he was angered at the failure of borrowers to repay his falle loans with grain or money interest, and worried about the future. Having cultivated a large amount of farmland, his investment funds were finished, and he was deeply dependent on borrowed funds. Then, he offered a neat summary of the previous two years:

> Two years ago, I had jali of N2,000. I spent N400 on the first marriage of my son, which failed. This year I spent N600 on his second marriage. I spent N200 marrying a woman in the dry season, who left me. I spent N400 on a plot in Malumfashi town, and N400 obtaining farms by purchase and by pledge. By the second month of this rainy season, the N2,000 was finished.

In saying this, he accepted without question the priority given to marriages in the use of his investment funds, and his ensuing dependence on credit.

We know now that he found the money for continued trading and paid off the patron's loan. This left him with ample funds for trade. But by the end of the Guineacorn Harvest, he once again faced a cash shortage: 'No money! I have given my jali to the other traders. House building and the marriage of my younger brother – these have taken my money.'

Note once again the prior claim of family responsibilities and trading friendships on his investible cash reserves. In early 1979, he expanded on his recent loans to trading friends, and said that in return, they stored produce for him. Then he laughed and added, 'Just as I give them rance, so they give rance to others.' He offered a revealing summary of his recent past: 'For four years, I have not postponed a marriage in my house – for myself, my son, and my brother Gambo. If not for this, I would have gone East [to Mecca].'

Note that he did not say, 'I would have had more money to buy farms or hire labourers.' In chapter 1, I described the competition among richer villagers of Marmara to go on pilgrimage to Mecca. In this case study, we have seen how expenditure on farmland and additional hired labour did not deflect M. from the consolidation and expansion of his household. Household (gida) and social responsibility (hidima), informed and guided by Islam (*musulunci*), furnished him with the ultimate definition of the desirable and the obligatory in his search for wealth.

Conclusion: The Analytic Uses of Biography

A General Analysis of Commercial Borrowing

In all three case studies, borrowing and lending were essential to the process of long-term wealth acquisition. We can invoke the notions of 'long', 'medium' and 'short' term to explain the different kinds of commercial credit.

Jali denoted a person's investment funds. However, it could equally refer to a trading loan without interest given in return for services rendered. Thus, the cost of the loan was not money interest, but labour time spent trading on the creditor's behalf. Jali was given at harvest and, notionally, was to be repaid before the start of the farming season. But since the underlying purpose of their relationship was mutual income growth, the creditor was not surprised when the borrower eventually ploughed the trading loan into farming, and only repaid it at the following harvest. Hence, I categorize jali as a long-term loan.

Rance is, strictly speaking, a loan without interest for a very short period of time – generally supposed to be a week or less. But where there was a long-standing trading friendship, the period of the loan could be extended to several months. Hence, I categorize rance as including both short-term loans – repayable after a week or less – and medium-term loans – repayable after several months.

Underlying the different terms were four loan cycles marked by different periodicities. First, there was the period established by trading in weekly or biweekly marketplaces. This defined the time for repaying 'short-term' loans. Secondly, there was the period set by two peaks in the agricultural year – harvest time (September–December), and the time when harvest produce stored against a price rise was sold (usually June or July). These peaks normally set the time limit on 'medium-term' loans to six months or less. Thirdly, there was the period from one harvest to the next – the time limit on 'long-term' loans. There was also a fourth loan cycle – the traditional period of off-farm activity in the postharvest dry season. Here, loans given at harvest were supposed to be repaid before the start of the farming season, lest they be sunk into farming. But as the case of M. showed, the medium-term loan cycle could easily become a long-term cycle.

These three main terms of credit can be related to a borrower's prior process of saving over time, his investment in trade and agriculture and the resultant growth in his income. Long-term credit enabled a borrower to divert an equivalent amount of his own funds from trade to the acquisition of farmland, because it did not have to be repaid until the following harvest. Medium-term credit at the start of the farming season could be used to meet the costs of farming if the borrower had stored produce since harvest, allowing him to postpone its sale until prices at his market outlet had risen to around their peak levels. The net contribution of medium-term credit to farming expenditure was thus the difference between trade earnings early in the farming season – when he would have had to sell stored produce if he had not had the credit – and trade earnings when prices reached peak levels in the middle of the season. Short-term credit enabled the borrower to expand his weekly turnover trading beyond the level possible with his own funds. This increased his weekly trading profits and as a result, the money available for spending on weekly farming.

The most interesting fact about commercial credit is that enormous sums were circulating in the rural areas without interest being charged. Islamic distinctions between lawful profit and unlawful interest, and injunctions against interest, were part of the reason for this.[11] However, the basic reason for the absence of a rate of interest on commercial loans is that borrowers were subject to such fluctuating claims on their own income – from kin, from other trading friends or from their own clients – that they could not guarantee lenders the reinvestment of borrowed funds over a specific period in such a way as to generate a reasonably predictable rate of return. In this respect, Table 7.5 – showing sharp weekly changes in one man's trade expenditure – contains the most revealing evidence of the chapter. Since borrowers and lenders were subject to the same set of diverse social pressures, it made little sense to charge interest on loans. Their attention was rather focussed on a concept of mutuality. Through clientage or trading friendship, they aimed by lending to generate a return flow of services or money credit in the longer term. They were aware that commercial loans helped them to surmount the fluctuating pressure of social claims.

The case studies reveal the existence of a flourishing capital market in rural southern Katsina. I use 'capital' in the restricted sense of funds for investment in activity which generates income. This market was guided by two principles. Firstly, borrowing proceeds through personal relationships governed by an ethic of reciprocal obligation, and secondly, these obligations make possible long-term wealth acquisition, but limit the rate at which investment funds can be continuously reinvested.

The Social Relations of Long-Distance Produce Trading

Against the familiar idea that personal relationships hobble the scale of transactions, the case studies show how different kinds of personal relationship enabled rural traders to break through the limits in their own funds. Five kinds of relationship controlled the flow of money, labour and supplies:

Under the *master-servant* relationship, a trader gave his all-purpose labour time in commerce, agriculture and, more generally, mediation between his master and the various people in whom the master had an interest. In return, he received long-term loans.

Through *clientage,* a trader engaged in weekly trading or bought produce and stored it against a price rise, on the instructions of his patron. In return, he received long-, medium- and short-term loans.

Groups of *closely related kinsmen* provided wealthy traders with supervisory labour, market information and skills in long-distance trading. In return, they received long- and medium-term loans and a wide variety of assistance for food provisioning and ceremonial expenditure.

Asymmetrical trading friendships linked big rural traders to government officials and city merchants as their superior trading friends. Officials and merchants gave these traders advances to buy produce at quoted prices, and then store it. In return, the traders received commissions, plus the use of the produce advances until such time as purchase prices had reached the quoted levels. Asymmetrical trading friendships also linked purely rural traders of different income. Typically, they traded in different lines, and the borrower received short- and medium-term loans.

Symmetrical or lateral trading friendships linked traders of similar income or power, operating in the same or different lines. They exchanged short- and medium-term loans and storage. Longstanding personal relationships between a rural wholesaler and the retailers at his outlet markets were a form of lateral trading friendship. Each gave the other preference in competitive marketing.

Flexibility pervaded these relationships. Patrons sought to expand their circles of clients. Clients could always seek out alternative patrons. Relations between suppliers and their buyers were never exclusive. The scope for ignoring the claims of clients or suppliers was therefore restricted. There was room for manoeuvre over credit volumes and repayment periods.

There was a broad distinction between master-servant, patron-client and kinship relations on the one hand, and the various kinds of trading friendship on the other. The former involved wide ties of mutual obligation; the latter were more strictly commercial, involving money or market transactions. In the former, the superior was buying the all-purpose labour time of the inferior with many kinds of help. In the latter, the lender was giving credit with the aim of cultivating an alliance marked by reciprocal borrowing; or he was lending to those poorer than himself because of an ethic of diffuse generosity which was reciprocal in the long run. Men who had begun their trading careers as net borrowers felt obliged to loan out ever larger sums of money as they became more successful.

The case studies suggest that the global amount circulating short term was much greater than the amount of medium- or long-term credit. Moreover, medium- and long-term credit was disbursed among a variety of social and economic objectives. Thus, the various forms of trading friendship were much more important than master-servant or patron-client relations in financing the rural grain marketing system.

We can now distinguish clearly between trading across space and across time. Trading across space, between economic regions, within a short period of time, was highly competitive. As a result, profit margins tended to be low (Table 7.4). Given low overhead costs, the producer's share of the retail price in final outlet markets tended to be high (Table 6.6).

Trading across time – storage against a price rise – was highly profitable (Table 7.4). Yet in the case studies, the percentage of annual volume stored against a price rise by the traders *for themselves* was less than 20 per cent. Traders' ability to participate was restricted by their investment funds. Moreover, uncertainty over the interseasonal price rise limited the willingness to engage in storage. But the crucial reason for its limited extent is suggested by our analysis: the global amount of medium- or long-term credit available for trading across time was much less than the amount of short-term credit for trading across space.

A Comparison of Three Farmer-Traders

The purpose of grain trading was the acquisition of wealth in two interconnected senses – the specific accumulation of farmland and the labour power to work it, and the broad-based acquisition of 'wealth' (dukiya). This latter included material assets of varying degrees of liquidity (from money to productive equipment) and human assets incorporated in social relationships of varying degrees of density (from household kinsmen to trading friends). The three case studies went far beyond grain trading to examine the range of traders' investments. We saw that grain trading was one of many investments in interlinked product markets; and in a spectrum of activities from farming through transport to urban property.

The three farmer-traders occupied different positions in the system of long-distance grain marketing. Because of the differences in their characteristic trading activities, they offered distinctive opportunities which drew other men into relations with them. The *marketplace trader* (R.) offered chances for profit making to the ruler of the town on which the marketplace abutted. The *intervillage wholesaler* (Alhaji Z.) no longer personally engaged in long-distance trading, but through his wide circle of kinsmen and clients, he offered advantages to urban merchants and government contractors. The *hamlet wholesaler* (M.), through his direct access to farmers, was one of the foundations on which rested the marketing system. It is all the more interesting, then, that the three men revealed common patterns. Standing back from the evidence, four themes repeat themselves.

All three were 'entrepreneurs': they accepted risk in the pursuit of profit. 'Profit' (riba) was seen as the balance of money revenues over money costs in a multiplicity of endeavours. In their everyday business they took three very real kinds of risk – in commodity markets, in cultivation and in personal relationships (since loans might not be repaid).

Their achievements were impressive in forward planning, expertise and general management. Their thinking showed great scope. They were making plans in terms of prices and product markets across the whole expanse of central and western Hausaland. They were balancing between rural and urban environments, contractors and market traders, political elite and common people.

All three exemplify the sheer prestige attached to building a large household. They saw their households as the centre of an expanding circle of personal relationships through which a wide range of future economic activities could be conducted.

The prior claim of personal relationships on their resources limited the speed of expansion of their landholdings and their capacity to hire farm labour. Therefore, these claims reinforced their need to borrow money for investment purposes. As a result, these claims actually re-produced the system of borrowing through personal relationships. Under these circumstances, it is not surprising that farmer-traders 'acquired wealth together'. There was an ethic of mutual help.

Investment in Trade versus Investment in Agriculture

Exploring a particular question highlights the process of wealth acquisition: why was investment oriented toward farming instead of trade? Why the emphasis on increasing the scale of agriculture rather than of trade? The case studies of R. and Z. show more successful farmer-traders than M. expanding the scale of both. The case study of M. shows that farming and trading were part of a broader strategy of multiple investments. The revised question becomes: why invest all or part of one's own funds in agriculture while relying on credit for trade?

Let us begin by comparing the returns to grain trading and agriculture, using M. as our example. During 1978, M.'s grain trading occurred in a regime characterized by a 35 per cent interseasonal rise in the retail price of guineacorn in his final outlet market (Table 6.6). He made most of his investment and realized most of his profits during the first six months. In farming, most investment was concentrated in the first six months, but most profit was not realized until May–June of the following year, when he sold the bulk of his output. Thus, the period of effective investment was longer for farming than for trade. Moreover, during the period of agricultural investment – from (say) February 1978 to May 1979 – local output prices actually fell.

During 1978, M. invested N1,255 in grain trading. The return to capital employed was 133 per cent. He invested N1,797 in farming – not including the cost of family labour. This generated a profit margin of N810. The return to capital employed was thus 45 per cent. However, the recurrent costs alone of maintaining family labourers and their dependents totalled over N850. This transforms profit into a loss. The real return to agricultural investment was (-)1 per cent (Table 7.15).

Table 7.15. M's returns to investment in trade and farming (N), Marmara, 1978

Trade:			
	460	Stocks stored for a price rise.	(*Table 7.4*)
	495	Average circulating capital.	(*Table 7.13*)
	300	Value of storerooms	(*Table 7.14*)
Capital employed	1,255		
Margin on sales	1,664		(*Table 7.4*)
Return:	**133%**		
Farming:			
	218	Initial farmland.	
	406	Additional farmland.	(*Table 7.14*)
	1,172	Operating costs.	(*Table 7.13*)
	851	Food and tax of family labourers.	(*Table 7.8*)
Capital employed	2,647		
Margin on sales	**(–) 41**	Sales margin in Table 7.8 (–) family food and tax.	
Return:	**(–) 1%**		

Given M.'s knowledge of risks and of the superior returns to trading, why did he shift his own funds from trading to farming? M. was very conscious of the recurrent costs and the long-term marriage expenses of his family workers. In raising his landholding from 6 to 22 acres, I think it reasonable to conclude that he was attempting to increase the marginal return of family labour – *because he would have had to bear its costs in any case*. To the extent that family workers are used primarily in farming, there will be a general tendency to shift funds from trade to farming. This is not a circular argument. As we have seen, extending the number of adult male dependents was a basic social value.

Comparing the hamlet wholesaler with the intervillage wholesaler, Alhaji Z., as landholding grew, the ratio of family to hired labour diminished. Thus, the amount of labour cost borne for the entire year declined as a proportion of the amount borne for specific tasks. Therefore, the return to investment in farming, after deducting the cost of family labour, increased. At the same time, as the scale of trade increased, family labour became more involved in the trading sector of the enterprise. Therefore, part of its cost must logically be deducted from the return to investment in trade. Despite a tendency to convergence between the returns to farming and to trading, as family labour was reallocated between the two sectors, the return to trading probably remained higher. Commerce was less labour intensive than agriculture.

Thus, the predilection for farming must be seen in terms of a *social* process of wealth acquisition. Reasons of security induced farm investment. Money invested in farmland was considered safe (*Asusu ke nan:* 'It's a money box.'). It was less liable than money in trading stocks to social claims. This reminds us of that other pattern: all three farmer-traders were outsiders, not indigenes. Wealth acquisition entailed strategies for the partial avoidance of others' claims on one's wealth.

Yet inevitably, increased material wealth brought in its train the rising pressure of an enlarged family and more clients, friends and kin. These were both the instrument for wealth acquisition and the constraint upon it. Borrowing was essential to overcoming the constraints.

Farmed land was the fundamental security on commercial loans. Basically, then, traders invested their savings in agriculture because by farming more land they raised their future borrowing capacity!

Economic Process and Social Value

I end with a more abstract statement of the process of long-term wealth acquisition. The fundamental problem facing farmer-traders was that labour power in agriculture and commerce was limited in relation to the demand for it. In consequence, subordinate workers attracted favourable terms. As a result, real profit margins, and therefore returns to investment, were reduced.

'Labour power' covers the wide spectrum from family to occasional hired labour. Chapter 4 analysed the underlying processes whereby the real rates for hired farm labour were rising over the period 1977–85. In consequence, rural employers placed high value on the enlargement of their family workforces through marriage and procreation. Moreover, they sought out client labourers to whom they were attached by wider obligations than the payment of labour rates. This chapter has shown how in 1979, traders attempted to reduce total labour costs by contracting acreage under cultivation, and unit labour costs by substituting high-yielding maize for guineacorn.

Concerning trade, it might be thought that the real problem facing potential investors was access to supplies. However, supplies could only be obtained through the skill of traders prepared to spend their time negotiating with farmers or handling produce. Even the hamlet wholesaler was reaching a level of turnover which required the storage facilities of other traders, and would soon have required their services in expanding the volume of his supplies from the hinterland. And at each level of the marketing system, competition for supplies raised the demand for trading skills.

To overcome these constrictions, farmer-traders were compelled to seek out investment funds. We may analyse the activities of borrowing, investment and saving as a staged process over time. The first stage can last for many years. The farmer-trader develops expertise, and a reputation for honesty in borrowing and generosity in lending. Gradually, he develops a circle of patrons and a group of trading friends upon whom he can rely for credit to expand the volume of his trading and, hence, the profits available for increased investment in commerce and agriculture. He increases his harvest output and stocks in trade. In so doing, he augments his own investment funds. He keeps them in four forms, on a scale of decreasing liquidity according to the conventions of Hausa rural society:

1. cash;
2. stocks in trade;
3. harvest grain – once this is stored, either as bundles in a traditional granary (*rumbu*) or as sacks in a storeroom (*shagu*), it is less subject to continuous social claims than money or trading stocks;
4. cattle – since purchased cattle are handed over to the pastoralists for herding, they are even less subject than harvest grain to the competing attentions of kin, clients and friends.

Nevertheless, his own investment funds expand slowly because he cannot ignore his social obligations, and labour is costly. It is all the more necessary that he supplement his own funds with those of others. Also, it is crucial that he develop a credit pattern whereby he borrows more than he loans out.

If he surmounts the possible hazards, he eventually reaches the second stage – a core group of trading friends whose wealth is sufficient to finance his weekly turnover trading. This releases his own investment funds for accelerated agricultural expansion. Part of his funds he invests in farmland. Part he invests in grain stocks for storage against a price rise, when they are sold to meet costs of agricultural production. Superimposed on this basic process – this shifting of his own funds from trading to farming – there are further interconnections between commerce and agriculture. The short-term credits which he receives for trading generate trading profits which he uses to buy inputs and pay farm labourers. The medium-term credits which he receives for farming he repays when he sells stored grain. By shifting his own funds from trade to agriculture, he builds up his farmland – the basis for prospective lenders' assessments of his credit worthiness. At the end of the year, the greatly increased harvest output resulting from this strategy can be invested.

Thus, reaching the second stage is the achievement of 'breakthrough' from the severe constraints on the growth of investment funds caused by social claims and costly hired labour. It is the most fascinating stage to study: hence the extraordinary detail in which I explored the case of the hamlet wholesaler. 'Breakthrough' cannot be ripped from its social context. Nor can it be conceived in the strictly material terms of money costs and benefits and rates of return. The shifting of the farmer-trader's own funds from trade to agriculture represents a conversion of 'soft wealth' into 'hard wealth'. During the first stage, the farmer-trader's own funds are so restricted, and his borrowing capacity so limited, that he must keep most of his own funds as cash and stocks-in-trade. During the period of 'breakthrough', his investment funds and, indeed, his total assets are shifted down the portfolio of liquidity (Tables 7.11 and 7.14). They enter a different moral sphere – less subject to erosion from social obligations.

The career of M., the hamlet wholesaler, is not the only path to 'breakthrough'. Different niches in rural society present different opportunities. M. was an immigrant Fulani in southern Katsina who maintained close ties with pastoral kinsmen and his area of origin, whither he continued to trade. His background led him into a combination of livestock and grain trading. His knowledge of marketplaces in northern Kano attracted the patronage of wealthy traders. His career was typical in that he started as a small-scale trader seeking patrons, atypical in that the growth of his enterprise was helped by his knowledge of cattle markets. The path to 'breakthrough' followed by R., the marketplace trader, was more unusual, since he began as the servant of a powerful ruler. There are very few of these notables in relation to the number of men seeking patronage in rural society. But in both cases, the cultivation of a range of kinds of personal relationship enabled them to borrow for trading, while transferring their own gradually accumulated funds to farming. Since R. was actually younger than M., we may perhaps infer that success in attracting the patronage of a single exceptional individual speeds up the transition to 'breakthrough'.

Although 'breakthrough' implies that wealth is held in forms that are more socially secure, risk remains real. There is always a tense balance between increasing resources and increasing family size. Risks also grow with the scale of enterprise. A combination of misfortunes – for example, the default of major borrowers, poor harvests or a collapse of market prices – may force a farmer-trader to sell off land in order to satisfy his creditors. Some forms of enterprise – for example, transport – are both more lucrative and more risky than others, since a single accident can remove the source of income. As we saw in Marmara, large farmers (with more than ten acres) were more exposed to the risk of selling land than middle or small farmers (chapter 3).

Analytically, a third stage of investment growth is reached when the farmer-trader's volume of turnover and scale of landholding are such as to attract the attention of urban merchants and government contractors. Alhaji Z. had long ago reached this stage. Physically, the farmer-trader no longer engages in long-distance trade himself, but relies on his core team of close kinsmen and his circle of clients. Economically, he attains a new position in the agricultural marketing system, functioning as the interface between urban and rural society, channelling investment funds in one direction and supplies in the other.

All three farmer-traders in the case studies were immigrants to southern Katsina. Immigrants are less exposed than indigenes to the claims of agnatic and affinal kin, and therefore more able to gradually enlarge their funds to the point of 'breakthrough'. This is not to say that indigenes cannot increase their material wealth. Those indigenes who begin their adult careers with a relatively large inheritance are in a good position to do so (chapter 3). Nevertheless, indigenes who begin with little land will find it hard to break through the overlapping costs of social obligation and labour to achieve sustained capital growth.

In all three stages of investment growth, the success of long-term wealth acquisition is defined and constrained by the social context. We saw this most clearly in the case of Alhaji Z, the wealthiest of the three farmer-traders. First, farming and agricultural marketing are labour-intensive forms of enterprise. As the scale of enterprise grows, so, too, does the sum total of claims from the inner circle of kinsmen, friends and clients. This constricts the investor's capacity to expand the volume of hired farm labour and, hence, the size of his effective landholding. Secondly, the burden of domestic dependents continues to grow irrespective of fluctuations in the growth of the farming-trading enterprise. This general statement of economic problems and their solution suggests a doctrine of limited material accumulation.

Having stated the doctrine, I must stand it on its head. For it implies that the cultivation of personal ties is a technique for overcoming labour scarcity in the interest of material accumulation (Bourdieu 1990: 111). This would entail that 'social values' exist mainly as verbal generalizations concerning strategic interest, incorporated in observable behaviour. On the contrary, I argue that the social value which gives priority to personal relationships is a moral belief. It is an inner mental state. Farmer-traders reflect about their moral beliefs, although I can only infer their inner states from verbal discourse and public action. This social value has a degree of causal efficacy; it places limits on the range of actions which are realistically possible in society. Moral beliefs constrain and even deflect the achievement of purely material self-interests. Farmer-traders were very conscious of this. *Continuous* changes in circumstance may eventually force a change in values. But in calling a value 'embedded', I imply that people will only abandon it tardily. Hence, it is neither obscure nor tautological to say that farmer-traders accumulate personal relationships because that is what they value.

Notes

1. For a fourth case study occupying a different marketing niche, of a market retailer supplied by traders from Malumfashi Division, see Clough 1985.
2. Grain porters from Marmara counted an average of 65 sacks per market day, weekly from Kankara and twice weekly from Yargoje, over two weeks in March and April 1976. From January through October, at an average rate of 65 sacks per market day, he would have purchased 8,580 sacks of produce – at a higher rate in the early farming season, when larger farmers sold big amounts to finance their farming and at a lower rate during the late farming season and minor harvests, when trade was slack. These porters said that during the Guineacorn Harvest, Z. would purchase at a much higher rate – about 200 sacks per market day at Yargoje and 300 sacks per market day at Kankara. On their information, he might have purchased some 5,600 sacks over eight weeks in November–December. In addition, each of his 17 kinsmen and clients might have been storing, on average, some 50 sacks for Z. (see Case Study III of his client, M.). Perhaps, then, Alhaji Z. purchased about 15,000 sacks of various types of produce for himself and others in the agricultural year 1975–76.
3. In March 1976, Z. told me he had stored about 200 sacks for himself.
4. This was in an agricultural year when the price of guineacorn in Kankara rose sharply (Chart 6.3). In 1978–9, when the price of guineacorn rose very little after harvest, his client M estimated that Z. was storing much less.
5. When I interviewed Alhaji in December 1985, he said that the majority of his labourers came from Daura and Danbatta: 'They do not plant their own crops there

until the first weeding has been done in southern Katsina, and they harvest their own crops early, before the harvest in southern Katsina.'

6. The overhead cost of hemp sacks was actually greater in the trade to nearby Funtua than in the trade to distant Danbatta, because at Funtua he always parted with them in the wholesale transfer.
7. For the sequence of farm operations, see Chart 4.2.
8. For the manner in which M. gave me the information, see chapter 5. For 11.4 acres, I recorded his spending on all farming operations. For 11 acres, I recorded only part of his spending, from land clearing through the first weeding; I estimated his spending from the second weeding through harvest. Spending on all inputs was fully recorded. His younger brother informed me of his output for each field.
9. The account is incomplete, for it does not include gifts and return gifts at wedding ceremonies, or his spending at the Salla festival on his wives and other female dependents. But it is very close to capturing the magnitude of the money flows to and from M.
10. His achievement was helped by the subsidy on artificial fertilizer.
11. In Hausa, the spelling of (lawful) 'money profit' and (under Muslim legal codes, unlawful) 'interest' is the same. (For Hausa-English dictionaries, see Robinson 1925 and Abraham 1962.)

Chapter 8

Economic Change from 1985 to 1998

Introduction

By probing rural Hausa institutions governing the transfers of land, labour, credit, produce marketing and the formation of working capital in trade and farming, chapters 3 through 7 have sought to demonstrate the constraints under which farmer-traders engaged in the long-term acquisition of wealth, and the corresponding vitality of smaller farmers, during 1977–85. These patterns emerged from the analysis of fieldwork focussed mainly on 1977–79, when the price and output of Nigerian petroleum was rising dramatically. The oil boom led to a vast increase in state spending and in the private importation of capital goods. The upward valuation of the currency caused a shift from the production of export crops like cotton to food crops like maize and guineacorn (chapters 1 and 6). The increased circulation of commodities – and of money – enabled farmer-traders to engage in all of the forms of accumulation. At the same time, it created new opportunities for smaller farmers to buy land and engage in outward-bound seasonal labour – counterweights to any process of appropriation by rural accumulators.

My research in 1996 and 1997–98 occurred during a period of drastic change in the macroeconomic environment. From 1986 onwards, under pressure from the IMF, the military regime implemented a wide-ranging Structural Adjustment Programme (SAP). Major policies included the sharp devaluation of the naira; a big cut in federal and state expenditures on health, education and agriculture; and in 1987, the abolition of the commodity boards that had effectively controlled producer prices for many staple crops.

From 1981 to 1993, the prices for Nigerian petroleum exports sank to 43 per cent of their 1981 level. A sharp depreciation in the value of the naira began in 1984, and by 1993 it had dropped to 12 per cent of its 1984 value. Over the country as a whole, consumer prices were estimated to have risen by 560 per cent from 1984 to 1993 (Forrest 1995: 134, 214, 242). There ensued huge shortages in many imported goods, most conspicuously in motor vehicle spare parts. Roads were no longer maintained.

However, the devaluation of the naira and the privatization of the marketing of staples like cotton stimulated a steady increase in agricultural exports. Policy changes included a reduction in controls on foreign investment. The effect of all these changes was new investment in agro-allied industries, e.g., maize milling and sorghum malting. If, during the 1980s, great urban hardship resulted from cuts in social spending, there was, at the same time, a shift in real income from the urban to the rural sector. Between 1991 and 1994, when industrial output fell by a quarter, agricultural output was estimated to have risen by 3.8 per cent per year, responding to the liberalization of trade and markets (Forrest 1995: 217, 242).

Thus, the crucial questions for this chapter are whether or not changes in the wider economy led richer farmers to concentrate on capital, as opposed to household and cliental, accumulation; and smaller farmers to depend more heavily on hired labour. With fewer controls on foreign capital, new investment in agro-allied industries and major cuts in state spending, changes in political economy created conditions for a deepening of capital accumulation in the rural areas. Put differently, did the research of 1996–98 show that reduced liquidity had changed:

- the patterns of long-term wealth acquisition,
- the relations between farmer-traders and smaller farmers, and
- the degree of viability of smaller farmers?

Method

In September 1996 and December 1997–January 1998, I returned to Nigeria and to Marmara for the first time since 1985. The first visit lasted three weeks, and the second, two weeks. In the earlier fieldwork, I had drawn on a range of methods – universal surveys of land and labour use, samples of farm expenditure and output from different strata of farmers, and case studies of lenders and produce traders. These different kinds of information were related to local conversations and to the variety of interactions which I experienced through the course of fieldwork. In the return visits of 1996 and 1997–98, I could not hope to replicate a comprehensive range of methods. I therefore decided to focus on a small set of case studies which were drawn from the three strata of farmers – Large, Middle and Small. These cases were in no sense a random sample of the farmers in each strata – rather, they were all people well known to me in the 1970s; indeed, some of them were close. Case studies of personally selected individuals cannot hope to demonstrate patterns for the whole stratum to which they belong. They can, however, be suggestive – pointing to ways in which the integrated analysis of economic institutions during 1977–85 contained in the previous chapters was, or was not, consistent with the course of their lives in the mid- and late 1990s. Thus, case studies can help ascertain whether or not there had been basic changes in the nature of rural economy.

By looking at particular individuals in these strata in some detail, my aim was to see if previous patterns still held for them. Moreover, by examining individuals whom I had known in the 1970s, I could trace personal histories of change or continuity. It was necessary to look at all of the strata because I was specifically interested in three patterns – of long-term wealth acquisition, of the relations between richer and poorer households and of the extent to which Small Farmers were viable.

At the same time, the two visits gave ample opportunity to be struck by general changes in economy and society. Thus, I embed the case studies in an account of the major public changes which were observable, and it is with these that I begin. They give necessary perspective to the case studies, and allow us to set them in a wider framework of change and continuity.

Finally, three notes on field technique. I benefited from friendship built up during my earlier fieldwork. Men and women across the range of incomes were happy to see me and eager to discuss changes in their lives and in those of others since 1985. People were pleased that I had taken the trouble to come back – and to remember them as individuals. Compared with my long stay of 1977–79, when I was trying to overcome many kinds of mistrust, the flow of answers to my questions was surprisingly open.

Secondly, we have seen (e.g., in chapter 5) that answers to questions put by a fieldworker cannot be taken at face value. Moreover, answers are more likely to be broadly accurate in some contexts than in others. As a result of my previous experience of Marmara, I tried as much as possible to follow up questions about occupation and income in the privacy of a person's room or when joining a man on a tour of his fields, where questions of present and future economic prospects preoccupied him. Lastly, the visits of 1996 and 1997–98 also allowed me to observe change and continuity in the patterns of public expression and interaction.

I identify all household heads in this chapter by reference to their index-numbered land rank in 1979 – or that of their retired or deceased fathers. The relative rank of some of these men must have changed since 1979. Moreover, the increase in the total number of Marmara household heads must have added new land users. Nevertheless, I will continue to use the land rank of villagers in 1979 in order to remind the reader of their relative land rank – from HH 1, the largest, to HH 108, the smallest – at that time.

Changes in Local Economy

New Dimensions of Community Life

The most immediately obvious change observable in approaching Marmara in 1996, for the first time in eleven years, was the deterioration in the highway linking Marmara with Malumfashi and with Katsina. Nevertheless, a multitude of old vehicles plied the road, kept in repair by local mechanics.

Marmara had grown greatly in size, from 120 households in 1979 to over 300 in 1996. Many had come from the rural hinterland behind Marmara, where they had been used to living dispersedly. The term 'hamlet' was still true of the settlement, as it was politically within the boundaries of the village of Yaba, but now seemed inappropriate of a place which had grown larger than the seat of the village head. Marmara people themselves liked to speak of their 'town' (*gari*).

Purely Hausa or Fulani in 1979, Marmara now included several Igbo households – headed by mechanics, shop keepers and a baker who supplied Malumfashi and other towns by van. All compounds had electric light. The number of indigenous people with very small shops – supplying soap, sugar, salt, radio batteries or, in other cases, cloth – had increased greatly. (There had only been two small shops in 1979.) A certain rise in the tempo of public life was the result. At night, youths gathered in front of several of the shops, and boys danced to the music from the radios inside.

The earthen mosque on the highway had been torn down and replaced by a much larger mosque constructed in cement. Another cement mosque had been built inside the village. A small dispensary was staffed by local government health workers, including an auxiliary from Marmara.

Marmara was now a centre of transport for villages up and down the Katsina road, because a young local entrepreneur had built up a small fleet of second-hand buses. Local men – only boys when I left the hamlet in 1979 – were the drivers. The ownership of oxen and ploughs, for hiring out as much as for own cultivation, was much more widespread than in 1979. Many more houses had corrugated iron roofs. A few of the younger household heads were proud of their electric fans and sofas, unheard of in 1979.

Nevertheless, the consumption of manufactured goods for individual use was still centred on the transfer of gifts in marriage. Returning to the village during the postharvest dry season of 1998, I found that social life still reverberated to the cries of the praise singers calling men to early-morning wedding ceremonies and whole families to evening gatherings for marriage gift exchange (*biki*).

As in 1979, economic life was pervaded by a plethora of off-farm occupations (chapter 1). A few new ones had been added: petrol selling, radio repair, and motorcycle repair. The material standard of living, from agricultural or off-farm income, was much as I had seen it in 1979: there was no evidence of a general decline. Women were well dressed. Children appeared well fed.

Thus, despite signs of decrepitude resulting from national economic crises – the mangled road, the empty Farm Service Centre of the once-thriving agricultural development project – the village had taken on new dimensions of community life.

Widening the Context of Wealth Acquisition

Between 1979 and 1996, several rich villagers had greatly expanded the size of their landholdings. If, in 1979, a stratum of Large Farmers could be delineated, with 10–50 acres of land, by 1996 there had emerged a stratum of 'Very Large Farmers' with much more than 50 and in some cases more than 100 acres. In the case studies below, I specify my knowledge of the conditions under which this expansion of landholdings had occurred. Here, I consider the changing context of wealth acquisition.

From 1983 through 1985, the banning by a military regime of the international trade in grains with the Niger Republic had led to a sharp fall in the amount of grain traded with Niger. But since then, the grain trade with Niger had resumed and once again become very large. In Marmara, HH 13 (a small-scale trader in 1979 – Table 6.5) specialized in the trade to the weekly marketplace of Jibiya on the border with Niger, sometimes carrying 200 sacks of guineacorn. This was far more than any trader had carried on a weekly basis in 1979 (Table 6.5).

There had been dramatic changes in the market destinations of grains purchased by the farmer-traders of Marmara. Danbatta in northern Kano State, and Sokoto, had declined sharply as markets compared with 1979. Jibiya, near the border with Niger, was now the major destination. With the deterioration in the road from Marmara to Kankara and Katsina, Kankara weekly marketplace was no longer a bulking centre for the smaller farmers of Marmara. In its place, the crossroads four miles away, linking Marmara with Malumfashi and Funtua, had blossomed from nearly nothing in 1979 to become the major local marketplace for grains, visited by lorries and traders from a wide area of central Hausaland. Another new development was that Very Large Farmers sold much grain to the breweries of southern Nigeria. Tighter linkages in a national economy had thus resulted from the development of agro-allied industries.

The privatization of cotton marketing had opened up new opportunities for cotton traders in the village. In the 1970s, they had been local buyers (*yan baranda*) for the licensed buying agents in Malumfashi town. But by 1996, they operated with large advances provided by a variety of merchants in the northern cities. Two of them, cotton buyers in 1979, each now had ten yan baranda working for them in the hinterland behind the village. Two were new entrants to cotton marketing. One of these, the oldest son of the largest farmer in 1979 (now deceased), controlled thirty yan baranda. The largest cotton buyer was the young entrepreneur with a small fleet of buses, who had forty yan baranda. Thus, the privatization of cotton marketing created a new opportunity for wealth acquisition, in which cotton buyers had much greater freedom to negotiate terms with urban merchants than they had formerly as buyers subject to the Cotton Board.

The ownership of commercial vehicles had undergone surprising transformations. In 1979, 4 men in Marmara had owned second-hand Ford passenger buses. With the exception of HH 20 (a dynamic young trader and farmer, now dead), these men were, or had been, among the largest landholders in the hamlet. In the early 1980s, during the petroleum boom, the number of vehicles owned in Marmara soared to

30, before dropping in 1985 to 14. Of the 11 owners in 1985, 3 were Middle Farmers and 2 were Small Farmers who had invested their savings as bus drivers in vehicles of their own. By 1996, the number of locally owned vehicles had expanded once again. Nine of the 11 owners were men who had been among the top 10 per cent of land users in 1979, or their inheritors. Thus, after a period during the petroleum boom when ownership of vehicles had widened considerably, it was once more concentrated among the largest farmers. Three cotton buyers owned between them 13 of the 32 vehicles. Clearly, rural cotton buying was lucrative in the privatized conditions of the mid-1990s, and led to the acquisition of commercial vehicles.

Labour Relations and Credit Relations

If the context in which some villagers acquired wealth had widened, what of their economic relations with poorer villagers and smaller farmers? As in 1979, there were two main types of labour agreement – piece rate (payment when the job agreed was finished) and payment for a long morning's work (now called *safiya*) until the early afternoon prayer. Observing labourers at the start of the maize harvest in September 1996, the majority were young men in their early twenties. This is consistent with the pattern I argued for the 1970s (chapter 4): the hired labour force consists mainly of young men because as men mature, they forsake hired labouring and develop various off-farm occupations. Nevertheless, there was agreement among all villagers questioned that the proportion of household heads who frequently laboured had increased considerably over 1979 – mainly for the long morning, leaving the afternoons free for work on their own farms.

Real rates of pay fluctuated with economic conditions over a wide area. From 1993 through 1996, piece rates bargained by groups of labourers with very large village farmers had increased by over 400 per cent (see the case study of HH 2 below). They declined in 1997 because drought in the far north of Nigeria and in Niger drove many farmers to migrate thence and seek seasonal work in southern Katsina.

As in 1979, there were two main forms of credit – money loaned without interest for very varying periods (*rance*); and money advanced in the 'hungry' month of August in return for money or harvest crops in December–January (*bashi*). As in 1979, bashi usually took the form of speculation by creditors on the price of future produce. The creditor would offer the potential debtor one half of the speculative harvest price per sack in return for a sack at harvest.

By 1996, however, a new form of bashi had become established. A number of creditors now followed what, to local mallams, was correct Muslim practice. They would offer potential debtors money equivalent to the August price per sack in return for the same sum at harvest. Since the harvest price was much lower than the August price, this enabled the creditor to buy much more than a sack with the money repaid. In purely money terms, however, there was no interest or profit built into this new form of bashi. Continued expansion of the market economy had been accompanied by a more self-conscious adherence to Islamic tenets in the supply of credit.

Changes in Local Society

Population Growth

Inquiries in 1996 and 1998 all pointed to the idea that family sizes were distinctly larger than in 1979. In 1979, Marmara had an estimated population density of approximately 470 persons per square mile, which, though high, still compared favourably with densities in most studies of the Sokoto or Kano Closely Settled Zones (Table 3.5). A rapid increase in family sizes since then would have dramatic implications for the future size of holdings of most villagers and for the pattern of land distribution.

I concentrate here on a comparison of family sizes between 1979 and 1996–98 of household heads in the age range thirty to thirty-nine. In this age range, it is easier to chart the number of children of any household head, since children have seldom matured to the point of 'marrying out' of the household. The number of children in the house can be taken as the total number, whereas in the houses of older household heads, the father may have raised and married off one set of children and now be rearing a second set by the same or other wives.

In 1979, 24 of 108 land-using household heads were estimated to be from 30 to 39 years of age (Appendix 1). While in this age group, the number of children per household head ranged from 6 to 0, it converged around a mean of 2.2 and a median of 3. In 1996 and 1998, I collected figures from 14 household heads aged 30 to 39. The mean number of children per household head was 7.8 and the median was 8 (Table 8.1). (These household heads are fewer than the total, and are likely to have more land than the average in that age range.)

A comparison of the two groups also suggests part of the reason for the increase in the number of children per household. In 1979,

Table 8.1. Household heads aged 30–39 in Marmara: Number of children

1979:	
Total number:	24
Number of wives:	Mean 1.4, Median 1
Number of children:	6–0, Mean 2.2, Median 3
1996–98:	
Sample size:	14
Number of wives:	Mean 2.6, Median 3
Number of children:	15–1, Mean 7.8, Median 8

two-thirds of the household heads aged 30 to 39 had one wife; the remainder had two. None had three wives. In 1996–98, all but one of the group of 14 had at least two wives, and 10 had three wives. The mean number of wives in this sample exceeds that of the highest decile of land users in 1979 (compare Table 8.1 with Table 3.19). In this respect, the five men in the 1996–98 sample whose fathers had been relatively poor are no exception: they all had three wives. There had clearly been a new development since 1979: young men were taking more women in marriage.

In my discussions with villagers, they explained that the proportion of men with two wives and many children had increased, and discussed the consequences. Touring his fields with me, HH 4 complained that 'people are now too many in Marmara. It is difficult to find a farm to buy. I can only find one to buy if I go far from the village.' Old HH 24, a reflective speaker on historical matters in my early fieldwork, volunteered that 'the area around Marmara as far east as Gora is full up [*cika*] with people, just like Kano has been for many years.' This led to a long discussion in which his crucial point was the importance of an off-farm occupation (*sana'a*) to provide for many children.

Indeed, the ways in which villagers talked provide, possibly, a context for understanding their reaction to rising population and scarce farmland. A son of the late HH 32, and the muezzin, HH 99, told me separately that in reaction to increasing land scarcity, some men had already left the village and moved south in search of farmland. Others responded more simply. The son of HH 52 (now independent) stated tersely that it was a matter of the will of God: '*Abun Allah ne*.' A son of HH 64 (also now farming on his own) admitted that the increasing size of his own and others' families created a severe problem for the future but stressed that children were the ultimate source of wealth: '*Allah Ya sa mu samu arziki wajen yara* (God grant us fortune through our children).' HH 45, who had raised nineteen children, said that men had already left Marmara and more would have to, especially if they had no education or skill and 'only knew how to farm.' The number of children was the dispensation of God. His detached comments were made as if this movement of events was part of a cycle both natural and divine.

These discussions suggest a cultural template through which villagers assess demographic change. There is the belief that children ensue from the activity of God. Moreover, people have an historical awareness of past change. Marmara was founded in the late nineteenth and early twentieth century by farmers escaping the high population densities in Kano Emirate (chapter 1); older villagers had shown me how the exodus of Fulani pastoralists in the 1950s, in response to increasing land scarcity, had enabled some villagers to expand their farmland (chapter 3). Furthermore, villagers evaluate the problems and prospects of population growth in terms of the value they place on polygynous marriage and on the number of children for which they shoulder 'responsibility' (*hidima*). It colours axiomatically their assessment of historical change. Lastly, they weave into their discussions of the problems of household provision, the importance of developing a special skill or off-farm occupation (*sana'a*). Population growth is not seen as an independent variable affecting action, but a reality resulting from the hierarchy of their own desires and beliefs, a change which they incorporate into their mental models of economy and society.

The tendency to translate material growth into more wives and children shows the continuing vitality of household accumulation as a dynamic element in the polygynous trajectory of accumulation. Marmara people continued to convert material values into the higher value of wives and children.

The Evolution of Islamic Discourse

As we saw in chapter 1, the roadside concentration of Marmara was established around 1960 out of dispersed rural compounds. It consisted of Maguzawa indigenes and Muslim immigrants. Shortly thereafter, most Maguzawa converted to Islam. They abstained from drinking guineacorn beer, a major focus of Maguzawa sociality. During my early research, only four of the household heads, and their wives, continued to brew and drink guineacorn beer. By 1998, in Marmara, there were no Maguzawa left. Many of the farmers who came to live in Marmara from the surrounding countryside had done so after conversion. Around Marmara there was the self-conscious sense that it is spiritually beneficial for a Muslim to live in a 'town' (gari) – a place where there are many mosques and mallams, evening assemblies of young and old studying the Qur'an and the pervasive sound of calls to prayer. In local thinking, town life – in however microcosmic a form – overlaps conceptually with Islamization.

Since 1985 the 'purist' or reformist Islamic movement, known in northern Nigeria as Yan Izala – with its emphasis on doctrinal understanding, Arabic literacy and strict ritual observance without Sufi accretions – had captured local support and become the dominant form of local Islam. Its discourse – the stress of its *tafsiri* (Islamic learned commentary) – emphasized the wider participation of all believers in the political order and the necessity of an informed public opinion.

The most learned local mallam in 1979, the only *mai tafsiri,* was still the intellectually dominant force in Marmara when I returned in 1996 and 1998. He was proud of his former association with the deceased founder and leader of the Yan Izala in Nigeria, Sheikh Abubakar Gumi. When I returned to Marmara in Ramadan of 1998, he was leading tafsiri in the main village mosque. It was noticeable that whereas in 1979, only a small group of villagers would gather to listen to his Ramadan commentary, in 1998, at least fifty villagers would devote two hours of their afternoons to this each day. Many were carrying the Quran – unusual in 1979 – and were trying to follow his reading. The mai tafsiri was surrounded by all of the mallams in the hamlet during these commentaries, and a local cadre of men dressed in a special uniform. Local Muslim practice had become more self-conscious than it was in 1979.

Concern to understand Islamic discourse in the original Arabic did not just reflect the local prestige of literate knowledge (this also applies to Western learning in Marmara). It was moreover seen as a key to power – supernatural as much as social power. The Yan Izala had always emphasized that understanding Muslim law – through the holy books of Islam – provides protection for the common people against the demands of the powerful and the rich. To appreciate this political dimension, I turn to the impact of Izala discourse in another sphere.

Yan Izala and Marriage Payments

Throughout northern Nigeria, one of the key criticisms levelled by the Izala against the 'traditionalist' Islam of the religious brotherhoods had been that indigenous custom encourages high marriage expenditures which take a toll on the resources of the poor (Gumi 1992: 162; Loimeier 1997: 286–307). In some Hausa areas, this criticism had been embraced by poorer farmers and young men anxious to limit socially necessary expenses (Loimeier 1997: 296). In other regions it had been condemned by rural people as a sign of the rupturing of kinship obligations (Masquelier 1996). In Marmara, however, the real burden of marriage expenditures appears to have remained constant. In 1979, *sadaki,* the gift required in Muslim law as part of the marriage transaction, was a tiny part of the total marriage expenditure undertaken by the bridegroom or his father. Other categories of expenditure had different names, and their money burden was easily enumerated (chapter 5). In 1998, I recorded marriage expenditures for four marriages among smaller farmers – one of whom was in the process of becoming a mallam of the Izala persuasion – and a marriage contracted by the richest trader in the village. The word *sadaki* had come to denote the substantial money payment made by the bridegroom or his father to the father of the bride. Essentially, a renaming of the various categories of marriage expense had occurred between 1979 and 1996.

In 1979, a Small Farmer would spend a total in the region of N500 on the marriage of himself or his son to a previously unmarried girl (*budurwa*). This was the money equivalent of 25 sacks of guineacorn in the local marketplace. A rich farmer's marriage expenses on a budurwa extended to N1,000 (Table 5.1). In 1998, ordinary marriage expenses of a bridegroom or his father would total between N30,000 and N50,000 in a much-changed currency. This was the money equivalent of 19–31 sacks of guineacorn. The richest trader in the village spent on the goods in *sadaki* alone N100,000. Real marriage expenses had not declined after villagers joined the Izala movement.

Villagers had negotiated their adherence to purist Islam in such a way as to avoid a radical change in their sense of kinship obligations (Clough 2009: 601–3). The local interpretation of Islam expressed what I have argued was their greatest desire, and highest value, in human relations – marital union. In this regard, it is crucial to bear in mind three features of the social economy (chapter 5). Rotating marriage gifts between *biki* (marriage gift) partners had always defrayed a significant portion of marriage expenses. Secondly, these partnerships linked richer and poorer villagers, men and women. Lastly, women had always been the key accumulators of small livestock, and had very often taken on the responsibility for providing their sons with the money to buy the bride's cloth and clothing (*lefe*), a key category of marriage expenditure. Thus, the preoccupation of Marmara villagers with reformed Islam was much less concerned with its impact on domestic economy than with its implications for political economy. Essentially, their concern was in a discourse of justice (*adalci*).

The Articulation of the 'Local' and the 'Regional' in Religious Discourse

Loimeier has provided an overview of the evolution of Izala campaigns against the religious brotherhoods, stressing their place in the Nigerian national articulation of Christian and Muslim 'ethnicities' (Loimeier 1997). However, the evidence from Marmara suggests that any 'global' movement is more complex than he describes, particularly when we observe the ways in which rural communities alter a global discourse in the process of preferring it. In Marmara, participation in wider discourses is part of a long tradition of political self-reflection and manoeuvre (chapter 1). A religious identity like 'Izala' is refracted along a spectrum of communities, from large to small. In a small place like Marmara, it is part of 'multiplex' relationships of kinship, friendship and clientage (Bailey 1969: 47–48). Changes in Islamic identity adopted by local communities reveal an effort to grapple with social problems and develop a moral economy wherein they have more power. This need not imply acceptance of the more sectarian tenets of the wider discourse.

Islamic identity in Marmara appears to have a collective political intent – the strengthening and wider extension of a 'community of obligation'. People are seeking to construct a terrain of force that can be brought to bear on the rulers. This gives some of the electricity to their attendance at tafsiri. They are aware that only by adopting the moral language of a wider community can they succeed.

The mesh between local and regional religious discourses allows us to understand a crucial element whereby villagers modelled their social universe over the periods of fieldwork. There was no sense in which rich village farmers occupied a privileged ideological space, or were linked to an urban class which did so. Rather, Large and Very Large Farmers were absorbed into a local, common, evolving moral economy. Put differently, there was no religious or political ideology of individualism by which they justified their actions. In this, they were unlike the pedlars of the Javanese *pasar*, who were swept up by the Islamic Reform movement of the early twentieth century and thus gained the elan to become businessmen (Geertz 1963: 28–81). The pondering of rural Hausa people on the nature of right, wrong and justice had not proceeded in a way to produce separate discourses of rural rich and rural poor.

Summary

Despite deterioration in the roads and in state provision, Marmara was in an agricultural area doing well. The demand for its grains from the Sahel continued to be strong. People had adjusted flexibly to devaluation of and change in the currency, to changing market destinations and to the resurgence of export crops like cotton. The area remained engaged in populist politics. The deepening of Islamic practice and knowledge which had grown with adherence to the Izala movement had a strongly populist dimension. Resulting from increases in the production of grains and cotton, material gains continued to be converted into the higher local value of wives and children.

Case Studies of Economic Change

The Large Farmers of 1979

The Sons of HH 1

In 1979, HH 1 had fifty acres of farmland, and was approximately sixty-five years old. By 1996 he had died. The inheritance was divided between fourteen sons and eleven daughters. According to his second son, the farmland had been divided equally, each child inheriting two acres.[1] The tractor and the bus had been sold, and the money divided on the principle that male inheritors together receive two-thirds of the money value of inherited assets apart from farms. The oldest son, in his forties, was a successful cotton agent operating with advances from urban merchants, and had some thirty buyers working for him in and around the hamlet. The second son concentrated solely on farming. About forty years old in 1998, he had expanded his inheritance of two acres to a holding of some ten acres, by purchasing farmland. With two wives and nine children, he said that he bought farms 'so that my children will have an inheritance'. In terms of food, clothing and the quality of their housing, the four oldest sons of HH 1 – all of whom he had sent on the Hajj – appeared to be well off, and were so regarded by other villagers. But none of them farmed on anything like the scale of their father.

HH 2

The most interesting case of economic expansion between 1979 and 1996 was HH 2 (hereafter, 'Alhaji Yakubu'). He had become the largest farmer in Marmara. This account of his economic growth derives largely from conversations with his oldest son, who was his chief manager. Approaching seventy years of age in 1996, Alhaji Yakubu was healthy and active. In 1979, he had 43 acres of farmland. He had three teams of oxen for ploughing his fields and those of other farmers. He owned a small passenger bus. He also bought cloth wholesale in Kano for retailing from his shop. By 1996, his landholding had expanded dramatically. His largest purchase was eight miles to the west of Marmara. It was in an area of open farmland, with fewer villages and hamlets than in the vicinity of Marmara. Accompanied by his oldest son, I measured this field in 1998 (hereinafter, the 'big farm'). It was approximately 123 acres. In addition, he had purchased three other fields nearby, which together almost equalled the big farm in size. Thus, he had added some 220 acres to the 43 acres of 1979, achieving a total of approximately 263 acres (106 ha.). This was an expansion of more than 600 per cent over seventeen years.

Alhaji Yakubu had purchased the big farm as one field from a merchant in Malumfashi town, a son-in-law of the district head, who had benefited from the district head's patronage. This merchant had begun by buying small adjoining fields and then, to consolidate a large farm, had offered local farmers on adjacent fields money to buy better, or larger, fields elsewhere. Thus, Alhaji had purchased an already-developed field.

Unlike in 1979, Alhaji Yakubu had contacts with six banks, some of which gave him small loans for farming. He sold most of his grain through a Hausa family enterprise in Lagos which specialized in the southern Nigerian grain market. He sold his cotton to various private ginneries. Because of his large output, he was sought after by companies in agro-allied industry. Unlike in 1979, he was now part of a commercial market which directly linked large producers in northern Nigeria with cotton dealers and (for grains) breweries in southern Nigeria. Furthermore, Alhaji had bought a tractor, a small truck for produce collection and local transport and a large trailer which carried to Lagos his own produce and that of other farmers. He also owned three small passenger buses. Alhaji had developed a multifaceted agricultural and transport enterprise. The underlying objective was the use of combined earnings to purchase additional farmland and deploy increasing amounts of hired labour.

An examination of revenues and costs on the big farm increases our understanding of the forms of accumulation in which Alhaji engaged. In December 1995–January 1996, this farm had yielded 120 tons of cotton. Total revenue from cotton sales was approximately 4 million naira. Of this, 2.2 million flowed into transport – to buy the trailer and repair other transport. In December 1996–January 1997, the big farm had yielded 125 tons of guineacorn. Eighteen tons were still in store a year later. This shows that output was adequate to meet the costs of production in the subsequent farming season *and* still leave a surplus. In using earnings from farming to buy new vehicles or repair existing ones, Alhaji was actually expanding his total income for reinvestment in agriculture.

Using costs estimated by his oldest son, a conservative estimate is that his profit margin on the big farm in December 1997–January 1998 was probably sufficient to cover its production costs in the subsequent farming season (Table 8.2). However, margins vary greatly from year to year. In 1997, labour rates averaged one-third of their

Table 8.2. Costs and revenues (N) on the big farm of HH 2, 1997

a)	Farm size: 123 acres (49.8 ha.)			
b)	Output: 80 tons of cotton (*down from 120 tons at harvest, 1995–96*)			
	Yield: 1.6 tons per hectare			
c)	Cash inputs: no fertilizer (unlike the preceding two years)			
	Seed cotton: 4 tons @ N16,000 per ton (September 1996) = N64,000			
d)	Labour Operations:			
	Planting		80,000	
	Ridging with oxen		40,000	
	First weeding[a]		250,000	
	Second weeding[a]		150,000	
	Third weeding[a]		130,000	
	Fourth weeding[a]		170,000[b]	
	Cotton picking		400,000[c]	
	Off-farm transport		95,000	
		Small truck: 1,000/day petrol, 50 days		
		Tractor: 900/day gas, 50 days		
		Basic costs[d]		1,379,000
		Revenue[e]		2,880,000–4,800,000
		Margin		1,501,000–3,421,000

a. Does not include the cost of lunch. See the text below.
b. Labour was harder to obtain than in the previous weeding.
c. N5 per kilo, 80 tons. Rates for picking began at N3 but rose to N10.
d. These do not include the costs of field preparation at the start of the farming season, or costs of bags, porterage and substitute transport when his own vehicles broke down, at the end of the season.
e. The low harvest price was 36,000/ton, the high postharvest price was 60,000/ton.

level in the previous year. But they had increased by over 400 per cent from 1993 through 1996. In addition, output prices are volatile. Cotton prices had dropped considerably from 1994 through 1996, and then increased in 1997. Also, the supply of fertilizer, and therefore yields, fluctuates greatly. As a result, Alhaji Yakubu's financial room for manoeuvre across his enterprise is more limited than basic costings might suggest. (For example, at the time of fieldwork in 1998, his trailer had been without wheels for a half year; and although a month had elapsed since harvest, he had still not stocked a newly built store with retail supplies.)

The acquisition of very large fields like the big farm had led to a change in the management of farm operations. Whereas in 1979 Alhaji had been solely responsible for management, by 1996 his three oldest sons constituted a management team essential to the operation of the large, distant farms. Alhaji had a certain commitment to the Western education of his sons. He had put nine of his thirteen male children through secondary schools of one form or another – though noticeably, none of his daughters. Western education increased the self-confidence of the sons in handling demands from town-based officials and in marketing their output in southern Nigeria.

Acquisition of very large fields had resulted in a constant demand for labour. As a result, the connections between Alhaji and other villagers – as employer to occasional employee – had increased. These changes can be seen in the complex of operations on the big farm in the farming season of 1996. His sons had to assemble hundreds of labourers from different places. In this, they were aided by two foremen (*wakilai*, sing. *wakili*) stationed in distant hamlets, who could contact labourers living near the fields. Labourers from Marmara would be transported in the truck; those from the hamlets would arrive on foot. The objective was to finish each operation as quickly as possible by assembling as many labourers as possible.

For the initial ridging of the big farm, over one hundred ploughsmen with oxen of their own were called. Each calculated his area of the farm and then bargained over his payment with the management team. For planting, men, women, youths and small children were called from many hamlets, the pay varying with age and strength. Nine supervisors from Marmara were paid four times the daily rate of adult labourers. They moved among them to ensure even spacing of the plants. With one exception, they were close kinsmen of Alhaji, with households and farms of their own (Table 8.3).

For weeding, prospective labourers would assemble in teams (sing. *kungiya*) under a chosen leader (*shugaba*). Bargaining with the man-

Table 8.3. The supervisors on the big farm of HH 2, 1996

1.	The son of a deceased junior brother of Alhaji
2.	The son of (1)
3.	The grandson of (1)
4.	The junior brother of the father of Alhaji
5.	The son of (4)
6.	A son of the junior brother of Alhaji
7.	The grandson of a senior brother of the father of Alhaji
8.	A kinsman of Alhaji living in the same quarter of Marmara
9.	A non-kinsman ('stranger')

agement team was intense. (In 1996, according to Alhaji's son, bargaining drove average agreements per team on the big farm significantly upwards; in 1997, there was much less bargaining pressure because of the influx of labourers from the north.) Apart from pay, the management team had to ensure that a lunch of millet and milk (*fura*) was provided to the respective teams.

Clearly, the organization of agriculture on the big farm dwarfed in scale anything occurring in 1979. A team of kinsmen from other households played a crucial role in ensuring the efficiency of planting and thus, the ultimate yield.

Total farm expenditure remained highly sensitive to the supply of labourers for weeding. There has been a change in the composition of the work force. According to Alhaji's oldest son, 'Some household heads now take labouring as a specialized occupation [sana'a].' However, the majority of labourers were employed on the big farm for a short time, and came from many places. Given their limited attachment to the enterprise of Alhaji, they tried to bargain up pay as much as possible.

Although he is responsible for all money payments, the oldest son of Alhaji does not calculate income from the farm in terms of profit (*riba*). Nor does he keep books with figures for expenditure or income. 'Since we take take [*dauka*] farming as a profession [sana'a], we know that a year of profit may be followed by a year of loss. If there is an increase in, for example, cotton or guineacorn over the previous planting, we will take it as "profit"; if there is a decline, we take it as a "loss".'

This physicalist approach to notions of 'gain' or 'loss' shows continuity with 1979 in management methods – involving kinsmen, lack of bookkeeping, and personal bargaining. Personal interactions remain essential to work in a form of production which remains largely premechanized. Thus, organization is based on an implicit idea of mutual dependence. Bargaining rests on collective, consensual comparisons by employer and employee of present with past rainfall, outputs, prices and labour rates. Moreover, a physicalist and personalist perspective on management objectives is accentuated by a labour regime in which there can be sharp fluctuations in labour rates over several years, ultimately the result of climatic variation. These render monetary and numerical predictions very difficult.

Under these circumstances, part of the product may be sold at harvest to buy new vehicles, without being sure that the money values for remaining output will be sufficient to cover costs of farm labour in the subsequent year. The mental process must be to visualize harvest earnings as 'transformed' into cumulative earnings from transport, which in turn feed back into the financing of farm operations. Numerical calculations are less important when management reasoning is based not on annual profit, but on an idea of the long-term growth of the enterprise.

The growth in Alhaji Yakubu's enterprise must be seen in the context of his growing household. During 1979–97, when his landholding had expanded sixfold, the number of people immediately dependent on Alhaji had grown threefold (Table 8.4). These included not only his three wives and many unmarried children, but also three married sons with their own large families. He was responsible for the feeding, marriage, naming ceremony and medical expenses of this total ensemble.

The increase in the number of his children involved more than a proportionate increase in expenditure. Many sons went to government boarding schools, involving extra expenses on provision and textbooks. He had built each of his married sons a separate compound. For the first marriages of his sons, he had undertaken all of the expenditure. For their subsequent marriages, he had provided the sadaki. When his daughters married, Alhaji was the recipient of sadaki. However, his ten married daughters were raising sixty young children between them, and for his grandchildren's naming ceremonies, Alhaji provided a ram or a sheep.

We must also consider the eventual subdivision of this landholding on the death of Alhaji Yakubu. If (as with the children of HH 1 in the previous case study) 263 acres were to be divided equally among his thirty-six male and female children, then each would receive less than 8 acres. (This excludes possible claims by other more distantly related kin. See Ross 1987: 230–31.) Additionally, there are lucrative

Table 8.4. The dependents of HH 2 in 1979 and 1997

1979:	1997:	Dependents' Wives	Dependents' Children	Other	Subtotal
Mother					
3 wives	3 wives				
4 unmarried sons:	3 married sons:				
Abdul	Abdul	2	4	1 (mother)	7
Musa	Musa	3	11	1 (mother)	15
Smaila	Smaila	2	5		7
Jamilu					
11 unmarried daughters	10 unmarried sons				
	13 unmarried daughters				
Total: 19	**58**				

non-farm assets to be divided – especially cattle and the sale value of vehicles.

If (as with the children of HH 1 in the previous case study) these are sold and two-thirds of their money value goes to the sons, then the sons would be in a position to buy back some farmland inherited by the daughters. Exchanges between children after the inheritance has been settled will leave some of them with larger landholdings than the other inheritors.[2] The oldest sons will also have advantages because of their greater management experience and knowledge of agricultural marketing.

There is nothing, moreover, to prevent Alhaji from transferring farmland as *inter-vivos* gifts to some sons, in order to avoid the worst effects of fragmentation.[3] After all land transfers among kin before as well as after Alhaji's death, the three oldest sons are likely to begin their lives as independent household heads with larger holdings than the remaining children. They will be better positioned than was Alhaji at his father's death. (In my land transfer record covering half of the mapped acreage of Marmara farmers [chapter 3], Alhaji had inherited seventeen acres.)

Nevertheless, the rural economy has changed much during the intervening period of forty years. Population densities are much higher.

The departing pastoralists who, in their exodus south, sold land to Hausa farmers, have long since left. Land purchase is much more costly than it was then. Accumulators must go far from Marmara to find large tracts of land. Moreover, since Alhaji's success has been partly the result of a long life, his sons will, necessarily, begin their independent careers at a later age than he – and with less time in which to achieve his scale of success. In circumstances of polygyny and increasing land scarcity, the subdivision of a very large landholding renders difficult the subsequent accumulation of capital for the inheriting generation.

A Son of HH 16

When I left Marmara in 1979, HH 16 was one of the more successful farmers of the time. He had twenty-four acres of farmland and headed a large family farming unit of five sons. He was approximately sixty years old. Later, he acquired a second-hand truck. Thereafter, he retired from farming. His third son – not more than thirty years old in 1996 – had become one of the most interesting cases of economic success in Marmara.

Abdullahi as a very young man had begun his trading career by buying and selling sugar cane. He also drove his father's truck. While transporting cotton, he became the client of a wealthy cotton trader. When delivering cotton to Kaduna, he became the client of a Hausa dealer who bought cotton for foreign companies. This man placed large sums of money in Abdullahi's hands. With these advances, he organized the largest network of cotton buyers in the area of Marmara. His good fortune (*arziki*) was not more than three years old. Yet during this time, he had built up a transport enterprise of eight second-hand buses. He had purchased the tractor inherited by one of the sons of HH 1 (case study above). Another son of HH 1 had become his main buyer, and thus, his client. These relationships with the sons of the late HH 1 signify a shift in wealth from the inheritors of one of the main accumulators of the previous generation, to a young entrepreneur in the present.

The purchase of cotton is concentrated during and after harvest, from January through March. In that period, Abdullahi went to Kaduna twice a week to obtain advances from his patron, because advances were quickly exhausted buying cotton. His patron gave him a commission per ton purchased. Moreover, the patron would stipulate the tonnage required from the advances (i.e., the price per ton) and if Abdullahi bought a larger amount (i.e., at a lower price) the additional cotton was his own to sell. He combined his cotton earnings, his income from transport and his net farm income to purchase farmland

– including a very large field behind a village five miles from Marmara, from the inheritors of its village head.

Travelling with Abdullahi, I observed his great dependence for cotton money on the Kaduna patron. In September 1996, he was anxious to obtain early advances, and had nothing to give to his buyers in Marmara. Some cotton grown on his own fields was also owing to the patron. This dependence suggests that he was investing his own earnings from trade and transport in fixed assets like farmland. His dependence also resulted from ambitious plans for expanding his household. Despite his youth, he already had three wives, and was seeking to marry a fourth. Abdullahi was in competition with other suitors. In 1997, he unsuccessfully spent over N100,000 in gifts on the woman and her kin. (This sum is significant when compared with the N500,000 he reported spending on all farm operations in 1996.)

His career exemplifies the wealth that could be made after the privatization of cotton marketing, because urban dealers were competing for rural clients who could be relied on to find cotton. Given his youth, he had no children involved in his enterprise. For management purposes, he had attached to himself several clients among the smaller farmers of Marmara. While he was engaged in the significant accumulation of capital when young *before* the onset of numerous household obligations, his clients expected him to take on the commitments of a patron.

This cotton trader can be linked in a common analysis with the three case studies of grain traders in chapter 7. There, I analysed their borrowing, investment and saving as a staged process over time. Breakthrough to accelerated investment – from the constraints of social obligation and expensive labour – is achieved when a man's core group of patrons or trading friends have sufficient wealth to finance his trading. This allows him to shift his own investment funds into fixed assets like farmland. The patronage of a single exceptional individual (as in the case of Abdullahi) can speed up this transition from slow to rapid growth of investment funds. At the same time, the trader remains inserted in a chain of risk between his lenders and his borrowers. This is particularly so because his dependence on others for commercial loans ensues from his own emphasis on expanding his family and his farming. These processes are also true of a young cotton buyer and transporter like Abdullahi. While patronage has enabled him to transfer trade earnings into farmland, he faces a future in which his dependents in a polygynous household, and his circle of clients, will multiply. The speed of his accumulation of capital can be set within a long-term trajectory involving household and cliental accumulation as well.

The Middle Farmers of 1979

A Son of HH 32

In 1979, HH 32 had 8.5 acres of farmland and was approximately sixty years old. After his death, his landholding of 8.5 acres was divided between two sons. From 1979 to 1998, his oldest son married a second wife and his total household expanded from three to twelve. His farm was not large enough to feed this household. However, he had continued with his off-farm occupation of bread selling, and used the earnings to gradually acquire three oxen and a plough, hiring out his ploughing services. Daily earnings from bread selling, and seasonal earnings from ploughing, provided him with enough money to feed his family and participate actively in the local networks of childbirth-and-matrimonial-gift exchange (biki). These off-farm income sources also provided the marriage expenses for his son.

HH 45

In 1979, HH 45 had farmed five fields (5.6 acres) and was approximately forty years old. He had two wives and seven young children. His main source of income was as a house builder in the nearby town of Malumfashi.

By 1998, house building in nearby towns had brought him considerable success. In conversation, he dwelt on the number of his children: he had nineteen, of whom eight were married women in separate households. He had two wives and ten children in his own house. He had increased his landholding to eight fields. They were farmed by his male family workforce. He had purchased three oxen and a plough. He had the 'capital [*jali*] to buy five cows', but planned to use it to set up his oldest son in a shop of his own.

He attributed his ability to provide for a large household to hard work and an urban reputation in his off-farm occupation; patronage for house building in the nearby towns; and the use of earnings to buy food grain cheaply immediately after harvest. Thus, he had avoided the need to buy it during the farming season, when prices were at their annual peak.

The Small Farmers of 1979

HH 63

In 1979, HH 63 had farmed 3.3 acres of farmland and was approximately forty years old. His career reveals circumstances which can lead to long-term economic decline. His adult life began well enough.

An indigene of the hamlet, his ancestors had been among those who had first farmed the area in the late nineteenth century. In 1977, he had 6.8 acres. But debts as a cotton buyer had forced him to pledge half of his land. Thereafter, he had worked as a dry-season migrant labourer and earned the funds to reclaim the pledged land.

Changes in the composition of his household show how in a polygynous society, the circulation of women between marriages can increase household size and intensify the economic pressure on male household heads. In 1979, he had a family of nine in his care. Then, he divorced his second wife and married a new one. By the time that I returned to Marmara in 1996, he had (except for his first wife who was still with him) an entirely new family of ten. His first wife had given birth to a boy, now in his teens. His new second wife had given birth to six children, the two oldest being also teenaged boys. The two oldest daughters of 1979 had married, and the two younger girls had died. Thus, in 1996, already in his mid-fifties, HH 63 had a family which was larger than, but as young as, the family which he had supported in 1979. Moreover, the three teenaged boys were a net drain on his income because he was trying to put them through secondary school.

By 1996, he had subdivided half of his holding among his sons as plots for their personal use. He had been obliged to sell nearby farmland because of the expansion of the village centre. He was reduced to farming two acres.

HH 63 exemplifies the problems that arise when a very small farmer marries a second wife and produces a new set of children, greatly increasing the financial pressures on a man with very limited acreage. He was in contrast to the trend in Marmara, at least during the earlier period of my research, when farmers with 3–3.9 acres tended to have one wife (Table 3.19).

His main problem was that for years, he had not had any remunerative off-farm occupation. He relied for income on his two acres and on seasonal work as a farm labourer. In the farming season of 1996, this was a reasonably secure strategy, because labour rates were more than sufficient to cover the daily cost of family food. However, in the farming season of 1997, this strategy no longer provisioned his household. Over the previous farming season, guineacorn prices had risen while labour rates had dropped considerably due to the influx of migrant labourers from the far north.

His other strategy was to plant his one remaining field with cotton, selling it at harvest and using the money to buy his annual requirement of family food grain at low postharvest prices. Again, this strategy was successful after the harvest of December 1995–January

1996. But at the harvest of December 1996–January 1997, his cotton yield and cotton prices dropped sharply compared with the previous year, while the price of guineacorn rose considerably. Before the next farming season, he had pledged half of his remaining farm to a wife in order to obtain funds for family food grain. At the harvest of December 1997–January 1998, the remaining acre yielded five sacks of guineacorn. One went to repay a creditor from the previous August. That left four sacks of guineacorn, against an annual family requirement of eighteen sacks.

Why was he able to still retain a hold on land? And how was he able to keep his sons in school, with its numerous expenses? The major reason for survival was the financial support of his wives. Both had small farms – some inherited, some provided by HH 63 himself years before. These yielded quantities of grains and vegetables which could be sold to finance various household needs – including loans without interest to their husband. Moreover, they occasionally employed him on their fields. Even more important, like many women they prepared and sold cooked food in the hamlet. This enabled them to give their children breakfast and their sons money for school expenses. They also used their earnings from the sale of cooked foods to buy goats and sheep. Thus, unlike their husband, they had a stock of savings on which they could draw to support their children.

A second reason for survival was that HH 63 had always had a friend of his own age in HH 12, a chicken trader who would return from market and give him small gifts of N10–20 (*alheri*, a 'kindness'), as well as employing HH 63 on his fields. Thirdly, among his regular creditors in the 'hungry' preharvest month of August, one followed Islamic practice and charged no interest on loans.

Hitherto, transactions with his wives and the support of friends had kept HH 63's annual burden of debt at a low level. And clearly, in keeping his sons at school he was pursuing a 'high-risk' strategy in the hope that they would eventually find urban jobs and help his household. But in the absence of a regular, off-farm source of income, it is difficult to see how HH 63 could avoid pledging his remaining land.

A Son of HH 64

In 1979, HH 64 had 3.3 acres of farmland and was approximately sixty years old. He frequently hired out his own labour and that of his three sons as a work team (Chart 4.4). He also had a regular income from his off-farm occupation as a skilled roof maker. By 1996, HH 64 had retired and divided his holding among his sons, each of whom had their own off-farm occupation.

In 1979, Yau, in his early twenties, was unmarried and part of the family work force of HH 64. He was a vigorous farm and general labourer. By 1996, he had built up a household of three wives and over ten children. He had acquired two oxen and a plough and had given up farm labouring. (He earned N600–1,000 per day as a ploughman compared with ordinary labour rates of N300–600 per day.) He estimated that during the farming season, he earned on average enough money to purchase a sack of guineacorn each day. This enabled him to store enough guineacorn to feed his family for most of the year, and to sell grain intermittently in order to buy soup ingredients (*cefane*). The small remaining shortfall in family grain requirements was met by selling cotton from his single field to buy guineacorn. The bran left over from pounding guineacorn for the evening porridge was fed to the oxen.

In September 1996, Yau estimated that his surplus of income over basic household requirements would enable him both to pay for the marriage expenses of a daughter and to buy an oxen-pulled cart which would give him additional income as a transporter during the post-harvest dry season. As of 1998, he had married off his daughter, but the illness of his father had drained income and prevented him from buying the cart.

Yau illustrates a theme of rural economy which emerged in my earlier fieldwork: many hired labourers, as they grow older, acquire an off-farm occupation and as a result, give up farm labouring. In Yau's case his earnings had also led to a large but financially viable household.

HH 66

In 1979, HH 66 farmed 3.2 acres and was approximately forty years old. Born and raised in a distant emirate, he had immigrated as a young man to Marmara, where his senior sister had married. For nine years he was the servant (*bara*) of the late HH 1. While in the house of HH 1, he learnt tailoring from a patron in a nearby village and purchased a sewing machine. HH 1 gave him neither money, nor a farm, nor a wife in marriage, so HH 66 decided to leave him, marry with his own money and buy a house.

By 1978, he had acquired a total of four fields. He had two wives and eight children. He did not work as a frequent labourer himself, but sent an adopted kinsman to perform hired labour.

By 1996, he farmed five fields. His household had grown to a total of twenty-four! It now included his two wives, six young children and the two wives *and* thirteen children of his married son. He continued as a tailor. Out of harvest earnings in 1995, he had purchased a second-hand passenger van, which was driven by his married son. He also gave this son money to rent (*aro*) three fields for farming. He had purchased three oxen and a plough, which he hired out.

Comments

The case studies above of two Very Large Farmers, Alhaji Yakubu and Abdullahi, show them making major acquisitions far from the village. Within the vicinity of the village, however, it was difficult to buy farmland. The one point at which purchases could be effected was at the time of the death of the owner, when his inheritors might sell. It is also interesting in the case studies that the largest fields of Alhaji and Abdullahi were purchased from other Very Large Farmers, or from their inheritors. To use the language of chapter 3, these were lateral transfers within the same category of landholder rather than transfers upward from Small or Middle Farmers.

In the case studies of Middle and Small Farmers, off-farm occupations remained crucial to household viability. They illustrate key themes of chapter 4: poor men tend to move with increasing age out of farm labouring and into off-farm occupations; personal energy in entering niches where there is demand for services enables household heads with small landholdings to achieve a measure of financial security in the provisioning of growing families. Wives can be essential to the financial viability of their husbands. All villagers were agreed that women owned most of the small livestock and fowl in the village. Thus, unlike many poorer men, they have a stock of savings on which they can draw to support their children, and provide loans to their husbands in time of need.

Change and Continuity

The most notable change emerging from these case studies is the emergence of landholdings far larger than any that were recorded in 1979. After the introduction of structural adjustment, closer linkages in a national economy must have strengthened the financial capacity of some accumulators to buy farmland, by selling grains in the southern Nigerian market to agro-allied industry (as in the case of Alhaji Yakubu) or by selling cotton to private ginneries and dealers (as in the case of Abdullahi). However, these accumulators were making their big land acquisitions from already successful accumulators rather than from Small Farmers. We might almost call it 'accumulation on the backs of previous accumulators'.

Returning to the village after an eleven-year interval makes it possible to focus attention on the diverse effects of economic success. I will call them medium term and long term. In the medium term, the successful accumulator (like Alhaji Yakubu) finds it impossible to separate domestic from commercial economy. He continues to think in terms of the overall management of 'wealth' (*dukiya*) as understood by the rural Hausa. The inseparability of domestic and commercial economy stems from the fact that under polygyny, an intrinsic purpose of capital accumulation is the provisioning of an expanding ensemble of wives and children. In the long term, the gradual accumulation of capital is followed by its fragmentation at death among numerous inheritors.

The case studies of 1996 and 1998 also suggest that in a noncapitalist trajectory of accumulation, two paths can be distinguished. Under a 'trade-oriented' path, the extent of patronage or trading friendship is crucial to the scale of accumulation (as in the cases of R., Alhaji Z., and M. in chapter 7, and Abdullahi in this chapter). Under a 'production-oriented' path, the initial extent of inherited farmland appears important to the eventual scale of accumulation (as with Alhaji Yakubu), although trading also fuelled accumulation. It is relevant that in the Land Transfer Record (covering half of hamlet farmland), Alhaji Yakubu inherited more land (seventeen acres) than any other household head except his full-sibling (nineteen acres).

Total patterns of accumulation result as much from relations between different categories of farmer as they do from the values and material opportunities among accumulators. The condition of Small Farmers tells us much about the chances for and constraints upon accumulation. The case studies of 1996 and 1998 suggest that four characteristics of small farming households continued to hold from 1977–85:

1. The tendency of Small Farmers who perform hired labour to acquire an off-farm occupation with increasing age and so drop out of the labour market. This tends to limit the supply of hired labourers to younger men. It therefore exerts long-term upward pressure on the price of labour power (chapter 4).
2. The contribution of off-farm occupations to the viability of small farming households. These even allowed some Small Farmers to be active participants in the land market (as in chapter 3 and the

cases of HH 45 and HH 66 above). As in 1977–85, accumulators were competing for land, and for a heterogeneous labour force, with limited land purchasers and with small-scale employers.

3. The continued widening of ownership of oxen and ploughs. Since 1979, at least four Middle and Small Farmers of the time, or their sons, had become ploughmen.
4. The contribution of women to the viability of their households. Women's farm produce, their income from house trade and the small livestock in which they invested provided a stock of savings which could be transformed into marriage goods for their sons and daughters. They thus played a vital part in the social reproduction of small farming households through marriage.

Given the viability of most small farming households, relations between them and Large or Very Large Farmers continued to be characterized (as in chapter 5) by a complex admixture of struggle (over labour rates), competition (over land acquisition) and cooperation (through marriage alliances and marriage-gift exchange networks) – and by a diversity of credit rates flowing from the mutual exchange of services between known persons. In consequence, the long-term acquisition of wealth remained an intersection of three processes – the polygynous expansion of households and their work forces; the expansion of circles of patrons, clients and trading friends; and the accumulation of capital.

Villagers across the spectrum of income remained part of a common, evolving moral economy. Chapter 1 described how Islamic conversion and community formation were overlapping mutations, as converts in the concentrated settlement of Marmara became exposed to immigrants from Kano with a much older tradition of belief. In this chapter, we have seen how the much greater enlargement of the village had been accompanied by an intensification of Islamic practice and learning. It was of a particular kind – the Izala movement, with its emphasis on the empowerment provided by Islamic literacy and learning. One result of the intensification of Islam was the wider practice of Muslim forms of credit. Yet this intensification had actually extended one older tradition among the mallams of Marmara – a call for greater reciprocity in exchanges between rulers and ruled, rich and poor. Despite inequalities, the people of Marmara continued to share the same populist political tradition.

Notes

1. This suggests that after the reduction of women's participation in land inheritance in the 1960s (chapter 3), women had once again become active in land inheritance. See endnote 2.
2. In her study of land distribution in a farming area with extremely high population density adjacent to Kano City, Hill argued that polygyny, together with the partible nature of inheritance, made it impossible for most children of rich men to be rich themselves (Hill 1977: 101). There, older sons tended to inherit more land than younger sons, despite the customary principle of 'equal division among sons' (1977: 126). An increasing number of women were exerting their rights under Muslim law, to half the share of their brothers (1977: 133). She maintained that Hausa rural communities lack a systematic attitude toward inheritance (1977: 125). In contrast, Ross, in his study of land distribution in another part of the Kano Closely Settled Zone in 1974–76, observed that the local population understood the widespread eligibility of various categories of kin under the Maliki version of Muslim law, and for that very reason, many inheritors were willing to delay actualization of claims in order to continue having usufruct (Ross 1987: 231).
3. In her study in 1966–67 of a village in northern Katsina Emirate with a much lower population density than Marmara in 1977, or today, Hill observed that no account was taken of previous *inter-vivos* gifts when property was divided on death (Hill 1972: 183).

Chapter 9

Continuity, Change – and Growth

Introduction

This book has argued that the concept of a *trajectory* of accumulation enables us to explain the particular economic changes which the people of Marmara experienced and enacted between 1977 and 1998. Different, discernible processes of accumulation were united through a local hierarchy of desires into an interrelated, moving whole. Because the model of a polygynous trajectory of noncapitalist accumulation has been tested through two markedly contrasting economic cycles, it is more likely that we are witnessing a durable order of desires with the power to absorb changes in economic circumstance. Through the period when rising petroleum wealth in the national economy increased liquidity in the rural areas, and *despite* the subsequent period when liquidity sharply contracted, we have seen the persistence of a particular pattern of acquisition and of relations between farmer-traders and households that do not trade. Had there been significant agricultural investment in the area by the traditional ruling class or by foreign or local capital, the trajectory might have been different. In its absence, local priorities and values determined the actual constellation of accumulative processes. Thus, the model developed in this book outlines the economics of the common people in a surplus-producing area of the African savannah where elite and capitalist landholding were not significant because farmer-traders had preempted the development of open spaces before the onset of high population density. But because population density was rising, they themselves had to go increasingly far to develop large landholdings of their own.

The concept of a trajectory assumes that there will be continuous interaction between preexisting scales of desire on the one hand, and one or more forms of accumulation that emerge sequentially in time. The outcomes of the interaction over time will depend on the relative material resources in each accumulative form that emerges – but *also* on the political consciousness and the ethical sense of the agents of accumulation. For example, the relative power, self-confidence and even militancy of different social classes shape the contours of any trajectory. It might be conjectured that a local or external capitalist class would have more space to develop large landholdings and, thus, its power over other classes, where population density is relatively low. Nevertheless, the availability of hired labour, and the attitude of the work force toward working for others for money, are also critical influences. Thus, it is always necessary to analyse the totality of relations and values in tracing the eventual overall pattern of accumulation. The concept of a trajectory is supple with respect to differences. It is sensitive to historical and moral particularity. It privileges accumulation over production and exchange in the explanation of economic change. For the mode of accumulation specifies the desires, intentions and moral attitudes toward interpersonal relations, that animate the modes of producing and exchanging.

Continuity

Interconnections

Chapters 3 through 5 described the processes and institutions governing land distribution, land transfers, labour relationships and credit relations as these had unfolded in the hamlet by 1979, with further evidence collected in 1985. They constituted a series of constraints on villagers engaged in the accumulation of land, labour power and other forces of production – and of possibilities for economic growth among small farming households – which, as chapter 8 indicated, continued to hold from 1986 through 1998, despite reduced liquidity in the rural areas.

Each generation of immigrants found less land available by purchase or pledge than the previous generation. Land accumulators were competing with buyers of limited amounts of land for the acreage available. As money wealth increased among villagers and was invested in farmland, it was also used to finance a larger number of wives and larger households. Thus, as money wealth increased, so, too, did the number of consanguineal and affinal kin, clients and trading friends. The greater a villager's money wealth, the more gift (*biki*) partnerships he established with poorer men, which helped to defray their marriage and naming ceremony expenditures.

The wide range of alternative credit outlets limited the levels of annual debt of Small and Middle Farmers – and consequently, their need to sell land to Large Farmers. Crucially, there were mechanisms for saving. Individual men and women invested small money sums in young goats and sheep, which grew into herds. A local collective method of saving, whereby women and men joined common savings clubs (*adashi*), aided this process. Moreover, women and men committed themselves to spending on biki partnerships, which yielded return gifts at the marriage and naming ceremonies in their own households. These various forms of saving helped insure smaller farmers against the high cost of life-cycle events. While most household heads ran out of food grain before harvest, the credit institution for meeting this deficit – *falle* – generally involved low and intrinsically variable real interest rates. This is because creditors and debtors were linked by a wide range of exchanges in a local economy marked by the personal, face-to-face nature of transactions. Moreover, real interest rates were influenced downward by the often low returns to commercial farming. Most village employers were caught between the relatively low yields of dry-grain agriculture and the rising price of hired labour power.

These very constraints on the individual accumulation of productive forces established the viability of most Small and Middle Farmers. They were 'viable' in two distinct senses: (1) they were able to finance the cycle of socially necessary expenses without selling land or borrowing heavily; (2) they had a range of means for economic self-advancement.

At a more general level of analysis, we can isolate the dynamics which had shaped economic relations between those who provided the various kinds of labour power and those who controlled it. Historically, the gradual in-migration of farmers and out-migration of pastoralists had enabled older farmers to acquire land on a scale unlikely to be repeated. This explains the degree of inequality in land distribution – and points to less inequality in the future.

A second economic dynamic was the continuous search by Hausa farmers for a new and more remunerative off-farm occupation (*sana'a*). The income from a sana'a raised the viability of 'smaller farmers' (those with ten acres or less), and enabled many of them to engage in limited land acquisition by purchase or pledge. Moreover, the development of a sana'a with increasing age tended to restrict the supply of frequent hired labourers to younger men. This raised the labour rates of men who frequently hired out their labour power. The restricted supply of hired labourers from the households of Small Farmers (with less than five acres) and Middle Farmers (with five to ten acres) and the uncertain supply of seasonally migrant labourers raised real labour rates for rural employers – subject to fluctuations in the availability of migrant labour from more northern areas. It reinforced the tendency of Large Farmers (with more than ten acres) to enlarge their family work forces and their circles of client labourers – with the concomitant financial obligations.

Ecologically, the existence of different rainfall zones in Nigeria enabled smaller farmers to earn extra income when not engaged in their own farming, through seasonal migration to areas with longer rainy seasons. At the level of social consciousness, ecological differences encouraged them to treat hired labouring as a *complement* to family farming.

Turning to the social dynamics, conversion to Islam, by withdrawing women of the household from most (though not all) farm work, increased the demand for hired labour power and the rates for male labourers. Secondly, villagers were altering the institutions governing land transfers, labour and credit, in response to changing circumstances. By comparing trends in Marmara with those reported by Hill and Ross from villages in Kano Emirate, we generalized the discussion of institutional change. Communities exist in rural central Hausaland. It is true that their juridical and corporate expression is limited, since villages and hamlets are organized hierarchically under traditional rulers imposed from above. In consequence, their methods of collective self-determination are usually informal. Nevertheless, a basic moral value gives form and meaning to institutional change: the circle of closely related kin ought to be provisioned and expanded so that it remains the focal point of transfers of land, labour, money and food. Thus, institutional change can be seen as moral praxis. Rather than dissolving under the impact of expanded commodity production, rural Hausa communities are in a continual process of becoming.

These various dynamics generate a puzzle. The evolution of rural economic relations had prevented farmer-traders from having at their disposal cheap supplies of land or labour power. As a result, it was difficult for those seeking enrichment to rapidly expand their investment funds. How, then, did they overcome the constraints on wealth acquisition?

Chapters 6 and 7 directly address this puzzle. They explore how some farmers overcame, or attempted to overcome, the constraints on wealth acquisition. Thus, I now shift attention from the complex economic relations of the rural community as a whole to the relations among farmer-traders; from the markets in land, labour and credit to the 'capital market' around Marmara. We have discerned two paths whereby farmer-traders sought to acquire wealth – a production-oriented path and a trade-oriented path.

The Production-Oriented Path

The clearest example of this path in Marmara was Alhaji Yakubu, now the largest farmer in Marmara. On the land transfer record, he inherited seventeen acres. He probably inherited more than this, since the record only covered the means of acquisition of farmland for half of all hamlet acreage (Table 3.21). As we saw in chapter 8, Alhaji Yakubu was heavily involved in trade. He was the leading cloth trader and retailer in Marmara. He had expanded his ownership of passenger vans from one in 1979 to three in 1996, and had acquired a trailer which enabled him to market his own produce and that of other farmers in southern Nigeria. The continual reinvestment of profits from trade and transport in agriculture, and of agriculture in trade and transport, had been the means for dramatically expanding an already large inheritance in local terms. However, his focus in this cycle was on the expansion of his farming.

At the same time, we can discern three processes in the expansion of Alhaji Yakubu's enterprise. Heavy disbursements on a growing household necessitated careful management of total wealth. This required constant calculation of the cash and kind flows from income-earning activities to domestic requirements. Alhaji's married sons referred to themselves as being 'in *gandu*' with him (for gandu, see chapter 4). Their loyalty depended upon his meeting a wide array of social obligations. The increasing scale of a successful polygynous family makes it difficult for the accumulator to conceptualize management of the enterprise separately from household management.

This recalls Max Weber's distinction between ideal types of 'rationality' in economic action – the *rational management of household accounts* versus *profit-making; acquisitive activity* versus *profit-making enterprise* (Weber 1978: 89–99). In both typologies, the former is oriented toward obtaining all advantages which enable the household to secure more goods and achieve greater security; the latter is directed to increasing advantages on the market for profit making. In the life of a rural Hausa accumulator, profit making cannot be divorced from the management of 'wealth' among the rural Hausa.

Secondly, continuous household growth was a strong incentive for Alhaji Yakubu to invest insistently in the expansion of enterprise. At least partly, capital accumulation is a response to the imperatives of increasing family size in a polygynous culture.

Thirdly, viewing the entire lifetime of Alhaji Yakubu, the expansion in the size of the polygynous household leads to *both* the cyclical accumulation and decomposition of capitals. The gradual accumulation of capital is followed by its fragmentation at death among numerous inheritors. This is not seen as a paradox among accumulators. For they culturally model the process of success, the acquisition of 'wealth', in terms of the accumulation of wives and children.

The Trade-Oriented Path

For villagers without large initial inheritances, and for immigrants to the area, it was through borrowing-for-trade that they overcame the constraints on the rapid development of investment funds, and the consequent accumulation of productive forces. Borrowing proceeded through vertical ties of patronage and clientage, and through horizontal ties of trading friendship between social equals. Borrowing-for-trade swelled trade margins that could be used to finance farming. It also included medium- and long-term loans that could be diverted from trade to agriculture. It further provided a stream of short-term credits for trading while the borrower diverted his own savings from trade to agriculture.

Clearly the success of this strategy in making possible agricultural investment depended on the borrower's ability to save – to gradually set aside trading profits from personal consumption and the many claims of kin, clients and friends. The rural Hausa practice of Islam encouraged an austere lifestyle. Compared with the drumming and drinking gaiety of Maguzawa communities, the Muslim hamlet was a quiet place. In summary, the interactive cycle of investment in trade and agriculture went beyond the investment of the profits from each in the other. The process was rather: long-distance trade – borrowing for own trade – trading profits invested in own agriculture – reliance on trading credits in order to divert own savings into agriculture. Commercial borrowing is the truly fascinating and understudied aspect of Hausa rural economy – not just because of its implications for rural economic organization, but also because of what it reveals about social relationships and values.

The case studies in chapter 7 of three farmer-traders in different niches of produce marketing, and of Abdullahi in chapter 8, show that borrowing-for-trade accelerated agricultural investment. Conversely, increased borrowing-for-trade actually depended on increasing farmed land, because traders were expected to repay trading loans out of harvest output if their trading ventures failed. The success of borrowing-for-trade as a strategy for agricultural growth depended on past savings and continuing austerity.

Agricultural Growth as Subordinate to the Social Process of Wealth Acquisition

Most Hausa Muslim villagers were eagerly acquisitive. Some farmer-traders were successfully so. It has therefore been relevant to relate commercial borrowing to agricultural growth, and show how borrowing helped overcome the constraints upon it. But this leaves open a more basic question. How did farmer-traders themselves construe their economic activity? Partly, this is a question of collective mentality. More broadly, it concerns the coherence of the model of a non-capitalist or polygynous trajectory.

In *Economics as Culture: Models and Metaphors of Livelihood,* Gudeman distinguishes between the 'universal' models of Western social theory and the 'local' or 'exotic' models of tribal and peasant societies. Universal models – whether neoclassical, substantivist or Marxist – assume some core traits of human economic behaviour which exist below the level of diverse social appearances (Gudeman 1986: 34). These models have a derivational form, in that they begin with axioms concerning behaviour which are held to be universally valid and, by means of operational rules, deduce theorems. 'Explanation' occurs when the data of fieldwork can be derived from the theorems. Thus, 'explanation' is the connecting of observed activities to an abstract scheme (Gudeman 1986: 29). 'Local' models of economy also purport to 'explain' economic activity but they do so by relating observed activity to vivid metaphors which reflect connections between nature and local society (Gudeman 1986: 44, 143–54).

Universal and local models share two characteristics. First, the axioms of the former and the metaphors of the latter reflect the assumptions of the modellers about the proper order of society. Secondly, axioms and metaphors are transformational. They transmute observations of economic activity into a different set of entities so that the modeller can *act* upon reality. Thus, all models contain schema for social action. Therefore, they are to be compared, not in terms of universal criteria of truth-value, but in terms of the social meanings and intentions that can be discerned in the models (Gudeman 1986: 37–43).

Gudeman's use of ethnographies by various authors (1986: 90–141) shows that he is attempting to reconstruct local models from the reported images and actions of rural peoples. In exploring the Hausa farmer-traders' model of their economy, I, too, am offering a reconstruction.

Let us begin by returning to the farmer-traders' notion of working capital (*jali*) – the assets available for investment in any activity which contributed to the growth of their 'wealth' (*dukiya*). We can arrange their material assets on a spectrum of liquidity (Chart 9.1). Partly, this reflects the technical ease with which specific assets could be transformed into cash. Partly, it reflects the degree to which different assets were transformable into cash because they were variably prone to claims of social obligation.

Sugar cane grown on the small available *fadama* acreage was sold immediately. Cotton, once mature, had to be sold for cash before it deteriorated. The minor crops could easily be stored, but in Marmara were produced in such small amounts, or for such a limited market, that they tended to be sold as they were harvested – some groundnuts being reserved for making groundnut oil. Once harvested, guineacorn was notionally divided into two parts: a part was considered saleable for luxuries (e.g., a bicycle, radio, new gown, or in the case of one of the richer farmers, a motorcycle); but the major part was reserved to repay debts or to meet expenses intimately associated with the social

Chart 9.1. Hausa farmer-traders' assets on a spectrum of liquidity

Assets:	Degree of Liquidity:
1. Cash	*Highest*
2. Trading stocks	
3. Sugar cane	
4. Cotton	
5. Minor crops – millet, rice, maize and groundnuts	
6. Small livestock	
7. The major crop – guineacorn	
8. Cattle	
9. Oxen and ploughs, buses and lorries	
10. Farmland	*Lowest*

reproduction of the household in its relations with other households. These expenses included food grain, the purchase of soup ingredients, the payment of labourers in house repair, gifts (*gudumwa*) to kin and friends and reciprocal contributions (biki) at weddings and naming ceremonies, Salla gifts to wives and children, spending on marriages and naming ceremonies, and the payment of farm labourers. The same approach was applied to small livestock. Indeed, guineacorn and small livestock were together regarded as the household's basic stock of saving. But we can assess small livestock as more liquid than guineacorn, because farmers would normally sell small livestock at the guineacorn harvest, but would wait until guineacorn prices had risen after harvest (and livestock prices had fallen) before selling guineacorn to buy small livestock.

Cattle could be sold more quickly than the remaining assets on the spectrum – oxen and ploughs, vehicles and farmland. However, cattle, oxen and ploughs, and vehicles were all reserved for sale to defray basic outlays in the cycle of social consumption; or they were sold to purchase other income-yielding assets (e.g., more cattle or farmland). The least liquid asset, farmland, was only sold to finance household marriages, or to meet pressing debts.[1]

Of the spectrum of assets, we can say, first, that all were saleable to meet marriage payments and pressing debts-in-trade. Participation in the circulation of money, labour, goods and services was put at risk if trading debts were not repaid or household marriages financed. Secondly, assets 1 through 5 (cash through the minor crops) were decidedly more liquid than 6 through 10 (livestock and guineacorn through farmland). Thirdly, small livestock was a social cut-off point with regard to the obligation to lend money. A man would not be expected to answer a call for a loan by selling small livestock, guineacorn, cattle, oxen and ploughs, vehicles or farmland. The pressure from others to lend money was reduced by converting assets 1 through 5 into 6 through 10.

The dilemma facing farmer-traders was the need to throw assets into circulation in order to achieve income growth; while, at the same time, to keep assets out of circulation lest they be dissipated in lending money. If throwing assets into circulation increased a man's assets, then the dilemma was partially solved by shifting his assets down the spectrum of liquidity. It was difficult to shift down the spectrum, as long as his total investment funds (jali) were limited – combining his own resources, his claims on others and the claims of others on him. But as his core group of patrons and trading friends expanded, he was able to do so by relying on them for credits to finance his trading.

When he shifted his assets into oxen and ploughs, or vehicles, he was sinking his funds into a social relationship with the ploughman or the driver. For they were normally free to make contracts with prospective customers, provided that they informed the owner and guaranteed him a regular stream of income. Through these particular investments, he was *institutionalising a capital sum in a social relationship* in order to protect it from dissipation. And when he shifted his assets into farmland, the resultant output of guineacorn was free from requests for loans.

In summary, different assets can be regarded as belonging to separate, though not insulated, moral spheres; they were subject to different claims of social obligation.[2] By shifting his assets down the spectrum of liquidity, the farmer-trader was trying to reduce the moral pressures to disburse them.

Yet, as we saw in chapter 7, the success of this strategy was never more than partial. The claims of dependents, friends and the various kinds of subordinate labourer drew the farmer-trader into continued lending. Seen from this perspective, shifting assets from more to less liquid forms, and especially into farmland, did not so much reduce the pressure of social claims. Rather, it increased the farmer-trader's attractiveness as a borrower by presenting lenders with potential security. Hitherto, we have argued that borrowing helped overcome the constraints on agricultural growth. But now, we can stand the thesis on its head. Because of the value placed on extending the range of personal relationships, agricultural expansion was itself designed to raise borrowing capacity. Stated thus, the social process of long-term wealth acquisition is left without an inner material cause – an economic 'ghost in the machine' – to which social relationships can be reduced. Instead, both borrowing and agricultural expansion expressed the structure of social relations. They reflected the moral emphasis placed on responsibility (*hidima*) for others.

Farmer-traders borrowed for trade in order to divert funds into agricultural expansion in order to borrow still more – a circular economic logic whose meaning was moral.

Change

The major change between the earlier period of research spanning 1977–85 and the more recent research of 1996–98 was the emergence of Very Large Farmers (with over fifty, and in some cases, over one hundred acres of farmland). This might suggest that there will be a growing bifurcation between the production-oriented and trade-oriented paths to wealth acquisition, leading to two distinct sectors – a capitalist sector marketing its output through agreements with agro-allied industry, and a noncapitalist sector trading through the many, and shifting, market destinations for grains.

However, the major reason for believing that Very Large Farmers will remain integrated within a common noncapitalist trajectory of accumulation is that polygyny is a core value shared by farmer-traders on both the production-oriented and trade-oriented paths to wealth acquisition. It generates a particular kind of enterprise, in which household, cliental and capital management are merged. In this connection, it is critical to remember that the Muslim prohibition on more than four wives does not stop the tendency for men to spend on more – and in the case of wealthy men, sometimes many more – than four marriages in a lifetime, because of the ease and frequency with which women divorce and remarry. As we saw in chapter 8, polygyny is so intrinsic to the beliefs and desires of this society that it sets up a dynamic of population increase and, as a result, there is increasing land scarcity. Farmers are increasingly unwilling to part with land and in consequence, production-oriented accumulators must look further afield to find the space to consolidate large landholdings.

A serious implication of this trajectory, with its emphasis on polygyny, is now manifest after the passage of time. The rapid increase in population resulting from polygynous marriage is likely to change the nature of land distribution. Given that the number of wives and children tends to increase with wealth (Table 3.19), most inheritors of present Large Farmers are likely to be Small or Middle Farmers. When the present Very Large Farmers die, among their numerous inheritors, only the senior male siblings are likely to have considerable farmland in village terms. When they themselves die, there would be a further subdivision among their own children of the land of the initial accumulators. With the death of the present generation of Middle Farmers, their inheritors will usually be Small Farmers. With the death of the present generation of Small Farmers, many of their inheritors will receive tiny holdings, approaching a condition of near-landlessness.

And yet, the increasing subdivision of farmland does not inevitably entail the emergence of a full-time, landless wage-labour force. Chapter 3 showed how local land tenure and inheritance patterns were flexible in response to changing circumstances. Male siblings could recombine as a single fraternal farming unit after the death of their father if there were increasing postponement by heirs of the subdivision of small holdings upon inheritance. To the extent that women become increasingly aware of their inheritance rights under Islamic law, this could be a further incentive for brothers to continue to farm the common inheritance while providing for their sisters. In other words, the family farming unit (gandu) would become stronger. As population densities increase, the findings of Paul Ross (Ross 1987: 233–47, and chapter 4 above) on changes in land tenure and family farming arrangements in the high-population-density area of the Kano Closely Settled Zone become ever more relevant.

Chapter 4 argued that villagers engage in a social praxis whereby they revise family labour institutions in the light of their understanding of a changing reality and their reference to continuing values. Thus, the alternative in the future to a class of permanent wage labourers may be a general process of involution or miniaturization. This would be accompanied by a growing emphasis on off-farm occupations.

The energy with which smaller farmers seek out off-farm occupations is relevant to the nature of future change. In 1996 and 1998, a striking feature of Small and Middle Farmers was the vigour with which they widened their participation in off-farm occupations – particularly ploughing services, but also transport and retailing. Thus, reduced average landholding need not cause poverty, where a population is open to innovation.

It is critical to remember that the need to generate marriage funds and to provision growing families pushes smaller household heads into the investment of some of the proceeds of their off-farm work in farmland (chapter 3). Tables 3.17 and 3.18 showed that as landholding increased in 1979, there was a distinct tendency for age to increase among those born in the hamlet. What the data for 1979 also uncover is that as age increased, the chances of becoming a Middle Farmer greatly increased among the indigenous population. Taking six acres as a clear indication of Middle Farmer capacity to meet basic household requirements (chapter 3), it is noticeable that the proportion of household heads having six or more acres increased from 18 per cent among those with an estimated age of thirty to 67 per cent among those with an estimated age of sixty (Table 9.1):

Table 9.1. Estimated ages with landholdings: Indigenes, Marmara, 1979

Age:	30	35	40	45	50	55	60	65	70
Number of household heads:	11	10	10	11	9	12	9	4	2
Per cent with six or more acres:	18	40	50	45	56	50	67	100	100

Source: Appendix 1

Fluctuation is evident between forty and fifty-five in the proportion of household heads that had six acres or more – the precise age range when a household head was likely to pledge land for his own second marriage and later, for the marriages of his children (see also Table 3.19 for farmers in Decile V, with four to six acres of land). Thus, *the amount of farmland inherited does not give us fixed economic positions for the inheriting generation.* For the rural Hausa tend to search for ever greater off-farm income, some of which is invested in farmland with increasing age.

Chapter 3 revealed a shift in the social structure of the population in the 1950s and early 1960s, as departing pastoralists sold their land to the present generation of farmers. That generation is beginning to pass away. When it does, a different kind of shift is likely. As of 1979, the top tenth of landholders controlled 40 per cent of land used by Marmara farmers within a three-mile radius of the hamlet (Table 3.2). Their inheritors are likely to control a smaller proportion. *Within the vicinity of any village,* the growing equality in land distribution predicted in chapter 3 is likely to occur. A few Very Large Farmers will develop out of the inheritors of large landholders. However, their farmland will be dispersed over a number of villages, corresponding to the area that can be reached by the employment of a dispersed and heterogeneous labour force. Under the impact of the polygynous expansion of family sizes, land distribution is likely to change from the present pyramid of Very Large, Large, Middle and Small Farmers (chapters 3 and 8), to a flatter distribution consisting mainly of Middle, Small and 'Very' Small Farmers – with nodal points of Very Large Farmers spread over the rural landscape.

A Market Economy without Local Capitalism

This book has argued that capital accumulation had proceeded through but been limited by household and cliental accumulation. As a result, economic relations between accumulators and other members of the community continued to be characterized by the feature of 'multi-strandedness'. For example, an accumulator will be related to a Small Farmer not only as employer to hired labourer, but also as biki partners, as customer for and provider of house repair or transport services, as giver and recipient of the Islamic charity of *zaka* or *sadaka* or as consanguineal or affinal kinsmen (chapter 5).

F.G. Bailey developed the idea of the multiple or 'multiplex' relationship among Indian peasants. When 'the transaction based upon calculations of interest and profit . . . is supplemented by, or even replaced by a bond of religion or of kinship or of both, the tie becomes a moral one, is less easily broken and commands much more generous terms of credit' (Bailey 1969: 47–48). Applying this insight to Marmara, the multistranded nature of economic ties has prevented labour relationships from being reduced to a cash nexus, wherein the various kinds of subordinate labourer are treated solely as units of labour power calculated in terms of the exchange value which they contribute to production.

The relatively high status and extended rights of the subordinate labourer in agriculture or commerce did not result from 'labour scarcity' – either in the demographic sense of high land/labour ratios, or in the ecological sense that 'labour-intensive systems of cultivation' have resulted from human adaptation to the physical environment of the savannah. Social values which gave priority to personal relationships in farming and trading made it easier for younger and poorer farmers to obtain interest-free short-term loans, develop off-farm occupations and retain or even acquire land. Therefore, subordinate labourers in agriculture or commerce could only be attracted by offering them a variety of rewards. Thus, there was no demographic or ecological determination of labour relationships. Deeply felt notions of the obligatory and the desirable channelled labour relationships. They actually *created* 'labour scarcity'.

This rural economy was innovative, among farmers Small or Large, in products, technology and occupations. It was entrepreneurial, for its accumulators were enterprising risk takers. Borrowing for trade through relations of clientage or trading friendship generated upward economic mobility and prevented 'social closure'. The category of farmer-traders was continuously open to the entry of new members, and reduced by the exit of those who failed to achieve the difficult balance between saving and spending, borrowing and lending.

Given these dynamic features of local economy, Very Large Farmers will have to continue competing with a wide range of other farmers for land and hired labour. As nodal points in a changing economic landscape, they will continue to be drawn into personal relations with other, less wealthy households.

The Impact of Islam on Social Relations

In his subtle depiction of Islamic consciousness and its connections to political and social structures in the Middle East and North Africa, Gilsenan gives us a complex picture. The ulema are significant, because people care that their social relations are authentically Islamic. At the same time, while being instrumental in defining Islamic knowledge, the ulema are not exclusively so, as ideas percolate through all of 'the capillaries of the social system', including markets (Gilsenan 2005: 49). Comparing late Ottoman society with contemporary Morocco, he shows that Islamic practice has been consistent with divergent political economies – the former 'modernizing and centralizing' the latter 'traditionalistic' and peripheral (2005: 43–49). Indeed, he comments that 'If the rulers enforce religious law in the "appropriate" areas, then a society can be claimed to be properly Islamic and to based on religion . . . Very different political and economic structures are thereby justified . . . or rendered "invisible"' (2005: 35).

This amounts to saying that socially and politically, there are different kinds of Islam. The point with regard to Marmara is that the mallams shared a common interpretation of Islam. It was highly critical of the hereditary ruling class, and so, entrenched villagers' consciousness as a common class vis-à-vis the rulers. It therefore contributed to a communitarian sensibility. It also confirmed and encouraged polygyny, and, indeed, many of the social practices of exchange between persons that predate Islam (with important exceptions: drinking alcohol is abhorred, as is the open work of women through all of the phases of the farming cycle).

The specific dynamics of conversion are also crucial to understanding the impact of Islam on local society. In Marmara, most people converted at the same time. This meant that in converting wholesale, they brought with them all social exchanges except those declared to be un-Islamic. This contrasts with Parkin's classic account of the Giriama of Kenya in the 1960s, at a time of rapid economic change. There, conversion was confined to a small minority – the young accumulators who were buying up palm trees and land in the thriving market for copra. To avoid the drains on their wealth that might ensue from clientage, they converted to Islam in order to achieve ritual distinctiveness. This was effected by abstaining from palm wine at the centre of traditional exchanges, from sharing meat which had not been ritually slaughtered, and in general, by avoiding commensality with non-Muslims. Parkin links this with other studies, for example, of conversion to the Tijjaniya Brotherhood in Ibadan (Cohen 1969), to outline an international strategy of detachment by the economically successful from the claims of others (Parkin 1972: 3). In Marmara, no such detachment occurred, since most people converted at the same time and most of the existing social exchanges were approved by the mallams. Even guineacorn released from circulation as beer had often to be sold to pay for the male hired labour which was needed to substitute for the withdrawal of women from most forms of farm work (chapter 4). If, among the Giriama, conversion was a cultural strategy in support of capital accumulation, in Marmara it immersed accumulators more deeply in polygynous marriage and the networks of marriage-gift exchange which tied them to the rest of the community.

How Markets Grow

In chapter 2, I ended my comparison of economic change in Marmara with that in other parts of rural Africa, by pointing to the historical and moral specificity of economic formations. In consequence, the spread of the market can be expected to have very different outcomes in different formations. Jane Guyer's *An African Niche Economy: Farming to Feed Ibadan 1968–88* demonstrates this theme through her analysis of agricultural change in the rural town of Idere, in the derived guinea savannah of southwestern Nigeria, some fifty miles from Ibadan. Despite the great differences between Marmara and Idere, her analysis is relevant because both communities have been undergoing rapid change and share a dynamic of enthusiastic commercialism.

A central and continuing theme of local Idere history is the importance of occupational associations. The continuing development of these to cover every aspect of the local economy is grounded in one of the most evocative processes of Yoruba culture, whereby the expanding repertoire of occupations is given names. This, in turn, is based in a deep sense that every person has a unique trajectory. Life careers are individuated through choices made before birth, the person being a reincarnation of an ancestor and the composite of his or her genealogy as far back as the fourth generation (Guyer 1997: 33–34, 37–40).

A history of widespread political participation and individual economic independence in a context of low population density distinguishes Idere from Marmara, with its long conflict between urban lords and country folk, its cliental relations and high, rising population density. Moreover, low population density in Idere is likely to structure the long-term dynamics of employer-labour relations, and the opportunities for Small Farmers, very differently than does high population density in Marmara. At a more general level, however, four kinds of similarity between the Idere and Marmara economies suggest that comparisons are useful: (1) As in Marmara, the Idere economy is embedded in labour flows between ecological zones. (2)

People in both areas think in terms of the contribution of off-farm occupations to total income. (3) Innovation in response to market incentives is characteristic of both. (4) Money-mindedness, and the propensity to sell all goods and services to available customers, are old traits in both.

Guyer argues that the 'market' in Idere must be understood as social totality – not just in terms of short-term price responses. Nor is it helpful to see the impact of the market as a process of commoditization, with its resultant differentiation, because 'Yoruba communities have been commercial and differentiated for as long as we have records'(1997: 222). Rather, patterns of economic change ensue from social dynamics and cultural history in a way that differs from capitalist logic. 'The major driving logic . . . is career enhancement' because of the local propensity to 'create *a multiplicity of niches*' [her italics] (1997: 223). By the morality of the niche economy, the principle which enjoins specialization enjoins, by extension, full participation by all specialists in the circulation of goods and services (1997: 228).

Throughout this book, I have examined the operation of a series of markets involving the people of Marmara – land, labour, credit, produce and 'capital' markets. The labour, produce and capital markets involve them in transactions with other regions of Nigeria. The shaping of these markets has been the product of particular social drives – to provision closely related kin and to develop polygynous households. This permits us to construct a model of the market as intrinsically inflected by cultural specificity. While the 'market' exists as a matrix of interlocking prices for products, labour and land, subject to the intersection of supplies and demands over a huge area from the Sahel to the Atlantic, supplies and prices are also negotiated through the language and moral priorities of local Hausa institutions.

Indeed, this economy has its own institutions for land, labour, produce and 'capital'. Land sales are less likely to arise among Small Farmers, and more likely to arise when Large Farmers become over-extended because of the growth of their households or their exposure to risk. Land pledging is usually a countercyclical mechanism whereby farmers obtain credit in bad times and reclaim the land in good times. Labour is frequently hired, but the core work force of any accumulator tends to be close kinsmen or clients because of the difficulty of attracting inexpensive hired labour in an economy marked by widespread access to land and off-farm occupations. A well-developed market in grain futures exists, whereby credit is extended to smaller farmers on the basis of speculation in the future price of produce. Investment funds flow through clientage ties (long-term credit) and trading friendships (medium- and short-term credit). Capital assets tend to be institutionalized in social relationships. The 'money cost of capital' does not consist of interest but of labour-time assigned to the service of a patron, and the provision of reciprocal credit or services to a trading friend. As we have seen in chapters 7 and 8, this economy achieves a scale of production and distribution that transcends the household unit through the relations of clientage and trading friendship.

Labour may be defined as the 'scarce' factor of production. But 'labour scarcity' is not given by demographic or ecological determinants. It results from the totality of social relations and values in rural southern Katsina.

Farmer-traders are risk taking. However, 'risk' includes both external factors and factors embedded in the social objectives of farmer-traders. We can distinguish between: risks on the 'market' – i.e., changes in global and local prices; risks which are the product of climatic and other physical uncertainties; and risks from expansion of the household and the circle of clients and trading friends. Thus, risk is not just an array of external material factors in terms of which farmer-traders do culturally conditioned calculations; it also arises from within the circle of culturally inflected economy. The peculiar and historically specific combination of polygynous, cliental and capital accumulation leads farmer-traders into risk-laden transfers. The goal is the development of multipurpose family enterprises, defined partly in terms of their material wealth, but also in terms of the density of their connections to other households.

This market has its disciplines. Some are typical of any market-based economy: people are compelled to produce for or supply services to the market and to flexibly adapt to changing conditions through hard work and careful calculation. More problematic in the case of the Hausa market economy is the Western idea of competition between individuals for resources that are intrinsically scarce in relation to wants that require satisfaction. This implies social distance between individuals. It is a very particular Western idea of the individual moral responsibility to compete, and of a restricted domestic circle of dependents *for whom* the individual competes. In contrast, the Hausa person is a success insofar as he or she *narrows* social distance. Social distance is bridged when a person extends credit in cash or in kind, or establishes a marriage-gift (biki) partnership. The various alliances established in Hausa markets involve a different kind of discipline from that associated with Western markets. There are big risks involved in lending or giving, which require a careful assessment as to whether or not a reliable mutual claim is being established over each other's time, energy and material resources.

There is competition. However, the notion of competition is heavily qualified by the idea of cooperation. The boundary between the domestic and the extradomestic is blurred. The multiplication of wives and children inside the domestic circle involves constant negotiation and gift exchange outside of the circle. The domestic relations of the polygynous accumulator are extended in a way that they are not in a monogamous society. In consequence they entail a different notion of competition. The attitude of the monogamous competitor implies an anxiously self-contained struggle against non-kin. In contrast, polygyny expands marriage relations so much, and the circulation of women between marriages is so great, that the distinction between 'kin' and 'non-kin' is more elastic than in a monogamous society. Competitors in trade are, potentially, kin by marriage. More than in monogamous societies, the idea of individual competition is inflected by the idea of actual or potential marriage alliance.

A Particular African Style of Growth

If the noncapitalist trajectory of accumulation is the engine of growth in this part of the African savannah, then the outcome is a particular style of growth. Growth has occurred in a matrix of ideas concerning what is ultimately desirable and obligatory. Engagement with land, labour, credit and produce markets has sought to achieve, not just the reproduction, but the expanded reproduction, of the household. A man's entrance into Muslim trading networks has aimed for the multiplication of personal ties of dependence through clientage and of mutual obligation through trading friendship. And, we can add, dependence is sought for: *it is no shame.*

Markets are continually being made and remade by local people through transactions which lead over time to the establishment of local economic institutions. What is fascinating, reviewing the evidence from Marmara for over twenty years, is that the result has clearly been material growth – in production, technical innovation and the spread of new means of transport; while at the same time, moral priority is given to two social realities – the expansion of the household and the development of multistranded ties between economically active people. Indeed, under this style of economic growth, more weight is given to the pleasures and responsibilities which multiply with social bonds than to individual material growth. I have tried to demonstrate that this balance in the style of growth is most clearly explained by seeing the strong acquisitive drive of this rural people as the product of a morally and historically specific accumulative trajectory. Ultimately, polygyny generates a paradigm of social action, moral obligation and collective desire that has profound effects on the course of economic growth.

Notes

1. Very occasionally, farmland would be sold by the more risk-taking farmers to buy other income-yielding assets, e.g., a bus.
2. The use of 'spheres of exchange' or 'economic spheres' as explanatory terms has a long pedigree, including Bohannan's classic statement (1959) and Barth's complex scheme for analysing the rural economy of Darfur (1967). Parry and Bloch's edited volume (1989) shows the continuing vitality of this idea in efforts to understand the uneven impact of Western money and of the circulation of commodities on non-Western economies.

Appendix 1

Basic Information on Household Heads, Marmara, 1979

Household Head	Age[a]	If Immigrant ('M')	Inheriting Brothers[b]	Off-farm Occupation(s)	1979 Holding (acres)	Wives	Household Size
				Decile I:			
1	65		7	Bus owner, cattle owner, 3 oxen teams, oxen hirer. Former grain trader	49.9	3	22
2	50		4	Bus owner, cloth trader, cattle owner, 3 oxen teams, oxen hirer	43.3	3	20
3	25[c]		2	Bus driver, cattle owner, 2 oxen teams, oxen hirer	41.5	1	17[c]
4	70			Oxen-cart transporter, 1 oxen team, oxen hirer	36	1	9
5	55		4	Cattle owner, 1 oxen team, oxen hirer. Former grain miller	35.4	2	13
6	55		2	Kolanut wholesaler	35	4	14
7	55	M		Grain trader	22.4	2	18
8	70			1 oxen team, oxen hirer	21.1	2	8
9	40			Grain miller, cotton buyer	19	3	17
10	50		2	Shopkeeper, cotton buyer, 1 oxen team, oxen hirer	16.4	2	14
11	60		3	None	16.3	3	10
				Decile II:			
12	40		2	Chicken trader	14.4	3	13
13	45			Grain trader, 1 oxen team, oxen hirer	13.2	2	14

Household Head	Age[a]	If Immigrant ('M')	Inheriting Brothers[b]	Off-farm Occupation(s)	1979 Holding (acres)	Wives	Household Size
14	45			Part-time grain trader, groundnut decorticator, 1 oxen team, oxen hirer	13.2	3	11
15	60			Donkey transporter	12.9	2	4
16	65		3	Part-time grain trader	12.6	3	13
17	50		4	None	12.3	2	9
18	45		4	None	12.3	2	10
19	55		3	1 oxen team, oxen hirer	12	2	10
20	40	M		Maize trader, cotton buyer, bus owner	12	2	7
21	35		4	1 oxen team, oxen hirer, hand-cart transporter, migrant labourer	11.8	2	12
22	40		4	None	11.6	2	8
				Decile III:			
23	55		6	Cassava seller	11.5	1	4
24	60		1	None until April 1979 (new hamlet head)	11.2	2	10
25	35			Goat trader, maize trader, grain miller, 1 oxen team, oxen hirer	10.2	1	5
26	35		4	None	9.9	2	5
27	50			Bus owner, cotton buyer, hamlet head until April 1979	9.9	3	7
28	50		4	Donkey transporter	9.6	2	7
29	60			Pillow and mattress maker	9.5	2	6
30	65		6	Unknown	9	2	4
31	45		4	Housebuilder	8.8	2	5
32	60		1	None	8.5	1	12
33	55		2	None	8.3	2	8
				Decile IV:			
34	25		3	1 oxen team, oxen hirer	7.7	1	6
35	65		1	House builder	7.4	4	16
36	45		3	Part-time general and farm labourer	7.4	2	7
37	35			Marketplace grain retailer	7	2	6
38	30		2	Kolanut retailer	6.9	1	5

House-hold Head	Age[a]	If Immigrant ('M')	Inheriting Brothers[b]	Off-farm Occupation(s)	1979 Holding (acres)	Wives	House-hold Size
39	40		4	Donkey transporter	6.8	2	6
40	55	M		Goat trader, butcher.	6.7	3	6
41	30		1	Farm labourer	6.4	2	4
42	65	M		Small table retailer (mai teburi)	6.4	1	5
43	60		3	Farm labourer, migrant labourer	6.3	1	12
44	55		6	Grain trader, 1 oxen team, oxen hirer	6.2	2	11
				Decile V:			
45	40		2	House builder	6.0	2	10
46	45		4	1 oxen team, oxen hirer	5.9	2	6
47	30		8	1 oxen team, oxen hirer	5.6	1	4
48	40		1	Farm labourer, grain porter	5.3	1	6
49	55	M		Kolanut retailer	5.1	2	6
50	50		2	Chief of the motor park	4.9	0	11
51	35		8	Donkey transporter	4.6	2	4
52	55	M		Shopkeeper	4.5	1	7
53	30			Tailor	4.5	2	5
54	60		6	Small table vegetable retailer	4.3	1	3
55	30			Bus driver	4	3	7
				Decile VI:			
56	50	M		Shopkeeper, tailor, smuggler	3.9	4	8
57	35		3	Unknown	3.8	1	3
58	45		3	Farm labourer	3.7	2	6
59	45		1	Donkey transporter, well digger, house builder	3.6	1	7
60	55		6	Chaff trader	3.6	1	7
61	30		1	Bus driver	3.3	1	4
62	60	M		Qur'anic mallam, primary school religion teacher	3.3	3	9
63	40		1	Cotton buyer, road survey assistant	3.3	2	9
64	55			Roof maker, farm labourer	3.3	1	10
65	55	M		Butcher	3.2	1	3
66	40	M		Tailor	3.2	2	7

House-hold Head	Age[a]	If Immigrant ('M')	Inheriting Brothers[b]	Off-farm Occupation(s)	1979 Holding (acres)	Wives	House-hold Size
				Decile VII:			
67	40		1	Farm labourer, barber, circumciser	3.1	1	6
68	30		1	Farm labourer, general labourer	3.1	1	3
69	30		8	Farm and general labourer	3.1	1	5
70	60			Rope maker, general labourer	3.0	1	3
71	55	M		Qur'anic mallam	2.9	2	8
72	45	M		Farm labourer, migrant labourer	2.8	0	1
73	35		8	Ploughman	2.7	2	7
74	70	M		Hides and skins and sugar cane trader	2.7	1	10
75	60	M		Liman	2.7	2	7
76	35		3	Farm labourer, migrant labourer	2.6	1	5
77	50		8	Kerosene retailer	2.6	1	4
				Decile VIII:			
78	30		8	Farm labourer, donkey transporter	2.5	1	4
79	55		1	Herbal medicine man	2.5	1	4
80	45		3	Farm labourer, general labourer	2.5	1	4
81	55		6	Small table vegetable retailer	2.3	1	4
82	55		3	Professional Lagos beggar	2.3	2	13
83	30		2	All-purpose commission agent	2.3	1	5
84	50	M		Unknown	2.2	1	4
85	55	M		Small table retailer (mai teburi)	2.2	1	5
86	40	M		Farm labourer, general labourer	2.2	0	1
87	40		4	Farm labourer, general labourer	2.1	1	6
88	35		1	Farm labourer, general labourer	2.0	1	5
				Decile IX:			
89	45	M		Qur'anic mallam	2.0	1	5

Household Head	Age[a]	If Immigrant ('M')	Inheriting Brothers[b]	Off-farm Occupation(s)	1979 Holding (acres)	Wives	Household Size
90	45		2	Farm labourer, general labourer	1.9	1	5
91	45	M		Qur'anic mallam	1.6	2	5
92	25		3	Petty trader, smuggler, marijuana seller	1.5	1	2
93	35			Farm labourer, general labourer	1.5	1	5
94	60		4	Wall-builder, general labourer	1.5	1	3
95	60	M		Farm labourer, general labourer	1.4	1	6
96	30	M		Farm labourer, grain mill operator for HH 19	1.3	1	2
97	50		2	Kolanut trader, fried fish seller.	1.3	2	5
98	55		1	Farm labourer, muezzin	1.3	3	7
99	50			Wall builder, muezzin	1.1	2	3
				Decile X:			
100	55	M		Farm labourer, bicycle mechanic	1.1	1	4
101	70	M		Qur'anic mallam	1.0	1	2
102	45	M		Qur'anic beggar	0.9	1	5
103	30		3	Bus driver	0.9	1	4
104	70	M		Well digger	0.8	1	2
105	45		2	Leather craftsman	0.8	3	8
106	40		4	Praise singer	0.6	1	3
107	45	M		Qur'anic mallam	0.6	0	1
108	35	M		Butcher	0.5	1	2
				Landless:			
109	35		2	Ploughman, farm labourer		1	3
110	35			Local authority road worker		2	9
111	55			Local authority road worker		1	2
112	30			Bus driver		1	3
113	55			Local authority road worker		2	2
114	30			Bus driver		2	4
115	35			Farm labourer, general labourer		1	3
116	40	M		Butcher		1	8

Household Head	Age[a]	If Immigrant ('M')	Inheriting Brothers[b]	Off-farm Occupation(s)	1979 Holding (acres)	Wives	Household Size
117	55	M		Blacksmith		1	2
118	40	M		Small table retailer, farm labourer		1	3
119	35	M		Butcher		1	7
120	35	M		Butcher		1	5

a. Estimated.

b. Including the household head. Of 75 nonimmigrant household heads with deceased fathers, the number of inheriting brothers is known for 66.

c. The inheritor of a large landholder who had died in 1977. He formed a joint household with his younger brother.

Appendix 2

INNOVATION, AGRICULTURAL EXTENSION AND YIELDS

The various farmers in Tables 1–3 are not 'representative' samples. They are simply the farmers who were willing to cooperate with me in my fieldwork. The group in Table 1 gives a more comprehensive picture of yields than the group in Table 2. With a mean acreage of 7.4, and a median of 6.3, the group in Table 1 is also closer to the mean acreage (7.8) and the median acreage (4.1) of all Marmara landholders as surveyed in 1979. The group in Table 2 gives a clearer picture of fertilizer use. With a mean acreage of 14.1 and a median of 10, it is also more biased toward Large Farmers. Table 3 demonstrates that the official distribution of fertilizer from the local FADP store was revised in 1979 to reduce the fertilizer given to richer farmers and increase that given to smaller farmers. Some richer farmers compensated for this change in policy by buying from other FADP stores where they were known.

Yellow maize, introduced by the FADP in 1975, was popular among farmers in Malumfashi Division for a reason in addition to its relatively high yield. Typically millet is harvested in late August, rice in September, groundnuts in October and guineacorn – the staple food – in December. However, millet yields are low in the soils of southern Katsina, and rice production is possible only on lower ground, where sufficient rainwater gathers. Groundnuts are eaten in many forms but hardly constitute a staple food. Under these circumstances, there is a long period during which farmers find it difficult to guarantee family food supply. Hence the popularity of yellow maize. Farmers in Marmara always stated that maize was ripe to cook from August, even though it was not dry enough to bag and sell until the end of September. For smaller farmers who obtained artificial fertilizer, yellow maize had become the stop-gap food from August until the guineacorn harvest.

Although yellow maize was being strongly promoted by the FADP, most farmers in Marmara applied significant quantities of fertilizer to sole-cropped guineacorn and to crop combinations. Part of the reason was that FADP-recommended quantities of fertilizer for guineacorn, groundnuts and rice were far less than that recommended for yellow maize. Thus, farmers could fertilize more extensive acreages of these other crops. But there were more important reasons why farmers distributed their fertilizer over guineacorn and other crops rather than concentrating it on maize. First, if guineacorn and yellow maize are ground and boiled in the customary way, guineacorn tastes much better. (It is difficult to detect whether high-yielding yellow maize has any taste at all.) Thus, the maize was regarded as *abincin miri-miri* – food to be taken occasionally, or else in the absence of other food.

Secondly, the market for maize was limited in comparison to the market for guineacorn. The main demand for the yellow maize of Malumfashi Division came from the northern markets of Katsina town, Mashi and Batsari. Two months of frenetic trading activity in October and November, when maize traders arrived and departed in droves, were followed by deep calm. Apart from that period, it was difficult for Marmara farmers to sell their maize. In contrast, the demand for guineacorn was large, growing and extended deep into Niger (chapter 6).

Agricultural extension staff saw themselves largely as agents for the distribution of fertilizer and for advice to richer village farmers, and this is how they were seen by the villagers among whom they lived. Since staff did not engage in much extension work, fertilizer use did not conform with FADP recommendations (Table 2). The fields measured by extension workers were mainly those of larger farmers listed as 'progressive' by the FADP, so the majority of farmers were not equipped to accurately assess fertilizer needs on their fields.

Extension workers were not imparting a knowledge of practices associated with fertilizer. Typically, farmers broadcast fertilizer over a whole field before ploughing, rather than concentrate it where seeds would be planted. Moreover, farmers placed maize plant stands at 2–2½ feet rather than the 1½ feet recommended by the FADP and guineacorn, even when fertilized, at the customary 2½–3 feet. These practices may in part explain why the maize yields projected by local

FADP staff (20 sacks per acre) were hardly ever achieved (6–9 sacks per acre was typical).

Lacking advice, farmers often experimented with solutions of their own to the problem of fertilizer application. As a result, farmers developed their own views: 'Fertilizer has the best effect when combined with cattle manure. Sulfa [calcium ammonium nitrate – recommended for rice] should be applied much more sparingly than in the recommendations because it is too "hot" for the soil.' There was much agricultural discussion among villagers in the evenings, or even while working on adjoining fields, and much observation of each other's farming performance.

From at least 1978 demand for fertilizer was high and widespread. The evidence does not support the 'trickle-down' theory that richer village farmers are inherently more innovative than Small Farmers. Smaller farmers used less fertilizer than richer farmers because there was less available to them from the FADP. The distribution policy of the FADP became more balanced in 1979 because richer village farmers mobilized smaller farmers in widespread protests against the tendency of FADP staff to sell fertilizer to wealthy outsiders (Clough and Williams 1987: 184–92, and for Marmara, Table 3 below).

Information from a group of eighteen farmers in Marmara for the 1977 crop year gives little reason to suppose that villagers had any basis for admiring the performance of relatively Large Farmers (Table 1). Using guineacorn grown *without* fertilizer as a standard of comparison, there was no clear tendency for yields to rise with a rise in the overall size of holdings. Indeed, grouping the farmers in Table 1 as Large, Middle and Small (see chapter 3), the *median* yield of guineacorn grown without fertilizer *fell* as holding sizes increased. Even when fields and crops on which fertilizer was used are taken into account and a weighted cereal yield is derived, there was no clear tendency for farmers with relatively large holdings to perform better than farmers with relatively small holdings.

Yields fluctuated greatly among farmers when ordered by size of holdings. Many factors affected yield – the quality of soils on particular fields; drainage; the size, health and strength of the labour force; the experience of the farmer; and the availability of cattle and household manure as well as artificial fertilizer.

Table 1. Aggregate cereal yields from all fields for eighteen farmers, Marmara, 1977 (sacks/acre)[a]

	Farmer[b]	1977 Total Holding (acres)	Adult Family Workforce	With Fertilizer			Without Fertilizer				Weighted Cereal Yield[c]
				G	M	R	G	M	R	MI	
1.	HH 6	26.6	3		4.2		2.6				3.3
2.	HH 21	13.9	2		5.2		2.0		2.8		3.8
3.	HH 19	12.0	6				10.4	3.9			6.3
4.	HH 20	11.6	1	4.6	13.0	7.9					10.1
	Large Farmers:		**Average**				**5.0**				**5.9**
			Median				**2.6**				**5.0**
5.	HH 39	7.8	1	5.3	9.8		2.0			3.3	4.5
6.	HH 35	7.4	3				6.3				6.3
7.	HH 37	7.0	1	4.0			2.6	4.0			3.1
8.	HH 63	6.5	1					6.5		2.6	6.2
9.	HH 42	6.4	1	2.5	1.7		3.2				2.5
10.	HH 7	6.2	5				3.5				3.5
11.	HH 47	5.6	1				5.0	5.5	3.9		5.0
12.	HH 45	5.6	1						2.1		2.1
13.	HH 49	5.1	3	4.1		4.0					4.0
	Middle Farmers		**Average**				**3.7**				**4.1**
			Median				**3.3**				**4.0**
14.	HH 56	3.9	2				3.5				3.5
15.	HH 66	3.1	2	5.6	3.3	7.8					4.6
16.	HH 74	2.7	3				4.9			3.8	4.6
17.	HH 79	2.5	1				5.7				5.7
18.	HH 93	0.7	1				2.1	1.6			1.8
	Small Farmers		**Average**				**4.0**				**4.0**
			Median				**4.2**				**4.6**
	Total		**Average**				**4.1**				**4.5**
			Median				**3.5[d]**				**4.2**

a. Farmers gave output information in terms of sacks (maize and rice) and either sacks or bundles (guineacorn and millet). For the weight of sacks of different crops, see Table 2, note d. When farmers spoke in terms of bundles, their conversion factor has been used when they gave it (normally 3–3½ bundles per sack). Where farmers did not give a conversion factor, the more conservative figure of 3½ bundles per sack has been used in calculating output of guineacorn or millet.

Table notes continued on next page.

Table 1 notes continued

b. Farmers are listed and described in terms of their land rank in the 1979 land survey. However, their actual 1977 holding is given above, since it is known for this group of farmers.
c. The weighted cereal yield is derived by adding the yields for each crop on each field, multiplied by the percentage of total cereal acreage on that field.
d. The median guineacorn yield without fertilizer in 1977 for this group (900 kg/ha) is more than the median guineacorn yield with fertilizer in 1978 for the group described in Table 2 (874 kg/ha). See the discussion of yields above.
G = guineacorn; M = maize; R = rice; MI = millet

Table 2. Fertilizer input and produce output for thirteen farmers on individual fields, Marmara, 1978

Farmer[a]	Total Holding[b] (acres)	Acreage of Designated Field	Crop(s)	Fertilizer Input Per Acre[c] (kg.)	(+)(=) or (−) FADP Advice	Main Crop: Rough Yield[d] (kg / ha)
1	50	14.6	Maize	342	+	2,073
6	35	2.0	Maize	300	=	2,698
		1.9	Guineacorne	79	+	933
		7.4	Guineacorn	54	=	622
7	22	0.8	Groundnuts/ guineacorn	125	+	531
		0.8	Guineacorn/ groundnuts	125	+	899
		1.7	Maize	294	=	3,027
		1.8	Guineacorn	139	+	719
		2.5	"	20	−	873
		3.0	"	33	−	642
		4.9	"	82	+	899
16	13	2.5	Maize	150	−	1,126
		3.5	"	150	−	1,341
17	12	1.0	Guineacorn	100	+	1,024
		1.3	"	77	+	590
		2.9	Maize	155	−	1,942
20	12	0.2	Maize	250	−	3,520
		0.6	Guineacorn	83	+	n.a.
		1.0	Cotton	250	+	651
		2.3	Maize	261	−	4,285
		2.7	Maize/rice	148	−	4,085
		3.3	Guineacorn	91	+	n.a.

f

28	10	1.0	Rice	10	–	n.a.
		1.0	Millet/cowpeas	50	=	n.a.
		2.0	Guineacorn	50	=	n.a.
		2.5	Maize	300	=	2,534
36	7	1.7	Guineacorn	59	=	1,054
42	6	1.4	Maize/groundnuts/ cowpeas	107	–	168
		1.9	Guineacorn	26	–	n.a.
45	6	1.4	Maize	48	–	503
		0.7	Rice	47	–	427
49	5	1.2	Maize	208	–	1,506
		2.0	Rice	75	–	1,344
63	3	0.4	Maize	260	–	1,833
66	3	0.9	Maize/guineacorn	278	–	1,304
		1.2	Guineacorn	42	=	874

a. Described in terms of their land rank in the 1979 landholding survey.

b. Rounded to the nearest whole number.

c. FADP recommendations were expressed in acreage terms:
(BSSP=boronated superphosphate; CAN=calcium ammonium nitrate)

Yellow maize: 200 kg BSSP and CAN (mixed) at first ridging, 100 kg CAN after 5 weeks = 300 kg/acre
Guineacorn: 50 kg CAN after 5 weeks = 50 kg/acre
Groundnuts: 50 kg BSSP at first ridging = 50 kg/acre
Rice: 50 kg BSSP at first ridging, 100 kg CAN after 2 weeks = 150 kg/acre

An alternative for maize was 100 kg of compound fertilizer at first ridging, followed by 100 kg of CAN after 5 weeks, but compound was not generally available in 1978. It was often stressed that if all advice were followed, a yield of 20 sacks per acre – 4,700 kg/ha – would be achieved.

d. The yields are estimates calculated from the number of sacks and fractions of sacks produced on these fields. Where two or more crops were intercropped, the yield refers to the first crop described. The weight of a sack depends on the crop and the number of *tiya* (large measures) which it contains. Farmers sold sacks containing 40 tiya at nearby marketplaces and to hamlet traders and sacks containing 38–39 tiya to outside traders – especially of maize. A conservative figure of 38 tiya is used above in figuring the weight of sacks. The approximate weights for sacks of 38 tiya are as follows:
guineacorn - 104 kg; maize – 95 kg; rice – 120 kg; millet – 104 kg; groundnuts – 86 kg; locust beans – 95 kg

e. Guineacorn was usually yellow guineacorn (*kaura*) but was sometimes *mori*, a variety considered superior. No new, high-yielding varieties of guineacorn were available in Marmara from the FADP.

Notes: 1. FADP recommendations were either followed or exceeded on 19 of 36 fields. However, fertilizer application was broadly equivalent to FADP advice on only 8 fields, suggesting that the clarity of extension advice, and the professional interaction between extension staff and farmers, were limited.

2. From this table it appears that as the size of landholdings declined, fertilizer application decreased from being above recommended quantities to being below recommendations. Of the 11 fields belonging to farmers with more than twenty acres, 9 had recommended or more than recommended usage. Of the 11 fields belonging to farmers with more than ten but less than twenty acres, 5 had recommended or more than recommended usage. Of the 14 fields belonging to farmers with ten acres or less, only 5 had recommended or more than recommended usage.

3. The yield of yellow maize was superior to that of all other crops. On the 12 fields sole cropped with maize, the average yield per ha was 2,200 kg, the median being 2,007. On the fields sole cropped with guineacorn, the average recorded yield per ha was 823 kg, the median being 874.

Table notes continued on next page.

Table 2 notes continued

4. The median yield of yellow maize is equivalent to 8.5 sacks per acre. The median yield of guineacorn is equivalent to 3.4 sacks per acre.
5. In his detailed survey of three Zaria villages, Norman found in two-crop mixtures of guineacorn and millet, average yields of 648 lb and 330 lb per acre respectively – 727 kg and 370 kg per ha (Norman 1973: 131, 136).

Table 3. Known fertilizer purchases by farmers in Marmara, 1978 and 1979 (50-kg bags)

		Total Holding[b] 1978 (1979) (acres)		1978				1979			
				FADP Stores:[c]				FADP Stores:[c]			
	Farmer[a]			Yaba	Other	Private	Total	Yaba	Other	Private	Total
1.	1	50		100			100	25	75		100
2.	2	43	50	143			143	25		25	50
3.	3	42		10			10	25			25
4.	6	35	33	20		30	50	25	22	19	66
5.	7	22	18	12		48	60	25			25
6.	10	16		20			20	25		25	50
7.	16	13	24	25			25	17			17
8.	17	12		5			2	13			13
9.	18	12		0		16	16	10			10
10.	19	12		0			0	5			5
11.	20	12	19	0		33	33				15[d]
12.	28	10		5		12	17	10			10
13.	32	9		0		6	6	10			10
14.	35	7		0				5			5
15.	36	7		2			2	5			5
16.	42	6	7	3			3	5			5
17.	43	6		1			1	4			4
18.	45	6		0		5	5	5			5
19.	47	6		0			0	5			5
20.	49	5		10			10	10			10
21.	63	3		0		2	2	0			0
22.	66	3		6			6	12			12
23.	76	2		0			0	7			7

Table 3 continued

a. Described in terms of their rank in the 1979 land survey.
b. 1978 figures list holdings as of April 1979, before the onset of the 1979 farming season. In May 1979, several farmers increased or reduced their holdings, as under the 1979 figures.
c. Includes fertilizer purchased privately in Marmara from farmers who had received it from Yaba FSC. Yaba FSC was the farm service centre and store which supplied Marmara.
d. The gap of a horizontal empty row separates Large Farmers from smaller farmers.

Notes:1. Official prices per 50-kg bag were as follows: boronated super-phosphate (BSSP) – N1.50; calcium ammonium nitrate (CAN) – N1.50; compound fertilizer – N2.00.
2. Richer farmers – those with around 20 acres or more – bought 383 bags in 1978 and 316 bags in 1979. But their FADP purchases fell from 305 bags to 247 bags. Farmers from the top quarter of landholders – those with over 10 acres – purchased 462 bags in 1976 and 376 bags in 1979. Their purchases from FADP sources fell from 335 bags to 307 bags.
3. Among the 12 farmers with 10 acres or less – a category which includes three-quarters of household heads – purchases from FADP sources rose from 27 bags to 78 bags.

Appendix 3

All Landholding Household Heads Grouped by Labour Practices During the Weeding Operation in the Farming Season of 1978

	1979 Land Rank	Off-farm Occupation(s)	1979 Holding (acres)	Age	Adult Family Workforce[a]
I. Own Labour (+) Hired Labour					
A.	Mainly Hired Labour: over one-half of weeding performed by hired labourers				
1.	HH 12	Chicken trader	14.4	40	1
2.	HH 14	Part-time grain trader, groundnut decorticator, 1 oxen team, oxen hirer	13.2	45	1
3.	HH 20	Maize trader, cotton buyer, bus owner	12	40	1
4.	HH 22	None	11.6	40	1
5.	HH 25	Goat trader, maize trader, grain miller, 1 oxen team, oxen hirer	10.2	35	1
6.	HH 27	Bus owner, cotton buyer, hamlet head until 1979	9.9	50	1
7.	HH 42	Small table retailer	6.4	65	1
8.	HH 45	House builder	6	40	1
9.	HH 55	Bus driver	4	35	1
10.	HH 61	Bus driver	3.3	30	1
B.	Much Supplementary Hired Labour: one-third to one-half of total weeding performed by hired labourers				
1.	HH 23	Cassava seller	11.5	55	1
2.	HH 28	Donkey transporter	9.6	50	1

	1979 Land Rank	Off-farm Occupation(s)	1979 Holding (acres)	Age	Adult Family Workforce[a]
C.	Small Supplementary Hired Labour: less than one-third of total weeding performed by hired labourers				
1.	HH 18	None	12.3	45	1
2.	HH 29	Pillow and mattress maker	9.5	60	1
3.	HH 37	Marketplace grain retailer	7.0	35	1
4.	HH 38	Kolanut retailer	6.9	30	1
5.	HH 39	Donkey transporter	6.8	40	1
6.	HH 53	Tailor	4.5	30	1
7.	HH 63	Cotton buyer, road survey assistant	3.3	40	1
	II. Own Labour (+) Family Labour (+) Hired Labour				
A.	Mainly Hired Labour: over one-half of weeding performed by hired labourers				
1.	HH 2	Bus owner, cloth trader, cattle owner, 3 oxen teams, oxen hirer	43.3	50	3
2.	HH 3	Bus driver, cattle owner, 2 oxen teams, oxen hirer	41.5	25[b]	3
3.	HH 4	Oxen-cart transporter, 1 oxen team, oxen hirer	36	70	4[c]
4.	HH 6	Kolanut wholesaler	35	55	3
5.	HH 9	Grain miller, cotton buyer	19	40	2
B.	Much Supplementary Hired Labour: one-third to one-half of total weeding performed by hired labourers				
1.	HH 1	Bus owner, cattle owner, 3 oxen teams, oxen hirer; former cloth trader	49.9	65	6
2.	HH 7	Grain trader	22.4	55	5
3.	HH 13	Grain trader, 1 oxen team, oxen hirer	13.2	45	2
4.	HH 15	Donkey transporter	12.9	60	2
5.	HH 19	1 oxen team, oxen hirer	12	55	7[c]
6.	HH 40	Goat trader, butcher	6.7	55	2
7.	HH 44	Grain trader, 1 oxen team, oxen hirer	6.2	55	2
C.	Small Supplementary Hired Labour: less than one-third of total weeding performed by hired labourers				
1.	HH 5	Cattle owner, 1 oxen team, oxen hirer. Former grain miller	35.4	55	4

	1979 Land Rank	Off-farm Occupation(s)	1979 Holding (acres)	Age	Adult Family Workforce[a]
2.	HH 8	1 oxen team, oxen hirer	21.1	70	2
3.	HH 10	Shopkeeper, cotton buyer, 1 oxen team, oxen hirer	16.4	50	3
4.	HH 11	None	16.3	60	7[c]
5.	HH 21	1 oxen team, oxen hirer, hand-cart transporter, migrant labourer	11.8	35	2
6.	HH 24	None until 1979 (new hamlet head)	11.2	60	3
7.	HH 36[d]	Part-time general and farm labourer	7.4	45	2
8.	HH 56	Shopkeeper, tailor, smuggler	3.9	50	2
9.	HH 62	Qur'anic mallam, primary school religion teacher	3.3	60	2
		III. Own Labour (+) Family Labour			
1.	HH 16	Part-time grain trader	12.6	65	6
2.	HH 17	None	12.3	50	2
3.	HH 32	None	8.5	60	3
4.	HH 33	None	8.3	55	7[c]
5.	HH 34	1 oxen team, oxen hirer	7.7	25	3
6.	HH 35	House builder	7.4	65	3
7.	HH 43[d]	Farm labourer, migrant labourer	6.3	60	3
8.	HH 46	1 oxen team, oxen hirer	5.9	45	2
9.	HH 49	Kolanut retailer	5.1	55	3
10.	HH 50	Chief of the motor park	4.9	50	2
11.	HH 52	Shopkeeper	4.5	55	2
12.	HH 54	Vegetable retailer	4.3	60	2
13.	HH 64[d]	Roof maker, farm labourer	3.3	55	4
14.	HH 66	Tailor	3.2	40	2
15.	HH 74	Hides and skins and sugar cane trader	2.7	70	3
16.	HH 75	Liman	2.7	60	4
17.	HH 80[d]	Farm labourer, general labourer	2.5	45	2
18.	HH 82	Professional Lagos beggar	2.3	55	2

	1979 Land Rank	Off-farm Occupation(s)	1979 Holding (acres)	Age	Adult Family Workforce[a]
19.	HH 83	All-purpose commission agent	2.3	30	2
20.	HH 95[d]	Farm labourer, general labourer	1.4	60	2
21.	HH 98[d]	Farm labourer, muezzin	1.3	55	2
		IV. Own Labour			
1.	HH 26	None	9.9	35	1
2.	HH 30	Unknown	9	65	1
3.	HH 31	House builder	8.8	45	1
4.	HH 41[d]	Farm labourer	6.4	30	1
5.	HH 47	1 oxen team, oxen hirer	5.6	30	1
6.	HH 48[d]	Farm labourer, grain porter	5.3	40	1
7.	HH 51	Donkey transporter	4.6	35	1
8.	HH 57	Unknown	3.8	35	1
9.	HH 58[d]	Farm labourer	3.7	45	1
10.	HH 59	Donkey transporter, well digger, house builder	3.6	45	1
11.	HH 60	Chaff trader	3.6	55	1
12.	HH 65	Butcher	3.2	55	1
13.	HH 67[d]	Farm labourer, barber, circumciser	3.1	40	1
14.	HH 68[d]	Farm labourer, general labourer	3.1	30	1
15.	HH 69[d]	Farm labourer, general labourer	3.1	30	1
16.	HH 70	Rope maker, general labourer	3.0	60	1
17.	HH 71	Qur'anic mallam	2.9	55	1
18.	HH 72[d]	Farm labourer, migrant labourer	2.8	45	1
19.	HH 73	Ploughman	2.7	35	1
20.	HH 76[d]	Farm labourer, migrant labourer	2.6	35	1
21.	HH 77	Kerosene retailer	2.6	50	1
22.	HH 78[d]	Farm labourer, donkey transporter	2.5	30	1
23.	HH 79	Herbal medicine man	2.5	55	1
24.	HH 81	Vegetable retailer	2.3	55	1

	1979 Land Rank	Off-farm Occupation(s)	1979 Holding (acres)	Age	Adult Family Workforce[a]
25.	HH 84	Unknown	2.2	50	1
26.	HH 85	Small table retailer	2.2	55	1
27.	HH 86[d]	Farm labourer, general labourer	2.2	40	1
28.	HH 87[d]	Farm labourer, general labourer	2.1	40	1
29.	HH 88[d]	Farm labourer, general labourer	2.0	35	1
30.	HH 89	Qur'anic mallam	2.0	45	1
31.	HH 90[d]	Farm labourer, general labourer	1.9	45	1
32.	HH 91	Qur'anic mallam	1.6	45	1
33.	HH 92	Petty trader, smuggler, marijuana seller	1.5	25	1
34.	HH 93[d]	Farm labourer, general labourer	1.5	35	1
35.	HH 94	Wall-builder, general labourer	1.5	60	1
36.	HH 96[d]	Farm labourer, grain mill operator	1.3	30	1
37.	HH 97[d]	Kolanut trader, fried fish seller, farm labourer	1.3	50	1
38.	HH 99	Wall builder, muezzin	1.1	50	1
39.	HH 100[d]	Farm labourer, bicycle mechanic	1.1	55	1
40.	HH 101	Qur'anic mallam	1.0	70	1
41.	HH 102	Qur'anic beggar	0.9	45	1
42.	HH 103	Bus driver	0.9	30	1
43.	HH 104	Well digger	0.8	70	1
44.	HH 105	Leather craftsman	0.8	45	1
45.	HH 106	Praise singer	0.6	40	1
46.	HH 107	Qur'anic mallam	0.6	45	1
47.	HH 108	Butcher	0.5	35	1

a. Including the household head, except HH 4 and HH 74.
b. Recent inheritor of his father.
c. Maguzawa: wives were in the workforce.
d. Frequent farm labourer: at least one-third of total weeding time was spent on the farms of employers.

Appendix 4

Household Consumption of Food Grain and 'Soup Ingredients' (*Cefane*)

Most household heads provided their dependents with at least two meals a day: (1) lunch usually consisted of a hand-mixed combination of cold, cooked millet balls (*fura*) and cow's milk (*nono*) purchased from Fulani women vendors; (2) the evening meal usually comprised hot guineacorn porridge (*tuwo*) dipped by the handful into a sauce of baobab leaves (*miyan kuka*) or okro (*miyan kubewa*).

Some household heads paced their annual consumption of guineacorn to allow for higher consumption during May through July, when their family workforces needed extra strength for farming. The majority of households reduced their consumption of guineacorn during the 'hungry month' of August, and to a lesser extent in September, two to three months before the December guineacorn harvest. They substituted various vegetable preparations, with or without groundnuts. In September, small sales of rice could provide the cash to buy guineacorn. Maize, though not ripe enough to harvest and bag until the end of September, was ripe enough to roast.

Cefane is translated by Abrahams and Robinson as 'soup ingredients', but in Marmara it was used more broadly to include the millet and milk for lunch. Typically, cefane for the evening meal included: salt, pepper, palm oil or (more expensive) groundnut oil, baobab leaves, okro, locust bean cakes (*daddawa*) used in cooking for thickening and flavouring the sauce, and a recent, almost universal addition, Maggi cubes. These ingredients were purchased from the small table retailers. However, daily money expenditure on cefane varied greatly between households according to whether they:

- had their own baobab trees or locust bean trees;
- had their own water supply, since there was extra expense if a porter were hired to carry water from the public well;
- purchased goat meat daily – a prestigious sign of well-being.

Moreover, even within any given range of cash income, there would be variations in taste and in the priority which household heads, influenced by their wives, gave to cefane expenditure. For example, HH 35, despite his large family, did not buy pepper, and also did not buy palm oil because it caused one of his wives to vomit. Thus, the following household heads can provide only a suggestive guide to cefane expenditure in the whole population.

These household heads were either personal friends or else they cooperated closely with me in my research. Their mean landholding was close to the hamlet mean (7.8 acres) though somewhat above the hamlet median (4.1 acres). Large Farmers and Small Farmers are slightly underrepresented, and Middle Farmers overrepresented, compared with the whole population (Table 3.20). They always discussed their requirements in terms of an average – of which they had a clear concept. They expressed guineacorn as a daily or monthly, and cefane always as a daily, average.

Table 1 arranges them in terms of landholding size, as a rough indicator of cash income, although clearly, purchasing power also varied greatly with the nature of off-farm occupations (Appendix 1). As landholding size increased, grain consumption tended to increase. But noticeably, even among household heads with very small holdings, reported grain consumption seldom dipped below one tiya per day (6 lbs, 2.7 kg). Partly, this may reflect their unwillingness to expose the degree of their poverty. But also, men normally ate the evening meal outside their compounds in small groups of friends and neighbours, each contributing a portion of porridge and sauce (chapter 1). Thus, there was a communal element in food consumption. This raised the daily requirements of most household heads.

As landholding size increased, cefane consumption tended to increase, though much more erratically than did guineacorn. The greater deviation from the trend, of cefane compared with guineacorn, is partly explained by the factors discussed above. But also, some household heads with relatively small holdings had ready access to meat (e.g., the butcher) or unusually large cash earnings (e.g., the bus driver).

Table 2 arranges the same household heads in terms of household size. The tendency of grain and cefane consumption to increase with household size suggests that broadly speaking, these reports are accurate. The similarity in trends derived from both tables is due to the general tendency for household size to increase with the size of landholding (Table 3.19).

Table 1. Average daily consumption of guineacorn and cefane, selected household heads, Marmara, 1979

	Acreage	Household Size	Household Head	Guineacorn (tiya)	Cefane (N)
1.	35.0	13	HH 6	2.0	4.00*
2.	22.4	18	HH 7	2.5	2.50
3.	12.0	7	HH 20	1.0	2.95**
4.	8.5	12	HH 32	1.5	1.10
5.	7.4	16	HH 35	2.5***	0.45
6.	7.4	7	HH 36	2.25	1.12*
7.	6.8	6	HH 39	1.5	1.15
8.	6.4	5	HH 42	1.0	0.65
9.	6.0	10	HH 45	1.6	1.10
10.	3.9	8	HH 56	2.0	1.34
11.	3.3	4	HH 61	1.0	2.02*[a]
12.	3.3	9	HH 63	1.5	1.15
13.	3.2	3	HH 65	1.0	1.60*[b]
14.	3.2	7	HH 66	1.5	1.10*
15.	2.7	10	HH 74	1.0	0.70
16.	2.5	4	HH 79	0.6	0.70
17.	1.5	5	HH 93	1.0	1.13
Means:	8.0	8.5		1.5	1.46
Medians:	6.0	7.0		1.5	1.13
6 or more acres (Large and Middle Farmers):					
Means:				1.8	1.67
Medians:				1.6	1.12
3.9 or less acres (Small Farmers):					
Means:				1.2	1.22
Medians				1.0	1.14

* Includes meat. ** Includes meat, butter and tomatoes. *** More in the farming season.
a. Bus driver. *b*. Butcher

Table 2. Average daily consumption of guineacorn and cefane, selected household heads, Marmara, 1979

	Household Size	Acreage	Household Head	Guineacorn (tiya)	Cefane (N)
1.	18	22.4	HH 7	2.50	2.50
2.	16	7.4	HH 35	2.50*	0.45
3.	13	35.0	HH 6	2.00	4.00**
4.	12	8.5	HH 32	1.50	1.10
5.	10	6.0	HH 45	1.60	1.10
6.	10	2.7	HH 74	1.00	0.70
7.	9	3.3	HH 63	1.50	1.15
8.	8	3.9	HH 56	2.00	1.34
9.	7	12.0	HH 20	1.00	2.95***
10.	7	7.4	HH 36	2.25	1.12**
11.	7	3.2	HH 66	1.50	1.10**
12.	6	6.8	HH 39	1.50	1.15
13.	5	6.4	HH 42	1.00	0.65
14.	5	1.5	HH 93	1.00	1.13
15.	4	3.3	HH 61	1.00	2.02**[a]
16.	4	2.5	HH 79	0.60	0.70
17.	3	3.2	HH 65	1.00	1.60**[b]
Means:	8.5	8.0		1.50	1.46
Medians:	7.0	6.0		1.50	1.13
Above 7 members (hamlet mean):					
				1.80	1.54
				1.70	1.12
Below 7 members (hamlet mean):					
				1.0	1.21
				1.0	1.14

* More in the farming season.
** Includes meat.
*** Includes meat, butter and tomatoes.
a. Bus driver.
b. Butcher.

Appendix 5

Trading Purchases, Sales and Margins of M., 1978

Table 1. Guineacorn: Purchases, sales and margins in trading of HH 7 (M.), Marmara, 1978

Week Ending:	Purchases sacks	@	N	Storage Balance sacks	N	Sales sacks	@	N	Over-heads[a] N	Sales N	Cost of Sales N	Margin N
1 Jan.	0			5	48[b]	0						
8 Jan.	10	18.00	180	10	138*	5	27.00	135	9	135	99	36
15 Jan.	30	22.00	660	17	264**	27	27.00	729	53	729	627	102
	4[c]	10.00	40									
22 Jan.	16	24.00	384	17	264	16	27.00	432	32	432	416	16
29 Jan.	unk					unk						
5 Feb.	19	28.00	532	17	264	19	30.00	570	37	570	569	1
12 Feb.	0			17	264	0						
19 Feb.	23	28.00	644	27	544	13	31.00	403	26	403	390	13
26 Feb.	7	28.00	196	17	264	17	30.00	510	33	510	509	1
5 March	30	28.00	840	24	334	30	30.00	900	59	900	899	1
	7[c]	10.00	70									
12 March	unk						unk					
19 March	unk						unk					
26 March	unk						unk					
2 April	50	27.00	1350	44	874	30	31.00	930	59	930	869	61
9 April	9	28.00	252	37	685	16	30.50	488	32	488	473	15
16 April	7	28.00	196	24	334	20	31.00	620	39	620	586	34
23 April	25	28.00	700	24	334	25	31.00	775	49	775	749	26
30 April	0		24	334	0							

Week Ending:	Purchases sacks	@	N	Storage Balance sacks	N	Sales sacks	@	N	Over-heads[a] N	Sales N	Cost of Sales N	Margin N
7 May	34	27.00	918	24	334	34	32.50	1105	67	1105	985	120
14 May	31	26.00	806	24	334	31	32.50	1008	61	1008	867	141
21 May	21	30.00	630	24	334	21	31.00	651	41	651	671	(–)20
4 June	29	30.00	870	25	364	28	34.00	952	57	952	857	55
11 June	28	30.00	840	25	364	28	32.00	896	62	896	902	(–)6
18 June	36	30.00	1080	25	364	36	33.00	1188	80	1188	1160	28
25 June	32	30.00	960	25	364	32	33.00	1056	69	1056	1029	27
2 July	27	30.00	810	15	450***	37	33.50	1240	80	1240	806	434
9 July	35	32.00	1120	0	0	50	34.00	1700	109	1700	1679	21
16 July	30	30.00	900	0	0	30	34.00	1020	65	1020	965	55
23 July	47	30.00	1410	12	360	35	33.50	1173	76	1173	1126	47
30 July	0			0	0	12	30.00	360	26	360	386	(–) 26
6 Aug.	20	28.00	560	0	0	20	32.00	640	43	640	603	37
13 Aug.	16	26.00	416	0	0	16	28.00	448	34	448	450	(–) 2
20 Aug.	10	24.00	240	0	0	10	28.00	280	22	280	262	18
27 Aug.	0	(rice only)		0	0	0	(rice only)					
3 Sept.	0				0	0	0					
10 Sept.	0	(rice only)		0	0	0	(rice only)					
18 Sept.	1	24.00	24	0	0	1	28.00	28	2	28	26	2
24 Sept.	6	24.00	144	0	0	6	27.00	162	13	162	157	5

Table 1 continued on next page

Table 1 continued from previous page

Week Ending:	Purchases sacks	@	N	Storage Balance sacks	N	Sales sacks	@	N	Over-heads[a] N	Sales N	Cost of Sales N	Margin N
1 Oct.	4	26.00	104	0	0	4	28.00	112	9	112	113	(–) 1
8 Oct.	2	26.00	52	0	0	2	28.00	56	4	56	56	0
15 Oct.	10	26.00	260	0	0	10	28.00	280	21	280	281	(–) 1
22 Oct.	20	26.00	520	0	0	20	28.00	560	42	560	562	(–) 2
29 Oct.	4	24.00	96	0	0	4	28.00	112	8	112	104	8
5 Nov.	0				0	0	0					
12 Nov.	0 (groundnuts only)			0	0	0 (groundnuts only)						
19 Nov.	0 (groundnuts only)			0	0	0 (groundnuts only)						
26 Nov.	20	20.00	400	15	300	5	23.00	115	11	115	111	4
3 Dec.	0			13	260	2	20.00	40	4	40	44	(–) 4
11 Dec.	0			6	120	7	22.00	154	15	154	155	(–) 1
17 Dec.	1	19.00	19	0	0	7	22.00	154	15	154	154	0
24 Dec.	14	15.00	210	0	0	14	22.00	308	31	308	241	67
31 Dec.	2	18.00	36	0	0	2	22.50	45	4	45	40	5
TOTAL	**744**		**20279**	**0**	**0**	**749**		**23226**	**1552**	**23226**	**21879**	**1347**

a. Overheads are rounded to the nearest whole number. See Table 4.

b. The year opened with 5 sacks in store, being sack repayments of preharvest loans given at N8 or N10 (chapter 5).

c. These sacks were repayments of preharvest loans given at N10 (chapter 5) and were put in store.

* Includes 5 sacks bought in the current week and only sold in the following week.

** Of 17 sacks in store, 8 were bought at current prices with money repayments of preharvest loans. 4 were sack repayments of preharvest loans given at N10 (chapter 5). 5 were the sack repayments of preharvest loans in store from 1 January.

*** 25 sacks were removed from storage and sold, being sack repayments of preharvest loans and sacks purchased with money repayments of preharvest loans (chapter 5). The 15 sacks in storage were bought in the current week and only sold in the following week.

Note: All sales were in Danbatta Marketplace, except on 11 December in Funtua Marketplace.

Table 2. Rice: Purchases, sales and margins in trading of HH 7 (M.), Marmara, 1978

Week Ending:	Purchases sacks	@	N	Storage Balance sacks	N	Sales sacks	@	N	Overheads[a] N	Sales N	Cost of Sales N	Margin N
1 Jan.	0			6	96[b]	0						
—	"			6	96	"						
7 May	0			5	80	1	28.00	28	2	28	18	10
14 May	0			4	64	1	28.00	28	2	28	18	10
21 May	0			0	0	4	28.00	112	8	112	72	40
—	0			0	0	0						
20 Aug.	3	22.00	66	0	0	3	28.00	84	7	84	73	11
27 Aug.	6	22.00	132	0	0	6	28.00	168	13	168	145	23
3 Sept.	0			0	0	0						
10 Sept.	19	18.00	342	5	90	14	26.00	364	30	364	282	82
17 Sept.	1	20.00	20	0	0	6	24.00	144	13	144	123	21
24 Sept.	3	20.00	60	0	0	3	24.00	72	7	72	67	5
1 Oct.	5	20.00	100	0	0	5	24.00	120	11	120	111	9
8 Oct.	6	22.00	132	0	0	6	28.00	168	13	168	145	23
15 Oct.	6	22.00	132	0	0	6	26.00	156	13	156	145	11
TOTAL	**49**		**984**	**0**	**0**	**55**		**1444**	**119**	**1444**	**1199**	**245**

a. Rounded to the nearest whole number. See Table 4.
b. Rice purchased at the September harvest.
Note: All sales were in Danbatta Marketplace.

Table 3. Groundnuts: Purchases, sales and margins in trading of HH 7 (M.), Marmara, 1978

Week Ending:	Purchases sacks	@	N	Storage Balance sacks	N	Sales sacks	@	N	Overheads[a] N	Sales N	Cost of Sales N	Margin N
1 Jan.	0			0	0	0						
—	"			"	"	0						
23 July	6	40.00	240	6	240	0						
30 July	0			0	0	6	40.00	240	13	240	253	(–) 13
6 Aug.	0		0	0	0	0						
13 Aug.	3	34.00	102	0	0	3	32.00	96	7	96	109	(–) 13
—	0			0	0	0						
24 Sept.	1	36.00	36	0	0	1	42.00	42	2	42	38	4
1 Oct.	0			0	0	0						
8 Oct.	1	32.00	32	0	0	1	36.00	36	2	36	34	2
15 Oct.	0			0	0	0						
22 Oct.	3	28.00	84	0	0	3	32.00	96	6	96	90	6
29 Oct.	2	26.00	52	0	0	2	32.00	64	4	64	56	8
5 Nov.	0			0	0	0						
12 Nov.	12	30.00	360	0	0	12	36.00	432	25	432	385	47
19 Nov.	8	30.00	240	0	0	8	36.00	288	17	288	257	31
TOTAL	**36**		**1146**	**0**	**0**	**36**		**1294**	**76**	**1294**	**1222**	**72**

a. Rounded to nearest whole number. See Table 4.

Note: All sales were in Danbatta Marketplace.

Table 4. M.'s overhead costs per sack, 1978

Period	Hemp Sack	Donkey Transport: Seller to Storeroom	Motor Transport to Outlet Market	Porters: Load Marmara	Unload Outlet Market	Total Per Sack
To Danbatta:						
1 Jan. – 14 Jan.:	.57	.30	.80	.10	.10	1.87
15 Jan. – 3 June:	.67	.30	.80	.10	.10	1.97
4 June – 10 June:	.73	.30	.80	.10	.10	2.03
11 June –24 June:	.73	.30	1.00	.10	.10	2.23
25 June – 7 Oct.:	.67	.30	1.00	.10	.10	2.17
8 Oct. – 3 Dec.:	.60	.30	1.00	.10	.10	2.10
4 Dec. – 31 Dec.:	.70	.30	1.00	.10	.10	2.20
To Funtua:						
11 Dec.:	1.10	.30	.50	.10	.20	2.20

Table 5. Summary: Purchases, sales and margins in trading of HH 7 (M.), Marmara, 1978

Season[a]:	Purchases		Storage Balance		Sales		Over-heads	Cost of Sales	Margin	
	sacks	N	sacks	N	sacks	N	N	N	N	%
GUINEACORN:										
End 1977			5	48						
PHDS[b]	237	6,044	24	334	218	6,492	428	6,186	306	5
FS	397	11,714	–	–	421	13,880	889	12,937	943	7
MH	73	1,856	–	–	73	2,038	155	2,011	27	1
GCH	37	665	–	–	37	816	80	745	71	9
Total	**744**	**20,279**	**–**	**–**	**749**	**23,226**	**1,552**	**21,879**	**1,347**	**6**
Storage for price rise:	25	364			25	838	54	418	420	50
% of all guineacorn sales:										3
% of total margin on guineacorn:										31
RICE:										
End 1977			6	96						
PHDS	–	–	6	96	–	–	–	–	–	–
FS	–	–	–	–	6	168	12	108	60	36
MH	49	984	–	–	49	1,276	107	1,091	185	14
GCH	–	–	–	–	–	–	–	–	–	–
Total	**49**	**984**	**–**	**–**	**55**	**1,444**	**119**	**1,199**	**245**	**17**
Storage for price rise:	6	96			6	168	12	108	60	36
% of all rice sales:										11
% of total margin on rice:										24
GROUNDNUTS:										
PHDS	–	–	–		–	–	–	–	–	–
FS	6	240	–	–	6	240	13	253	–13	–5
MH	10	306	–	–	10	334	21	327	7	2
GCH	20	600	–	–	20	720	42	642	78	11
Total	**36**	**1,146**	**–**	**–**	**36**	**1,294**	**76**	**1,222**	**72**	**6**

a. PHDS: postharvest dry season (1 January–30 April) FS: farming season (1 May–6 August) MH: minor harvests (7 August–5 November) GCH: guineacorn harvest (6 November–31 December).
b. 4 weeks not known, ending 29 January, and 12–26 March.

Appendix 6

Land Sales and Labour Use, Marmara, 1978 and 1979

Table 1. Sales of land by known farmers to the users of 1979, Marmara, data collected in 1979

		Sellers*1	Buyers*1	Field size
Small to Large Farmers:		0	0	0 acres
Small to Middle Farmers:	1	HH 103	HH 25	1.1 acres
	2	HH 79	HH 25	2.0 acres
	3	HH 94	HH 38	0.8 acres
Small to Small Farmers:	4	HH 105	HH 45	2.7 acres
	5	HH 94	HH 51	0.2 acres
	6	'SF'*2	HH 56 (M)	1.3 acres
	7	HH 92	HH 62 (M)	1.3 acres
	8	"SF'*2	HH 66 (M))	1.4 acres
Middle to Large Farmers:	9	HH 50	HH 2	3.6 acres
	10	HH 63	HH 6	0.1 acres
	11	HH 59	HH 9	2.1 acres
	12	HH 59	HH 9	2.0 acres
Middle to Middle Farmers:	13	HH 80	HH 25	2.5 acres
Middle to Small Farmers:	14	HH 36	HH 25	0.8 acres
	15	HH 34	HH 40 (M)	2.0 acres
	16	HH 46	HH 49 (M)	1.7 acres
Large to Large Farmers:	17	HH 16	HH 2	0.4 acres
	18	HH 16	HH 3	0.5 acres
	19	HH 82	HH 6	9.5 acres
Large to Middle Farmers:	20	HH 27	HH 7 (M)	1.5 acres
	21	LFNH 1*3	HH 20 (M)	2.3 acres
	22	HH 50	HH 40 (M)	1.7 acres
Large to Small Farmers:	23	FNH 2*3	HH 7 (M)	0.8 acres
	24	HH 59	HH 42 (M)	1.9 acres
	25	LFNH 3*3	HH 64	2.3 acres
TOTALS:		**19 Sellers**	**17 Buyers**	**46.5 acres**

*1 Described in terms of their index-numbered land rank in 1979 but grouped according to their positions at the actual times of transaction.

*2 Deceased in 1979.

*3 Large Farmers in neighbouring hamlets.

Note: (M) denotes 'immigrant'. All others were indigenes.

Source: Field notes and mapping for the land transfer record.

Table 2. Patterns of labour use among household heads for the weeding operation, Marmara, 1978

Types of labour use		Acreage		Adult workers		Acres	
		Mean	Median	No.*1	Age*2		
I. Own and hired							
A. Mainly hired	**10**	9	10	1	41	90	11%
B. Much supplementary hired	**2**	(11,10)		1	(55,50)	21	3%
C. Small supplementary hired	**7**	7	7	1	41	49	6%
II. Own, hired and family							
A. Mainly hired	**5**	35	36	3	48	174	22%
B. Much supplementary hired	**7**	18	13	4	56	123	15%
C. Small supplementary hired	**9**	14	12	3	53	124	15%
*3Frequent hired labourers (*under II.c*)	1	7		2	45	7	
III. Own and family	**21**	5	4	3	54	107	13%
*3Frequent hired labourers (*under III.*):	5	3	2	3	55	13	
IV. Own	**47**	3	2	1	44	121	15%
*3Frequent hired labourers: (*under IV*):	17	3	2	1	38	44	
Total:	**108**	8	4	2	47	**809*4**	**100%**
Total acreage:						←	
Percentage of hamlet acreage:							←

*1 Indicates the mean number of workers including the household head.
*2 Mean age of household head.
*3 Labourers who spent at least one-third of total weeding time on the farms of employers.
*4 The total is different from Table 3.1 because the acreages of farms have been rounded.

Table 3. The frequent labourers among household heads, Marmara, 1978

		Farm	Family size and dependent workers			
Farmer	**Age**	**Acres/*per capita***	**Size**	**Workforce**	**Off-farm occupation**	
HH 36	**45**	7.4/*1.1*	**7**	2	General labourer	I
HH 41	**30**	6.4/*1.6*	**4**	1	*none*	I
HH 43	**60**	6.3/*0.5*	**12**	3	Migrant labourer	I
HH 48	**40**	5.3/*0.9*	**6**	1	Grain porter	I
HH 58	**45**	3.7/*0.6*	**6**	1	*n.k.*	I
HH 64	**55**	3.3/*0.3*	**10**	4	Roofmaker	I
HH 67	**40**	3.1/*0.5*	**6**	1	Barber	I
HH 68	**30**	3.1/*1.0*	**3**	1	Migrant labourer	I
HH 69	**30**	3.1/*0.6*	**5**	1	General labourer	I
HH 72	**45**	2.8/*2.8*	**1**	1	Migrant labourer	M
HH 76	**35**	2.6/*0.5*	**5**	1	Migrant labourer	I
HH 78	**30**	2.5/*0.6*	**4**	1	Donkey transporter	I
HH 80	**45**	2.5/*0.6*	**4**	2	General labourer	I
HH 86	**40**	2.2/*2.2*	**1**	1	General labourer	M
HH 87	**40**	2.1/*0.3*	**6**	1	General labourer	I
HH 88	**35**	2.0/*0.4*	**5**	1	General labourer	I
HH 90	**45**	1.9/*0.4*	**5**	1	General labourer	I
HH 93	**35**	1.5/*0.3*	**5**	1	General labourer	I
HH 95	**60**	1.4/*0.2*	**6**	2	General labourer	M
HH 96	**30**	1.3/*0.6*	**2**	1	Grain mill labourer	M
HH 97	**50**	1.3/*0.3*	**5**	1	Kolanut trader	I
HH 98	**55**	1.3/*0.2*	**7**	2	*n.k.*	I
HH 100	**55**	1.1/*0.3*	**4**	1	Bicycle mechanic	M
Means: 42					I: 78%,	
Median: 40					M: 22%	
Hamlet:	**47 Means**				I: 75%,	
	45 Median				M: 25%	
					Indigene (I), or Immigrant (M):	

Table 4. The adult family workforce of gandaye, Marmara, 1978

	Farmer*1					Adult Family Workers						
						Married				Unmarried		
	Age	Decile	Holding	Dependents holdings*2	Gandu type*3	Sons	Brothers	Male kin	Wives	Sons	Brothers	Adult workers
MAGUZAWA:			**Acres**	**Acres**								
HH 4	70	**I.**	36.0	4.8	**P**	**1**			**3**			4*4
HH 11	60	**I.**	16.3	20.8	**K**			**1**	**5**			7
HH 19	55	**II.**	12.0	27.6	**P**	**1**			**5**			7
HH 33	55	**III.**	8.3	10.5	**P**	**2**			**4**			7
MUSLIM:												
HH 1	65	**I.**	49.9	5.5	**P**	**2**				**3**		6
HH 3	25	**I.**	41.5	1.4	**F**		**1**				**1**	3
HH 5	55	**I.**	35.4		**P**	**1**				**2**		4
HH 7	55	**I.**	22.4	3.5	**C**	**1**	**1**	**1**			**1**	5
HH 8	70	**I.**	21.1	3.8	**P**	**1**						2
HH 9	40	**I.**	19.0		**F**		**1**					2
HH 10	50	**I.**	16.4		**P**	**1**				**2**		4
HH 13	45	**II.**	13.2	0.6	**P**	**1**						2
HH 16	65	**II.**	12.6	2.8	**P**	**2**				**3**		6
HH 17	50	**II.**	12.3		**P**	**1**						2
HH 21	35	**II.**	11.8	3.0	**K**			**1**		**1**		2
HH 24	60	**III.**	11.2		**P**	**1**				**1**		3
HH 32	60	**III.**	8.5	3.4	**P**	**2**						3
HH 35	65	**IV.**	7.4	6.0	**P**	**2**				**1**		3
HH 36	45	**IV.**	7.4		**P**	**1**						2
HH 40	55	**IV.**	6.7		**P**	**1**						2
HH 43	60	**IV.**	6.3	2.2	**P**	**1**				**1**		3
HH 49	55	**V.**	5.1	0.7	**P**	**2**						3
HH 50	50	**V.**	4.9	0.9	**F**		**1**					2
HH 56	50	**VI.**	3.9		**F**		**1**					2
HH 62	60	**VI.**	3.3		**P**	**1**						2
HH 64	55	**VI.**	3.3		**P**	**1**				**2**		4
HH 74	70	**VII.**	2.7		**P**	**2**				**1**		3*4
HH 82	55	**VIII.**	2.3		**P**	**1**						2
HH 95	60	**IX.**	1.4		**P**	**1**						2

*1 Listed according to their index-numbered land rank, as in other tables.

*2 This list includes both gayauna and personally acquired fields. It is incomplete, as gayauni were sometimes measured as part of gandu heads' fields.

*3 P = paternal, F=fraternal, K=kin, C=composite

*4 Does not include the aging household head. All others include the household head.

Glossary of Key Hausa Words in the Text

I. *Talakawa*	sing. *Talaka.* The people without entitlement to the political offices of the Hausa-speaking emirates; more generally, the 'common people'.
II. *Masu sarauta*	sing. *Mai sarauta.* The people holding any political office (*sarauta*), with the corresponding powers, of the Hausa-speaking emirates; more generally, the rulers (see *sarakuna*, below).
aboki	pl. *abokai.* A friend.
abokin ciniki	A commercial friend; more specifically, a person with whom is exchanged, on the basis of trust, services useful to trade (including borrowing facilities).
adashi	A rotating contribution club organized by women, in which each member agrees to pay a fixed money sum, weekly or biweekly, a different member drawing the total amount on each occasion, until each has had her/his share.
alkali	pl. *alkalai.* An official judge for the administration of Islamic law.
attajirai	sing. *attajiri.* A wealthy merchant.

aure	Marriage.
azumi	The Muslim month of fasting, or Ramadan.
bashi	A loan, usually though not necessarily of money, which is not repayable for some time; in Marmara, use of the term implied that some form of interest, or return apart from the loaned sum, was due to the lender.
bara	pl. *barori.* A 'servant', in a sense which implied more complete subordination and dependence than the looser term *yaro* (below).
bawa	pl. *bayi.* A slave.
bazawara	A formerly married woman; a divorcee.
biki	pl. *bukukuwa.* (1) A feast in celebration of a marriage or naming ceremony. (2) Linked gifts in cash or kind, given at marriage and naming ceremonies, as part of a voluntary, reciprocal gift relationship between two persons, often unrelated by kinship.
budurwa	An unmarried girl of marriageable age.
cefane	(1) The ingredients for the sauce into which the porridge (*tuwo,* below) of staple grain is dipped. (2) In Marmara, daily living requirements for eating and drinking apart from the staple grain; it included meat, water and (when used) firewood.
ciniki	Trading, a trade transaction, or the process of bargaining.
dillali	pl. *dillalai.* (1) A broker. (2) Someone who specializes in acting as an intermediary in a particular line of trade, in order to earn commission (*la'ada*).
dukiya	Wealth.
gandu	pl. *gandaye.* (1) The customary labour relationship in farming between the head of a household and his adult dependents, involving mutual obligations. (2) Any of the large fields of a farmer.
gayauna	pl. *gayauni.* A farm plot allotted by a household head to a dependent member of his *gandu* group (above), for the dependent's own use; rights over the output appear

	to vary with the locality that has been researched (see Chapter 3).
gida	pl. *gidaje*. (1) The people who constitute a household by living together, sharing the same food supply, and acknowledging a common authority figure or household head. (2) The buildings and courtyard wherein these people live.
gudummawa	(in southern Katsina, also *gudumwa*) (1) Help. (2) A gift given, especially by close kin, to those responsible for organising a marriage or naming ceremony. In Marmara, the term implied a general obligation for the recipient to reciprocate at the donor's ceremonies, but not the standardized pattern of gift and return-gift characteristic of *biki* (above).
hali	(1) Character. (2) Circumstances.
hakimi	pl. *hakimai*. (1) Before the colonial period, a high official appointed by an emir to supervise, and collect taxes from, an area. (2) Since the colonial period, a district head. A generic term, the specific local title attached to the office is often used (e.g., *Galadiman Katsina* for the *hakimi* of Malumfashi District).
haraji	The annual community tax levied on all able-bodied males aged sixteen and over. As recently as 1966, the amount varied between individuals, being determined by the village head (Hill 1972: Glossary); but by 1977, the same sum was due from every adult male.
hidima	(1) The responsibility of one person to another. (2) The service of one person to another.
jali	(1) Trading capital. (2) Investment funds. (3) A medium- or long-term loan given as funds for investment.
jingina	The pledging or pawning of an item or a field in return for a sum of money.
la'ada	A commission paid to any broker in a transaction.
mai gari	(1) The official headman of a town or village (*gari*), responsible to the *hakimi* (above) for tax collection. (2) Since the colonial period, a village head.

mai gida Household head.

mai unguwa pl. *masu unguwa*. The official headman of the third and smallest area of jurisdiction in the Hausa-speaking emirates, responsible to the village head for tax collection; in rural areas, *unguwa* refers to a 'hamlet' and in urban areas, to a ward. Whereas district heads and village heads are drawn from families among the *sarakuna* (below), hamlet heads are usually appointed from among the common people – the *talakawa* (above).

malam pl. *malamai* (anglicized to 'mallam', 'mallams'). (1) An Islamic religious teacher or scholar. (2) Any person with some Islamic learning. (3) Any teacher. (4) A respectful form of address to any educated man or official, whether or not he has Islamic education.

rance The universal term for a short-period loan of money or of a thing not itself to be returned, to tide the borrower over until he acquires the means to repay by earning cash or selling an item; in Marmara, periods of repayment were flexible.

riba (1) Money profit (legal by Muslim law). (2) Money interest (illegal by Muslim law). (The spelling is the same for both uses, though the pronunciation given in dictionaries is slightly different for each. See Abraham 1962 and Robinson 1925.)

sadaka The general term for charity or alms; in Marmara, it was also used to indicate any small gift given in the name of God.

sana'a Any occupation, trade or profession apart from farming.

sarki (1) Any official chief (including an emir) or official headman in charge of an activity. (2) Formerly, an informal term for the leader of a group activity (e.g., *sarkin gandu,* or 'head of the farming unit [on behalf] of the household head'). (3) Currently, a title given by an emir to a man who has distinguished himself in an activity (e.g., *Sarkin Noma* [to a prominent farmer]).

sarakuna (1) Plural of *sarki*. (2) Those people who are eligible for the traditional political offices of the Hausa-speaking

	emirates; more generally, the ruling class, in contradistinction to the common people (*talakawa,* above). Ruling class families speak Hausa as their primary or only language, but they are descended from *malamai* (above) and pastoralists whose primary language was Fula and who conquered the Hausa-speaking Maguzawa kingdoms in the early nineteenth century.
shari'a	The Islamic legal code, as interpreted by the Muslim judges (*alkalai,* above).
suna	(1) Name. (2) Muslim naming ceremony.
tafsiri	Learned commentary on the Qur'an.
tuwo	The porridge made from the flour of guineacorn, millet, maize or rice; it resembles a well-set pudding, and is usually dipped by the handful into a sauce (*miya*), but it may be cut and served in slices.
uba	Father.
uban gida	(1) Literally, the 'father of the house'. (2) Patron. (3) The master of a 'servant' (*bara,* above).
uwa	Mother.
uwar gida	(1) Senior or only wife. (2) Respectful form of address to any wife of a household head.
yarinya	pl. *'yam mata.* (1) A girl. (2) An idiom for a marriageable young woman.
yaro	pl. *yara.* (1) A boy. (2) A client. (3) A general term for any male subordinate or dependent.
zaka	The Islamic religious tithe on farm produce, now voluntary, payable to the *malamai* (above) and the poor of the donor's choice.

Bibliography

Published Books and Articles

Abbott, J. 1987. *Agricultural Marketing Enterprises for the Developing World.* Cambridge: Cambridge University Press.

Abraham, R. 1962. *Dictionary of the Hausa Language.* London: University of London Press.

Adeleye, R. 1971. 'Hausaland and Borno 1600–1800', in J. Ajayi and M. Crowder (eds), *History of West Africa,* vol. 1. London: Longman, pp. 264–301.

Anderson, P. 1978. *L'Etat Absolutiste: Ses Origines et Ses Voies.* Paris: François Maspero.

Andrae, G., and B. Beckman. 1987. *Industry Goes Farming: The Nigerian Raw Material Crisis and the Case of Textiles and Cotton.* Research Report No. 80. Uppsala: Scandinavian Institute of African Studies.

Anthony, K., and B. Johnston. 1968. 'Field Study of Agricultural Change: Northern Katsina'. Preliminary Report No. 6: Economic, Cultural and Technical Determinants of Agricultural Change in Tropical Africa. Food Research Institute, Stanford University (cyclostyled).

Anyang' N'yong'o, P. 1981. Editorial, and 'What "the friends of the peasants" Are and How They Pose the Question of the Peasantry'. *Review of African Political Economy* 20: 1–7, 17–26.

Bailey, F. 1957. *Caste and the Economic Frontier: A Village in Highland Orissa.* Manchester: Manchester University Press.

———. 1969. *Stratagems and Spoils.* Oxford: Blackwell.

Bailey, F.G. 1964. 'Capital, Saving and Credit in Highland Orissa (India)', in R. Firth and B. Yamey (eds), *Capital, Saving and Credit in Peasant Societies.* London: George Allen and Unwin, pp. 104–32.

Barkow, J. 1973. 'Muslims and Maguzawa in North Central State, Nigeria: An Ethnographic Comparison'. *Canadian Journal of African Studies* 7.

Barth, F. 1964. 'Capital, Investment and the Social Structure of a Pastoral Nomadic Group in South Persia', in R. Firth and B. Yamey (eds), *Capital, Saving and Credit in Peasant Societies*. London: George Allen and Unwin, pp. 69–81.

———. 1966. *Models of Social Organisation*. London: Royal Anthropological Institute, Occasional Paper No. 23.

———. 1967. 'Economic Spheres in Darfur', in R. Firth (ed.), *Themes in Economic Anthropology*. A.S.A. Monographs No. 6. London: Tavistock, pp. 149–74.

Bayart, J-F. 1991. 'Finishing with the Idea of the Third World: The Concept of the Political Trajectory', in J. Manor (ed.), *Rethinking Third World Politics*. London: Longman, pp. 51–71.

———. 1993. *The State in Africa: The Politics of the Belly*. London: Longman.

Beckman, B. 1987. 'Public Investment and Agrarian Transformation in Northern Nigeria', in M. Watts (ed.), *State, Oil, and Agriculture in Nigeria*. Berkeley: Institute of International Studies, University of California, pp. 110–37.

Bernstein, H. 1977. 'Notes on Capital and Peasantry'. *Review of African Political Economy* 10: 60–73.

———. 1979. 'African Peasantries: A Theoretical Framework'. *Journal of Peasant Studies* 6(4): 421–43.

———. 2005. 'Considering Africa's Agrarian Questions'. *Historical Materialism* 12(4): 115–44.

Berry, S. 1985. *Fathers Work for Their Sons: Accumulation, Mobility and Class Formation in an Extended Yoruba Community*. Berkeley: University of California Press.

———. 1993. *No Condition Is Permanent*. Madison: University of Wisconsin Press.

Bohannan, P. 1955. 'Some Principles of Exchange and Investment among the Tiv'. *American Anthropologist* 57(1): 60–70.

———. 1959. 'The Impact of Money on an African Subsistence Economy'. *Journal of Economic History* 19(4): 491–503 [reprinted in G. Dalton (ed.). 1967. *Tribal and Peasant Economies*. New York: Natural History Press].

Bohannan, P., and G. Dalton (eds). 1962. *Markets in Africa*. Evanston: Northwestern University Press.

Boissevain, J. 1974. *Friends of Friends*. Oxford: Basil Blackwell.

Bourdieu, P. 1990. *The Logic of Practice*. Cambridge: Polity Press.

Buntjer, B. 1970a. 'The Changing Structure of Gandu', in M. Mortimore (ed.), *Zaria and its Region: A Nigerian Savanna City and Its Environs*, Occasional Paper No. 4, Department of Geography, Ahmadu Bello University, Zaria, Nigeria.

———. 1970b. 'Aspects of Change in Rural Zaria'. *Samaru Agricultural Newsletter* 12(2). Zaria, Nigeria: Institute for Agricultural Research: 26–29.

Clammer, J. (ed.). 1978. *The New Economic Anthropology*. London: Macmillan.

Clough, P. 1981. 'Farmers and Traders in Hausaland'. *Development and Change* 12(2): 273–92.

———. 1985. 'The Social Relations of Grain Marketing in Northern Nigeria'. *Review of African Political Economy* 34: 16–34.

———. 1999. 'The Relevance of Religion and Culture to Commercial Accumulation: Fieldwork on Muslim Hausa Exchange and Agricultural Trade in Northern Nigeria', in B. Harriss-White (ed.), *Agricultural Markets From Theory to Practice*. London: Macmillan: 305–22.

———. 2003. 'Polygyny and the Rural Accumulation of Capital: Testing a Model Based on Continuing Research in Northern Nigeria'. *Etnofoor* 16(1): 5–29.
———. 2009. 'The Impact of Rural Political Economy on Gender Relations in Islamizing Hausaland, Nigeria'. *Africa* 79(4): 595–613.
———. 2012. 'Immunology, the Human Self, and the Neoliberal Regime'. *Cultural Anthropology* 27(1): 138–43.
Clough, P., and G. Williams. 1987. 'Decoding Berg: The World Bank in Rural Northern Nigeria', in M. Watts (ed.), *State, Oil, and Agriculture in Nigeria.* Berkeley: Institute of International Studies, University of California, pp. 168–201.
Clyde Mitchell, J. 1983. 'Case and Situation Analysis'. *Sociological Review* 31(2): 187–211.
Cohen, A. 1969. *Custom and Politics in Urban Africa: A Study of Hausa Migrants in Yoruba Towns.* London: Routledge and Kegan Paul.
Cooper, R. 1978. 'Dynamic Tension: Symbiosis and Contradiction in Hmong Social Relations', in J. Clammer (ed.), *The New Economic Anthropology.* London: Macmillan, pp. 138–75.
Cowen, M. 1981. 'The Agrarian Problem'. *Review of African Political Economy* 20: 57–73.
Cox, T. 1984. 'Class Analysis of the Russian Peasantry: The Research of Kritsman and His School'. *Journal of Peasant Studies* 11(2).
de Waal, A. 1989. *Famine That Kills.* Oxford: Clarendon Press.
Dupre, G. and P.P. Rey. 1980. 'Reflections on the Pertinence of a Theory of the History of Exchange', in H. Wolpe (ed.), *The Articulation of Modes of Production.* London: Routledge and Kegan Paul, pp. 128–60.
Edel, M. and A. Edel. 1959. *Anthropology and Ethics.* Springfield: Charles C. Thomas.
Elster, J. 1989. *Nuts and Bolts.* Cambridge: Cambridge University Press.
Ensminger, J. 1992. *Making a Market: The Institutional Transformation of an African Society.* Cambridge: Cambridge University Press.
Flynn, P. 1974. 'Class, Clientalism, and Coercion: Some Mechanisms of Internal Dependency and Control'. *Journal of Commonwealth and Comparative Politics* 12(2).
Forde, D. 1946. 'The North: The Hausa', in M. Perham (ed.), *The Native Economies of Nigeria,* vol. 1. London: Faber, pp. 123–215.
Forman, P., and T. Riegelhaupt. 1970. 'Market Place and Marketing System: Toward a Theory of Peasant Economic Integration'. *Comparative Studies in Society and History* 12.
Forrest, T. 1981. 'Agricultural Policies in Nigeria, 1900–1978', in J. Heyer et al. (eds), *Rural Development in Tropical Africa.* London: Macmillan.
———. 1986. 'The Political Economy of Civil Rule and the Economic Crisis in Nigeria 1979–84'. *Review of African Political Economy* 35: 4–26.
———. 1993 (1995, rev. ed.). *Politics and Economic Development in Nigeria.* Boulder: Westview Press.
———. 1994. *The Advance of African Capital: The Growth of Nigerian Private Enterprise.* Edinburgh: Edinburgh University Press for the International African Institute.
Foster, G. 1965. 'Peasant Society and the Image of the Limited Good'. *American Anthropologist* 67(2).

Foster-Carter, A. 1978. 'Can We Articulate "Articulation"?', in J. Clammer (ed.), *The New Economic Anthropology*. London: Macmillan, pp. 210–49.
Foucault, M. 1972. *The Archaeology of Knowledge*. London: Routledge.
———. 1978. *The History of Sexuality, vol. 1*. London: Penguin.
———. 1983. 'Afterword: The Subject and Power', in H. Dreyfus and P. Rabinow, *Beyond Structuralism and Hermeneutics*. Chicago: University of Chicago Press, pp. 208–26.
Frank, A.G. 1967. *Capitalism and Underdevelopment in Latin America*. New York: Monthly Review Press.
———. 1969. *Latin America: Underdevelopment and Revolution*. New York: Monthly Review Press.
Frankenberg, R. 1967. 'Economic Anthropology: One Anthropologist's View', in *Themes in Economic Anthropology*, A.S.A. Monographs No. 6. London: Tavistock, pp. 47–89.
Geertz. C. 1963. *Peddlers and Princes*. Chicago: University of Chicago Press.
———. 1973. *The Interpretation of Cultures*. New York: Basic Books.
———. 1984. 'Culture and Social Change: The Indonesian Case'. *Man* (n.s.) 19: 511–32.
Gilsenan, M. 2005. *Recognizing Islam: Religion and Society in the Modern Middle East*. London and New York: I.B. Tauris (rev. ed.).
Gluckman, M. 1961. 'Ethnographic Data in British Social Anthropology'. *Sociological Review* 9: 5–17.
Goddard, A. 1970. 'Land Tenure and Agricultural Development in Hausaland'. *Samaru Agricultural Newsletter* 12(2). Zaria, Nigeria: Institute for Agricultural Research: 30–39.
———. 1973. *Changing Family Structures among the Rural Hausa*. Samaru Research Bulletin No. 196. Zaria, Nigeria: Institute for Agricultural Research, Samaru.
Goddard, A., D. Norman, J. Fine, W. Kroeker and D. Pryor. 1976. *A Socio-economic Survey of Three Villages in the Sokoto Close-settled Zone. Part 3*. Input-output study Vol. I: Text. Samaru Miscellaneous Paper 64. Zaria, Nigeria: Institute for Agricultural Research.
Goodman, D. and M. Redclift. 1981. *From Peasant to Proletarian: Capitalist Development and Agrarian Transitions*. Oxford: Basil Blackwell.
Graziano, L. 1973. 'Patron-Client Relationships in Southern Italy'. *European Journal of Political Research* 1.
Greenberg, J. 1941. 'Some Aspects of Negro-Mohammedan Culture-Contact among the Hausa'. *American Anthropologist* 43.
———. 1946. *The Influence of Islam on a Sudanese Religion*. New York: Monograph of the American Ethnological Society.
———. 1947. 'Islam and Clan Organization among the Hausa'. *Southwestern Journal of Anthropology* 3: 193–211.
Grove, A. 1957. *Land and Population in Katsina Province with Special Reference to Bindawa Village in Dan Yusufu District, 1952*. Kaduna, Nigeria: Government Printer.
Gudeman, S. 1986. *Economics as Culture: Models and Metaphors of Livelihood*. London: Routledge and Kegan Paul.
———. 2001. *The Anthropology of Economy: Community, Market, and Culture*. Oxford: Blackwell Publishers.

——. 2008. *Economy's Tension: The Dialectics of Community and Market*. Oxford and New York: Berghahn Books.
Gumi, Sheikh Abubakar, with Ismaila Tsiga. 1992. *Where I Stand*. Ibadan: Spectrum Books.
Guyer, J. 1993. 'Wealth in People and Self-Realisation in Equatorial Africa'. *Man* (n.s.) 28(2): 243–65.
——. 1995. "Wealth in People/Wealth in Things: An Introduction." *Journal of African History* 36: 83–90.
——. 1997. *An African Niche Economy: Farming to Feed Ibadan 1968–88*. Edinburgh: Edinburgh University Press for the International African Institute.
——. 2004a. *Marginal Gains. Monetary Transactions in Atlantic Africa*. Chicago: University of Chicago Press: 115–30.
——. 2004b. 'Niches, Margins and Profits: Persisting with Heterogeneity'. *African Economic History* 32: 173–91.
Guyer, J. and S. Eno Belinga. 1995. 'Wealth in People as Wealth in Knowledge. Accumulation and Composition in Equatorial Africa'. *Journal of African History* 36: 91–120.
Guyer, J. and E. Stiansen (eds). 1999. *Currency, Credit, and Culture: African Financial Institutions in Historical Perspective*. Uppsala: Nordic African Institute Publications.
Hammersley, M. 1992. *What's Wrong With Ethnography*? London: Routledge.
Harriss, B. 1982. *The Marketing of Foodgrains in the West African Sudano-Sahelian States*. Economics Program Progress Report No. 31. Andhra Pradresh, India: ICRISAT.
Hart, K. 1982. *The Political Economy of West African Agriculture*. Cambridge University Press.
Hays, H. 1975. *The Marketing and Storage of Food Grains in Northern Nigeria*. Samaru Miscellaneous Paper 50. Zaria, Nigeria: Institute for Agricultural Research.
Helleiner, G.K. 1966. *Peasant Agriculture, Government and Economic Growth in Nigeria*. Economic Growth Center at Yale University. Homewood: Irwin.
Hill, P. 1970. *Studies in Rural Capitalism in West Africa*. Cambridge: Cambridge University Press.
——. 1972. *Rural Hausa: A Village and a Setting*. Cambridge: Cambridge University Press.
——. 1977. *Population, Prosperity and Poverty: Rural Kano 1900 and 1970*. Cambridge: Cambridge University Press.
——. 1982. *Dry Grain Farming Families: Hausaland (Nigeria) and Karnataka (India) Compared*. Cambridge: Cambridge University Press.
——. 1986. *Development Economics on Trial: The Anthropological Case for a Prosecution*. Cambridge: Cambridge University Press.
Hobsbawm, E.J. 1964. *Introduction to Karl Marx – Pre-capitalist Economic Formations*. London: Lawrence and Wishart.
Hogendorn, J. 1976. 'The Vent-for-Surplus Model and African Cash Agriculture to 1914'. *Savanna* 5(1): 15–27.
Hopkins, A.G. 1973. *An Economic History of West Africa*. London: Longman.
Horton, R. 1967. 'African Traditional Thought and Western Science'. *Africa* 37(1).

——. 1971. 'African Conversion'. *Africa* 41(2).
——. 1975. 'On the Rationality of Conversion'. *Africa* 45(3): 219–35.
Hunwick, J. 1976. 'Songhay, Borno and Hausaland in the Sixteenth Century', in J. Ajayi and M. Crowder (eds), *History of West Africa*, vol. 1. London: Longman, pp. 264–301.
Iliffe, J. 1971. *Agricultural Change in Modern Tanganyika*. Historical Association of Tanzania Paper No. 10. Nairobi: East Africa Publishing House.
——. 1979. *A Modern History of Tanganyika*. Cambridge: Cambridge University Press.
——. 1995. *Africans: The History of a Continent*. Cambridge: Cambridge University Press.
Ingold, T. (ed.). 1996. *Key Debates in Anthropology*. London: Routledge.
James, W. 1996. '1990 Debate: Human Worlds are Culturally Constructed – For the Motion', in T. Ingold (ed.), *Key Debates in Anthropology*. London: Routledge: 105–12.
Johnson, M. 1970. 'The Cowrie Currencies of West Africa'. *Journal of African History* 11(1 and 3): Part I, pp. 17–49, and Part II, pp. 331–53.
Kaduna State of Nigeria. 1976. *Statistical Yearbook*. Kaduna: Ministry of Economic Development, Statistics Division.
Kahn, J. 1975. 'Economic Scale and the Cycle of Petty Commodity Production in Western Sumatra', in M. Bloch (ed.), *Marxist Analyses and Social Anthropology*. A.S.A. Studies No. 2. London: Malaby, pp. 137–58.
Kautsky, K. 1980. 'Summary of Selected Parts of Kautsky's The Agrarian Question' (translated by J. Banaji), in H. Wolpe (ed.), *The Articulation of Modes of Production*. London: Routledge and Kegan Paul, pp. 128–60.
King, J. 1939. 'Mixed Farming in Northern Nigeria'. *Empire Journal of Experimental Agriculture* 7.
Kohnert, D. 1979. 'Rural Class Differentiation in Nigeria – Theory and Practice: A Quantitative Approach in the Case of Nupeland'. *Afrika Spectrum* 79(3): 295–315.
Kriesel, H. 1968. *Cotton Marketing in Nigeria*. Consortium for the Study of Nigerian Rural Development. East Lansing: Michigan State University.
Laclau, E. 1971. 'Feudalism and Capitalism in Latin America'. *New Left Review* 67.
Last, M. 1967. *The Sokoto Caliphate*. London: Longman.
——. 1970. 'Aspects of Administration and Dissent in Hausaland, 1800–1968'. *Africa* 40.
——. 1979. 'Some economic aspects of conversion in Hausaland (Nigeria)', in N. Levtzion (ed.), *Conversion to Islam*. New York: Holmes and Meier, pp. 236–46.
LeClair, E. 1968. 'Economic Theory and Economic Anthropology', in E. LeClair and H. Schneider (eds), *Economic Anthropology*. New York: Holt, Rinehart and Winston, pp. 187–207 [reprinted from *American Anthropologist* 64: 1179–203].
Loimeier, R. 1997. 'Islamic Reform and Political Change: The Example of Abubakar Gumi and the Yan Izala Movement in Northern Nigeria', in D. Westerlund and E. Evers Rosander (eds), *African Islam and Islam in Africa*. London: Hurst, pp. 286–307.

Long, N. 1975. 'Structural Dependency, Modes of Production and Economic Brokerage in Rural Peru', in I. Oxaal, T. Barnett, and D. Booth (eds), *Beyond the Sociology of Development*. London: Routledge and Kegan Paul.

——. 1977. *An Introduction to the Sociology of Rural Development*. London: Tavistock.

Lovejoy, P. 1978. 'Plantations in the Economy of the Sokoto Caliphate'. *Journal of African History* 19(3): 341–68.

Lovejoy, P. and J. Hogendorn. 1993. *Slow Death for Slavery: The Course of Abolition in Northern Nigeria*. Cambridge: Cambridge University Press.

Lutz, C. and L. Abu-Lughod. 1990. Introduction to C. Lutz and L. Abu-Lughod (eds), *Language and the Politics of Emotion*. Cambridge: Cambridge University Press, pp. 1–10.

Marx, K. 1967 [1848]. *The Communist Manifesto*. London: Penguin.

——. 1976. (1867). *Capital, vol. 1* (trans. Ben Fowkes). Harmondsworth: Penguin Books.

Masquelier, A. 1996. 'Identity, Alterity and Ambiguity in a Nigerien Community: Competing Definitions of "True" Islam', in R. Werbner and T. Ranger (eds), *Postcolonial Identities in Africa*. London: Zed Books.

Mauss, M. 1925. (translated by I. Cunnison, 1954). *The Gift*. London: Cohen and West.

Meek, C.K. 1949. *Land Law and Custom in the Colonies*. London: Oxford University Press.

Meillassoux, C. 1980. 'From Reproduction to Production: A Marxist Approach to Economic Anthropology' (reprinted from *Economy and Society* 1[1]), in H. Wolpe (ed.), *The Articulation of Modes of Production*. London: Routledge and Kegan Paul, pp. 189–201.

——. 1981. *Maidens, Meal and Money*. Cambridge: Cambridge University Press.

Miers, S. and I. Kopytoff (eds). 1977. *Slavery in Africa: Historical and Anthropological Perspectives*. Madison: University of Wisconsin Press.

Mommsen, W. 1987. 'Personal Conduct and Societal Change', in S. Lash and S. Whimster (eds), *Max Weber, Rationality and Modernity*. London: Allen and Unwin.

Mortimore, M.J. 1968. 'Population Distribution, Settlement and Soils in Kano Province, Northern Nigeria, 1931–62', in J. Caldwell and C. Okonjo, (eds), *The Population of Tropical Africa*. London: Longman.

Nadel, S. 1942. *A Black Byzantium*. Oxford: Oxford University Press.

Nicolas, G. (n.d.) 'La pratique traditionnelle du credit au sein d'une societe subsaharienne (Vallee de Maradi, Niger)'. *Cultures et Developpement*. Catholic University of Louvain.

——. 1964. *La vallee du Gulbi de Maradi: enquete socio-economique*. Documents des Etudes Nigeriennes No. 16 IFAN-CNRS, Editions du Centre Universitaire de Polycopiage de l'A.G.E.B., Bordeaux (cyclo-styled) (co-author G. Mainet).

——. 1968. *Problemes poses par l'introduction de techniques agricoles modernes au sein d'une societe africaine: Vallee de Maradi, Niger*. Faculty of Letters and Human Sciences, University of Bordeaux (cyclostyled). (Co-authors H. Magaji and M. dan Mouche).

Njonjo, A. 1981. 'The Kenyan Peasantry: A Re-assessment'. *Review of African Political Economy* 20: 27–40.

Norman, D. 1967 (1973). *An Economic Study of Three Villages in Zaria Province: 1. Land and Labour Relationships; 2. Input-Output Relationships; 3. Maps.* Samaru Miscellaneous Papers 19, 23, 33. Zaria, Nigeria: Institute for Agricultural Research.

———. 1970. 'Rural Economy in the Zaria Area, with Special Reference to Agriculture', in M. Mortimore (ed.), *Zaria and Its Region: A Nigerian Savanna City and Its Environs.* Occasional Paper No. 4, Department of Geography, Ahmadu Bello University, Zaria, Nigeria.

North, D. 1981. *Structure and Change in Economic History.* New York: Norton.

———. 1990. *Institutions, Institutional Change and Economic Performance.* Cambridge: Cambridge University Press.

Paine, R. 1963. 'Entrepreneurial Activity without Its Profits', in F. Barth (ed.), *The Role of the Entrepreneur in Social Change in Northern Norway.* Bergen: Norwegian Universities Press.

———. 1974. *Second Thoughts About Barth's Models.* Royal Anthropological Institute, Occasional Paper No. 32.

Pallot, J. 1982. *Social Change and Peasant Land-holding in Pre-Revolutionary Russia.* Research Paper No. 30, School of Geography, University of Oxford.

Parkin, D. 1972. *Palms, Wine, and Witnesses: Public Spirit and Private Gain in an African Farming Community.* London: Intertext Books.

Parry, J. and M. Bloch (eds). 1989. *Money and the Morality of Exchange.* Cambridge: Cambridge University Press.

Pearse, A. 1971. 'Metropolis and Peasant: The Expansion of the Urban Industrial Complex and the Changing Rural Structure', in T. Shanin (ed.), *Peasants and Peasant Societies.* Harmondsworth: Penguin Books.

Plattner, S. (ed.). 1989. *Economic Anthropology.* Stanford: Stanford University Press.

Pocock, D.F. 1986. 'The Ethnography of Morals'. *International Journal of Moral and Social Studies* 1(1): 3–20.

Post, K. 1963. *The Nigerian Federal Election of 1959: Politics and Administration in a Developing Political System.* London: Oxford University Press.

Pratt, J. 1994. *The Rationality of Rural Life: Economic and Cultural Change in Tuscany.* Chur: Harwood Academic Publishers.

Ranger, T. 1978. 'Growing from the Roots: Reflections on Peasant Research in Central and Southern Africa'. *Journal of Southern African Studies* 5(1).

Raynaut, C. 1975. 'Le cas de la region de Maradi (Niger)', in J. Copans (ed.), *Secheresses et Famines du Sahel,* vol. 2, *Paysans et Nomades.* Paris: Maspero.

———. 1976. 'Transformation du systeme de production et inegalite economique: le cas d'un village Haoussa (Niger)'. *Canadian Journal of African Studies* 10(2): 279–306.

———. 1977. 'Circulation monetaire et evolutions des structures socio-economiques chez les Haoussas du Niger'. *Africa* 47.

Richards, P. (n.d.) 'Local Strategies for Coping with Hunger: Central Sierra Leone and Northern Nigeria Compared'. *African Affairs.*

———. 1985. *Indigenous Agricultural Revolution.* London: Hutchinson.

Robinson, C. 1925 (4th ed.). *Dictionary of the Hausa Language.* Cambridge: Cambridge University Press.

Ross, P. 1987. 'Land as a Right to Membership: Land Tenure Dynamics in a Peripheral Area of the Kano Close-settled Zone', in M. Watts (ed.) *State, Oil, and Agriculture in Nigeria.* Berkeley: Institute of International Studies, University of California, pp. 223–47.

Rural Economy Research Unit (RERU). 1972. *Farm Income Levels in the Northern States of Nigeria.* Samaru Miscellaneous Paper 35. Zaria, Nigeria: Institute for Agricultural Research.

Ruxton, F.H. 1916. *Maliki Law.* London: Luzak.

Sahlins, M. 1974. *Stone Age Economics.* London: Tavistock.

Schatzl, L. 1973. *Industrialization in Nigeria.* Munich: Weltforum Verlag.

Schumpeter, J. 1976 [1943]. *Capitalism, Socialism and Democracy.* London: George Allen and Unwin.

Scott, J.C. 1976. *The Moral Economy of the Peasant.* New Haven: Yale University Press.

———. 1985. *Weapons of the Weak: Everyday Forms of Peasant Resistance.* New Haven: Yale University Press.

Shenton, R. 1986. *The Development of Capitalism in Northern Nigeria.* London: James Currey.

Shenton, R., and L. Lennihan. 1981. 'Capital and Class: Peasant Differentiation in Northern Nigeria'. *Journal of Peasant Studies* 9(1).

Shenton, R., and M. Watts. 1979. 'Capitalism and Hunger in Northern Nigeria'. *Review of African Political Economy* 15/16.

Silverman, S. 1965. 'Patronage and Community-Nation Relationships in Central Italy'. *Ethnology* 4(2).

———. 1970. '"Exploitation" in Rural Central Italy'. *Comparative Studies in Society and History* 12.

Smith, A. 1976. 'The Early States of the Central Sudan', in J. Ajayi and M. Crowder (eds), *History of West Africa,* vol. 1. London: Longman, pp. 152–95.

Smith, M.G. 1955. *The Economy of Hausa Communities of Zaria.* Colonial Research Series No. 16. London: HMSO.

———. 1959. 'The Hausa System of Social Status'. *Africa* 22.

———. 1962. 'Exchange and Marketing among the Hausa', in P. Bohannan and G. Dalton (eds), *Markets in Africa.* Evanston: Northwestern University Press.

———. 1964. 'Historical and Cultural Conditions of Political Corruption among the Hausa'. *Comparative Studies in Society and History* 6.

Smith, M. 1954. *Baba of Karo: A Woman of the Muslim Hausa.* London: Faber and Faber.

Stenning, D. 1958. 'Household Viability among the Pastoral Fulani', in J. Goody, *The Developmental Cycle of Domestic Groups.* Cambridge: Cambridge University Press, pp. 92–119.

Tiffen, M. 1971. *Changing Patterns of Farming in Gombe Emirate.* Samaru Miscellaneous Paper No. 32. Zaria, Nigeria: Institute for Agricultural Research.

Todorov, T. and M. Bakhtin. 1981. *Le Principe Dialogique, suivi des Ecrits du Cercle de Bakhtin.* Paris: Seuil.

van Apeldoorn, J. 1981. *Perspectives on Drought and Famine in Nigeria.* London: George Allen and Unwin.

Vansina, J. 1990. *Paths in the Rainforests: Toward a History of Political Tradition in Equatorial Africa.* Madison: University of Wisconsin Press.
Vigo, A. 1965. *A Survey of Agricultural Credit in the Northern Region of Nigeria.* Nigeria Ministry of Agriculture, Kaduna (microfilm in the Institute for Agriculture Library, Samaru, Nigeria).
Wallace, T. 1978. 'The Concept of Gandu: How Useful Is It in Understanding Labour Relations in Rural Hausa Society?' *Savanna* 7(2).
Wallis, J. and D. North. 1986. 'Measuring the Transaction Sector in the American Economy, 1870–1970', in S. Engerman and R. Gallman (eds), *Long-Term Factors in American Economic Growth.* Chicago: University of Chicago Press, pp. 95–161.
Watts, M. 1983. *Silent Violence: Food, Famine, and Peasantry in Northern Nigeria.* Berkeley: University of California Press.
——, (ed.). 1987. *State, Oil, and Agriculture in Nigeria.* Berkeley: Institute of International Studies, University of California.
Weber, M. 1949 [1904]. '"Objectivity" in Social Science and Social Policy', in E. Shils and H. Finch (trans. and eds), *Max Weber: The Methodology of the Social Sciences.* Glencoe: Free Press, pp. 49–112.
——. 1978. *Economy and Society, vol. 1.* Los Angeles: University of California Press.
——. 1992 [1930]. *The Protestant Ethic and the Spirit of Capitalism.* New York: HarperCollins Academic.
Williams, G. 1976 (1985, rev. ed.). 'Taking the Part of Peasants: Rural Development in Nigeria and Tanzania', in P. Gutkind and I. Wallerstein (eds), *The Political Economy of Contemporary Africa.* Beverly Hills: Sage.
——. 1981. *Inequalities in Rural Nigeria.* Occasional Paper No. 6. Norwich: University of East Anglia, School of Development Studies.
——. 1988. 'Why Is There No Agrarian Capitalism in Nigeria?' *Journal of Historical Sociology* 1(4): 345–98.
Williamson, O. 1975. *Markets and Hierarchies: Analysis and Anti-trust Implications.* New York: Free Press.
——. 1985. *The Economic Institutions of Capitalism: Firms, Markets, Relational Contracting.* New York: Free Press.
Wolf, E. 1966. 'Kinship, Friendship and Patron-Client Relations in Complex Societies', in M. Banton (ed.), *The Social Anthropology of Complex Societies,* ASA Monographs No. 4. London: Tavistock, pp. 1–22.
Wolf, E. 1966. *Peasants.* Englewood Cliffs: Prentice Hall.
World Bank. 1981. *Accelerated Development in Sub-Saharan Africa: An Agenda for Action* [Berg Report]. Washington, DC: World Bank.
Yeld, E. 1960. 'Islam and Social Stratification in Northern Nigeria'. *British Journal of Sociology* 2 (June).

Unpublished Manuscripts, Papers and Dissertations

Bryceson, D. 1983. 'A Clientage Mode of Production'. Paper, Oxford.
Clarke, J. 1979. 'Agricultural Production in a Rural Yoruba Town'. PhD thesis, University of London.

Clough, P. 1976. 'The Relationship between Rural Poverty and the Structure of Trade'. School of Basic Studies, Ahmadu Bello University, Zaria, Nigeria.

———. 1980a. 'Indebtedness among the Rural Hausa: A Case-Study'. Report to the Department of Research and Consultancy, Institute of Administration, Ahmadu Bello University, Zaria, Nigeria.

———. 1980b. 'History, Culture, and Rural Economy of Ruvuma Region'. Investment Centre Working Paper 14/1980, FAO, Rome.

———. 1986. 'The Production and Marketing of Cash Crops and Grains in Northern Nigeria, 1985: A View Based on Village Research'. Consultancy report, Western Africa Regional Office, World Bank, Washington, DC.

———. 1996. 'The Economy and Culture of the Talakawa of Marmara'. D.Phil. thesis, Oxford University.

Giles, L.C. 1937. 'The Hausa Village and Co-operation'. Ms. in Rhodes House Library, Oxford.

Nigerian Cotton Board. 15 February 1983. '1983/84 Market Prospects'. Funtua, Nigeria.

Usman, Y.B. 1974. 'The Transformation of Katsina: c.1976–1903. The Overthrow of the Sarauta System and the Establishment and Evolution of the Emirate'. PhD thesis, Ahmadu Bello University, Zaria, Nigeria.

Watts, M. 1980. 'Peasantry, Merchant Capital, and International Firms in Northern Nigeria'. Conference paper. Dakar.

Index